RESURRECTING POMPEII

Pompeii has been continuously excavated and studied since 1748. Early scholars working there and in other sites associated with the AD 79 eruption of Mount Vesuvius were seduced by the wealth of artefacts and wall paintings yielded by the site, meaning that the less visually attractive evidence, such as human skeletal remains, was largely ignored, and its archaeological value unrecognized and compromised.

A number of skeletons were used as props for vignettes of the tragic last moments of the victims, made to impress dignitaries visiting the site. They were also used to creatively reconstruct the lives of the victims in literary works, such as Edward Bulwer-Lytton's 1834 novel *The Last Days of Pompeii*, where the skeletal evidence is presented through storytelling with a thin veneer of science. This work in particular has had a profound influence and has driven the agenda of many Pompeian and Campanian skeletal studies into the twenty-first century.

Recognizing the important contribution of the human skeletal evidence to the archaeology of Pompeii and studying the reasons for the scientific neglect of the human remains, *Resurrecting Pompeii* provides detailed information about what the skeletal record can actually provide. Estelle Lazer demonstrates that the biological evidence does not support the detail of the stories that have been told to date, but it does yield tantalizing glimpses into the lives and deaths of the victims, providing students of archaeology and history with an essential resource in the study of this fascinating historical event.

Estelle Lazer is an Honorary Research Associate at the University of Sydney. Her research interests include forensic archaeology and Antarctic cultural heritage management. She has spent seven field seasons working on the human skeletal remains at Pompeii.

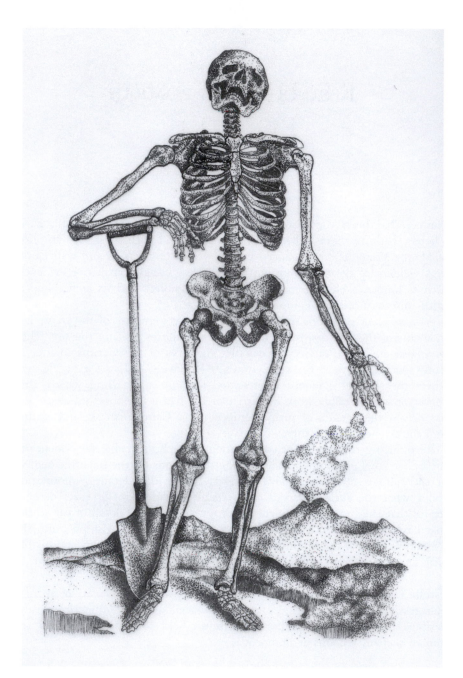

Frontispiece With apologies to Vesalius – adapted from Vesalius' first book of the *De Humani Corporis Fabrica c.* 1543 (Reproduced in Saunders and O'Malley, 1982, 85).

RESURRECTING POMPEII

Estelle Lazer

Routledge
Taylor & Francis Group

LONDON AND NEW YORK

First published 2009
by Routledge
2 Park Square, Milton Park, Abingdon, Oxon OX14 4RN

Simultaneously published in the USA and Canada
by Routledge
270 Madison Ave, New York, NY 10016

Routledge is an imprint of the Taylor & Francis Group, an informa business

© 2009 Estelle Lazer

Typeset in Garamond by Taylor & Francis Books
Printed and bound in Great Britain by
CPI Antony Rowe, Chippenham, Wiltshire

British Library Cataloguing in Publication Data
A catalogue record for this book is available from the British Library

Library of Congress Cataloging in Publication Data
Lazer, Estelle.
Resurrecting Pompeii / Estelle Lazer.
p. cm.
Includes bibliographical references and index.
1. Pompeii (Extinct city) 2. Excavations (Archaeology)–Italy–Pompeii (Extinct
city) 3. Human remains (Archaeology)–Italy–Pompeii (Extinct city) 4. Naples
Region (Italy)–Antiquities. I. Title.
DG70.P7L39 2008
937'.7256807–dc22
2008047753

ISBN13: 978-0-415-26146-3 (hbk)
ISBN13: 978-0-203-88516-1 (ebk)

FOR RUTH, ASHER, CAROL, SIMON,
JENNIFER, MEGAN AND SUZANNE

CONTENTS

FIGURES

TABLES

ACKNOWLEDGEMENTS

It is not possible to adequately acknowledge the numerous people who have assisted and encouraged me during the course of the research and the writing of this book, but the following must be mentioned.

I would like to thank the current Superintendent of Pompeii, Professor Pier Giovanni Guzzo, for his continued permission to obtain access to skeletal material and for his generous support of this work and for granting me permission to reproduce photographs I have taken of skeletal material on site. Thanks are also due to the previous Superintendent, Professor Baldassare Conticello, for initially granting me permission to work on the human skeletons from Pompeii. I am grateful to all the staff at the *Soprintendenza Archeologica di Pompei*, in particular, Dr Antonio D'Ambrosio, Grete Stefani, Dr Antonio Varone, Vittorio Boccia, Vincenzo Matrone and Mattia Buondonno. The custodians who facilitated my research deserve a special mention, most notably the late Luigi Matrone and Ciro Sicignano, as well as Franco Striano.

Professor Andrew Wallace-Hadrill, Head of the British School at Rome and leader of the Herculaneum Conservation Project, has provided endless support and assistance, for which I am extremely grateful. I would also like to thank the Herculaneum Conservation Project Manager, Jane Thompson, and research and outreach coordinator, Sarah Court, for their patience in answering questions about the ethics and management of the human skeletal remains at Herculaneum.

I am beholden to Emeritus Professor Richard Green, from the Department of Classical Archaeology at the University of Sydney, for suggesting that I write this book and for his unfailing support and encouragement during the writing process.

I am very much indebted to the Discipline of Architectural Science in the School of Architecture, Design and Planning for appointing me as an Honorary Research Associate. The level of collegiality has been wonderful and I am particularly grateful to Dr Simon Hayman for his assistance with the statistical analysis of the data, as well as his comments and criticism of the text, and to Dr Jennifer Gamble, for her acts of gratuitous kindness, especially with regard to the seemingly endless task of referencing the work. I also want to express my gratitude to Megan Haig and Suzanne Roberts for their comments and criticism of the text. I deeply regret that Emeritus Professor Henry J. Cowan did not live to see the manuscript completed. He was a wonderful mentor to me. I would also like to thank the excellent IT team, Julian Tam, Joe Nappa and Leslie George, for their continuous assistance throughout the project. Thanks are also due to Bruce Forwood, Professor Warren Julian, Dr David Leifer, Professor Richard Hyde, Kim Beecroft, Mark Neil, Sharon Dubos, Jennifer Ryan, Dr Densil Cabrera, Sharon Perritt, Dr onacloV, Anne Christian, Rick Moss, Phil Granger, Ken Stewart, John Elliot and Bruce Hyde for their continued support and assistance.

This work could not have been completed without the support of the staff of the former Architecture Library (now SciTech library), who could not have been more helpful. They always treated my more obscure requests for interlibrary loans as a challenge rather than a nuisance. Particular mention must be made to Lise Roberts, Michael Arndell, Lindy Collien, Margaret Harvey, Helen Campbell, Dr John Wu, Michelle Harrison, Rebecca Goldsworthy, Elizabeth Quilty, Michael David Hoggard, Lily Li and Sue Gong.

Friends and colleagues across the University of Sydney also made a significant contribution to this work, especially Dr Sarah Colley from Archaeology, Dr Kathryn Welch from Ancient History and Monika Dzidowska from Psychology. Dr Murray Smith, then of Econometrics, generously provided assistance with the statistical analysis of the data and Associate Professor Cedric Shorey guided my training in anatomy.

Special mention must be made of the team of people who were involved in the x-ray analysis of the cast of the 'Lady of Oplontis' in 1994. My thanks especially go to the late Dr Mario Benanzio, orthopaedic surgeon, who helped me apply for permission to do this work, organized logistic support and assisted with the interpretation of the x-rays, Dr Michael Houang, radiologist, who provided access to the x-ray and CT-scanning facilities, x-ray film, radiographic support and interpretation of the x-rays, and Dr Chris Griffiths, of the then NSW Forensic Institute for organizing the dental x-rays and their interpretation. I appreciate their provision of permission to reproduce some of these x-rays in this book. Thanks are also due to Ian White, from the then NSW Forensic Institute, Dr Greg Doran, then from Anatomy and Histology, University of Sydney, and the team of radiographers. The staff at the Australian Museum, where the body was housed as part of the travelling exhibition, Rediscovering Pompeii, were wonderful in providing logistical support, especially Ross Clendenning, Colin MacGregor, Liz Wilson and Liz Pearson.

Numerous scholars generously provided me with information and advice, including forensic dentists, Dr Alain Middleton and Dr Sue Cole, as well as forensic pathologist, Dr Chris Lawrence, Professor Marshall Becker from West Chester University, USA, Dr Corinne Duhig, University of Cambridge, Dr Jonathon Musgrave, then from Anatomy, University of Bristol, Professor Valerie Higgins of the American University of Rome, Dr Vincenzia Iorio, then of

Pompeii, Dr Penelope Allison, University of Leicester and Amanda Claridge and Professor Grahame Barker, former Deputy Director and former Director of the British School at Rome. I am eternally grateful to Professor Emeritus Peter Garnsey, Department of Classics, for his continued encouragement and support.

For their endless patience and continuous assistance, I would like to thank Richard Stoneman, Amy Laurens and particularly Lalle Pursglove, who saw the book to completion.

Finally, I would like to express gratitude to my family and friends for their moral support and comments and criticism of the text. In particular, I would like to thank Ruth, Asher and Dr Carol Lazer, Ian Chapman, Vicki Parish, Sean Volke and Leigh Dayton.

INTRODUCTION

Making sense of death

As humans, we suffer from the double whammy of being both sentient and mortal. We may attempt to defy our chronological age with Botox and plastic surgery, but whatever we do, we will eventually die. Death is a taboo subject in modern Western society and has largely been removed from view. Denial does not change the fact that our ultimate demise is an unavoidable rite of passage. The most common question I overheard from passing tourists during my years of fieldwork in Pompeii was, 'So where are the dead bodies?' Perhaps this can be interpreted as a recognition of a need to view one's fate rather than just a gratuitous act of voyeurism.

The human remains from Pompeii have always been a major attraction for visitors to the site. They have been one of the key factors that separated Pompeii from Herculaneum, which did not have a culture of bodies due to the minimal number of skeletons found there before the 1980s. There are several reasons for the fascination with the remains of individuals who perished in a mass disaster almost two millennia ago. One of the most important is that the event that killed the victims was also responsible for preserving their living context, from the most humble domestic items to substantial, largely intact structures. Another is that the negative forms of a number of bodies were preserved, which when cast, can provide a detailed image of individuals at the time of their death. Visitors can gaze at death without seeing the actual body. These human remains are also more accessible than those from other contexts, like Egyptian tombs or plague pits. This is because Pompeii is an above-ground site where we can see all the minutiae that made up a lifestyle to which a modern Western person could easily relate. Ultimately, the human remains from Pompeii are compelling because of their context. They are not too confronting because they are removed by time and, in the case of casts, they present a tangible reflection of identifiable individuals without the disturbing reality of soft tissue.

This book explores the fascination with human remains from Pompeii from the first discovery of skeletons in the eighteenth century to the realization that the forms of the bodies were also preserved.

The first part of the book considers why there was so much interest in this material and yet only minimal research was undertaken until the latter part of the twentieth century. The sample of available skeletons was severely compromised, partly because a number of the skeletons were used to create

1

vignettes of the tragic last moments of victims. Initially, human remains were not considered to have much other value than as props, both physically and for the creative reconstruction of the lives of the victims. There was no appreciation of their intrinsic research value. As a result, many of the skeletons were disarticulated over time and stored in ancient buildings.

The second part of the book deals with the information that the skeletal material and casts can provide. It is particularly concerned with the problems associated with a compromised sample. Some scholars abandoned this material as a result of the post-excavation dismembering of the collection. The value of the Pompeian material was also considered to be diminished by the discovery of a large number of skeletons in the nearby site of Herculaneum in the 1980s. Despite their proximity and destruction as a result of the AD 79 eruption of Mt Vesuvius, Pompeii is essentially a different site and the finds from one cannot be seen as interchangeable with the other. The Pompeian material provides unique information and with some effort yields incomplete but tantalizing glimpses into the lives and deaths of the inhabitants of this town.

This book is more about storytelling and investigative procedure than an attempt to produce the definitive work on the human remains from Pompeii. The most vital part of the process of studying human skeletal material is the collection of basic data from measurements and observations. These data and their use to establish the sex ratio, range of ages-at-death, general health and population affinities of the sample, provide baseline information that underpins all future studies of the material at the macroscopic, microscopic and molecular level. The limitations of the techniques and the problems associated with dealing with biological material are also discussed. Some of the recent literature on the Vesuvian sites gives the impression that the evidence provides us with more certain information about the past than is actually the case. Knowledge of the limitations of the evidence and the techniques that are used for its interpretation is an essential tool for an assessment of claims about the victims of the eruption. The level of information presented enables the non-specialist to appreciate the degree of uncertainty associated with skeletal identification and should help determine when the evidence has been pushed beyond its potential and speculation begins.

The approach taken in this book is multidisciplinary. There is no assumed specialist knowledge and, while this is not a textbook, the information required to understand and critically assess this and other works, especially in osteoarchaeology, is explained in detail in the text. A glossary and illustrations have been included to make the book easy for the non-specialist to use without having to resort to other sources.

Part I

THE LAST DAYS
OF POMPEII

1

SKELETONS AS ARTEFACTS

On 7 April 1768 the Austrian Emperor Joseph II visited Pompeii. To mark the occasion, a house was named in his honour and he was invited to witness the excavation of its contents. As he watched the workmen remove the pumice stones that covered the kitchen on the lower level of the house, a human skeleton was revealed. Perhaps the bones were draped just a little too artistically over several amphorae. Whatever the reason, it was instantly apparent that a deception had been perpetrated and that it was not of the highest order. Joseph II was not impressed.[1]

This occurrence was not unique, though other dignitaries were more gullible than the Austrian Emperor and failed to recognize that the scenes of the final moments in the lives of victims that emerged from the pumice and ash had been faked.

Such tableaux were the result of the tendency for those in charge of the site in the eighteenth and early nineteenth centuries to re-excavate spectacular finds and produce vignettes for the benefit of celebrity guests; for example, the *Casa del Chirurgo* (House of the Surgeon) (VI, i, 10) was 'discovered' three times in the presence of royalty. The designated area was liberally salted with valuables, such as coins and statues, and then re-covered with ash and pumice stones or lapilli. Skeletons were often employed as they provided wonderful props for this kind of entertainment.[2]

Elements of this approach to the site have continued to the present, albeit in a less ostentatious form. In this context, the bones of the Pompeian victims have been treated as artefacts rather than as a class of archaeological evidence. That this happened in the eighteenth and even in the nineteenth centuries is perhaps not so surprising. The continuation of this tradition and the fact the skeletal material found at the site was not subjected to the types of analysis routinely used for human remains from other sites until the latter part of the twentieth century requires some explanation. The nature of the destruction of Pompeii, the history and philosophy of the excavations and the close relationship between popular culture and skeletal finds had considerable bearing on the study and presentation of human remains from this site.

encourage them to develop a taste for the classical art that they had admired during their travels in Italy. The Society of Dilettanti provided assistance to members of the British aristocracy who wished to establish collections of antiquities whilst on their obligatory Grand Tour. William Hamilton had worked for the society in this capacity. The society also supported the publication of scholarly works on the classical world.[12]

Gell became famous as a classical topographer, describing Greece and Asia Minor, Rome and Pompeii. His first volume of the *Pompeiana* series was published in 1817. These works were very popular as they provided the first account of the excavations in English. In fact, very little had been published on Pompeii in any language in the first fifty years of excavation. In a letter to the Society of Dilettanti in 1834, Gell complained about the politicking amongst those responsible for the excavations. He stated that on-site petty rivalries were responsible for preventing the documentation of finds either by the excavators or visitors to the site. He attempted to alleviate this situation by recording everything he saw as he watched the excavations progress. This information was included in the 1832 and 1852 editions of *Pompeiana*. Eventually, he was thwarted in this aspect of his work as he could no longer afford the bribery necessary to ensure him access.[13] His contribution to the dissemination of knowledge about Pompeii in a period of poor documentation cannot be overrated. Nonetheless, he was criticized for concentrating his efforts on architecture at the expense of the more portable finds.[14] This is certainly true for the skeletal evidence. The skeletons he described from the excavations he witnessed were generally only those that were discovered with gold coins or other valuables.[15] This is hardly surprising as skeletal finds were not a major priority of the primarily *beaux-arts* interested Society of Dilettanti.

Even though the need for systematic planning and recording of the sites had been recognized, for example by Karl Weber, Francesco la Vega and Caroline Murat, the appointment of Giuseppe Fiorelli, first as inspector in 1860 and then as director of the excavations in 1863, marked the commencement of a rigorous approach to archaeological work in the Campanian region. He has been credited with a large number of improvements in the excavation and documentation of the sites, including the instigation of systematic excavation and regular documentation of all new finds. He enabled finds to be accurately mapped by dividing the site into regions made up of architecturally defined blocks or *insulae* which, in turn, were subdivided into numbered houses. This system is still in use. He also developed a policy of leaving objects and wall paintings *in situ*, where possible.[16]

Most importantly for a review of the history of the treatment of skeletal finds in Pompeii, it was Fiorelli who first applied a technique that had been used to reveal the forms of furniture and other objects made from wood to the human victims from Pompeii. Liquid plaster of Paris was used to fill cavities in the ash where organic material had decomposed over time. When it dried the surrounding ash was removed, leaving a cast of the form of the organic material. The first human casts were made in 1863.[17] The impact of Fiorelli's casting technique on the popular imagination was profound. It is telling that prior to 1994, the scientific potential of these casts had never been exploited (see Chapter 10).[18] Ironically, it was probably the seductive nature of the strong images produced by the casts that ensured their relegation to the status of entertaining artefacts. Conversely, the scientific contribution of the botanical remains had been appreciated for some time.[19]

One of the advantages of Fiorelli's policy of not removing panels of wall paintings for museum display was that they could be studied in their original context. This enabled another nineteenth-century scholar, August Mau, to influence the course of Pompeian research. His main contribution to Pompeian studies was the classification of Pompeian wall paintings into four separate decorative systems in 1873. The details of his system of classification were elucidated in his 1882 publication *Geschichte der decorativen Wandmalerei in Pompeji*. These so-called 'four styles' were thought to be more or less chronologically distinct. They are still employed as a standard for the study of Pompeian paintings, though their chronological relationship is the subject of some controversy.[20] Like his compatriot, Winckelmann, Mau's work reinforced the art historical approach to Pompeian scholarship. His continuing influence can be seen in the number of works devoted to the classification of Pompeian paintings.[21]

The methods of excavation and documentation established by Fiorelli were continued into the twentieth century by Sogliano (1905–10), Spinazzola (1910–23) and Maiuri. Amedeo Maiuri, who directed the excavations from 1924–61, further developed Fiorelli's approach and techniques with the aim of presenting the site as it looked at the time of its destruction. Buildings were restored and domestic objects were left *in situ*. The policy for human remains was also that, where possible, they be left *in situ*.[22] Maiuri's successors in Pompeii essentially continued this approach, especially with casts, as can be seen in the case of a number of fugitives that were discovered in 1989, cast and left *in situ* in the *Casa di Stabianus* in Region 1, Insula 22 (Figure 1.1).[23]

It is notable that site management was often personality-based and driven by politics. Nonetheless, the history of these excavations reflects the development of the history and philosophy of classical archaeology.[24] This overview highlights the continued emphasis on art and architectural history as a research priority at Pompeii. It partially explains why the human skeletal remains from the site were considered to be of marginal relevance to Pompeian archaeology for over two centuries.

A culture of bodies

From the first skeleton that was unearthed in Pompeii on 19 April 1748, the human remains in Pompeii captured the imagination of the public, possibly as a result of the enormity of the disaster and the way in which the bodies

Figure 1.1 Fugitives from the Casa di Stabianus in Region 1, Insula 22, found in the ash
layer above the lapilli of the first eruption phase

were preserved. This probably was a major contributing factor for the retention of so many bodies in a period in the history of classical archaeology
when skeletal finds were routinely discarded.[25] Another factor, which made
the discovery of human remains so desirable, was that they were often found
with precious items with which they had attempted to make their escape
from the devastated town. The above-mentioned skeleton, for example,
which was found only about two months after excavations officially commenced, was discovered with a number of coins. Associated finds often provided the main reason for the documentation of skeletal finds.[26]

While the skeletons themselves were not seen to have any intrinsic value,
their potential as props for the construction of theatrical displays for the
amusement of visiting dignitaries was soon realized. Within a comparatively
short space of time a culture of bodies was established. This was manifested in
several ways, most notably through vignettes, myths and popular literature.

Vignettes

Over time, the use of skeletons of Pompeian victims for the manufacture of
tableaux was expanded from being exclusively for regal visitors to more
common use to entertain the increasing number of tourists to the site. A good
example that demonstrates this activity in the twentieth century is the treatment
and presentation of the skeletal finds housed in Room 19 in the *Casa del
Menandro* (I, x, 4).[27]

Amedeo Maiuri excavated the *Casa del Menandro* between 1926 and 1932.[28]
He found the remains of three individuals at ground level in Room 19 near the
entrance from the peristyle. He identified them as two adults and a juvenile.

10

Figure 1.2 Detail of skeletons displayed in Room 19, *Casa del Menandro* (I, x, 4). Note the bronze lantern and the reconstructed wooden shafts of the pick and hoe

The juvenile was thought to be female because a gold ring was found on one of its fingers. A hoe and a pick were found in association with these bodies.[29] In a narrow vestibule in corridor L on the other side of the west wall of this room, another ten or so, mostly adult, bodies were discovered. They appeared to have collapsed on top of each other, and their bodies were so intertwined that Maiuri stated that it was difficult to distinguish individuals.[30] They were found 2.5 metres above the ground. A large cylindrical bronze lantern was found in association with these bodies. Artificial light would have been necessary as this phase of the eruption was associated with darkness.[31]

By the time these two groups of victims tried to escape, the deposit of ash and lapilli had reached a depth where it occluded the ground-floor exits. Maiuri suggested that the group in Room 19 probably used the pick and hoe to make an opening in the wall through which they could escape.[32] Three holes that could have been made with such tools can be observed in the southern and Western walls of Room 19.[33]

Maiuri[34] stated that the group of skeletons from the vestibule were transported in their precise positions to the adjacent room where the other three bodies had been removed. The bodies from the vestibule can still be observed in a glass case at the southwest end of Room 19. In addition to the bronze lantern, the above-mentioned pick and hoe with restored wooden handles have been placed with these bodies. In 1988 I was invited to examine the skeletons in this case for a publication on the *Insula del Menandro*.[35]

It has been presumed in the popular literature[36] that the bodies from the vestibule were encased *in situ* and that they belonged to looters who had returned to Pompeii after the eruption only to be killed by poisonous fumes that had been trapped in the ash. The holes in the southern and Western walls have been cited as further evidence for this theory. The powerful imagery of these bodies *in situ* has been stronger than the academic literature and a number of scholars have developed theories about the skeletons, apparently without reference to the original reports.

There is a further complication in association with these skeletal remains. Despite Maiuri's statement that the positions of the bodies were not altered during their removal to Room 19, it became obvious on inspection that the skeletons had been manipulated. That these changes occurred in Maiuri's time can be implied from the fact that the area around the bones was consolidated with plaster that was sprinkled with ash when it was damp, thus maintaining the impression of bones in their excavation context. This technique, which usually involves the consolidation of exposed, but only partially excavated remains, had been employed for some time in Pompeii. Some of the bones near the surface were loose. The remainder were embedded in the compacted ash and plaster. A comparison between my measured drawing of the bodies[37] and the photograph in Maiuri's publication[38] indicates that, with few exceptions, the arrangement of the skeletons has remained unchanged since they were enclosed in the glass case. The fact that various bones were partially embedded in plaster hampered analysis of these skeletons.

The skeleton associated with Skull Number 1 was found to have two left femora. The post-cranial remains associated with Skull Number 8 included one juvenile and one adult humerus. Skull Number 9 belonged to a young child, whilst the associated vertebrae were adult. A calcaneus had been placed where the patella should have been on the skeleton associated with Skull Number 10. This last piece of creative anatomy clearly post-dated Maiuri's involvement, as evidenced by comparison with the photograph in his 1933 publication.

A small rectangular pit had been dug in the northeast corner of the exhibit. This was presumably used to deposit the bones that were left over after the skeletons had been reconstructed.

Perhaps the most remarkable alteration to the group was demonstrated by Skull Number 5, which had been totally faked. It was observed in the Sarno Bath collection (Chapter 5) that the form of any missing parts of skulls buried in fine compacted ash would be preserved as a result of ash filling the cranium and hardening over time. This phenomenon was exploited in the creation of Skull Number 5. The cranium was formed by pieces from several different skulls. The dentition included a combination of adult and recently erupted juvenile permanent teeth. The area around the orbits had been hand moulded in wet ash and the nose was composed of a vertebral body. It is not certain when this addition was made. It apparently post-dates Maiuri's time

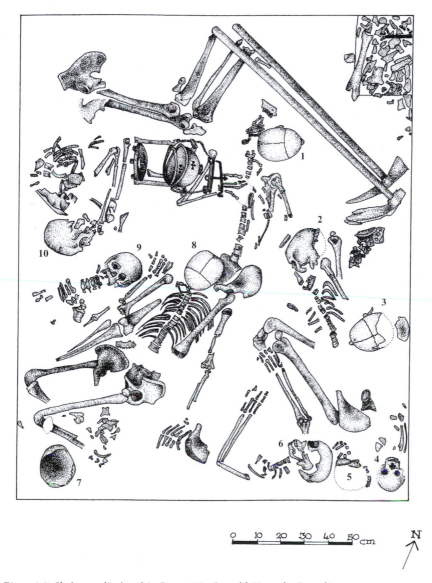

Figure 1.3 Skeletons displayed in Room 19, *Casa del Menandro* (I, x, 4)

as the comparably located skull in the photograph in Maiuri's book[39] appears to be considerably more complete than Skull Number 5.

With the exception of Skull Number 5, it is clear that there was no attempt at deception in the restoration of this group of victims in a place that was not the original find spot as Maiuri documented all his actions. The

13

novel rearticulation was probably the result of the work being undertaken by untrained people with no knowledge of anatomy. Nonetheless, this resulted in the loss of information as the sample was essentially disarticulated. The alterations that post-date Maiuri are more disturbing. The inclusion of the bronze lantern, which, even though it was found with these victims, does not appear in the photograph in Maiuri's publication, along with the addition of the restored tools that were found with the three victims in Room 19, was a conscious attempt to create both a tableau and a past that would appeal to visitors to this house.

This, and the earlier examples of vignettes mentioned above, indicates that the Pompeii that was presented to visitors from the eighteenth century to, at least, the first part of the twentieth century, hardly reflected the finds in their actual contexts, but instead was a product of wish fulfilment where the popular perceptions of the site were formed and realized. As a result, the Pompeii in the scholarly literature does not always resemble the extant remains. Since the eighteenth century, Pompeii has essentially been two separate sites; the archaeological site and that which was displayed to the nobility and the general public. Remains that have been presented to tourists and scholars as *in situ* have sometimes been manipulated or rearranged for better effect, thus simultaneously creating and challenging the concept of the site as a moment frozen in time (see Chapter 4).

The mythology of Pompeian bodies, or never let the evidence get in the way of a good story: victims real and imagined

Regardless of supporting evidence, stories based on specific Pompeian skeletal finds have become embedded in popular consciousness over time. The skeletons that formed the basis of these mythological reconstructions of Pompeian deaths tended to be those with associated artefacts because they provided excellent props for storytelling. These artefacts were usually precious, though objects of lesser value, like medical instruments, could also render a skeleton interesting enough for inclusion. Skeletons could also be singled out if they were found in contexts that inspired a spectacular story.

One of the best-known examples involved the alleged discovery of a skeleton in niche 21, on the left exterior side of the Herculaneum Gate. It was claimed that in 1763, a skeleton was found in a sentry box at this location, holding a lance and surrounded by armour and other finds associated with a soldier. The widely accepted interpretation was that this skeleton represented a soldier who was so disciplined that he did not leave his post, even when his world was crashing down around him.[40] The story had wide appeal and the hapless soldier appeared in various forms of popular culture, including Edward Bulwer-Lytton's *The Last Days of Pompeii* in 1834[41] and Edward John Poynter's painting *Faithful unto Death* in 1865 (Figure 1.4). This illustration by Lancelot Speed from an 1897 edition of *The Last Days of Pompeii*[42] is clearly based on Poynter's painting. The latter became one of the best-recognized images in Victorian painting. This image had particular resonance in England where it was used both as an exemplary case of unyielding dedication to duty and as a metaphor for the support due to the British Empire.[43] The political potential of this tale was also exploited by Fiorelli. He invoked the story of the soldier who had considered death a better option than desertion in a letter of support for King Ferdinand II's Constitution to the newspaper *Il Tempo* in March 1848.[44]

In the second half of the nineteenth century, Dyer dismissed this story as fiction.[45] He not only doubted the veracity of the interpretation; he also questioned whether a skeleton was even found at this location as he could not find evidence of such in the excavation journals. Moreover, he pointed out that the structure in question was not a sentry box, but the funeral monument of *M. Cerinius Restitutus*, as evidenced by an inscription. This account was supported in other nineteenth-century publications but that did not put an end to literary and other references to this tragic scene.[46]

Scholars who have grappled with the possibility that this often-reported skeleton may have existed have suggested that instead of an interpretation of a loyal soldier, it was probably that of a victim seeking shelter in a tomb.[47]

There is no argument that skeletons were found in and around the Temple of Isis (VIII, vii, 27–28), though their interpretation has been somewhat fantastic. The temple was excavated by Francesco la Vega between 1764 and 1766. Two victims were found in the temple and one nearby with a quantity of precious goods, presumably from the temple. The popular myth that was woven about these victims is thought to date to the first decades of the nineteenth century. As the remains of eggs, fish and bread were found on a table in a room behind the temple, it was thought that the priests' meal was interrupted by the violence of the onset of the eruption. Some of the priests fled with treasure from the temple; the one carrying the sack being toppled by the collapse of the colonnade in the Triangular Forum. The priests who remained inside the temple became trapped by the pumice build-up and could not escape, eventually succumbing to asphyxiation. Before he was overcome, one of the priests took up an axe and attempted to create an escape route by hacking through walls but was defeated by a very solid piece of masonry. It was claimed that he was discovered with the axe still in his hands.[48] Bulwer-Lytton included this fable in his novel *The Last Days of Pompeii* (Figure 1.5).[49]

A recent description of the human finds from the temple is far more conservative. It merely states that one skeleton was found in the kitchen of the residential complex and the other was found in the *ekklesiasterion*. There are insufficient associated artefacts to further indicate the part they played in the functioning of the temple, though it has been suggested that one may have been a priest and the other a servant.[50]

Perhaps the most famous skeleton to become part of the mythology of Pompeii is that of the supposed woman in the gladiators' barracks. The

"*Amidst the crashing elements: he had not received the permission
to desert his station.*"

Figure 1.4 Illustration by Lancelot Speed from an 1897 edition of *The Last Days of Pompeii*
by Edward Bulwer-Lytton (opposite p. 374)

"With desperate strength he attempted to hew his way through."

Figure 1.5 Illustration by Lancelot Speed of a priest from the Temple of Isis from an 1897 edition of *The Last Days of Pompeii* by Edward Bulwer-Lytton (opposite p. 372)

quadroporticus of the theatres (VIII, vii, 16–17) was sporadically excavated over thirty years from 1766. It was thought that this space originally served as a foyer for the theatres but was transformed into gladiators' barracks in the last years of occupation, presumably after the AD 62 earthquake. This interpretation was primarily based on finds of substantial numbers of weapons as well as bronze greaves, helmets, sword belts and shoulder guards. Numerous skeletons were found in this location but only one was really considered worthy of special attention. This skeleton was found in 1768 in one of the rooms in the *quadroporticus* and was adorned with armbands, earrings, rings and a very impressive necklace, which incorporated twelve emeralds. It was immediately assumed that this was the skeleton of a woman, purely on the basis of the associated artefacts. And not just any woman; this was clearly the skeleton of a wealthy matron who had made an unfortunately timed tryst with her gladiator lover and was caught in a compromising situation. A human skeleton near the bones of a horse that was found in the vicinity of the barracks was for some reason assumed to have been that of her servant, whose job was to protect her from harm. What isn't usually mentioned is that the bejewelled skeleton was not found in a context that would have been conducive to intimacy as eighteen other skeletons were also found in the same room. In another version of the legend, this much-maligned individual was thought to have merely been at the barracks to service the inhabitants.[51]

A more recent interpretation is that this person was just one of a group of fugitives trying to make their escape from Pompeii via the gladiators' barracks. It has been suggested that this individual was probably the last to enter the room as the skeleton was found near the entrance. It is unfortunate that we no longer have access to this and the other skeletons that were found at the barracks so that they could be identified using forensic techniques. It has spuriously been argued that some of the eighteen other skeletons that were reported to have been found in the room must have been children on the grounds that the room was far too small to hold that many adults.[52]

The casts of the impressions of human forms that were made from 1863 on inspired equally extravagant storytelling involving careers, status and the relationships between individuals in groups (see Chapter 10).

Pompeian victims in literature

A whole genre of literature in the nineteenth century was inspired, either directly or indirectly, by the human remains that were found in Pompeii.[53] A number of literary works were based on specific skeletal discoveries. The work that had the most profound influence on both the popular consciousness and interpretation of human skeletal finds from the sites destroyed by the AD 79 eruption was Edward Bulwer-Lytton's novel *The Last Days of Pompeii*.

The Last Days of Pompeii

The Last Days of Pompeii was published in 1834 and has probably been the most widely read novel about Pompeii. It was hugely successful when it was first published and its popularity has been continuous and widespread, as evidenced by numerous editions, translation into many languages and various interpretations in different media. The novel provided the inspiration for many nineteenth-century paintings, including Lawrence Alma Tadema's 1867 work *Glaucus and Nydia*[54] and Paul Falconer Poole's *The Destruction of Pompeii* in 1835.[55] It also spawned a number of film versions, including one in 1900, two in 1913, releases in 1926 and 1948, a stunning version in 1959 with Steve Reeves in the lead role and a mini-series that was made for television in 1984.[56] While the story is compelling, Bulwer-Lytton's writing style can be challenging and the poems that are littered through the novel are truly awful. He is justly famous for his purple prose,[57] many examples of which can be seen in this novel, such as:

> 'Oh? is that you — is that Glaucus?' exclaimed the flower-girl in a tone almost of transport; the tears stood arrested on her cheek; she smiled, she clung to his breast, she kissed his robe as she clung.[58]

It would be unkind to subject the reader to examples of his poetry.

The Last Days of Pompeii is essentially a love story with the bonus of a volcanic eruption near the end. The setting and the knowledge that there will be a tragic outcome for a number of the characters are among the appealing aspects of the book. The story can be simplified by concentrating on the key characters.

Glaucus, the hero, is from Athens and resides in the house commonly known as the House of the Tragic Poet (VI, viii, 3), most famous for the mosaic of a dog accompanied by the words *Cave canem* (Beware of the dog) at the principal entrance. He is infatuated with Ione who lives in an unspecified house with her brother Apaecides. Her guardian is the evil Egyptian priest of the Isis cult, Arbaces, who wants Ione for himself and wishes to eliminate his rival. Conveniently for Arbaces, Glaucus is very handsome and has two other female admirers he can enlist, intentionally or otherwise, to help him achieve his goal. One of these is Julia, the wealthy and beautiful daughter of Diomedes, who inhabits the so-called Villa of Diomedes beyond the Herculaneum Gate. The other woman who loves Glaucus is a blind slave called Nydia. Arbaces obtains some poison from a witch who lives in a cave on the slopes of Mt Vesuvius. The witch is more than happy to supply this to Arbaces as she recently had the misfortune to offer shelter to Glaucus and Ione during a storm, during which Glaucus managed to wound her familiar. The witch also has a talent for prophecy and predicts the imminent destruction of Pompeii. Arbaces manages to pass the poison off as a love potion to Julia. He instructs her to administer it to Glaucus to make him more attentive to her. Nydia learns of this and steals the potion to give to

"*Arbaces, pausing for a moment, gazed on the pair.*"—*Page* 51.

Figure 1.6 Illustration by Lancelot Speed of the main protagonists of *The Last Days of Pompeii* by Edward Bulwer-Lytton (1897, Frontispiece)

A partir de ce moment, ils se virent chaque jour.

Figure 1.7 Illustration by Clérice Frères from a French edition of *The Last Days of Pompeii*, by Edward Bulwer-Lytton, published in 1936 (Frontispiece)

Glaucus herself. As it has neither colour nor odour, Glaucus is not aware that his water has been spiked. Instead of making him fall in love with Nydia, however, it temporarily turns him into a raving lunatic. He roams the streets in this state and is found ranting next to the lifeless body of Ione's brother who has just been murdered by Arbaces. Apaecides had converted to Christianity and was attacked by the priest for having abandoned the cult of Isis. Arbaces merely transforms the stylus of the incoherent Glaucus into a blood soaked 'murder weapon', which he plants by the corpse. Glaucus is duly taken into custody. He recovers from the poison only to discover that he is incarcerated and is about to fight a lion that is being starved in anticipation of the forthcoming games in the amphitheatre. He denies having committed any crime but he is ignored. With only one exception, his circle of young male friends, with whom he regularly partied, offer no support and leave him to his fate.

Meanwhile, Arbaces has managed to trap and hold Ione and Nydia captive in his home, along with a priest from the Temple of Isis, Calenus, who witnessed the foul deed and has threatened to expose the true criminal. Confident that everything is going according to plan, Arbaces heads off to the amphitheatre to watch the demise of his rival but Nydia manages to get a message to Glaucus' last remaining male friend, the loyal Sallust. He duly liberates Ione, Nydia and Calenus, who make their way to the amphitheatre to exonerate Glaucus and expose the actual culprit. Glaucus is saved just in the nick of time but the lion is still hungry. Arbaces is about to become an alternative meal when Mt Vesuvius erupts. Numerous characters and unnamed Pompeians die in the course of the following pages but Glaucus and his true love, Ione, have the perfect guide to lead them to safety through the unnaturally dark and chaotic streets in the form of the blind slave girl who has always operated in darkness and has learned to navigate her way through the town. After justice is meted out to Arbaces in the form of a large column that crushes him to death, the protagonists are led to the shore and escape on a boat. Nydia, feeling that she cannot compete with Ione, and indeed does not deserve Glaucus after giving him the poisonous draught, jumps overboard. Glaucus and Ione marry, convert to Christianity and live happily ever after.

Bulwer-Lytton based this book on extensive research at Pompeii in 1832–33. He was inspired to create the character of Nydia as a result of a conversation with an expert on the ruins, who suggested that a blind person who knew their way around Pompeii would have had the best chance to escape the eruption.[59] One of the key devices employed by Bulwer-Lytton was the use of skeletons that he saw *in situ* or heard about when he was conducting his study as the basis for a number of the characters in the novel. He re-animated these skeletons and gave them characters of his own invention and interpreted their last moments from their positions and associated artefacts.[60] The character of the foreign villain, Arbaces, was based on a victim whose body appeared to have been severed by a falling column. Under the influence of Spurzheim, one of the founders of the so-called science of phrenology, it was determined that the skull of this individual displayed remarkable intellectual properties, along with a propensity for evil.[61]

The character of Julia was inspired by the form of a woman that had been preserved in the ash in the so-called Villa of Diomedes. Her father, Diomed, was drawn from a skeleton found in the vicinity of a bag of coins in the portico of the garden. The skeleton was reported to have had an iron key in one hand and a gold ring on a finger. Burbo, a minor character, was created from the axe-wielding priest in the Temple of Isis myth and Calenus was based on the skeleton found near the sack full of treasures taken from the temple.[62] It is notable that though Bulwer-Lytton employed the skeletons from a number of famous myths, including the faithful sentry near the Herculaneum Gate, he did not mention the salacious story of the woman in the gladiators' barracks. The repopulation of the site with re-animated corpses and with purely imagined individuals, often inhabiting houses that could be identified by any visitor to the site, contributed to the success of the novel and had a long-reaching impact on the interpretation of human remains destroyed by the AD 79 eruption.

The objectification of the objects of his desire: Theophile Gautier and Arria Marcella

Bulwer-Lytton was by no means the only author who used these devices in their reconstruction of Pompeian life and death. Shortly after his novel appeared, he was accused of plagiarism by Sumner Lincoln Fairfield, an American writer who had produced a lengthy poem called *The Last Night of Pompeii* in 1832.[63] A better-known work that utilized the Bulwer-Lytton approach, and even some of the same bodies, was Theophile Gautier's *Arria Marcella*, which was published in 1852. Though not as influential as *The Last Days of Pompeii*, Gautier's piece is worth recounting.

The story opens with a visit to the finds from Pompeii in the Naples Museum by three French tourists, Octavian and his friends Fabio and Max. Octavian is smitten by the impression of a woman's bosom and hip preserved in the compacted ash. This leads to a reverie about how entire ancient cultures had been lost, whilst the form of these mammaries had survived the millennia.[64]

The friends then continue on to Pompeii where they procure a guide. As part of the tour, the guide takes the visitors to the Villa of Diomedes and shows them the exact spot where the cast of the woman they had viewed in the museum was found. The guide's description moves Octavian so that:

> His breast heaved, his eyes were moist; the catastrophe effaced by twenty centuries of forgetfulness impressed him like quite a recent

misfortune; the death of his mistress or of a friend would not have moved him more, and a tear, two thousand years late, fell … upon the spot where had perished, stifled by the hot ashes of the volcano, the woman for whom he felt himself filled with retrospective love.[65]

That night, the three men engage in a discussion of their ideal woman. Octavian confesses a preference for inaccessible women, usually in the form of statues, or dead or mythical individuals.[66] He then went on to provide examples. On seeing the Venus de Milo in the Louvre, he was inspired to exclaim: 'Oh who will give you back your arms, so that you may press me to your marble breasts.'[67] On another occasion, he uses a medium to attempt to return the spirit of a woman, using a few head hairs he has obtained. The one thing that links his forays into love is that they are all marked by failure. Still, this does not deter him in his quest for love.

Octavian, his poetic heart beating fast, decides on a nocturnal visit to the site. He finds Pompeii strangely restored to its previous incarnation as a living town and realizes that he has been transported back to the days of Titus. He establishes the AD 79 date from the graffiti on the walls and he is struck with the notion that the woman whose impression he so admired in the Naples museum must now be alive and it might be possible for him to find and speak to the owner of those 'divine contours'.[68]

Luckily, Octavian is an award-winning Latin scholar and has little trouble conversing with the local Pompeians, though he is instantly marked as a foreigner by his odd nineteenth-century garb and his Parisian accent. In fact, his accent is so strong that his first acquaintance offers to speak to him in Greek.

His new friend invites him to see a performance at the theatre. He is distracted from the play by the sight of a pair of breasts that appear to correspond to the imprint in the ashes on display at the Naples Museum. He is so aroused by these bosoms restored to life that not only is he convinced that they must be the very pair that he observed in reverse in the Naples Museum but that they also belong to his first and only true love. His passions appear to have been reciprocated and, by means of her slave, the owner of the divine assets entices Octavian to follow her home. Octavian has correctly identified her and she is introduced as Arria Marcella, the daughter of Arrius Diomedes. He is so mesmerized by Arria Marcella's extraordinary anatomy that he barely registers the fact that he is following her through parts of Pompeii that have not yet been excavated.[69]

Octavian is taken to Arria Marcella's chamber where he finds her reclining 'in a voluptuous, serene pose'.[70] She explains that his desire for her has restored her to life. Just as they are improving their acquaintance, Arria Marcella's father bursts into the chamber. Diomedes has converted to Christianity and is rather fervent. He proceeds to berate his daughter for continuing her dissipation beyond her lifetime by bombarding her with a series of questions:

'Can you not leave the living within their sphere? Have your ashes not cooled since the day you died unrepentant under the volcano's rain of fire? Have two thousand years of death not quieted you and do your greedy arms still draw to your heartless bosom the poor mad men intoxicated by your spells?'[71]

Diomedes then proceeds to exorcize Arria Marcella and to Octavian's horror she is returned to the state she was in when she was discovered during the excavation of the villa, 'a handful of ashes and shapeless remains mingled with calcined bones, among which gleamed bracelets and golden jewels'.[72] Octavian reacts by swooning and only regains consciousness when his worried friends find and rouse him the next day.

Octavian never recovers from his adventure. He is haunted by Arria Marcella. He keeps returning to Pompeii for moonlight visits but is never able to relive his previous experience, though he goes with a heart filled with hope. Despite his wishes and desires, 'Arria Marcella obstinately remained dust'.[73]

Finally he marries a young English girl who is madly in love with him. She feels that despite being a good husband, he displays evidence of being in love with another. She investigates to the best of her ability but can never find evidence of a rival, but who would imagine that her rival is a long-dead corpse?

Part soft-core pornography, part travelogue, this work was too idiosyncratic to have the impact of *The Last Days of Pompeii*. Like Bulwer-Lytton, Gautier provided detailed, almost didactic, descriptions of the site. He also employed the same human remains as those used by Bulwer-Lytton as inspiration for the characters of Julia and Diomed, though in Gautier's story they are imbued with different personalities and are called Arria Marcella and Arrius Diomedes. These same skeletons were also used for the characters in Ferdinand Gregorovius' poem *Euphorion: eine Dichtung aus Pompeji*, which was published in 1858. In his tale, the skeletons retain the relationship of father and daughter. The father is still Diomedes but the daughter is now called Ione. They vary from the reconstructed individuals in the other works in that Diomedes is portrayed as an entrepreneur and Ione is much more gentle than either Julia or the siren portrayed in *Arria Marcella*.[74]

The skeletons found in the so-called Villa of Diomedes were found over the course of two years and had all the appropriate attributes for inclusion in Pompeian literature; they were numerous and they were found in interesting contexts with valuable and evocative associated artefacts. In 1771, the skeleton routinely interpreted as Diomedes, the *dominus* or master of the house was, as described above, found in the portico surrounding the garden, holding a key and accompanied by one of the most impressive collections of coins found in Pompeii. The remains of another individual were discovered near this skeleton, and were interpreted as being those of a slave. A large group of skeletons was discovered a year later in the *cryptoporticus* corridor.[75] A clearly female form could be discerned, impressed in the ash around the bones of one of the skeletons (see Chapter 10).[76] This became the ever-changing daughter of Diomedes. There is no compelling reason, apart from the circumstantial evidence of the key and the coins, for the interpretation of the skeleton as the *dominus*, and there is even less evidence to support the assumption that the skeleton whose form was preserved was this person's daughter.

Impact of popular literature on academic research in Pompeii and other Campanian sites

Possibly as a result of the history of the Campanian excavations, especially with respect to the problems associated with the documentation of the sites, the distinction between popular and academic literature on Pompeii and Herculaneum tends to be somewhat blurred. As stated above, it was often only through popular writing, like that of William Gell, that information was made available at all in the early periods of excavation. Much of the information for these years was recorded and disseminated by gentleman scholars, like Hamilton and Gell, who observed the progress of the excavations. This perhaps created a precedent for a popular rather than a scientific approach to these sites. The legacy of this can be clearly seen in the tremendous influence that popular culture has exerted on the perception of the sites. It can be demonstrated through an examination of the influence of Bulwer-Lytton's novel *The Last Days of Pompeii* on the interpretation of the skeletal evidence from Pompeii and Herculaneum.

It can be argued that *The Last Days of Pompeii* has been the single most influential work in relation to how the site and, more specifically, the victims, have been interpreted. Bulwer-Lytton did not envisage his novel to be seen as mere entertainment; he considered that it should also have an instructive component. In the preface to the first edition, he stated that it was important to integrate scholarship with creativity.[77] The book had some of the hallmarks of scholarship, like the use of footnotes. His attitude to his work is reflected in a footnote about the form of the eruption[78] where he stated that accuracy was not sacrificed for the sake of romance.

Bulwer-Lytton studied classics at school in Ealing and completed his education at Cambridge University. Throughout his life he was respected as both a scholar and a writer. *The Last Days of Pompeii* demonstrates a combination of these skills. It was based on thorough research, much of his information being obtained from detailed inspections of the remains along with discussions with William Gell and the Italian archaeologist Antonio Bonucci. Most critics acknowledge that, for the most part, it reflected what was considered historically and archaeologically accurate in the first half of the nineteenth century, even though his characters and their story were the product of his imagination.[79] He attempted to synthesize the available knowledge and present it in a form where it could be easily understood. Perhaps this is one of the more dangerous aspects of this book in terms of its relationship to Campanian scholarship. Because of its perceived accuracy in some areas, the boundaries between fantasy and reality have become confused and there has been a tendency to assume the romance has some veracity.

The effect of this novel on the perception of the site was almost immediate. William Gell, for example, wrote in a letter to the Society of Dilettanti in March 1835 that, after reading the book, he mentally peopled the site with the characters from the novel and could not look at the House of the Tragic Poet as belonging to anyone else than Glaucus, the protagonist of *The Last Days of Pompeii*.[80] Nearly thirty years later, a description of some of the first casts that were made was prefaced by the suggestion that they would have provided the basis for an excellent scenario by the talented author of *The Last Days of Pompeii* (see Chapter 10).[81]

The continued impact of this work is observable in the tendency to 'reflesh' the skeletons of victims and describe their last moments. There are numerous examples of the direct influence of this novel on twentieth- and twenty-first century Campanian scholarship, though just a few will suffice to illustrate its impact.

Corti described the impact of the eruption on Pompeii as his own version of *The Last Days of Pompeii*.[82] He embellished skeletal and other evidence to provide a narrative of the event. Not surprisingly, his account also included many of the legendary skeletal finds, as well as those from the Villa of Diomedes.

Ciprotti, in an article tellingly titled *'Der letzte Tag von Pompeji'*, stated that the only way to reconstruct the individual tragedies of how the victims met their fate was to use their remains as a guide. Like Bulwer-Lytton, he used the technique of reconstruction from the body and its context. He considered that the value of the skeletons, and more importantly the casts, was that they could be used to increase knowledge of the 'horrific drama of the eruption'. He stated that the bodies demonstrated 'universal scenes of horror and madness' as well as individual scenes of heroism, selfishness and plunder. Ciprotti consciously included the bodies from the so-called Villa of Diomedes in the series of vignettes of the demise of particular victims because of their connection with nineteenth-century literature. Despite the fact that this was published as a scholarly work, the interpretations given to groups of casts and skeletons are essentially romantic and sentimental. Examples include: the interpretation of a skeleton found with cases of surgical implements in the vicinity of two groups of bodies near the amphitheatre as an example of altruism; manacled individuals who were unable to escape as a result of 'heathen cruelty' to slaves; and a male and female skeleton discovered along with the remains of a 'weak youth' who was thought to have suffered either from rickets or a hunchback, as a case where devoted parents perished in their attempt to rescue their son.[83]

The legacy of Bulwer-Lytton's work is so ingrained in the culture of Pompeian studies that it is likely that scholars are not always consciously aware of the influence of *The Last Days of Pompeii* on their work.

The skeletons that were discovered in this house were studied by a multinational and multidisciplinary team in the last years of the twentieth century.[111] This work included an attempt to extract DNA from these bones.[112] While it was possible to detect the presence of human DNA, there was insufficient preservation to identify any genetic relationship between individuals found in this house. Relationships between individuals were, therefore, based on direct observations and measurement of the skeletons. Three tentative adult couples were postulated amongst these samples, solely on the basis of sex, age at death and their possible proximity at the time of death. The last was little more than a guess, as the skeletons had been removed from their original-find spots and stored in boxes. These assumed couples form the basis of the popular reconstructions already discussed, though the authors suggest a number of possibilities in terms of their relationships to each other as well as their status.[113] Regardless, all these interpretations are highly speculative and are not supported by any clear evidence.

The only biological evidence that could possibly be used to argue for a genetic relationship between any of the individuals found in the house was the apparent discovery of spina bifida occulta on two of the sacra of the victims. However, it should be noted that the sacrum of one of these skeletons was incomplete and the identification of this abnormality was equivocal.[114] Spina bifida occulta is the least significant form of spina bifida, which is the result of failure of the neural tube to fully close in the embryo. A number of conditions can occur when the neural tube fails to close. The cranial vault and the brain do not form if the tube does not close at the head end of the embryo. This condition is known as anencephaly and it is not compatible with survival after birth. If the tube fails to close at the tail end of the embryo, a range of spina bifida conditions with varying degrees of severity occur. Spina bifida occulta involves incomplete fusion of the posterior neural arch and can affect one or more segments of the sacrum. It tends to be clinically insignificant, as the underlying neural tissue tends not to be involved; only the bone of the neural arches fails to fuse. It is often only discovered incidentally when an individual is x-rayed, though the skin in the sacral region is generally marked by a hairy patch. The expression of spina bifida occulta is based on both genetic and environmental factors. It has been observed with a frequency of between 5 and 25 per cent in modern populations.[115] Assuming that there were actually two cases of this disorder in the skeletal sample from the House of Julius Polybius, it was argued that the two afflicted individuals were closely related. They were the pregnant female, who was aged between 16 and 18 years of age and a child who was aged between eight and nine years. It was argued that the pregnant girl had returned to her parents' house with her husband for the delivery of her baby.[116]

Another point that requires comment is the capacity of the pelvis to provide information about the number of children a woman has borne. It has been argued that it is possible to establish the number of pregnancies that have come to term from looking at the degree of pitting on the dorsal surface of the pubic symphysis of a female pelvis – the more pitting the more pregnancies.[117] The pitting has been said to be a reflection of lesions caused by stress to the ligaments that connect the pelvic bones during birth. Even if this were the only reason for such bony changes, it is likely that the most damage would occur with the first birth and, at best, all the changes could tell would be that, at least, one pregnancy had come to term.[118] However, there clearly must be other factors involved in the production of such pits as they can occasionally be seen on the pelvic bones of males and women who have never reproduced. The structure of the human female pelvis is a compromise between the need to have a pelvic outlet that is big enough to enable a baby's head to exit and the fact that a narrow pelvis is the most efficient shape for bipedal locomotion. Wide female pelves can result in stress on ligaments, which presents as bony lesions indistinguishable from any produced by a pregnancy that has come to term (see Chapters 6 and 8).

The vignettes that appear in recent popular literature tend to be based on both the legendary skeletal discoveries and recent academic publications of both the Pompeian and Herculanean skeletons. The final chapter of Butterworth and Laurence's book parallels the chapters on the eruption in the *Last Days of Pompeii*, with detailed descriptions, not only of the final moments in the life of the inhabitants of the House of Julius Polybius but also those of the priests in the Temple of Isis,[119] the Villa of Diomedes[120] and many other locations. It is notable that the recent work of physical anthropologists who have published material from Pompeii and Herculaneum can so easily be applied to such an approach. This is partially due to the fact that a number of the authors of academic publications both neglect to include information about the constraints of the discipline and extend their interpretations beyond the limitations of the evidence. As discussed above, establishing sex, age-at-death and interpretation of pathological change is fraught with difficulties. Attempts to determine genetic relationships are even more problematic (see Chapter 9) and the interpretation of marital relationships or social status solely from the skeletal record is probably futile.

Ultimately, popular culture has driven the agenda of Pompeian skeletal studies and, perhaps even more remarkably, those of Herculaneum. The influence of *The Last Days of Pompeii* has been so pervasive that much of the skeletal evidence continues to be presented by storytelling with a thin veneer of science.

2

AN EGYPTIAN INTERLUDE

Egyptian mummies and tomb finds

To highlight the unique position of Pompeii in terms of the way that popular culture has driven research on human remains, a comparison can be
made with ancient Egyptian tomb finds. This material provides the closest
parallels to Pompeii in terms of remarkable preservation and a long tradition
of popular culture, especially evident in film and literature. But the similarity ends with the way in which the material has been dealt with in relation
to research and general scientific investigation. Unlike the case in Pompeii,
popular culture has not impeded the quality of scientific studies of mummies. In fact, since scientific analysis of Egyptian mummies commenced, it
has always been cutting edge and has provided a benchmark for all studies of
ancient human remains.

Mummies: early contact with the Western world

Mummies entered the west as a result of their perceived medicinal qualities.
The word mummy is derived from the Persian word *mûm*, later *mûmiyá*, which
has variously been translated as pitch or bitumen. The belief that this substance possessed medicinal qualities can be traced as far back as the Classical
era. Pliny the Elder, for example, recommended the use of pitch or bitumen
for gout, leprosy, toothaches and dysentery. Medieval apothecaries expanded
the definition, possibly as a result of a mistranslation, to include 'pitch'
obtained from Egyptian mummies. The 'pitch' observed on mummies actually was a by-product of the resins used in the embalming process. Over
time, actual human tissue from mummies was ground up and sold as a drug.
It was so popular that demand outstripped the supply of available ancient
mummies. This resulted in the looting of graves of comparatively recent
Egyptians, whose bodies were oven dried, disarticulated and sold as *mumia*.[1]

Complete mummies were transported to Europe as collectors' items from
the seventeenth century. Popular belief has it that the first such mummy to
arrive in England was the property of Nell Gwynn, the mistress of Charles

II. This mummy is now allegedly housed in the British Museum. The first reliably documented case of a mummy finding its way into the British Museum collection, however, was one that was transported from Egypt as a curiosity in 1722 by a Mr William Lethieullier.[2]

The 1798 campaign to Egypt, led by Napoleon Bonaparte on behalf of the French Republic, is generally considered to have created the impetus for mummy studies in the European world. In addition to soldiers, Napoleon included 167 scholars in his entourage. He founded a Commission of Science and Art and an Egyptian Institute to guide the documentation of the monuments, technology, geography, flora and fauna of the country. The *Description de l'Égypte*, the Commission's ten-folio-volume illustrated account of the country, played a major role in the development of Egyptomania. This was manifested in the production of arts, crafts and a general fascination with Egyptian culture, which, in turn, promoted the growth of Egyptian collections in major museums, such as the British Museum. Associated with this was an increase in tourism to the area. And with tourism came the need to return home with an authentic piece of ancient Egypt to amuse and delight one's friends.[3]

Mummies were possibly the most sought after trophies. It was practically *de rigueur* for visitors to Egypt in the early nineteenth century to souvenir a portion of mummy, or even better, a complete mummy to display in a prominent place as a conversation piece. Unfortunately, for pilferers, the export of mummies from Egypt was beset with problems. One man, for example, was nearly arrested for murder when a mummy was found in his possession on a train as he tried to transport it across Europe. Sometimes modern bodies were mistaken for those of Ancient Egyptians as in a case reported by Flinders Petrie, when a tourist discovered that they had, in fact, souvenired the body of an English engineer who had perished in Egypt. Pettigrew documented the case of an Egyptian who made his living by manufacturing mummies for gullible buyers.[4]

As with house re-excavation in Pompeii, the mummy industry was associated with the seeding of areas with mummies, to ensure that no really important tourist went home disappointed. As in Pompeii, 'special excavations' were arranged for the benefit of noble visitors. A good example was the 1869 visit of the Prince of Wales (later Edward VII), who was treated to the unearthing of about 30 mummies in a tomb in Western Thebes of the 25th and 26th dynasties. The sarcophagi and mummies were transported to England and dispersed in various collections. It was later discovered that these bodies had been brought together from different sources and placed in a previously excavated tomb that had only yielded one sarcophagus in the 1830s. A further parallel can be drawn with Pompeii in that this type of fakery was continued, but on a lesser scale for mass tourism by people like Thomas Cook.[5]

The first real divergence from Pompeii was in the way bodies were treated once they arrived in the European world. For the most part, human remains in Pompeii were not considered an essential souvenir, though parts of skeletons certainly were collected (see Chapter 5). Mummies did not just serve as conversation pieces. Many formed the basis of theatrical after-dinner amusements. Mummy unwrapping became a popular form of Victorian parlour entertainment. A number of unwrappings were performed to a fee-paying audience as a cynical, money-making exercise.

One of the earliest unwrappings was in 1698 when Louis XIV's consul in Cairo performed the honours for a group of French tourists. He recorded some of the amulets that he found but neglected to discuss any other finds or make any observations about the mummy itself. This was common practice during the ensuing centuries, though there were some exceptions. In 1718, for example, an apothecary by the name of Herzog unwrapped a mummy and published a number of his observations. He also ground the mummy up and sold the powder as a novel way of financing this research. The famous physical anthropologist and physician Blumenbach unwrapped a number of mummies in England during the 1790s. His work involved mummies from both private and public collections. One of his key discoveries was that a substantial number of these mummies were fakes. The fakery was not only modern. Animals, single bones or rags bound up to give the appearance of mummified children, were occasionally used to construct mummies in antiquity.

The first investigation that could really be described as scientific was undertaken in 1828 on the so-called 'Leeds Mummy'. Chemical analysis was attempted and, though there were no conclusive results, it marked a shift in attitude and provided a basis for a more scientific approach to future mummy unwrappings. Belzoni famously unwrapped some mummies for the public with the assistance of one Thomas Pettigrew. Pettigrew then moved on to unwrap mummies on his own. To develop his professional skills, Pettigrew purchased a few mummies that he unwrapped in private where he could take notes about his observations and conclusions. He then commenced public unwrapping to audiences who paid for the privilege of viewing these spectacles. The first of these took place in the lecture theatre of Charing Cross Hospital in 1833. Amongst the audience were antiquarians, Egyptologists, artists, peers, royalty, diplomats, physicians, army officers and anyone from the great unwashed who could afford the admission price. These were sell-out events, with people being turned away at the door. These ethically questionable exercises, nonetheless, did yield valuable information about the various types of mummies and methods of mummification. In 1834, Pettigrew published his *History of Egyptian Mummies*, one of the first academic publications on the subject.[6]

Mummies for fun and profit

Another point of divergence with Pompeii is the industry that developed around mummies. While some unscrupulous people collected human remains from Pompeii as souvenirs, they did not appear to be considered of any value outside a private context. The situation was quite different in Egypt where the mummy trade formed part of the nineteenth century economy. The precedent for the mummy industry was its popularity as a drug and the use of mummy for medicinal purposes continued into the nineteenth century. A huge number of mummies found their way to Europe to satisfy the demand, despite the fact that this trade was not sanctioned by the Egyptian authorities.

Apart from the above-mentioned mummies that were exported for unwrappings, they were also used for various, and sometimes unexpected, purposes. They were, for example, used in the manufacture of the artist's oil paint known as Mummy Brown. It has been claimed that cat mummies were used as ballast in ships and then when they reached their European destination they served as fertilizer until the public sensibility created enough pressure to stop this trade. They were also traded as curios and most museums that were in existence in the nineteenth century would have housed at least one mummy, or portions of mummies, in their collection. There is an apocryphal story of the use of mummy wrappings for the manufacture of the brown paper used by butchers and grocers in North America. The paper was ostensibly used for wrapping produce until the industry was put to a halt by a cholera out-break that was thought to have originated in the mummification by-product.

The mummy industry was not merely the realm of insensitive Europeans. In Egypt, mummies served as firewood as the population had little other fossil fuel at its disposal. Similarly, mummified arms and legs were claimed to make excellent torches. Mark Twain famously made the spurious sugges-tion that they were also burnt to power locomotive engines.[7]

Mummies for science and entertainment

Amazingly, large numbers of mummies survived the nineteenth-century onslaught and subsequently could be employed to better understand the people of ancient Egypt.

As mentioned above, Napoleon's campaign inspired interest in ancient mummies, which led to organized expeditions to excavate and loot the ancient contents of tombs. This activity continued into the twentieth century.

Politics obviously played an important role in the growth of the excavation and plundering of tombs. When Mohammed Ali came to power as the ruler of Egypt at the beginning of the nineteenth century, he encouraged a large European presence in his country, as he was anxious to gain access to Western technology and trade. He also was very enthusiastic about improved diplomatic ties with Europe. A number of diplomats took the opportunity to amass antiquities for personal, as well as national, gain. Two of the major protagonists in this area were Giovanni Battista Belzoni, who worked for the British repre-sentative Henry Salt and the Consul General for France, Bernardino Drovetti.

Belzoni is the better known of these two characters, partly because he was more careful in his work and partly because of his remarkable history. He started his career as a strongman in a circus. He then trained as an hydraulic engineer and arrived in Egypt in 1816 to sell the new ruler of the country an irrigation pump. The demonstration of the pump was far from successful and Belzoni was forced to make an abrupt career change. His skills in moving large objects proved extremely valuable for his new role as excavator and tomb robber. He eventually returned to England with a large collection of mummies, some of which were used for very successful public mummy unrollings.[8]

Like Pompeii and other Vesuvian sites, the early history of Egyptian tomb excavation was marked by its similarity to a mining operation. The initial excavations primarily served to line the coffers of the people who excavated and commissioned such work. There were some notable exceptions and a more rigorous approach began to prevail by the middle of the nineteenth century.

In the early years of the twentieth century, American-funded expeditions were carried out under the aegis of the Egyptian Antiquities Service. These expeditions were a forerunner to international expeditions to Egypt, which became fairly common as the century progressed. Projects were undertaken by American and European institutions as well as independent wealthy individuals who were able to obtain permits. Flinders Petrie, for example, led a number of expeditions both for the English-based Egypt Exploration Fund and the British School of Archaeology in Egypt. Petrie is generally credited as the founder of scientific archaeology in Egypt. He was responsible for the excavation of numerous tomb sites, some of which yielded important information in establishing the history of mummification. Other archaeologists, like John Garstang, who worked in the ensuing decades could be accused of expending far less effort on documentation and analysis of the human remains than the grave goods.

Straight-out tomb robbing still continued throughout the late nineteenth and early twentieth centuries despite the fact that it was illegal. Objects obtained from tombs would always find buyers and major institutions, like the British Museum, were amongst the worst culprits when it came to making the job of the tomb robber worthwhile.

Perhaps the single find that most influenced the popular imagination in the twentieth century was the discovery of the tomb of Tutankhamun in the Valley of the Kings by Howard Carter in 1922. As the first intact royal burial to be exposed, it provided important information about the range of objects that accompanied a royal person to their grave. Also, although the young king was only a minor player in Egyptian history, the discovery of his tomb had an enormous impact on popular culture, influencing clothing, furniture, cinema and even confectionary design, as well as inspiring music.[9]

The mummy in popular culture

From the time of Napoleon's expedition, artefacts found in Egyptian-tomb contexts inspired the arts and the design of objects used in daily life. As already discussed, this was also the case with finds from the sites destroyed by Mt Vesuvius. Well-preserved human remains have continuously exercised influence in all media associated with popular culture. As with Pompeii, the macabre finds of mummies spawned numerous novels, and later, films. If anything, mummy finds in Egypt exerted greater influence on popular culture than the bodies of the victims from Pompeii. In film alone, mummies provided the inspiration for around 50 productions between 1909 and 2001.[10]

The mummy in literature – Mr Gautier again

Apart from the occasional incidental appearance of mummies in Tudor literature, such as Shakespeare's *Macbeth* and *Othello*, the mummy doesn't appear as a key character in novels until the nineteenth century.[11] Since then, there has been a plethora of mummy literature.[12]

Most notable, for the purposes of this study, is the presence of Theophile Gautier's works in the mummy literature. Gautier was one of the pioneers of this genre. He produced two works on Egyptian mummies, *The Romance of a Mummy* in 1857 and a short story, *The Mummy's Foot*, in 1863.[13] The latter obliquely refers to the practice of collecting portions of mummies as souvenirs. Like *Arria Marcella*, this story involves a hero with a disconcerting tendency to form attachments with portions of older, long-dead women.

The Mummy's Foot has the most obvious parallels with *Arria Marcella*. The story is fabulous enough to warrant gratuitous retelling: the tale opens with the protagonist idly entering a curio shop in Paris. His fancy is taken by a beautiful foot, which at first he mistakes for a fragment of a bronze statue. To his surprise, the foot is made of flesh. It transpires that it is, in fact, a portion of a mummy. And not just any mummy; it is an extremity of the Princess Hermonthis. Despite the fact that the foot is human, the hero desires to use it as a paperweight. The wizened old shopkeeper considers that a novel application, which would certainly have surprised the Princess's father, the Pharaoh.

Undeterred, our hero purchases the foot and takes it home wrapped in a piece of old damask. He is uncommonly delighted with his purchase and immediately puts it to use, placing it on a pile of papers. When he retires that night, he falls into a deep slumber and dreams that he is in his room. Everything appears normal until he notices his paperweight, which has started moving about and hopping amongst his papers. He is somewhat disturbed by this as he prefers 'sedentary paperweights'.[14]

The curtains then begin to move and he hears a sound like a person hopping around on one foot. This is followed by the appearance of the single-footed Princess Hermonthis herself. She is unable to catch her bounding loose foot until she speaks with it. The foot somehow manages to explain to her that it has been bought and no longer belongs to her unless she can repay the price of purchase. Our hero gallantly offers the princess her foot as he has no desire to cripple such a lovely individual. She is then able to reunite her severed foot to her leg. To thank our unnamed hero, she offers to present him to her father, as she is certain that he will be pleased that her foot has been restored. She also replaces his missing paperweight with a figure of Isis that she wears around her neck.

They are transported to a vast chamber in a granite mountainside. There he sees a whole collection of dessicated mummies – kings, their retinues and their mummified animals – returned to life. They all appear to be delighted that the princess is again intact. The Pharaoh asks our hero to name his reward. He asks for permission to marry the princess as it strikes him that it would be appropriate to replace her 'foot with her hand'.[15]

Taken aback by this request, the old Pharaoh inquires about his age and provenance. He replies that he is 27 years old. The assembled masses are shocked that one so young could consider matrimony with a woman who is 30 centuries his senior. The Pharaoh informs him that the age discrepancy is just too great to allow the marriage even to be considered. Even a two-thousand-year-old would be a trifle on the young side for such a venerable individual. The ancient Egyptian bemoans the fact that youngsters like him appear to be unable to preserve themselves and he really thinks that his daughter should have a husband who has the capacity to last over the millennia. Our hero awakens and finds himself back in his own apartment but the mummy's foot is no longer there. It has been replaced by a green clay statue of Isis.

What separates Egyptian popular culture from that of Pompeii is that it really did not have a significant impact on research output. Popularizing ancient Egypt obviously increased interest in tomb sites and the collection of antiquities, including mummified remains. This would have had an impact on funding of expeditions but it did not determine the direction of research. It is in stark contrast with the considerable and continued influence of popular literature, especially *The Last Days of Pompeii*, on the interpretation of human skeletal finds from Campania.

Egyptian mummies and science

Initial anthropological studies on Egyptian remains were limited to mummy unwrapping and craniometric studies. The latter were the most common analyses performed on skeletal material in the nineteenth century and were undertaken to establish so-called racial types (Chapter 3). One of the key nineteenth-century craniometric studies on Egyptian material was by Morton. Phrenological studies were also carried out until this type of research was duly discredited. It is notable that this type of work did not take advantage of the research possibilities provided by preserved soft tissue. This was set to change. The emphasis for future work would shift from typology to more medically oriented research.[16]

A fortuitous sequence of linked events provided the impetus for the first rigorous and systematic examinations of Egyptian mummies. Government reaction to public outrage over the construction of the first Aswan Dam in 1902 was a catalyst for this work. When the reservoir behind the dam was filled in 1903, the First Cataract on the Nile and Philae were lost and much of the valley of the Nile was flooded. Many monuments, burials and other artefacts were destroyed both as a direct result of the flooding and because of the ensuing seepage. There was considerable public resentment for these losses. This was exacerbated by a proposal from the Egyptian government to increase the height of the dam by a further seven metres in 1907, as it would result in massive flooding of a considerable area. To stave off criticism about the desecration of Egypt's cultural heritage, the government made the politically sensible decision to commission a systematic survey of the region prior to the planned deluge. Under this scheme, all monuments were to be documented. Burials were to be excavated and their contents removed before areas were submerged. In addition, all burials were to be recorded in detail, photographed and their contents subjected to analysis.[17]

Another key factor that determined the direction of Egyptian mummy research was the combination of British dominance and involvement in the foundation of the English-language Government School of Medicine in Cairo. It also established the agenda for mummy research, which to this day is mostly focused on palaeopathology. This medical institution was able to provide both the expertise and the resources to conduct mummy research. Three of the professors at this school exerted a profound influence on the study of mummies in the twentieth century. They were Grafton Elliot Smith in anatomy, Alfred Lucas in chemistry and Armand Ruffer in bacteriology. Elliot Smith only spent seven years in Egypt but continued his research when he moved to England. Ruffer established techniques for the examination of mummified soft tissues for evidence of disease, especially at a microscopic level. Some of his techniques, including that for the rehydration of desiccated soft tissue, are still in use. Among other things, Lucas worked on the chemical analysis of finds from Tutankhamun's tomb and performed experiments to determine the methods used in mummification.[18]

When the tomb of Tuthmosis IV was discovered in 1903, the mummy of the ruler was subjected to a public unwrapping for the benefit of the upper echelons of Cairo. Unfortunately, this was more an entertainment than a scientific exercise and yielded little useful information. Elliot Smith later was able to conduct a more rigorous study of this mummy, including the use of x-ray analysis to determine age-at-death.

The discovery of rays that were to become the basis of the new method of visualizing internal structures through x-ray technology in 1895, by Roentgen, a German physicist, took mummy research in a new direction. Early mummy investigations involved unwrapping the bandages and ultimately compromising the fabric of the mummy. This new technique had the huge advantage of being non-destructive. This meant that signs of trauma and disease could be recognized without performing an autopsy. It should be noted that the early use of x-rays was at least as important for the discernment of associated artefacts, such as amulets and jewellery, as for the understanding of the lives and deaths of the mummies.

A gentleman by the name of Koenig was responsible for performing the first x-ray investigations of human and animal mummies in Frankfurt in 1896. Flinders Petrie was responsible for the next x-ray of a human mummy, which was undertaken in 1897 and published in the following year. When Elliot Smith undertook to x-ray the mummy of Tuthmosis IV, the only x-ray machine in Cairo at that time was in the nursing home. Elliot Smith and Howard Carter had to transport the deceased pharaoh to this destination, stretched across their laps, in a taxi. Elliot Smith followed this study with an examination of the royal mummies from Deir el-Bahri and the tomb of Amenophis, as well as numerous other mummified individuals.[19] By the 1920s and 1930s, x-raying was an established technique for mummy research.[20]

The research that resulted from the raising of the Aswan Dam required more staff than the Government Medical School could provide and additional English scholars were employed. The two most notable of these were Frederic Wood Jones and W.R. Dawson. Douglas Derry succeeded Elliot Smith as professor of anatomy and was responsible for the examination of the body of Tutankhamun. Large numbers of mummies were subjected to autopsy in the first quarter of the twentieth century.

Outside of Egypt, work was also taking place on mummies in museum collections, most notably in Manchester. In 1908, Margaret Murray, the curator of the Manchester Museum, instigated a multidisciplinary study of two mummies from the same tomb. She worked with a physician, three chemists and two textile experts. This was the precursor of the type of approach that would dominate research in the latter part of the twentieth century.[21]

This period of intense activity was short lived and mummy studies dwindled for some decades before the next wave of research commenced. There are a number of reasons for this decline. Major events, such as the Depression, World War II and the Middle East conflict, clearly played a large role but other factors also had an impact on mummy studies. Political and economic changes during World War II affected the way excavations were funded and organized, which led to preference being given to non-funerary sites. This was paralleled with an increased emphasis on linguistic evidence.[22]

Though on a much smaller scale, research did continue. In the 1930s Boyd and Boyd undertook serological studies to attempt to determine blood types from mummy tissues and Moodie x-rayed mummies and identified skeletal pathology from the Chicago Field Museum collection.

One of the by-products of World War II was the development of new technologies, which could then be modified for non-military applications. Electron microscopes, for example, were used to examine mummified tissue by the end of the 1950s.

The 1960s saw new interest in the potential of human remains to provide evidence about the past. The fascination with scientific techniques that could be applied to human remains, including hair and soft tissue, is reflected in the publications of Brothwell and Sandison.[23] New developments in blood antigen serology meant that further studies could be made in an attempt to establish familial relationships between mummified individuals. The effect of changes to human tissue after death, desiccation and time on interpretation of ancient remains was also addressed.[24]

This work led the way to a revival of mummy investigations in the 1970s. The dissection of a number of Egyptian mummies in Detroit by Cockburn and a huge interdisciplinary team of scientists, led to the formation of the Palaeopathology Association.[25] Other major mummy projects were also carried out in the US and UK. Perhaps the most notable was that of the Manchester Museum. Rosalie David reinstated the interdisciplinary programme commenced by Margaret Murray in the first decade of the twentieth century. This type of investigation of mummies in museum collections has now become a global exercise.

Scholars quickly appreciated the benefits non-destructive x-ray technology provided when it became available. Similarly, CT (Computed Axial Tomography) scans found favour soon after the technique was developed. CT scans enable the production of three-dimensional images. Further, the associated software enables specific features to be isolated. Density differences can be used to produce soft tissue images. Numerous other techniques have been developed and employed since the 1970s to gain information about diet, genetic relationships, diseases and methods of mummification.

The problem of post-mortem changes to some cells initially limited the use of electron microscopy but this has been mitigated by coupling it with an electron probe that is capable of energy dispersive x-ray analysis, known as EDXA. This technique is especially useful in the diagnosis of ancient pathology, as are immunohistological studies and endoscopy. Stable isotope ratio studies in skeletal and soft tissues provide some indication of diet. Small sequences of DNA have been recovered and amplified from ancient soft tissue. These may provide evidence of both genetic relationships between mummies and infectious agents, such as bacteria.[26]

The main limitation to recent mummy research has been cost. One of the factors that assisted cutting-edge research on Egyptian mummies is the fact that mummies were transported trans-globally during the nineteenth century and eventually found their way into museum collections. This provided two distinct advantages, which enabled research that would not have been possible on finds from a site like Pompeii. First, there were numerous accessible mummies and, second, the expense of working on discrete collections could be more easily borne by individual museums or research institutions. Until comparatively recently, researchers were not compelled to obtain permission from Egyptian authorities to perform x-ray or other analysis on mummies held in collections around the world. This contrasts strongly with the majority of the skeletal material from Pompeii, where access is limited and controlled by the Italian Superintendency. While it is essential for a country to control its heritage, obtaining permission to undertake analysis was limited until the latter part of the twentieth century, when a policy that encouraged scientific research was implemented.

Conclusion

Human skeletal remains found in archaeological contexts have not always been treated with respect and their potential as a source of evidence was not appreciated by early excavators. Skeletons were routinely discarded from numerous archaeological sites right into the twentieth century. Human finds from both Pompeii and Egypt were unique for a number of reasons. The survival of the forms of bodies in Pompeii and the actual soft tissue in Egypt, coupled with the remarkable preservation of their contexts and the impressive array of associated artefacts, gave these sites unrivalled appeal. The initial treatment of human finds both in Pompeii and Egypt was similar. Skeletons and mummies were used as props for vignettes or re-excavations that were produced for the edification of visitors. Human finds from both Pompeii and Egyptian tomb sites inspired popular literature and film.

A fortuitous series of circumstances in Egypt produced an environment that was conducive to scientific research. This resulted in mummy research providing a benchmark for all investigation of ancient human remains, especially in the field of palaeopathology. Numerous mummies have been subjected to analysis with no reference to the huge body of popular culture based on mummy finds. In contrast, there was no associated culture of science in Pompeii and it was, therefore, more likely that popular culture would have a greater impact. Pompeian research on human remains not only lagged behind that of Egypt but was also palpably influenced by one particular work of fiction, *The Last Days of Pompeii*. So the key difference between the study and interpretation of human remains from Pompeii and Egypt up to the final decades of the twentieth century is that in Pompeii skeletal investigation remained bound with popular culture, whilst in Egypt popular culture and scientific research had a parallel existence with no apparent overlap.

3

AN ANTHROPOLOGICAL RESOURCE

The middle of the nineteenth century was marked by a discernible shift in attitude to the human skeletal remains that had been exhumed from Pompeii. Instead of merely functioning as props for either literary or physical reconstructions, this material was now recognized as having value as a scientific resource. The first scholarly examination of the Pompeian human skeletal material was published a little over a hundred years after the first official excavation of the site.

The impetus for the initial investigations was the establishment of the Commission for the Reform of the Royal Bourbon Museum and the Excavations of Antiquities of the Kingdom in 1848. This commission was set up by Ferdinand II under political pressure, as there were serious problems with the management of archaeological sites in the region around Pompeii. Raphaele d'Ambra reported to the Commission later in that year that bones and other finds had been neglected and remained in deposits without any attempt to ensure their preservation. Further, permission had been denied to a French chemist, Jean Pierre Joseph d'Arcet, to conduct research on the human remains. The Commission made 11 proposals to facilitate the reopening and subsequent protection of the archaeological area of Pompeii. One of these proposals was to open a gallery of Pompeian skeletons, which would involve the donation of skulls and other skeletal material to the Royal University of Studies in Naples. This was the first real acknowledgement that the human skeletal remains were of anthropological significance. Unfortunately, the liberal political climate was altered by the restoration of the monarchy, which meant that the proposals of the Commission were never put into practice.[1]

Early investigation

Stefano Delle Chiaie revived interest in the issues associated with storage and research on the Pompeian skeletons in 1853. He was responsible for the establishment of a sizable collection of skeletal material in the Anatomical Museum of the Royal University of Naples and undertook the first study of the bones that were available.

The first major publication of the human skeletal remains from Pompeii that included raw data and systematically presented results appeared in 1882. It involved the research of Giustiniano Nicolucci, the founder of the Institute of Anthropology of the University of Naples.[2] Nicolucci summarized and reviewed the studies on the human bones from Pompeii that preceded his work.[3] His literature review is revealing as Nicolucci was very much a man of his era. To him craniology, and more specifically craniometry, was paramount in anthropological studies and works that were not devoted to measurement and discussion of skull form were not considered important. He was fairly dismissive of the 1854 publication of Delle Chiaie. This was partly because its main focus was on a description of the pathological changes that he observed. It also contained two analyses of the chemical composition of Pompeian bones, which were undertaken by Lehman for comparison with the chemical composition of modern bones. Nicolucci was apparently not interested in the pathology and lamented that craniology scarcely received a mention in this work, there merely being a short note stating that some skulls were globular, others ovoid and that a few were oblong in form. The final type of skull observed in this work was interpreted as African, probably representing slaves who were in the service of the wealthy citizens of Pompeii.[4] Nicolucci was very critical of this work and stated that he thought that this brief description did not shed much light on 'the natural history of Pompeian man', especially since it did not include measurements. He stated that all Delle Chiaie's work revealed was that there was no uniform skull shape in the sample and that one could divide the skulls into specific types. Nicolucci, however, did not appear to be convinced that enough evidence was produced to establish these assertions, especially with regard to the so-called oblong or African crania.[5] Delle Chiaie's publication certainly tends towards being data-free, which does limit its scientific value.

Nicolucci also expressed reservations about the Pompeian skull that was illustrated in the work of Sandifort as it also had not been measured and there had been no attempt to compare it to other crania. Conversely, he considered that the publication of another Pompeian skull by Vrolik and Van der Hoeven provided an accurate description. This skull had been affected by osteo-sclerosis and displayed extreme brachycephaly, with a cephalic index of 87.3. These two scholars interpreted this skull as Greek in form, based on the work of the nineteenth-century Swedish anatomist Retzius, who defined and popularized the cranial or cephalic index. This is the ratio of maximum width to maximum length of the cranium and it was applied in the nineteenth and the first half of the twentieth centuries as an indicator of 'race'. Skulls that were described as long-headed, or dolicocephalic, had an index of no more than 75, whilst those that were more short headed were classified as brachycephalic and had an index of, at least, 80. Retzius classified the Greeks to be among the brachycephalic populations in

Europe. Nicolucci, as a typical nineteenth-century anthropologist, accepted the cephalic index as a reliable criterion for 'race' determination. However, he chose to disagree with the famous Swedish anthropologist's pronouncements as Retzius did not examine the skeletal remains of ancient Greeks. Retzius only used modern skulls, whereas Nicolucci found from his experience that the skulls of ancient Greeks were generally dolicocephalic. While Nicolucci considered that the judgement of the nationality of the Pompeian skull by Vrolik and Van der Hoeven was not exactly correct, he stated that he was certain that it did not represent one of the Pompeian types. He considered that its excessive brachycephalism was also partially due to pathological change.[6]

Presuhn published an article on Pompeian anthropology in 1881. This work was based on a minimal number of skulls. All that was stated was that they were big and robust with a strong and protuberant occiput, the facial angle was open, the face was full and the nose large. He considered that the stature of the Pompeians was medium, like other South Italians, and the hair was generally brown or almost black.[7]

Though it was apparent that Nicolucci was unimpressed with the fact that Presuhn formulated his description of the ancient Pompeians from virtually no skeletal evidence, he did not comment on the reconstruction of features that cannot be determined from the skeletal record, like hair colour. At best, such attributions could only have been based on extrapolation from ancient paintings or observations of the modern population. There was a long tradition for such reconstructions, which extended well into the twentieth century. Angel, in his work on skeletal material from Attica, for example, demonstrated a remarkable ability to detect not only hair but also eye colour from skulls. This can be seen in his description of people he classified as Nordic-Iranian from their skulls as 'probably … tawny haired, blue-or-green eyed blondes as well as brunettes'.[8] Such an approach negates the value of any study since the conclusions are drawn prior to commencement from preconceived 'types', presumably recognizable in modern populations.[9]

It is possible that Nicolucci's preference for things cranial explains why he neglected to mention the examination of a single right femur by Amabile, which was found to have an untreated compound fracture that had healed at right angles.[10]

Despite his obvious bias, Nicolucci presented a critical summary of the first studies of the Pompeian skeletal collection. It is apparent that he perceived the need for a more systematic study based on a large sample as compared to the essentially antiquarian approach of his predecessors.

The work of Nicolucci

Nicolucci's work provides a very good case study of nineteenth-century physical anthropology. It deserves detailed consideration as it was the major publication on the Pompeian skeletons in the nineteenth century and continued to be considered the seminal work on this material until this type of cranio-metric approach was challenged in the latter part of the twentieth century.

The skeletal remains that Nicolucci used for his study were either dis-played in cabinets or stored in special rooms in the anatomical museums in the University of Naples. Nicolucci did not state whether these collections comprised complete skeletons or merely crania but it is notable that he considered that the main purpose of this material was to provide information about the cranial form, and, therefore, enable scholars to determine the exact 'type' of the Pompeian skulls. These could in turn be compared with ancient Italian crania from known populations to establish the relationship of the Pompeian victims with the other ancient populations in the region. Nico-lucci also considered that this work would be of value in the determination of the cranial and physiognomic variability of ancient and contemporary Campanian people. He stated that this aspect of the study could be guided by observations from Pompeian wall paintings.[11]

Nicolucci described the history and ethnology of Pompeii to provide a context for his craniological study. His ethnological description was based on the ancient literary sources, like Strabo and Pliny the Elder (Chapter 4). He did not use the skeletal record to test the literary sources.[12] Their accounts were accepted as fact. This approach to written evidence in relation to physical evidence has been typical until comparatively recent times. Nicolucci also subscribed to the notion that the old, the very young, the infirm and women made up the majority of the victims, even though it was unencumbered by evidence.[13]

Sex and age-at-death of the sample

Nicolucci studied a sample of 100 skulls, 55 of which he determined to be male and 45 female. He considered that the entire range of ages was repre-sented in his sample, with the majority being between the ages of 60 and 90 (Chapters 6 and 7).

Non-metric traits

Nicolucci only commented on the presence of three non-metric traits asso-ciated with the skulls he examined. These were metopism, wormian bones and inca bones (Chapter 9). It is significant that Nicolucci related these findings to cephalic index and cranial capacity, which were considered to be the most important population indicators in the nineteenth century. From his conclusions from the data on metopism, it was obvious that he con-sidered that non-metric traits also provided a contribution as population descriptors. Nonetheless, his presentation of the cases of wormian and inca bones in the sample was more antiquarian in nature, where incidence was apparently noted for curiosity value and no conclusions or comparisons were drawn, though it is possible that comparative data were available at that time.[14]

Metric observations

Nicolucci stated that his classification of Pompeian skulls was based on the work of Linnaeus. In the mid-eighteenth century, Carl Linnaeus constructed the first formal classification scheme of different human groups as part of his greater taxonomy of living organisms. He identified four separate types: Europaeus albus (European white), Asiaticus luridus (Asiatic yellow), Americanus rufus (American red) and Africanus niger (African black). This work, like others of its period, incorporated perceived cultural characteristics with the physical traits.

Nicolucci emphasized the importance of the cephalic index in relation to the other metric data he collected by discussing it in a separate section. He determined that 14 per cent of the sample he studied was dolicocephalic, 43 per cent mesocephalic and 43 per cent brachycephalic, with a mean index of 77.7, which is in the mesocephalic, or moderate-headed, range. He noted that there were differences in the proportions of this index between the males and females in the sample, with males having a relatively higher incidence of dolicocephaly, whilst the females tended to be more mesocephalic and brachycephalic. The mean cephalic index for the female sample was 78.1 whilst that for the males was 77.3. He concluded that the variation he observed in the cranial index in this sample did not reflect, as some scholars before him had suggested, foreign forms. He considered that all the Pompeian skulls conformed to a common type, which he called the 'Pompeian' or 'osco-campano' type. This information, in conjunction with the rest of the large set of metric data that Nicolucci collected, was used to describe the features of the 'Pompeian' type.[15]

The Pompeian type

From his cranial analysis, Nicolucci considered that he was able to identify a Pompeian 'type'. This 'type' was considered to be specifically Southern Italian and was comparable to other regional 'types', like the Oscan or Samnitic 'type'. It presented under the various cranial forms, dolicocephalic, mesocephalic and brachycephalic, though, in general, mesocephaly was found to be predominant, followed by brachycephaly and then dolicocephaly. Nicolucci considered that brachycephaly was more frequently found in the female than in the male cranial series, whilst there was a higher incidence of dolicocephaly in the male series. The mean cranial capacity for males was calculated at 1500 cc for the males and 1323 cc for the females. The majority of the males were found to have a cranial capacity higher than the overall mean of 1412 cc, whilst most of the females were observed to have a cranial capacity below this figure. The forehead was not found to be very broad and apparently was less than that observed on Roman crania. The breadth of the anterior part of the skull was said to be a distinguishing feature of Roman skulls. The top of the frontal bone was observed to generally take a more or less ogival or pointed arch form, a characteristic that was considered to be a regional constant through time.

The form of the face was described as more or less oval, with cheekbones that only projected minimally. The jaw of the Pompeian type was considered to be rather large, heavy and high, the net result of which was a lengthened chin. The nose was characterized as high, large and narrow, or leptorrhine, with a nasal index of less than 48. The orbits were observed to be rounded and slightly slanted at the external edge. They were of moderate aperture. The orbits were found to be proportionately larger in the female sample.[16]

It is worth noting that though Nicolucci claimed that the population was mostly mesocephalic, there actually were equal numbers of brachycephalic and mesocephalic skulls in his sample. The sample mean was mesocephalic. Perhaps the reason for Nicolucci's tendency to present the population as more mesocephalic than the evidence actually suggested was that he had a preconceived idea of the features of the people from this region. The so-called Mediterranean 'race' that was first fully described by Ripley in 1899 supposedly included the people who occupied the area around Pompeii. This 'race' was characterized as relatively 'longheaded'. Kroeber noted that despite the fact that this would mean dolicocephaly, most European 'racial' groups described as 'longheaded' were, in fact, mesocephalic. It is likely that these notions about regional differences predated Ripley, which may explain Nicolucci's attempts to massage the data.[17]

The contribution of art

Nicolucci claimed that the wall paintings that had been revealed during the excavations in Pompeii provided an additional source of information about Pompeian anthropology and physiognomy. He stated that the different indigenous types were well illustrated in these paintings. He argued that even though most of the paintings showed depictions of Greek mythological scenes, local models were used. He presented examples from the Italian Renaissance to demonstrate his point. He considered that Raphael's Madonna was an example of Umbrian beauty and that Titian's voluptuous Venus was a reproduction of the form of a typical Venetian woman. He further claimed that the indigenous Pompeian type could still be observed in the modern populations in the region around Pompeii. He included a plate of lithographs in his monograph, which he described as 'faithful reproductions' of faces from Pompeian wall paintings. He used these to illustrate the faces of the local Pompeian types, which, not surprisingly, were noted as mostly mesocephalic (Figure 3.1).[18]

The idea that the wall paintings reflect the features of the ancient Pompeians has persisted, as exemplified in the writing of Conticello, a previous Superintendent of Pompeii, who described the various indigenous

Figure 3.1 Illustration of the Pompeian Type as identified by Nicolucci from Pompeian wall paintings (Nicolucci, 1882, 24–25)

components that he considered were detectable in the wall paintings from the Villa of P. Fannius Synistor in Boscoreale: 'The Campanian element is seen in the soft, flabby physiognomies, the large dark eyes, the familiar facial features and the indolence of the heavy, thick-skinned bodies that lack inner tension.'[19]

There has been considerable discussion about whether Pompeian paintings comprise portraits or idealized images.[20] It has been suggested that whilst portraits can be identified amongst Pompeian wall paintings, for example that erroneously identified as Paquius Proculus and his wife, the term cannot be used in the modern sense. Current wisdom is that portraits were supposed to be read, first, in terms of the context in which they were found and, second, in terms of the style and the attributes associated with the subject. These attributes provided information about the profession and status of an individual, as can be seen in the presumed portrait of Paquius Proculus, which shows the subject holding a writing implement, waxed tablets and a scroll, thus indicating literacy.[21] It is difficult to determine whether these portraits are actually representational. It does, however, seem unlikely that the illustrations Nicolucci chose for his work represent specific individuals or even generalized images of members of a population. The suggestion that the

53

works of Renaissance artists reflect regional types can also be questioned. A comparison, for example, between the work of Leonardo da Vinci and Botticelli, two fifteenth-century artists who were both trained in Florence under the same master, Verrocchio, demonstrates that they were not painting the same 'types' of individuals. The features of Leonardo's so-called Mona Lisa, which is purported to be a portrait of a Florentine woman, are demonstrably different to those of the women in Botticelli's Primavera.[22] It is rather simplistic to assume that idealized models of women owe more to regional form than the idiosyncratic personal preferences of the artist. As can be seen from Conticello's description, the interpretation of indigenous types from paintings appears to be based on preconceived ideas, like the notion that South Italians are dark and swarthy.

Evidence of foreign cranial types in Pompeii

Nicolucci considered that four of the hundred skulls he studied presented a type, which he described as very close to that of the ancient Romans. All four were male, two being mesocephalic and two brachycephalic. According to Nicolucci, there were a number of characteristics that suggested a Roman origin for these crania. He determined that these four crania were fuller, anteriorly wider and more flattened than the other Pompeian heads. The brows and orbits were larger, and the jaws almost circular in form. The cranial capacity was equal to the mean of the Roman crania, which was calculated at about 1525 cc. He also observed what he considered to be Pompeian traits on these skulls, such as the lack or minimal protrusion of the frontal sinuses, the lack of or slight depression of the nose at its root and 'the singular delicacy of all the contours of the skull'. He speculated that these people were not purely Roman but instead were the result of intermarriage between Romans and the indigenous Pompeian population. He also proposed as an alternative explanation, that fusion of types he observed might relate to the common origin of the Roman and Campanian populations.

One skull in particular claimed Nicolucci's attention. It was interpreted as that of a young male, notable in Nicolucci's eyes for its considerable length and laterally protuberant zygomatic bone as well as for its smooth temples, prognathic maxilla and large and heavy mandible. The facial angle was found to be about 70 degrees. He calculated its cephalic index to be 68.8 and its cranial capacity to be just below 1351 cc. Nicolucci considered that this skull had no European parallel and that its characteristics could only be seen in the so-called negroid type associated with people from the African continent. The principal measurements of this skull were compared with the mean measurements of the dolicocephalic male Pompeian skulls. Nicolucci found the proportions of this skull to diverge significantly from those of the other Pompeian dolicocephalic skulls and all other Italian dolicocephalic skulls.

Nicolucci primarily based his classification of this skull on a figure in Retzius' *Ethnologische Schriften* as well as Hartman's *Die Nigritier* since he did not have any African skulls for comparison. The figure Nicolucci consulted in Retzius' publication was of an old Abyssinian who had been in the service of a European family. He considered that the proportions of the different parts of the head in Retzius' publication corresponded very approximately with those of the skull from Pompeii. He suggested that there was, therefore, a high probability that the cranium in the Pompeian sample belonged to an individual from this region. Nicolucci did not consider the discovery of a 'negro' skull in an ancient Roman city at all remarkable since slaves from conquered countries were a well-known element of the Roman economy. In addition, he cited the identification of 'negro' features on a plaster cast of a victim stored in the museum in Pompeii.

Nicolucci concluded that the population of Pompeii in AD 79 was heterogeneous, incorporating an indigenous population along with people from other provinces, such as Rome, and from countries beyond Italy, as evidenced by the skull he identified as 'negroid'. He noted that though there were a number of cranial forms as reflected by the presence of the three types of cephalic index, they combined to form a specific Pompeian 'type' which was comparable to that identified as the ancient Oscan 'type' in other parts of Southern Italy.[23]

Nicolucci's contribution to knowledge of the ancient Pompeians

Nicolucci's work differed from that of his predecessors in that he chose to work on a large sample of material. The work that preceded him was often antiquarian in nature, generally involving only a few examples from which conclusions were drawn or single specimens that were thought to be of interest for some specific feature, such as pathological change. Like most other nineteenth-century physical anthropologists, Nicolucci considered that it was possible to characterize a population solely on the basis of skull shape (see below). He made a battery of measurements on an apparently statistically valid sample. His statistical treatment of the data was very basic, mainly involving the determination of means for specific measurements and indices.

The most significant contribution Nicolucci made to physical anthropology was the publication of the raw data he collected so that it could be compared to and incorporated into contemporary skeletal studies (see below and Chapters 6, 7 and 9). The interpretations he made from this data are generally not relevant in terms of modern skeletal studies as most of the notions he held about the value of craniometry for the determination of European population types are no longer considered valid. For example, the majority of the differences that Nicolucci invoked to separate the Pompeian from the Roman 'type' are almost certainly too superficial to be more than artefacts.

A point to consider when assessing a nineteenth-century analysis of skulls is the demonstrated tendency for such works to be used to reinforce commonly held beliefs about the status of different 'races' and sections of society. Nicolucci's work is distinguished by the absence of value judgements, especially when compared to the work of Linnaeus, which provided the basis for his study.[24]

It is notable that the cranial capacity of the skull Nicolucci interpreted as a 'negro' male is much lower than the male mean for the Pompeian sample. In fact, it is barely higher than the mean that he calculated for the female sample. Most nineteenth-century scholars believed that cranial capacity was a reflection of the size of the brain and, hence, intellectual capability. Groups were ranked hierarchically by the means of their cranial capacity. Such an approach can be seen in the work of Morton. This notion has since been discredited as no evidence has been found to link brain function with size.[25] In the same vein, the difference between the male and female means for cranial capacity is so great that, even though it is not stated in Nicolucci's paper, it is possible that this feature was used as a major criterion for sex determination, as it was commonly assumed that female cranial capacity is significantly lower than that of males (Chapter 6).

Nicolucci did not state what he used to measure cranial capacity. It has been demonstrated that there can be considerable variation in this measurement as a result of the use of different materials; for example in 1841 Morton revealed that white mustard seeds produced more variable results than lead shot. Morton observed differences of up to four cubic inches on remeasurement of skulls with mustard seeds and a margin of error of only one cubic inch with one eighth inch diameter lead shot.

Gould considered that it was possible that Morton may have exercised unconscious bias in the interpretation of measurements made before he forsook mustard seeds. It is possible that Morton unintentionally favoured results which reinforced his preconceived notions of what the cranial capacity ranking of the skulls should have been. That any bias on his part was unconscious was borne out by the fact that Morton presented both his raw data and described his methods.[26] Nicolucci's work is harder to scrutinize as he did not document his materials and methods. While it is likely that the interpretations of the skulls were directly related to the cranial capacities he calculated, consideration should be given to the possibility that Nicolucci's method of measurement could have unconsciously provided him with the results he expected for both sex and 'race'.

Historical overview of population studies

To appreciate Nicolucci's contribution to our understanding of the Pompeian population, his work needs to be viewed in the context of the development of the discipline of physical anthropology. From the eighteenth to the second half of the twentieth century, the main focus of population studies, based on human skeletal remains was taxonomic, where human groups were separated into so-called 'races' by anthropologists, including Nicolucci, Angel and Fürst. The word 'race' was initially introduced into scientific literature as a zoological term by Buffon in 1749. 'Race' was first used in a classificatory sense for humans in 1775 by Johann Friedrich Blumenbach, a German doctor and anatomist who is credited as a pioneer in physical anthropology and founder of craniometry. The impetus for the taxonomic approach to describe human variation was the work of Linnaeus. Traditionally craniometric analysis of the skull was used to provide this information, though non-metric traits could also be used as population markers.[27]

Blumenbach considered race to be a useful tool for classification. He did not invest too much meaning into his system as he considered it to be arbitrary. This appears to have been a reasonable approach, which is borne out by recent studies. In general, he described human variation as continuous, with relatively trivial differences between groups. The classification of people into specific groups is dependent on the criteria that are selected. Various criteria, such as retention of the enzyme lactase into adulthood, the presence of the gene for sickle cell anaemia or different fingerprint patterns all produce sets of groups which are composed of totally different collections of people. Despite Blumenbach's attitude to race, the concept became politicized. In the nineteenth century, there was a tendency to use racial classification to rank different human populations, usually with the group with which the investigator was affiliated at the apex. The Parisian Société d'Anthropologie, founded by Paul Broca in 1859, institutionalized craniology as the basis of anthropological research.[28]

Nineteenth-century racial classification systems were based on several assumptions; most importantly, that skeletal traits were immutable and that the divisions between races were hierarchical. The notion of immutability was challenged by Boas in 1911 when he published his findings of cephalic index measurements, a popular race descriptor, on the children of European immigrants to America. He discovered that environment played a significant role in the determination of this index, as it varied between the children and their parents. Subsequent studies in different parts of the world have confirmed the plasticity of certain traits as a result of altered environment.[29]

The whole concept of racial classification was reassessed at the conclusion of World War II and in the following years, when it became apparent that it had been used as a justification for genocide. The agenda of bioanthropological studies was reconsidered and the majority of scholars abandoned racial studies. The issue of the validity of this form of classification, especially for the so-called European races, was discussed at length. Some anthropologists, like Coon and D'Amore et al., continued to use the racial classification systems, even though most scholars would no longer consider them appropriate, especially for the description of European populations.[30]

Biologically, different races are categorized on the basis that they display a tendency to become separate species. One of the features of human populations is that there is no evidence that speciation is occurring. This can be demonstrated by the fact that individuals from populations that have been geographically and temporally separated for many millennia can reproduce and produce fertile offspring. It is now recognized that there are no human 'races' and that population differences are not discrete but continuous. The use of the term 'race' is no longer considered acceptable by most scholars as it is biologically inappropriate. In addition most researchers would prefer to distance themselves from the nefarious applications of racial studies in the past.[31] Nonetheless, there are, albeit superficial, differences between populations that can provide clues to origin. These result from various processes, including adaptation, genetic drift, small foundation populations and inbreeding groups. While it may seem precious to use other descriptors, like ancestry or population affinities, for current studies that attempt to identify different human groups, they do reflect a more appropriate scientific terminology.

The twentieth century

Barnicot and Brothwell

Barnicot and Brothwell[32] used the data collected by Nicolucci for the males in his sample as comparative material for a statistical study of ancient and modern bones from various regions in an attempt to characterize the ancient Etruscans and to establish their origins. The Penrose statistic was used to determine the distance between populations in terms of size and shape, based on the measurements for maximum cranial length, breadth and height. They found that the Pompeian male sample was close to the Etruscan and modern Roman samples, as well as those of modern Basques and Iron Age Greeks and Britons. When the set of measurements was increased to ten, the Pompeian, along with Roman, Basque, British and Greek Iron Age skulls were found to be further removed from the Etruscan skulls in terms of shape. In contrast, the addition of more characters had the general effect of reducing the distance between the samples in terms of size.

Consideration should be given to the exclusion of female skulls in this population study. Traditionally, skeletal population studies were based on males because, as Barnicot and Brothwell state, 'there are ... systematic differences in size and shape between male and female skulls'.[33] Barnicott and Brothwell accepted Nicolucci's sex attributions without question. This is not surprising in the light of the fact that their only interest in Nicolucci's work was that it provided a data set of an ancient Italian population that could be used to compare with skeletal material of ancient Etruscans. Since Nicolucci did not publish his criteria for sex determination, it is impossible to assess the degree of confidence one could have in his sexing. This means that even if one accepts the assumption that population differences are best represented by one sex, the validity of this work can be questioned on the basis of uncertainty as to the accuracy of sex separation.

The work of D'Amore, Mallegni and Schiano di Zenise

D'Amore, Mallegni and Schiano di Zenise made an examination of the human skeletal remains in Pompeii to mark the 1900th anniversary of the eruption of Mt Vesuvius in 1979. Given the status of such studies by the latter part of the twentieth century, it seems remarkable that the main aim of their study was the 'racial' classification of the ancient Pompeian population. They based their work on an examination of 123 skulls. They concentrated their efforts on crania for convenience because the skull has traditionally formed the basis of most anthropological studies. The crania which formed their sample were in relatively good condition, though they lacked mandibles. Skulls were selected from the skeletal deposit in the Sarno Baths. They were cleaned and then moved to the Forum Baths. Each skull was arbitrarily assigned a number.

Numerical and qualitative observations were made for each skull in the sample. Non-metric or epigenetic traits were also described in accordance with the definitions of Testut, which date to 1917. The epigenetic results have not yet been published.[34]

This study was undertaken as a companion piece to the work of Nicolucci which they described as 'very accurate and detailed'.[35] One of the aims of D'Amore et al. was to check their results against those obtained by Nicolucci. Despite a concerted effort, involving searches in both the *Istituti biologici della Facoltà di Scienze di Napoli* and in the areas of bone storage in Pompeii, they were not able to locate the skulls that Nicolucci examined. They also applied for but were denied access to the skeletal collection in the *Istituto di Antropologia* in Naples where they thought Nicolucci's sample might be found.

Some of the skulls in the sample they collected from the Sarno Baths had large numbers drawn on the frontal bone. They thought it was possible that these bones had been studied by Nicolucci. However, when they checked the measurements against those recorded by Nicolucci they found that there was no concordance. They concluded that the excavators of the skeletons were responsible for these numbers and that these numbered skulls had never been studied.[36]

Sex attribution and determination of age-at-death

D'Amore et al.'s first article involved the examination of the sample of 123 skulls to determine their sex and age-at-death (Chapters 6 and 7). They classified 43 skulls as female and 80 as male and calculated that 35 per cent of the sample they studied were female and 65 per cent were male. They concluded that there was probably considerable overlap between the sexes for the features that they chose for sex separation in their sample of Pompeian skulls. They interpreted two skulls as juvenile, 24 males and 25 females as adult, 45 males and 17 females as mature adults and nine males and one female as senile. Pooling the two genders the percentages were: 1.62 per cent juvenile, 39.84 per cent adult, 50.4 per cent mature and 8.3 per cent senile.[37]

'Racial' classification

In their second paper, D'Amore et al. presented the preliminary results of their 'racial' typology of the Pompeians.[38] They did not consider that their conclusions were radically different to those reached by Nicolucci nearly a century earlier when he described the 'Pompeian type'. Their aim was to examine some aspects of the Pompeian crania in greater depth to build on Nicolucci's original study.

D'Amore et al. described the Pompeian sample they studied in terms of four indices, namely, horizontal or cephalic, vertico-longitudinal, superior facial (or frontal) and nasal. They considered that these provided the basis for an initial 'racial' diagnosis. They defined the 'types' for males and females from the means they obtained for each index. The males were described as mesocephalic, orthocranial, mesosemial and mesorrhine, while the females were described as brachycepalic, orthocranial, mesosemial and leptorrhine. The modes produced the same results. The main difference between the males and females was that the females had rounder heads and finer noses.

They presented their transformed data in a series of four tables. Unfortunately, they did not exclude the two juvenile crania from their study. Juveniles are not usually used for population studies as measurements and proportions alter during the period of growth.

The first table summarized the results obtained for the four indices they calculated. The number of male and female cases for each division of an index were published, along with their percentages, means and standard deviations. The number of cases for certain measurements did not justify this treatment; for example, the provision of a percentage, mean and standard deviation for two to three females for several classifications is of questionable statistical value. No statistical procedures were undertaken to test significance.

The other three tables showed the relationship between the data for different indices. Relative and absolute frequencies were compared with the data obtained for the cephalic and vertico-longitudinal indices, the cephalic and frontal indices and the vertico-longitudinal and frontal indices. No comparisons were made with the nasal index due to the comparatively small number of measurements that could be made to the facial region as a result of post-mortem bone loss. D'Amore et al. concluded from their assessment of the tabulated associations between the three cranial indices that the 'type' they described for their Pompeian sample really did exist and was reflected by the coexistence of mesocephaly, orthocrany and mesosemy. It is worth noting that these are the features which, according to the authors, define the males in the sample.

The final section of this paper involved the 'racial diagnosis' of the Pompeian skulls in this sample. D'Amore *et al.* classified the skulls as Mediterranean, the 'race' that they thought represented Southern Italian populations, albeit with some variation. They suggested that the cephalic index, within certain limits, provided a general guide for 'racial' identification. More certain identification was supposedly provided by the other cranial features, whilst local variation was thought to be reflected in the features of the face. The population was considered to be essentially mesocephalic. The relatively high incidence of brachycephaly was attributed to an earlier indigenous type in the region rather than the result of contact with short or roundheaded populations from Eastern countries, like Anatolia, Mesopotamia and Palestine.[39]

This paper can be criticized on a number of levels. The most important of these is that the basic premises upon which this study was based had been called into question in the preceding decades and 'racial' studies, especially those concerning the so-called European 'racial groups' had been discredited. Further, D'Amore *et al.*, like Nicolucci, interpreted the data so that they would yield the results they expected, namely that the Pompeian sample reflected a mesocephalic population consistent with a Mediterranean 'racial' attribution. While it was perfectly reasonable for a scholar like Nicolucci to make such a study in a nineteenth-century context, it is remarkable that one hundred years later a similar analysis could be conducted so uncritically, and without any reference to the considerable body of recent literature on this topic.

Pompeian skeletal studies from the latter part of the twentieth century to the present

While it took a century for human skeletons to be recognized as an anthropological resource, it required considerably more than an additional century for them to also be seen as a class of archaeological evidence. This meant that, where possible, skeletons would be examined in their excavation context and they would be interrogated in such a way that they would yield answers to questions that actually were of interest to archaeologists. Prior to that, research primarily involved classification. Most archaeologists did not consider this work to be of great relevance to their research and the anthropological studies of Nicolucci and D'Amore and her team were largely ignored in the archaeological literature.

By the time I commenced my work on the human skeletal remains in Pompeii in 1986, all attention had turned to the large collection of victims, which had been discovered four years previously on the beachfront in Herculaneum. These complete skeletons could be carefully excavated and studied in relation to their archaeological context, essentially eclipsing the badly stored piles of bones stored in Pompeian bathhouses (Chapter 5). There was certainly no competition to gain access to the Pompeian material and my work was, at best, considered virtuous, though in general I was just seen as a quaint character working on fairly inferior archaeological material. Sara Bisel told me that she wouldn't touch the collection of Pompeian skeletons with a bargepole.

Ten years later the situation changed, and despite the compromised nature of the sample, the scientific potential of Pompeian skeletons was recognized and they were again considered worthy of examination. Since my investigation, a number of other scholars have studied these bones. Projects have included revisiting the sample of stored bones in the Forum and Sarno Bath complexes, work on new skeletal finds and previously unstudied skeletons, such as those from the House of Julius Polybius (IX, xiii, 1–3). In addition, there have been attempts to undertake histological examination of the bones and to apply techniques like DNA analysis.[40]

Herculaneum

Only 32 human skeletons were discovered in Herculaneum prior to the 1980s. The lack of bodies was interpreted as evidence that the majority of the inhabitants managed to escape the eruption of Mount Vesuvius, either by sea or by travelling north to Naples. It was assumed that they had this opportunity as they were not exposed to the pumice and ash that covered Pompeii. This material was considered to have been responsible for the large number of victims that were found at the latter site. It was suggested that the people of Herculaneum fled so quickly that they were forced to abandon those that were vulnerable as evidenced by the fact that the few victims found in the urban section of Herculaneum included individuals who could not fend for themselves, such as a baby that was discovered in a wooden cradle in the House of the Gem (Insula orientalis II, n.10). The skeletons of these victims were generally left *in situ*.

In 1982, a number of skeletons were uncovered on the ancient beachfront and in nearby boat chambers. By 2002, an estimated total of 350 individuals had been discovered in this area. The management of human skeletal finds was completely revised with these new finds (Chapter 11). Giuseppe Maggi, the Director of Herculaneum initiated a collaborative project with the National Geographic Society, which included the provision of an American physical anthropologist, Sara Bisel, who was responsible for excavation, restoration, conservation and scientific investigation of the human skeletal remains. She was ultimately responsible for the curation and publication of 139 of the victims.[41]

The work of Bisel

Bisel's pioneering work on the human skeletons in Herculaneum was the first attempt to really integrate physical anthropological and archaeological research. There is no doubt that skeletal studies at Herculaneum benefited from the majority of human remains having been found at a time when the value of bones as an archaeological resource was appreciated. This meant that there was the potential for the application of a more rigorous approach to an examination of the remains of these victims.

Sara Bisel was well positioned to study this material for *National Geographic,* as she was comfortable using an approach that was appropriate for the popular magazine (Chapter 1). She was under considerable pressure to individualize the skeletons she studied, giving them names and investing them with personalities that they never had. This, unfortunately, was not limited to the articles that appeared in *National Geographic*. Her approach, which sometimes included extending the evidence to the realm of speculation, intruded into her scientific publications (Chapters 1 and 8). Nonetheless, the work of Bisel represents a significant shift in attitude from that of her predecessors in Campania, who were primarily interested in physical anthropology, especially craniometry, to an interest in the broader archaeological issues. Her work, in part, reflects the interests of her mentor J. Lawrence Angel who, after having worked on 'racial' typology of the ancient Greeks in his early career, became one of the pioneers of palaeodemography after World War II.[42]

As it was customary for the dead to be cremated in the first century AD in Italy, Bisel considered that these skeletons were of particular value, since they provided the first sizeable sample of an articulated Roman population from that period. In contrast, she argued that the Pompeian skeletal sample was of little academic value because the bones of individuals had become disarticulated over time from the poor storage techniques in the eighteenth and nineteenth centuries.[43] She used traditional anthropological techniques to establish sex, age-at-death, stature, stress indicators, population affinity and evidence of pathology and also undertook trace element analysis. Her aim was to examine the Herculaneum bones to determine the health and nutritional status of the population, as well as to gain insight into the occupations and social status of individuals.[44] The results of Bisel's study and those of subsequent researchers at Herculaneum are presented in Chapters 6, 7, 8 and 9.

The work of Capasso

By 1985, the remains of 229 individuals had been recovered from the area around the ancient beachfront. Luigi Capasso and his team commenced a study of 162 of the Herculaneum victims in 1993, which was published in an enormous volume in 2001.[45] An additional 54 victims were examined by Torino and Fornaciari.[46] Capasso's sample included the 139 skeletons studied by Bisel. He estimated that he examined about 30,000 bones over a period of seven years.

4

CONTEXT OF A MASS DISASTER

The remains of Pompeii are often described as reflection of a frozen moment in time. This is the basis of the so-called 'Pompeii premise', which argues that Pompeii is the ideal archaeological site, providing a standard against which all other sites can be measured. The premise is underpinned by the notion that Pompeii was a thriving town that was destroyed quickly and without warning. This concept undoubtedly owes its origins to popular perceptions of the site rather than academic research.[1]

The idea of Pompeii as a frozen moment can probably be traced back to the early excavations, when, for example, the first skeleton was found with a small collection of coins that appeared to have just been dropped.[2] It was reinforced by subsequent discoveries, including those of 1765, when the Temple of Isis was uncovered. On the altar were the remains of the last animal sacrifice and in a room to the rear of the sanctuary, a skeleton was found next to a plate full of fish bones, assumed to be this person's last meal.[3] Such images provided the inspiration for the Romantic movement, as can be seen in Madame de Staël's early nineteenth-century novel *Corinne, ou l'Italie*.[4] With Bulwer-Lytton's *The Last Days of Pompeii*, the perception of Pompeii as a time capsule became enshrined in popular consciousness.

While most scholars who work in Pompeii would acknowledge that the concept of Pompeii as a static moment in time is far too simplistic,[5] a number of academic works on Pompeii nonetheless treat the site as such.[6] It is notable that Pompeian scholars who demonstrate awareness of the complexities of the site persist in invoking the imagery of a frozen moment in their works for a more general audience as exemplified by the following description:

> In no other ancient site is the past as intensely present as in Pompeii where the clock of history stopped so abruptly. Gazing at the breakfast which is still on the table, at the paint and brushes just prepared by the painter about to start his work, or at the slogans in the streets for the forthcoming municipal elections the visitor feels like the prince entering Sleeping Beauty's castle.[7]

Pompeii is far from the perfect site. The 'Pompeii premise' is a romantic ideal that neither Pompeii nor any other site could fulfil. The complexity of the site and its interpretation can be observed on a number of levels. These include the possible impact of the major earthquake experienced by Pompeii in AD 62 and the impact that subsequent seismic activity may have had on the population and the size of the population in AD 79. In addition, it is necessary to consider the form and time span of the AD 79 eruption and how it would have influenced survival prospects of individuals, as well as post-eruption and post-excavation alterations to the site. Examination of these issues enables the parameters of knowledge about the site at the time of its destruction to be established. Since the nature of the sample has been determined by these factors, this information is necessary for the interpretation of the skeletal material.

Impact of the AD 62 earthquake

Pompeii was not an important town in antiquity and only really achieved immortality as a result of the disasters it suffered. The first of these was an earthquake, which was recorded by two ancient writers, Seneca[8] and Tacitus.[9] Tacitus' account is very brief and notes extensive damage to Pompeii. Seneca described the event in more detail, stating that Pompeii in particular was devastated, though the whole Campanian region was affected. He noted that many of the country villas were so badly damaged that they could no longer be occupied. Though there is some disagreement about the date, most scholars now accept that this event occurred on 5 February, AD 62.[10]

While there is no doubt that this earthquake had a major impact on Pompeii and other Campanian sites, there is no consensus as to the exact nature and degree of change brought about by the catastrophe. All signs of damage, partial or completed repairs and rebuilding in Pompeii were traditionally attributed to the AD 62 earthquake. These include: damage and interruption to the water supply, villas and houses which had been damaged so badly that they were virtually uninhabitable, partial or complete destruction of public buildings, like the Capitolium and the Temple of Venus in the region of the Forum and reconstruction of the temples of Vespasian and Isis. Many of the larger houses were roughly repaired and subsequently subdivided into what appear to have been separate apartments. Some were also converted for commercial or industrial uses, such as the modification of a house into a fuller's shop, the *Fullonica Stephani* (I, vi, 7). Houses that were restored were supposedly recognizable by a new system of wall decoration, the so-called Fourth Style. Some houses were totally rebuilt, such as the *Casa dei Vettii* (VI, xv, 1–2).[11]

Much of this evidence cannot be unequivocally associated with the AD 62 earthquake. For example, an inscription commemorating the rebuilding of the Temple of Isis after it was damaged by seismic activity is generally

shifts in national and religious importance of the town over time, increasing industrialization and the development of certain trades in specific areas.[28] The conversion of some larger houses into apartments in Pompeii, for example, may simply have been a reflection of economic change. There is no need to invoke disasters to explain all the alterations in occupation and building usage in Pompeii.

Composition of the population of Pompeii in the last period of occupation

Perhaps the most difficult factor to assess in relation to changes between AD 62 and 79 is whether there was significant abandonment of the settlement by certain sections of the community and whether it had any impact on the composition of the population. The notion of abandonment probably dates back to Seneca,[29] who railed against survivors for emigrating and refusing to return to the region. This, in turn, influenced Winckelmann in the eighteenth century. From the little he had been able to observe on his early abortive visits to Herculaneum, he considered that there was evidence for the abandonment of Pompeii and Herculaneum by a large number of the inhabitants after the AD 62 earthquake.[30] The idea that Pompeii may have been entirely deserted after the earthquake was proposed in the second decade of the nineteenth century, but was rejected after much debate.[31] The notion of partial abandonment has sporadically been suggested and has been resurrected in more recent literature.[32]

The lack of certain expected finds at Pompeii was traditionally interpreted as evidence of post-eruption looting.[33] For example, numerous statue bases were found in the forum, though no trace remained of the statues that should have surmounted them. In addition, there was no evidence of most of the marble flagstones and veneers that once covered buildings in the forum. The possibility that this negative evidence could reflect pre-eruption abandonment has been offered as an alternative explanation. A number of scholars have argued that this resulted in a diminution of the population size in the last seventeen years of occupation.[34] It has even been suggested, though only in popular literature, that the skeletons that have been discovered in the Campanian sites could represent the entire population in AD 79.[35]

While it is quite possible that there was a decrease in population size in the last seventeen years of Pompeii's existence, it is extremely unlikely that the entire AD 79 population was killed by the eruption, given the literary references for survivors and the stratigraphic evidence that indicates the possibility of escape in the first phase of the eruption (see below). In addition, instigation of construction programmes that have been dated to the last 17 years of occupation, such as the building of a new bath complex, the so-called Central Baths or *Terme Centrali* (IX, iv, 5–18), implies that the population could not have been all that depleted. Evidence of continued occupation of structures during reconstruction adds weight to the argument that Pompeii was not abandoned in the years between the AD 62 earthquake and the eruption. Scholars, like Dobbins, argue that such extensive construction work, especially in the Forum could be interpreted as a reflection of growth rather than decline.[36] It has been suggested that it was only in the period immediately preceding the eruption that a considerable number of private residences were fully or partially abandoned as a response to intensified seismic activity.[37]

In terms of the interpretation of the human skeletal remains unearthed in Pompeii, there is no need to establish when abandonment occurred as the key issue is the determination of whether the sample of victims is likely to be representative of the AD 79 population.

The possible importation of labour for public building programmes and reconstruction work could also have contributed to alterations in the population structure in the last 17 years of occupation. These issues should be considered in the light of what is understood about the original composition of the Pompeian population.

The exact origins of Pompeii are uncertain. There is no conclusive evidence for its first settlement, though a number of scholars consider that it was initially occupied by an Italic population, the Oscans.[38] The first century AD geographer Strabo wrote that Pompeii and Herculaneum were occupied over time by various groups of people: Oscans, Etruscans, Pelasgians, Samnites and Romans.[39] The archaeological evidence for the earliest period is only now being revealed as there was a policy of not digging below the AD 79 layer prior to the last decade of the twentieth century to preserve the town as it appeared when it was destroyed.[40]

The earliest structural evidence at Pompeii, a supposedly Doric temple in the Triangular Forum (Reg VIII), was generally interpreted as Greek and said to date to the sixth century BC. On the basis of these remains and the introduction of the cult of Apollo from the Greek colony of Cumae, it was suggested that Pompeii was used as an outpost by the Greek colonists in South Italy to enable them to control the port associated with the town.[41] Research and excavation of the structure in the Triangular Forum at the end of the twentieth century led to a reinterpretation of this temple as Etrusco-Italic. This in turn has resulted in a reassessment of the issue of Greek dominance in Pompeii in the sixth century BC.[42]

Pompeii was dominated by the Samnites in the fifth century BC. The Samnites who settled in this region were known as the *Campani* and spoke the Oscan language. They were an Italic people who originated in the mountainous areas of the Abruzzi and Calabria. Pompeii remained an essentially Samnite centre, despite being an ally of Rome, until it became a Roman colony in 80 BC. The dictator, Sulla, imposed a colony of between two and four thousand veteran Roman soldiers and their families on Pompeii in that year as a punishment for earlier resistance.[43]

It has been generally assumed that Pompeii in AD 79, with its mixed background and its function as a river port, housed a heterogeneous population.[44] The evidence to support this view has largely come from epigraphy. Oscan inscriptions etched on plaster, ostensibly dating to the last seventeen years of occupation, have been cited as evidence of the presence of Italic people. The identification of Greek names in a list of accounts and Greek inscriptions on walls and amphorae were seen as a reflection of a Greek element in the population. Similarly, names like Martha and Mary on wall inscriptions have been interpreted as Jewish and inscriptions on amphorae as Semitic.[45] While such evidence has been considered proof of the presence of a Jewish community in Pompeii,[46] it should be noted that certain scholars, like Mau, were circumspect about the interpretation of names inscribed on amphorae as they could reflect either the dealers of commodities or the owners of the estates where they were found.[47] Wall paintings that have been interpreted as depictions of Old Testament subjects, such as the Judgment of Solomon[48] have also been used as evidence for the presence of a Jewish community in Pompeii. More spurious is the identification of some sculptures as representations of Semitic types on the questionable basis of stereotypical features associated with Jews, like the shape of the nose. It has also been suggested that the discovery of a temple dedicated to Isis provided proof for the presence of Egyptians at Pompeii.[49] Alternatively, it could be argued that this, like all the evidence cited above, merely implies that there was contact between different cultures.

It is possible that the Pompeian population was never as heterogeneous as suggested by the literary sources, which refer more to diversity in language and culture than genetic identity. Ultimately there is no certainty about the original make-up of the population. As a result, it is not possible to do more than postulate the types of changes that may have occurred in the final years of occupation.

It has been presumed that the people who chose to abandon the town were, on the whole, the members of the upper strata; people who were financially independent and whose economic base was not totally reliant on working the land in the Campanian region. A case has been mounted for some wealthy owners to have left their properties in the hands of their household staff during rebuilding.[50]

Evidence has also been presented to support the notion that the old aristocracy was replaced by *nouveaux riches* individuals, such as the Vettii brothers who were credited with the reconstruction and refurbishment of the so-called *Casa dei Vettii* (VI, xv, 1–2). Similarly, it has been suggested that the *Villa dei Misteri* changed hands to a Greek freedman called Zosimus after the earthquake, either because of abandonment or the death of the previous owner. It should be noted that the basis for the determination of the status of the presumed owners of property is often subjective and open to question. For example, it has been claimed that the Vettii brothers were wine merchants because of representations of Mercury and his attributes in the *Casa dei Vettii*.[51]

It is simplistic to assume that entire sections of the population abandoned Pompeii after AD 62. The discovery of a tomb enclosure outside Pompeii, for example, coupled with inscriptions found in Pompeii have been used to support the argument that, at least one élite family continued to exert influence in Pompeii after the AD 62 earthquake.[52]

It has also been suggested that though there may have been an initial drop in the population after the earthquake, growth would have resumed along with reconstruction. It is possible that new arrivals may have come from outside the region to meet the increased demand for people with building and wall painting skills in the final years of occupation.[53]

Although the archaeological evidence for this period is difficult to interpret, it does appear likely that there was some level of change to the Pompeian population in terms of size, and perhaps also composition, between AD 62 and 79. The available data suggest that the response of the population to the AD 62 earthquake and subsequent seismic activity was complex and varied. Ultimately, there is insufficient evidence to draw firm conclusions about the degree of alteration that may have occurred.[54]

Size of the population in AD 79

It barely needs to be stated that the value of a population study of the Pompeian skeletal remains would be greatly enhanced if we had some idea of the proportion of the community that was killed by the eruption. To determine this, it is necessary to know the size of the population at the time. We should also know the number of skeletons that have been uncovered over the last two hundred and fifty odd years.

There are no accurate figures for the size of the population of Pompeii on the eve of its destruction in AD 79. No ancient census information exists and estimates of the number of inhabitants vary widely between authors. The size of the population of Pompeii has been estimated to range between 6,400 and 30,000. The arguments for the various estimates have been discussed by a number of authors.[55] The population figures of various scholars and their underlying rationales warrant a brief examination to demonstrate the problems associated with attempting to calculate population for this or any other ancient site.

The earliest estimate of between 18,000 and 20,000 Pompeian inhabitants in AD 79 was based on a calculation of the seating capacity of the amphitheatre.[56] Fiorelli argued against this high figure as he considered that the space of about 40 cm that was allowed per person was too small. His recalculation of the number of individuals that the amphitheatre could hold was 12,807, based on the assumption that the space occupied by each person was 55 cm. This allowance is more generous than the 50.8 cm that is recommended for modern ergonomic bench design.[57] There is no reason to assume that the requirements of the ancient users of the amphitheatre were substantially different to those of a modern population.

The choice of the amphitheatre as a guide to population size was almost certainly inspired by the account of Dio Cassius, which stated that all the inhabitants were assembled in this edifice to watch a game when Vesuvius erupted.[58] Even though Dio Cassius' description post-dated the event by about 150 years and despite the fact that no supporting archaeological evidence was found at the amphitheatre, archaeologists were not deterred from using it as the basis for population reconstruction.

Regardless of the number of people that the amphitheatre could hold, this structure does not provide a reliable indicator of the size of the Pompeian population. The literary evidence indicates that this building provided entertainment for the entire region. Tacitus records that in AD 59 the Roman Senate banned the use of the amphitheatre for ten years after riots broke out between Pompeian and Nucerian spectators at a gladiatorial event where more blood was spilled in the stands than in the arena.[59]

Fiorelli made a separate population calculation of 12,000, based on an extrapolation of his estimate of the number of excavated rooms onto the area of the site still to be excavated. The figure he obtained was based on the premise that the number of people who occupied the site was proportional to the number of rooms in a dwelling. His calculations were devised on the premise that most of the public buildings had already been excavated.[60] The underlying assumption is clearly flawed as it can be readily demonstrated from various cultures in different geographical areas that the number of rooms in a residence does not necessarily relate to the number of occupants.

Nissen concluded that there had been about 20,000 inhabitants in Pompeii. His figure was also derived from rough calculations based on his observations of room and house numbers. He considered that Fiorelli's figure was too low as he did not include upper storeys, which were not represented in the archaeological record.[61] This population estimate has remained popular.[62] Mau, for example, subscribed to this figure as a population minimum while Maiuri was slightly more circumspect and placed a ceiling of 20,000 for the size of the population.[63]

Beloch initially accepted Nissen's figure but later recalculated Pompeii's population as more modest in size. He obtained a figure of 15,000 by assuming that there was a population density of 230 people per hectare within the walled area of the town.[64] Frank suggested that there were about 25,000 occupants, whilst Cary and Scullard claimed that as many as 30,000 people inhabited Pompeii at the time of the eruption.[65] Russell estimated a population density of 100–120 people per hectare, which yielded an estimate of between 6,400 and 6,700 individuals for the town with the possibility of another few hundred individuals inhabiting the suburban regions.[66] Eschebach incorporated the results of excavations by Jashemski which revealed vineyards and gardens in the south-eastern part of the town in his determination of the number of Pompeian inhabitants in AD 79. He concluded that there would have been between 8,000 and 10,000 inhabitants. La Rocca concurs on this population range on the basis of the same evidence.[67]

Jashemski emphasized the need to exercise caution in the application of such estimates, as in the absence of ancient Pompeian population records, they could never be considered reliable. She subscribed to the view that the best way to estimate the size of the Pompeian population would be to undertake an investigation of land use in the city, and of the relative density of the buildings in relation to the quantity of open space. Jashemski favoured the lower figures for the Pompeian population as more reasonable in view of the above-mentioned discovery of agricultural usage of the land in the south-eastern region of the site. The higher estimates of previous scholars were based on the assumption that this area, like that already excavated, would yield evidence of urban occupation.[68] Jongman and Wallace-Hadrill shared Jashemski's reservations about the reliability of population estimates for Pompeii and criticized the methodologies for the calculation of population size.[69]

Jongman noted that urban population density is variable and archaeological evidence cannot be employed to take account of differences between populations. He stated that it would be impossible to assess the tolerance of the Pompeian population to cramped living conditions. Russell's low figures, which were based on the assumption that the Pompeian urban population density was not likely to have been higher than that of medieval Europe, were criticized on the grounds that the structure of these two societies was not equivalent. Jongman gave qualified support to a population range of between 8,000 to 12,000 individuals. The discovery of agricultural property within the walled precinct meant that the high estimates of scholars like Nissen were untenable. These higher figures also suggested that Pompeii's level of urbanization was comparable to that of Rome, which Jongman suggested was unlikely.[70]

Wallace-Hadrill also questioned the validity of the extrapolation of data from medieval towns onto Roman sites for the determination of population density as this practice denies temporal and cultural differences. In addition, he tackled the difficult issues of population changes over time and the period in Pompeian history that these population estimates are meant to reflect. All of the estimates that have been made of Pompeii's population have, by necessity, been simplistic and could not take into account fluctuations in occupation levels in different periods. The calculations that have been made to reconstruct the population size of Pompeii in its last period of occupation have apparently not incorporated the possibility that the population may have been considerably reduced or otherwise altered as a result of the AD 62 earthquake and subsequent seismic activity. Wallace-Hadrill endorsed the notion that the destruction of Pompeii was not confined to the eruption of Mt Vesuvius in AD 79, but was probably a lengthy process, which commenced with the AD 62 earthquake. He also noted the fact that most scholars when presenting their population estimates do not indicate whether these figures are meant to reflect the population on the eve of the AD 79 eruption or in the pre-earthquake years of the first century AD.[71]

Wallace-Hadrill argued that had the archaeological data been better recorded, it may have been possible to gain a more accurate idea of the population size. He revisited the work of Fiorelli on the use of the number of rooms in each house as a basis for calculating population size. He considered that if it were possible to establish room function, it would be possible to reconstruct the size of households from the numbers of bedrooms, beds and so-called bed niches in walls. By his own admission, this approach has some problems, such as a degree of uncertainty as to the number of people who occupied each bed and whether all the beds were in constant use.[72] No matter how carefully recorded, the archaeological evidence could never provide answers to these questions. Ultimately, Wallace-Hadrill concluded that the determination of an absolute figure for the size of Pompeii's population was a futile exercise, though he did incline towards a figure of about 10,000.[73]

At best, population estimates can only provide a very rough guide to the size of Pompeii's population.[74] Such figures should be used with extreme caution as they tend to be based on simplistic and sometimes spurious assumptions.

Number of individuals thought to have perished and number of bodies that have been discovered

There is no reliable figure for the number of individuals who perished as a result of the AD 79 eruption in Pompeii. Gell estimated that at the time of publication of the second edition of his work in 1832, about 160 skeletons had been uncovered. He calculated that, in relation to the proportion of the site that had been excavated, this constituted about one eighth of the number of victims that could be expected to be found and, therefore, put a figure of 1,300 for the number that died.[75] It is notable that Bulwer-Lytton, who relied on Gell and Bonucci for information about the site, only two years later gave an estimate of 350 to 400 for the number of skeletons that had been discovered.[76] This suggests that estimates based on the poorly documented skeletal finds were variable and that the conclusions drawn from them were of limited value.

By the latter part of the nineteenth century, the estimate of the number of victims had risen to 2,000. This figure was calculated by Fiorelli and was also based on an extrapolation of the ratio of the estimated number of bodies that had been found to the area of the site that had been uncovered.[77] The figure of 2,000 as an approximation of the number of dead has never been revised and has been accepted virtually without question in the majority of publications on Pompeii.[78] It should be noted that this number has also been used variously to describe the number of bodies that have been found.[79]

So powerful is the number 2,000 in the popular perception of the site that it has even been used for the number of survivors, rather than the number of deceased.[80]

Blong, who relied on sources that claimed that the number 2,000 referred to the number of individuals recovered, made a similar extrapolation to those made in the nineteenth century and calculated that, altogether, about 2,700 people were killed in the eruption. Russell also arrived at this figure, though he considered that the 2,000 skeletons thought to be in storage in Pompeii included several hundred from the region around Pompeii.[81]

Until recently,[82] this number had never been subjected to the same scrutiny as the population estimates and virtually achieved the status of a magic number in Pompeii. The only exception to the use of this number can be seen in the estimate presented by Herbet and Bardossi. They claimed that the number of victims of the eruption totalled 16,000.[83] No information was included as to how this figure was derived or whether it referred specifically to Pompeii or the entire region around Vesuvius.

There is no evidence to suggest that any estimate for the number of victims based on the extrapolation of the bodies found in a portion of the site would be reliable, because this assumes an even distribution of bodies across Pompeii.

As mentioned above, there was minimal documentation during the first century of excavation and estimates of the number of skeletons that were found during this period were not altogether reliable. The diaries of the excavations provide the key source of information for the period prior to 1860. The initiation of systematic recording by Fiorelli in the latter half of the nineteenth century could not compensate for the loss of information from the preceding generations of excavators. The skeletons that have been unearthed cannot be counted to provide an accurate total because of the post-excavation treatment of skeletal material, including reburial, poor storage and removal of some of the material to be stored in collections that are not easily accessible.[84]

Despite these problems, De Carolis and Patricelli[85] undertook the gargantuan task of examining all the available literature in an attempt to determine the best approximation of the number of bodies that have been revealed by the excavations in Pompeii. They have been able to account for 1047 individuals, including three victims that were found in 2002. This figure is based on the official Pompeii diaries and excavation reports where exact numbers were provided. A number of reports only give a rough guess of the number of skeletons found in a group or merely indicate that several skeletons were revealed at a particular location without any attempt at quantification. De Carolis and Patricelli estimated that despite the lack of precision in reporting, probably no more than 1150 skeletons have been found during the course of excavations at Pompeii. They note that this number still falls somewhat short of the 2000 victims usually mentioned in the literature.

The information that has been presented regarding the size and composition of the Pompeian population prior to the eruption underlines the difficulty of interpreting a sample of bones that merely represent the victims of the eruption. To gain some appreciation of what sort of sample these victims may represent, it is necessary to examine issues that relate to the possibility of survival from this eruption, such as the form it took and its duration.

The eruption of Mt Vesuvius in AD 79

It has generally been assumed that the inhabitants of the region around Vesuvius were unprepared for the AD 79 eruption.[86] Ancient sources indicate that they were unaware that Mt Vesuvius was an active volcano. This is largely based on Strabo,[87] who described Vesuvius as an extinct volcano and Pliny the Elder who considered Vesuvius to be a benign element in the Campanian landscape.[88] The stratigraphic evidence, which reveals that the volcano was dormant for at least 700 years before the AD 79 event, supports the notion that there was no historical memory of the mountain as a potential source of danger to the region.[89] It has often been suggested that the Pompeians made no association between the earthquake of AD 62 and renewed volcanic activity on Mt Vesuvius.[90]

The main ancient literary source for the eruption comes from two letters written by the Younger Pliny to Tacitus.[91] The first deals with the events that lead to the death of his uncle, Pliny the Elder, as a direct result of the eruption. The second deals with his own experiences at Misenum, about 30 kilometres to the west of Mt Vesuvius. Though Pliny the Younger was an eyewitness to the events of AD 79, the reliability of his account of Vesuvius' eruption needs to be assessed. First, the letters were probably written some time between AD 104 and 107, at least 25 years after the event. Second, Pliny's perception of the eruption was of a less devastating event than that experienced by towns like Pompeii and Herculaneum, as he witnessed it from a significant distance in a region that suffered comparatively little damage.[92] Third, despite the fact that Pliny the Younger's description has been lauded as a well-observed, valuable volcanological account,[93] it is apparent that this was not the principal agenda for the letters.

Pliny the Younger's first letter was written in reply to Tacitus' request for information about the death of his uncle, who was well known both as an encyclopaedist and the commander of the Roman fleet in Misenum. Pliny the Elder's initial aim was to inspect and record the eruption from close quarters. This was altered in response to a request for help from his friend, Rectina, whose only means of escape from her villa at the base of the mountain was by sea. Not only did he fail in his rescue attempt but he also did not manage to return with a first-hand account of the event. His mission was an unmitigated failure and ultimately led to his demise. It is generally presumed that Pliny the Elder died of respiratory complications at Stabiae. Eco[94] argued that the first letter of Pliny the Younger was primarily written to vindicate the actions of his uncle. The Younger Pliny obviously desired his uncle to be remembered as a hero who was martyred to the cause of science rather than an incompetent rescuer.

Another concern about the accuracy of Pliny's description of the event is that stylistic similarities have been observed between his letters to Tacitus and the so-called Etna poem. The latter is an anonymous work, which describes an eruption of the famous Sicilian volcano in AD 40. It has been suggested that Pliny the Younger based his letters on the poem, which may have exerted some influence on his account.[95]

Dio Cassius[96] also wrote of the AD 79 eruption. His account postdated the volcanic event by about 150 years and is rather more fanciful than that of the Younger Pliny. He claimed that prior to the eruption, numerous huge men were observed wandering over the earth and flying through the air, and that their shapes could be seen in the smoke emanating from Mt Vesuvius. All this was apparently accompanied by the sound of trumpets. Suetonius gave a passing mention to the eruption, in terms of the aid Titus proposed to give to the survivors.[97]

The date of the eruption

While there has been some discussion of the year in which Mt Vesuvius erupted, most scholars accept that it occurred in AD 79.[98] Establishing the actual date of the event is more controversial. Despite the fact that the majority of authors writing on Pompeii confidently ascribe a date of 24 August for the eruption,[99] the evidence is not conclusive. This issue is worthy of consideration for a study of the human remains from the site as knowledge of the season in which the eruption occurred could provide some insight into the composition of the population of Pompeii at the time of its destruction.

It has been generally assumed that villas owned by wealthy Roman citizens were mostly used as summer resorts. This assertion is probably based on the knowledge that a number of these coastal properties were, at various times, owned by citizens who were obviously based in Rome, like the dictator Sulla, who had a villa near Cumae, and the Emperor Augustus, who had a retreat on Capri.[100] Strabo stated that the whole Bay of Naples appeared like a continuous town as a result of the number of villas that lined the coastline.[101] Many of these villas were owned by Romans. For example, the Younger Pliny had six villas, Cicero three, and it is thought, on the basis of evidence from inscriptions, that the Villa of Oplontis near Pompeii may have at one time belonged to Nero's wife, Poppaea. Chance finds that included inscriptions have also been employed as evidence to suggest that the family of the latter, the Poppaei, were the owners of the so-called *Casa degli Amorini dorati* (VI, xvi, 7) and *Casa del Menandro* (I, x, 4) in Pompeii, though it must be noted that these attributions are problematic as they tend to be based on spurious evidence.[102] If it were possible to establish the exact time of the year when Mt Vesuvius erupted, we could infer whether or not there was likely to have been a significant presence of Roman residents among the victims who would only have been living there in the summer months.

The various versions of the letters of Pliny the Younger that have survived suggest dates of either 3, 23 November or 24 August. It has been claimed that the August date came from a more reliable version of Pliny's text.[103] Dio Cassius[104] mentioned autumn as the season of the eruption, but one must bear in mind that he wrote a considerable time after the event. Also, there is no consensus with respect to the length of this season in the ancient world. Opinion varies and suggestions have been made that autumn ranged from mid-August to mid-December or from mid-September to mid-November. Contradictory archaeological finds of seasonal fruit and other plant remains, evidence of wine-making activities, carpets and braziers, have been used to support claims for both summer and late autumn. The venerable scholar Mau,[105] supported 24 August as the first day of the eruption and despite the lack of any definitive evidence, this date gained acceptance. The bombing of Pompeii on 24 August 1943 may have given further weight to the choice of this date as a result of a superstitious belief that there was some significance associated with this coincidence.[106] The debate was reopened in the 1990s by Pappalardo, who argued for the November date. In addition to the traditional arguments for an autumn eruption, he claimed that the impressions of clothing on casts of the bodies of Pompeians suggested the use of heavy materials, more consistent with cooler weather than that generally encountered in August. This argument was supported by the discovery of a skeleton in 1984 at Herculaneum with traces of a fur beret.[107]

Apart from the problems associated with interpretations of clothing on casts (see Chapter 10), there may be another explanation for such discoveries. It is possible that the inhabitants may have donned heavier clothing as protection against falling debris. Pliny the Younger's first letter to Tacitus[108] mentioned that people tied pillows to their heads for this purpose. Similarly, the bodies in the garden of the *Casa del Criptoportico* (I, vi, 2) were discovered with roof tiles covering their heads.[109]

This contentious issue may well have been resolved by the recent publication of a silver denarius by Grete Stefani.[110] It was found in a context that could be securely dated to the AD 79 eruption level below the *Casa del Bracciale d'Oro* in the *Insula Occidentalis* (VI, xvii, 42). This coin was found in 1974, along with 179 other silver and 40 gold coins, a gemstone and a ring, which were carried by victims in flight. The coin in question is a denarius of Titus and the inscription refers to his 15th imperatorial acclamation, which, according to Dio Cassius, occurred as a result of Agricola's conquests in Britain. Stefani cites epigraphic evidence with 7 and 8 September dates, which only attribute 14 acclamations to Titus. She convincingly argues for the versions of Pliny the Younger's letters that indicate an autumn date as the coin must have been minted after 8 September in AD 79.

The eruption sequence

An understanding of the form of the eruption enables us to establish the principal causes of death of the AD 79 victims. It also helps determine the potential for individuals to have escaped. Until the last few decades, opinion was divided about the exact nature of the event that destroyed the towns in the region of Mt Vesuvius in AD 79. Traditionally, it was considered that the rapid build up of air-fall ash and pumice, known as tephra, accounted for the majority of deaths.[111] This approach is exemplified in the volcanological work of Bullard, who described the AD 79 eruption as a classic example of a Vulcanian type of eruption. There are several types of eruptions, each associated with specific phases and types of eruption material.[112] Bullard's classification is consistent with Pliny the Younger's description of the eruption process.[113] Pliny employed the shape of a Mediterranean umbrella pine as a metaphor for the shape of the cloud that rose above Vesuvius. Pliny's description of what he viewed from Misenum has been considered to be a valuable contribution to volcanology and is commemorated by the descriptor 'Plinian' for explosive eruptions that are characterized by high eruption columns of ash pumice and volcanic gases.[114]

The second school of thought has become the accepted interpretation. This argues that there were, in fact, two phases in the AD 79 eruption. The first was a Plinian period of pumice and ash fall. This was followed by a phase of *nuées ardentes*, or pyroclastic density currents, after the collapse of the eruption column. *Nuée ardente* is a blanket term that has been used to cover both pyroclastic surges and pyroclastic flows. These are respectively dilute turbulent clouds of particles that are suspended in gas and hot air and dense avalanches of concentrated particles. They are composed of pumice, ash and gas. The direction of a pyroclastic flow is determined by the underlying topography, whilst that of the low density, highly turbulent surge is not dependent on ground features. As a result, a surge can spread radially from the crater at greater speed than a pyroclastic flow.[115] The notion of the AD 79 event as a two-phase eruption dates back to the eruption of Mt Pelée, Martinique in 1902, when an estimated 29,000 people were killed by a series of hot gas avalanches and has provided the term 'Peléan' for similar types of events. Parallels with the AD 79 Vesuvius eruption were recognized as early as 1903 and various scholars have propagated this view.[116] The definitive work was done by Sigurdsson and his team, who made a detailed stratigraphic examination of the region, with specific reference to the AD 79 layers and were able to clearly identify the different phases from the strata.[117]

The only real criticism that can be levelled at the work of Sigurdsson is his almost unquestioning use of the letters of the Younger Pliny as a totally reliable source for the sequence and chronology of the eruption.[118] This is probably the result of the influence of the key aim of his initial research project in the Vesuvian region, which was to tie in the evidence of Pliny the

81

Younger's account with the excavations in Herculaneum and Pompeii.[119] The widely accepted[120] hour-by-hour, and sometimes even half-hour, chronology is essentially based on two events.[121] The first is the time that Pliny the Elder's sister is said to have pointed out the umbrella pine shaped cloud.[122] This has been used to determine that the first violent phase of this explosive eruption began at about one o'clock in the afternoon. The second is the account of events in Pliny's second letter.[123] The current interpretation of this text is that he and his mother were forced to flee Misenum by a surge at about eight o'clock on the morning of the second day of the eruption. At the very least, it is misleading to describe the precise time of each event in the eruption sequence, as it gives the impression of greater certainty than is provided by the available evidence. The use of this chronology is problematic as it is predicated on the accuracy of Pliny the Younger's memory after an interval of about a quarter of a century.

Most of the literature that deals with eyewitness accounts concerns crime scenes but the results of this work are still appropriate for appraising Pliny the Younger's account. Memory is complex and can be unintentionally distorted to fulfil the expectations of the witness. Consequently, eyewitness memory is notoriously unreliable as demonstrated by numerous studies.[124] Various factors affect central and peripheral memory and what is perceived as such, and, depending on the event, it is possible that central and peripheral information can be interchangeable. Details that are not of primary interest tend not to be so well remembered.[125] The provision of a description of the eruption was by no means the principal agenda of Pliny the Younger's account of his uncle's death and the timing of the event was of even less importance. The reliability of Pliny's retrieval of information that was so peripheral to the main story, especially after such a long period of time, can be questioned.

It is notable that the influence of an earlier interpretation of the account of Pliny the Younger probably was responsible for scholars, like Bullard, discounting the possibility that *nuées ardentes* were a feature of this eruption.[126] The weight given to Pliny's account is a reflection of the emphasis that has traditionally been placed on primary literary sources over physical evidence.

According to Sigurdsson, the first phase of the eruption, as it was experienced in Pompeii, occurred over a period that he arguably estimated to have lasted at least eighteen hours and resulted in a layer of ash and pumice up to 2.8 metres. Since air-fall deposits do not tend to be lethal, Sigurdsson considered that there probably would have only been a relatively small number of deaths in this phase as a result of roofs collapsing due to the weight of lapilli. He estimated that ash and pumice were deposited in the first seven or eight hours at Pompeii at a rate of 12–15 cm an hour. The accumulated weight would probably have caused roofs to collapse after several hours, probably when about 40 cm had been deposited. It has been suggested that roof collapse would probably have provided substantial incentive for people who had taken refuge in their houses to consider evacuation of the town.

Falling volcanic debris may also have been responsible for some loss of life. In addition to the ash and pumice, there were lithic clasts which are pieces of rock that derive from the walls of the vent of the volcano. They are far more dangerous than pumice due to their greater density. It has been estimated that some of the lithic clasts at Pompeii were travelling at speeds of 50 metres per second when they hit the ground. Nonetheless, Sigurdsson argued that these would not have accounted for many deaths as they were only observed in very small numbers in the deposit, thus lowering the probability of individuals being hit.[127]

Sigurdsson suggested that this phase was not only associated with a minimal number of fatalities but that the phenomenon of the ash fall would have alerted the inhabitants of the danger to which they were being exposed and encouraged most of them to escape before the lethal second stage of the eruption. He did concede that escape would have been difficult as fugitives from this phase of the eruption would have had to contend with a thick layer of loose pumice in a dark environment.[128]

The second eruption phase was marked by a series of hot gas avalanches or *nuées ardentes*. This was the most lethal period in the eruption as evidenced by the number of bodies that were found above the layer of pumice. It has been observed that *nuées ardentes* are associated with a particularly high death to injury ratio, especially when compared with other types of natural disasters.[129]

Sigurdsson and his team examined the stratigraphy of the entire region that was affected by the AD 79 eruption. He concentrated on establishing the cause of death of the victims from Herculaneum but argued that his findings were also applicable to Pompeii. He considered that variation in the physical appearance of the remains in the two sites only reflected differences in post-eruption groundwater levels (also see Chapter 10). All the human bodies that were discovered at the waterfront of Herculaneum from the 1980s on were found in association with what Sigurdsson identified as the first surge layer (S1). The stratigraphic evidence indicates that the majority of the Herculaneum victims were killed by this surge (S1), which did not extend as far as Pompeii. A superficial examination of the positions of the bodies suggested that they met their fate fairly rapidly.

The second and third surges that Sigurdsson identified also did not affect Pompeii. The fourth surge (S4) reached Pompeii some hours later, followed only minutes later by the fifth surge (S5). The fourth surge was lethal and Sigurdsson argued that it would have been responsible for the death of any occupants who had remained in the town. It was observed that the majority of the documented victims have been found within the layers of the fourth and fifth surges (S4 and S5). The bodies of these victims were subsequently covered by the thick deposit associated with the sixth surge (S6). This surge was extremely destructive and was responsible for the collapse of the walls of the highest buildings and the displacement of building materials, as well as a few of the bodies of victims.[130]

Figure 4.2 Cast of the so-called 'Lady of Oplontis', which displays a 'pugilistic' pose (Photograph courtesy of Associate Professor Chris Griffiths)

exposure to extremely high temperatures at or about the time of death. The poses of the casts of the Pompeian victims appeared very similar to those of more recent eruptions, such as those of Mt Pelée, Martinique in 1902 and Mt Lamington, New Guinea in 1951. The corpses from these eruptions were observed in a number of different positions, though the majority were prone with the hands against the face or with an extended spine and flexed limbs (see Figure 4.2).[152] This latter position is described as 'pugilistic' in the forensic literature and is considered typical of perimortem exposure to at least 200–250 degrees Celsius. Muscles can be charred or coagulated when heated intensely and this may cause muscular contraction, which can be observed as flexion of the limbs. Contraction occurs as a result of the effect of heat on protein. Differential contraction occurs at the joint, the direction being determined by the more powerful muscle with the greatest surface area. Clearly, such poses do not necessarily reflect the final position of the body in life. The observed frequency of its occurrence in Pompeii is consistent with that from modern forensic contexts.[153]

The non-pugilistic poses that can be observed in the Pompeian cast collection require different explanations. It appears that a few of these victims (for example, Figure 4.3) were preserved in the positions they had assumed at the time of death. Though this phenomenon, known as cadaveric spasm, is not altogether understood, it has been explained in terms of total muscle contraction in the body at the time of death, specifically in cases of sudden and violent death. It would be expected to wear off, along with normal rigor mortis about 18–36 hours after death.[154] In the case of the Pompeian victims, the effect of thermal coagulation of the muscles may have been a factor

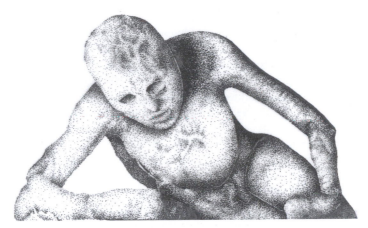

Figure 4.3 The pose of this cast from the *Orto dei Fuggiaschi* (Garden of the Fugitives) (I, xxi) has been interpreted as an example of cadaveric spasm

in preservation of poses, though the fact that the bodies would have been covered fairly soon after death was probably also significant.

Surveys of historic volcanic disasters reveal that pyroclastic density currents account for the greatest number of deaths directly related to the eruption process.[155] The main causes of death associated with these have been identified as fulminant shock, asphyxia, thermal lung injury and deep thickness burns. Documentation from more recent eruptions demonstrates that few individuals survive pyroclastic density currents. It has been observed that such individuals tended to have been exposed to the more dilute parts of the current or were in some way able to obtain shelter, usually indoors. There have been a few reported cases of survival outdoors but only at the margins of currents. Nonetheless, all such survivors have been found to be at risk from fatal pulmonary or laryngeal oedema resulting from respiratory burns and deep thickness skin burns. Individuals can receive substantial burns to the skin and respiratory tract without any damage to their clothing due to the short exposure time to hot ash.[156] It should be noted that, according to studies of the pyroclastic density currents associated with the AD eruption by Giuroli *et al.*, there could have been localized cooler zones in the lower part of the current, which may have increased the chances of survival for a few Pompeians.[157]

It has been argued that it is somewhat simplistic to assume that most of the deaths from the AD 79 event would have been from asphyxiation as it can be demonstrated that in these circumstances hyperthermia, or overheating, can also be a significant cause of death. Comparisons between the bodies of victims examined after the eruptions of Soufriére Hills volcano, Montserrat in 1997, Mt Pelée, Mt Lamington, Mt Vesuvius and Mt St Helens led Baxter to conclude that the bodies in the latter were not exposed to as much heat as those of the former four eruptions since there was no evidence of pugilism in the poses of the corpses from Mt St Helens. In addition, the survival of various cultural objects, such as paint, colour film and polystyrene insulation, suggests that they were not exposed to very high temperatures. Three of the four bodies found just outside the perimeter of the direct flow zone of the *nuée ardente*, about fifteen kilometres distant from the summit of Mt St Helens, were found with clear airways. This indicated that death occurred almost instantaneously as a result of extreme hyperthermia. Baxter therefore concluded that many of the individuals exposed to the greater heat intensity of the former three eruptions would have ceased to breathe before asphyxiation could have occurred.[158]

Determination of the exact cause of death provides an indication of the length of time that it would have taken to die. Though it is generally accepted that the fourth surge, as described by Sigurdsson, was responsible for the majority of Pompeian deaths, not enough physical evidence has survived to establish exactly how most individuals met their fate. It is likely that hyperthermia was a major cause of death in the second phase of the eruption and that many victims would have died rapidly, though it should be noted that the poses of the casts do not provide clear supporting evidence as it is possible that the bodies were only exposed to heat after death.[159]

Herculaneum

Further excavation at the Herculaneum beachfront in the two decades since the groundbreaking work of Sigurdsson and his team has revealed numerous additional victims and contributed to the discussion about regional differences in the experience of the event. Over three hundred skeletons were exposed by 2005. The majority were found in the barrel-vaulted boat-chambers beneath the Suburban Quarter. Fifty-nine individuals were found on the beach. A large number of the skeletons lie directly on the beach, while others lie within the surge deposit, between five and fifteen centimetres above the original surface of the beach. It was initially argued that all the skeletons that were found in the first surge deposit (S1) showed no signs of being carbonized, whilst those where portions of the victims protruded and were exposed to the greater heat of the second surge (S2) show signs of carbonization.[160]

Capasso undertook a multidisciplinary approach to establish cause of death of the victims at the sea front, which included examination of the taphonomic, anthropological and archaeological evidence.[161] Based on the position of the bodies, the distribution of burnt areas and histological changes in bone tissue, he concluded that differences could be observed in the manner of death between victims on the beach and those in the boat sheds. According to Capasso, the victims on the beach experienced the dehydrating effects of the surge, which resulted in the complete burning of bones. X-ray analysis indicated that the cracking patterns were not consistent with very high temperatures, though macroscopic and microscope studies produced results that indicated exposure to temperatures between 350 and 400° Celsius. A few cases were observed where high temperatures had caused rapid evaporation of the brain, which had caused the sutures of the skull to open. He argued that on the basis of histological studies, the bones of the individuals he observed in the boat sheds were also exposed to similar temperatures but, because of slower dehydration in a more protected environment, some soft tissue was preserved. He did not find any evidence of damage to skulls from evapora-tion of the brain but interpreted skull fractures that he observed as being consistent with post mortem damage from projectiles associated with the second surge. Like Sigurdsson, he considered that asphyxiation could have been a likely cause of death for a number of those victims who sought shelter in the boat sheds, though thermal shock would have accounted for a few cases.

Eighty skeletons from four of the 12 boat-chambers were recently exam-ined in a multidisciplinary study headed by Mastrolorenzo.[162] In contrast, the results of this research have led to the claim that rather than dying of asphyxiation, these victims died from fulminant shock. This means that their vital organs ceased to function so abruptly there was no time for conscious reaction. The poses of these individuals have been used to confirm this interpretation as there are no signs of defensive gestures or positions that would suggest suffering. From palaeomagnetic analysis of a tile collected outside chamber 12 and what has been interpreted as heat damage to the bones and teeth of the victims, it has been suggested that the first surge was associated with a temperature that may have been as high as 500 degrees Celsius. Exposure to such heat would have caused almost instantaneous death. A number of the skeletons have fractures that are commonly observed on incinerated bodies, such as transversal clear-cut fractures with blackened edges and longitudinal fractures on the shafts of the long and flat bones. Like Capasso, Mastrolorenzo et al. noted that some of the skulls displayed black-ened surfaces on cranial openings, inner skull surfaces and open sutures, which they interpreted as a reflection of high temperatures causing the brain to boil. Cracking of the dental enamel and changes in colour of the bones were also consistent with incineration.

While ongoing debate reflects a lack of consensus on the details of the deaths of the victims of the AD 79 event, it is clear that individuals who were killed by pyroclastic density currents met their deaths quickly from exposure to high temperatures and severe particle pollution.

Survival factors

Whether people knew of Mt Vesuvius' status as a volcano with the potential for eruption or appreciated the danger to which they were being exposed once the process commenced would have been significant in the determination of the need to escape. This is a relevant consideration for assessing the validity of more recent volcanic events as models for the possible behaviour of the Pompeians at the outset of the disaster.

An argument has been presented to suggest that the residents of the Campanian region may have been aware of the potential danger of Mt Vesuvius, though there is ultimately no compelling evidence to prove this point.[163] Ancient literature, including Diodorus Siculus,[164] Suetonius[165] and the Etna Poem,[166] have been cited to demonstrate that volcanic activity was known and understood by Romans in the first century AD. Diodorus Siculus, as a Sicilian, was familiar with the volcanic activity of Mt Etna and he recognized that Mt Vesuvius had been a volcano in the past. He did not suggest that it was still capable of activity and his writing implies, as does that of Strabo,[167] that the mountain was seen to be extinct. Modern scholars have dated the Etna poem to the years preceding the AD 62 earthquake because the poet considered Campania was not volcanically active.[168] This has been used as a basis for the questionable assumption that an understanding of the relationship between the earthquake and the commencement of a renewed volcanic cycle must, therefore, have existed after the AD 62 event.[169] Though Pliny did observe that earthquakes tended to portend major events, there is certainly no suggestion of any knowledge of Mt Vesuvius being a volcano in any of the Elder Pliny's work.[170]

Conversely, it has been reasoned that the Pompeians could not have been aware of the risk of Mt Vesuvius erupting as refugees from volcanic activity on Ischia in the fourth century BC settled on its slopes.[171] Plutarch's account of Spartacus,[172] who sought shelter from the Roman army on the summit of Mt Vesuvius in 73 BC after he escaped from Capua with 78 other gladiators, has also been presented as evidence that the mountain was not considered to be dangerous prior to the AD 79 eruption. It should be noted that the strength of the argument based on these examples is tempered by the fact that they predate the AD 79 eruption by a considerable time and that it is possible that there could have been a better understanding of volcanic risks by the first century AD. The Younger Pliny's first letter presents more convincing evidence for this view.[173] Pliny stated that it was not initially known which mountain was associated with the phenomenon that he and his uncle observed from Misenum. This letter certainly implies that the event was unexpected. The fact that the Elder Pliny immediately prepared to go to sea to investigate at closer range suggests that he did not comprehend the risks this posed.

Whatever the case, it does appear that a number of people did manage to escape as demonstrated by the literature and implied by the comparatively small number of skeletons that have been found in a town of this size.[174] It should be borne in mind that the majority of excavations to date have been within the walls of Pompeii and it is possible that many victims are yet to be found outside Pompeii.[175]

Though instructive when used to establish the possible causes of death, recent events like the eruption of Mt St Helens in 1980 are probably of limited value for gaining an insight into the types of people who would have been more likely to perish. The Mt St Helens eruption apparently differed from that of Vesuvius in AD 79 in that there was sufficient warning to enable most of the inhabitants to be evacuated before the lethal phase. Victims included thrill seekers and journalists.[176] It is possible that there were some equivalent individuals in the AD 79 eruption, the most likely historical candidate being the Elder Pliny. There is no doubt, however, that such victims were in the minority. Other recent eruptions, such as Taal, Philippines (1965) Galunggung, Indonesia, Rabaul, Papua New Guinea (1983–85), El Chichón, Mexico (1982), Rabaul (1994) and Parícutin, Mexico (1943), cannot be used to reconstruct the behaviour of the Pompeians, though they do give some indication of the range of possible behavioural responses to such a disaster.[177]

One can only speculate as to whether certain sections of the community were more predisposed to becoming victims in the AD 79 eruption. There is no conclusive archaeological evidence to suggest that particular groups chose to either remain or flee from Pompeii during the initial non-lethal period of the eruption. It is quite probable that the decision was arbitrarily made across all strata of the population. This view is supported by studies of modern disasters, which demonstrate that all levels of a community tend to be equally affected by this kind of event.[178]

If the effects of this eruption were egalitarian, it would imply that the Pompeian victims present a good reflection of the AD 79 population. This can be tested by examination of the skeletal evidence for particular biases, such as skewing of the sample to a specific age range, certain pathologies or one sex (see Chapters 6 and 7). It is not possible to test for class biases as the skeletal record does not usually provide reliable information about the social status of individuals from ancient populations (Chapter 1) but other population features, such as heterogeneity versus homogeneity, may be revealed.

Evidence for post-eruption interference at Pompeii

Another issue that is of relevance to the composition of the skeletal sample is whether there were post-eruption visits to the site. This also potentially challenges the concept of the 'Pompeii Premise'. There has been considerable debate as to whether the site was completely sealed after the eruption as a 'frozen moment' or if it were possible for people to return to Pompeii to collect valuables.[179] This activity could have been dangerous as excavation has been said to release pockets of poisonous gas, known as *mofeta*, that were trapped in the volcanic deposit during the course of the eruption.[180] Skeletons of individuals who perished in this way, either in the period after the eruption or in the eighteenth century, when it was difficult to control unauthorized excavation, could present a source of bias to the sample. The traditional view is that Pompeii, unlike Herculaneum, which was sealed in a solid deposit, was visited shortly after the eruption by both looters and residents who wished to salvage what remained of their belongings. This notion was first proposed in the 1760s by Winckelmann and has since received wide support.[181]

The possibility of such an occurrence is contingent on the fact that it was possible to identify at least part of the site after the volcanic event. It has often been claimed that the upper portions of walls were visible.[182] Certain scholars, however, have argued that it would not have been likely that residents or looters could have easily re-located the site, let alone specific houses, after the eruption as volcanic deposits of tephra compact by about 50 per cent in the first two weeks after an eruption.[183] It appears that knowledge of the exact location of Pompeii was lost some time after the eruption, though the collective memory of an ancient site in the region was commemorated by the name *Civita* for the general area.[184]

The lack of bronze statuary and much of the marble in the forum have been cited as archaeological evidence for post-eruption looting and salvage work.[185] It should be noted, however, that the paucity of certain classes of evidence has been questioned. Large quantities of marble, for example, were actually found in the forum, though there were problems both with documentation and robbery at the time of excavation.[186] It has been suggested that looting may not have been a major post-eruption activity, on the basis of information from contemporary eruptions, which revealed no escalation of the crime rate after volcanic disasters.[187]

Reports of mixed stratigraphy and the discovery of holes in walls by the excavators have often been invoked as evidence for people returning to the site in antiquity.[188] Some of this can be explained in terms of undocumented eighteenth-century excavation.[189] Finds, including ancient lamps that have been dated to periods after the AD 79 eruption[190] and the skeletal remains with a lantern and pick that are now in room 19 of the *Casa del Menandro*, have also been used as evidence of post-eruption visits to the site.[191] While the accuracy of the dates for the lamps cannot be questioned, the use of these skeletal finds as evidence of post-eruption intruders requires some comment. The skeletal group under discussion was not originally found either with a pick or in this context (see Chapter 1). Further, the skeletal evidence does not suggest looters. Three of the individuals in this group were identified as children equivalent in development to juveniles under the age of six in a modern European population.[192] The three skeletons that were originally found in this room in association with the abovementioned implements were also reported to include juvenile remains, though they were not available for examination. In addition, three holes can be observed in the south and west walls of this room. These have also been interpreted as evidence of looting, though it is apparent that they were cut from inside the room, probably by the three victims in an attempt to escape after the normal exits were blocked by the build-up of ash and lapilli.[193] Similar arguments have been used to explain the presence of holes in the walls of other houses.[194]

Other skeletal finds from the upper strata of Pompeii, especially the northwest quarter, have also been interpreted as looters.[195] Many of these were found with associated artefacts, such as coins or jewellery. Richardson considered that these individuals were clearly pillagers and not victims fleeing the eruption with their valuables, though he did not present any evidence to substantiate this claim.

These examples demonstrate the complexity associated with the interpretation of evidence for post-eruption visits to the site. Nonetheless, there is clear evidence that Pompeii was visited for some period after the eruption. Along with the lamps mentioned above, post-eruption salvaging can be seen, for example, in the form of holes in the north and south walls of Room c in the *Casa del Principe di Napoli*, along with disarticulated skeletal remains which had apparently been disrupted during exploration some time after the death and decomposition of the victims.[196] While one cannot discount the possibility of post-eruption skeletons in the Pompeian collection, there are no known unequivocal discoveries of ancient skeletons that do not date to the initial destruction. Whatever the case, it is unlikely that the contamination rate would be significant.

In conclusion, the evidence is such that it probably will never be possible to determine exactly what happened in the final period of occupation in Pompeii. Similarly, precise details about the people who became victims, or were able to escape, is unlikely to be established. It is clear that the site of Pompeii is not simply a sealed deposit of a thriving town, stopped in its tracks by the AD 79 eruption. While the AD 62 earthquake did not result in complete abandonment of the site as evidenced by rebuilding projects, it is clear that some changes did occur as suggested by Seneca's writings and other archaeological evidence. It is impossible to assess the degree of change or whether the nature of the population was altered, though it is likely that the population was dynamic in the last 17 years of Pompeii's history.

It is apparent that the responses of individuals to events like the AD 62 earthquake and the AD 79 eruption are likely to have been varied and defy simplification into models. It is not possible to determine the percentage of the Pompeian population that is represented from the skeletal remains. The volcanological evidence suggests that a number of Pompeians, probably the majority, escaped from the walled section of the town. As has been revealed by the limited excavation of the area around Pompeii, a proportion of these people became victims during their attempted escape from the region.

locked in for the duration of each working day. This captivity entailed certain physical discomfort.

Access was also limited by the climate. It was more practical to carry out the bulk of the field work during summer and autumn as winter work conditions were far from ideal. The temperature and light levels inside the ancient buildings drops considerably during winter and the humidity rises. The length of each season varied from five weeks to six months, over a period of five years, the average lasting about three months.[13]

Sample size

The literature variously suggested that approximately 2,000 individuals either lost their lives or had already been excavated (see Chapter 4). Such a large sample from a documented destruction is virtually unknown from antiquity.

Fewer individuals were available for study than suggested by the literature. It is known that a considerable number of bones were removed to the *Regia Università di Napoli* in 1853 for study by Chiaie. It is not known whether the hundred skulls that formed the basis of Nicolucci's examination came from this collection or were additionally removed from the site.[14] There has been no documented major removal of skeletal material from the site since these early anthropological studies. As many of the bones that are currently stored in Pompeii were probably excavated after the middle of the nineteenth century, it is likely that they would form a representative sample of the victims.

The sample has also been depleted by souvenir hunters and novel forms of secondary usage. Edward Bulwer-Lytton, for example, chose to grace the desk of his Knebworth house in Hertfordshire with a skull he collected from the excavations. Its shape and dimensions convinced him that it must have belonged to a man of great intellect and talent, a man like the evil Arbaces of his *Last Days of Pompeii*.[15] Hester Lynch Piozzi, who published an account of his visit to Pompeii in 1786, observed a French tourist pocketing a human bone as a memento.[16] In 1776, François de Paule Latapie commented on people who felt the need to have a piece of a Pompeian victim in their private collections and admitted to having removed skeletal material from the site for this purpose.[17] This is an historical problem that, to some extent, still exists in cases where bones have been left *in situ*. For example, the bones of two skeletons were left as they were found in the *Casa del Fabbro* (I, x, 7)[18] and were made available for the present study. Over a period of three years the number of bones in this house dwindled markedly. Apparently, tourists have managed to gain entry to the house and have purloined bones, such as mandibles, for souvenirs.

Some time ago, a 'cottage industry' was set up in the Sarno baths. This involved the transformation of human femora excavated at Pompeii into hinges for the reconstruction of ancient furniture found on the site. The original hinges were made of turned horse metatarsals which often required replacement for restoration.[19] This has contributed a novel source of sample bias to the femur collection (see Chapter 6).

It is possible that the sample has been contaminated by a small number of tomb burials from the region outside the walls of Pompeii. A previous director of archaeology at Pompeii stated that the level of contamination in the bone deposits would be minimal[20]. His premise is based on a number of reasons, such as the fact that until the final decade of the twentieth century, excavations were mostly directed at the AD 79 level. In addition, a great deal of the pre-AD 79 excavated skeletal material was lost during World War II bombing raids on the site. Any contamination would be so small in relation to the number of skeletons in this sample that it would probably have very little effect on the general statistical trends.

Site recording was erratic, especially during the early excavations, which means that it is virtually impossible to determine the exact number of bodies that have been uncovered. Although there is a tradition that two thousand individuals were found, recent work indicates that we can only account for just over half this number (Chapter 4).

The Pompeian skeletal project

The problems associated with the Pompeian skeletal remains limit the amount of information that they can yield, but they do not diminish the

Figure 5.2 Box of bone hinges stored in Pompeii

value of the material as an archaeological resource. These remains reflect previously unexplored aspects of an important classical site. Unlike other skeletal samples from this era, this represents a mass disaster rather than the more commonly encountered cemetery populations. Cemetery populations often cover large time spans and may be defined or skewed by sex, age, cultural practices, such as segregation, or pathology, as in the case of plague burials.

The Pompeian skeletal remains, along with those found from other sites destroyed by the eruption of Mt Vesuvius, form a sample with a number of features that are not often found in the archaeological record. They reflect a living population, which can yield valuable information about the people who inhabited Pompeii on the eve of its destruction. The major asset of these collections of bones is that they provide a relatively large sample of skeletal material from the ancient world where two variables, time and the cause of death, are already known.

The human remains from Pompeii, along with the skeletal material from Herculaneum[21] and other Vesuvian sites, are also important because they provide a major source of information about Roman populations in Italy in the latter part of the first century AD. In this period, cremation was the most popular form of disposal of the dead and while it is possible to learn about the characteristics of individuals and populations from cremated bone, the success of analysis of burnt material is dependent on the amount of bone and the number of diagnostic features that survive in each case. Burnt bone tends to be warped or otherwise distorted and can shrink. This makes the evidence far more difficult to interpret than complete skeletal elements.

When I started to work on this material in 1986, it was seen to be of minimal value by most contemporary scholars. It was apparent that any study would be an improvement on leaving this neglected collection to further deteriorate. The research design for this project had to be developed with respect to the limitations of the sample and the site. It was also constrained by a very small budget, which limited the amount of time that could be spent in the field and the laboratory work that could be undertaken. As a result, the majority of the work was based on gross observations and measurements. Such data provide the most important basic information that can be obtained from any skeletal sample and are a prerequisite for any further analyses, such as DNA or stable isotope analysis.

The project was designed to construct a population profile in order to address questions about the sample of Pompeian victims. One of the key aims was to test the commonly held assumption that the sample of victims would be biased towards the old, the infirm, the very young and women.[22] In the absence of complete skeletons available for study, I decided to concentrate on statistical studies based on large numbers of particular bones. This obviously influenced the nature of the research questions. The bones selected for study were chosen for their ability to provide specific information. For the determination of sex, the best skeletal indicators are the pelvis, femur, humerus, skull and teeth. Age-at-death was based on pelves, teeth and skulls. Another issue that was addressed was whether the sample of victims reflected a heterogeneous population, as suggested by ancient writers who described the inhabitants of Pompeii and the surrounding region.[23] The bones chosen for population studies were skulls, pelves, femora, humeri and tibiae. Because the skeletons were disarticulated, the femur was chosen as the most reliable single long bone for the reconstruction of height.

The most useful skeletal indicators for each feature under study could then be employed as controls for the determination of population norms for the other bone types in the Pompeian sample. For example, because of its bio-logical function, the pelvis is the most reliable indicator of sex. Other bones, such as the femur, humerus and skull, also reflect sexual dimorphism but the degree of difference between males and females can vary between populations due to cultural and genetic differences. By using the most useful sexual marker as a baseline, it was possible to establish the sex-related parameters for other bones in the Pompeian sample.

The first priority of this study was to obtain the maximum amount of information from a large sample of different individuals. Initial long bone measurements and observations were carried out on left bones to ensure that each bone represented one individual. Where possible, this work was also carried out on samples of bones from the right side. Observations from both sides are particularly important for the determination of frequencies of post-cranial non-metric traits and supposed stress markers, such as tibial flatten-ing or platycnemia. Such traits appear to be side related in certain popula-tions. Due to time and access restrictions, it was not possible to complete both sets of observations and measurements on all bones.

Preparation and recording of the material

Before the bones could be catalogued and measured, they had to be sorted, cleaned, coded, described and, where appropriate, photographed.

The first task was to organize the material into a form where it could be used. The disarticulated bones in the Sarno Baths were sorted into groups of skulls, mandibles, sacra and left and right long and pelvic bones. Bones that were not likely to provide useful information in terms of the aims of this study were placed in separate piles. Bones with evidence of pathological changes were segregated from the rest of the skeletal material. In some cases it was possible to reconstruct individual bones from fragments on the basis of pathological change, as in the case of the skulls of individuals with hyper-ostosis frontalis interna (Chapter 8). The unboxed bones in the Forum Baths had already been sorted, though it was necessary to separate left and right long bones. The conditions inside both the Sarno and Forum Baths meant that bones had to be recleaned each field season.[24]

Figure 5.3 Sorted piles of bones in the *Terme del Sarno* (VII, ii, 17)

Labelling the skeletal material under investigation involved some consideration. Evidence of the remains of labels from previous examinations of the skeletons suggested problems for long-term projects. A number of skulls display large numbers painted directly onto the frontal bone. These probably date from nineteenth-century investigations.[25] This method of labelling is obviously durable but tends to obscure certain anatomical features, which makes scoring some of the non-metric traits problematic. Also, modern practice requires that any method of labelling is reversible, especially with regard to skeletal remains. Disfiguring skeletal material in this way would now be seen as a sign of disrespect (Chapter 11). There was a lack of clearly defined labels dating to Nicolucci's study. This was deplored by D'Amore *et al.*[26] as it meant that they could not remeasure the bones he used in his work. D'Amore *et al.*[27] used adhesive paper labels. This suited their purpose of a one-season study. By the time I commenced my research, the adhesive had mostly failed and it was impossible to associate labels with specific bones. This limited comparisons with previous studies on the bones to general trends rather than specific cases.

I initially used tie-on tags for the long bones as this form of identification is less time consuming than painting numbers onto a treated area of the bone surface. After the discovery of a mouse with a penchant for paper inhabiting the femur pile, I decided that numbers applied with Indian ink on a cleaned bone surface coated with clear nail varnish would be more likely to survive from one season's study to the next. Each bone was marked with small numbers in a place that would not be too apparent and would not obscure any diagnostic features. The nail varnish was used so that marking was reversible as it could be removed with acetone, leaving no trace of ink on the bone. This method of identification was used for all the bones under examination.[28]

The sample

As mentioned above, the available sample of skeletons was considerably smaller than the number of discoveries claimed in the archaeological literature. It was not possible to select a sample as a percentage of the total since the exact number of individuals excavated was not known. For this reason I decided to examine the largest representative sample for each type of bone.

Almost all the bones stored in the Forum and Sarno Baths were inspected during the course of cleaning, which permitted assessment of the scope of the remains. As it was not logistically possible to fully record all the available Pompeian skeletal material, I decided to concentrate on the Forum Bath sample for the majority of skull and long bone studies. There were several reasons for this choice. First, I thought that the bones in the Forum Baths would provide a good random sample that I had not chosen. Comparison with the cranial and long bone remains in the Sarno Baths suggested that the Forum Bath sample was representative of the Pompeian material that had been recovered. Second, the Forum Bath bones were specially chosen for their completeness. Many of the Sarno Bath bones were incomplete and a number of the skulls had been deformed by the pressure of the ash under which they had been buried. Third, it would be possible to make a general comparison with the results of the 1979 study of the Forum Bath collection. In addition, these bones required less preparation for examination as they had been cleaned previously[29] and were stored in conditions which did not require the same amount of annual cleaning as the Sarno Bath bones. Finally, the Forum Baths provided a more desirable working environment since there was a table and some access to artificial light.

It is difficult to assess the exact number of individuals that are housed in the two bath buildings. The sample in the Sarno Baths appears to be strongly biased towards cranial remains. It would be very time-consuming to attempt to establish a minimum number of individuals from the skulls as many of them have been broken into small fragments which have been scattered about the building. At least 360 individuals could be identified from the combined crania in both the Forum and Sarno Bath collections. One possible explanation for the higher representation of skeletons by cranial rather than other remains is that the skull was the part of the skeleton most easily recognized by excavators that were not schooled in anatomy. Another is that the skull was considered the most important bone by nineteenth-century anthropologists (see Chapters 3 and 9) and that other, or post-cranial, skeletal remains were not thought worthy of preservation. A possible problem that could be associated with this skewing was whether the skull sample chosen for analysis was comparable to the samples chosen for other bones. The sample sizes chosen for each type of bone, however, were large enough to be statistically significant. In addition, the analysis suggested that there was enough consistency between the results to generally dismiss sample bias between bones as a problem.

The sample also seems to be strongly skewed towards adult bones with a total absence of neonatal bones and few young juveniles. Under-representation of neonates and infants is a recognized problem in archaeology and is thought to primarily result from small and fragmentary bones either being ignored as they are not recognized by excavators or disintegrating in the ground prior to excavation.[30]

The method of storage also appears to be a contributory factor for the absence of neonatal skeletal remains and the relative scarcity of young juvenile bones. This notion is supported by the comparative frequency of juvenile bones in collections of skeletons that have been left *in situ* for display purposes and the number of juveniles represented in the collection of casts (Chapter 10)

I decided to concentrate on issues associated with adult bones to circumvent the problem of a sample biased against juvenile remains. Juvenile skulls, teeth and pelves, however, were recorded to give an indication of the proportions of different age groups represented in the available sample. These particular bones were chosen because they were useful for the determination of juvenile age-at-death. Also, sufficient numbers of each bone were available for examination to provide a representative sample of the age spectrum of Pompeian victims stored on the site.

All the pelves in the Sarno Baths collection were examined. All the available teeth and as many skulls as possible from both stores were studied. While juvenile skulls were not sexed or used for the metric study, they were examined for epigenetic traits (see Chapter 9).

Two groups of skeletons from the Insula of the Menander that were supposedly *in situ* were to be studied as a control sample of intact individuals (see Chapter 1). It soon became clear that the main group of about ten bodies had been tampered with for display purposes by people with limited anatomical knowledge and that the individuals had been, in effect, disarticulated. The other group of two bodies was not complete.

Measurements

A range of basic measuring instruments was employed, such as vernier callipers, spreading callipers and an osteometric board.[31] The choice of measurements was based on a survey of the then current literature. It should be noted that the *Standards for Data Collection from Human Skeletal Remains*[32] was not published when these data were collected. Nonetheless, measurements and observations were recorded in sufficient detail to enable them to be applied to this sample. The main criterion for each measurement taken was that it would yield information about sex, height, age-at-death, pathological alteration of bone, or population affinity.

Reliability of the measurements

A problem that is frequently associated with the metric analysis of archaeological bones is that they tend to be incomplete or eroded as a result of post mortem damage. The areas around the landmarks on bones, which are used to define measurements, are often damaged and a certain degree of guesswork may be required to make a measurement. An assessment of reliability or confidence level in each measurement would therefore be prudent, although it is not often undertaken in skeletal studies. The scoring system that was employed for this study also acted as a reflection of the degree of preservation of the bones.

One of the major concerns in dealing with this sample was whether it was representative of the Pompeian victims or was biased towards the more robust bones, which are generally associated with males (see Chapter 6). If the sample were found to be representative, there was still the problem of whether the more gracile bones, generally assumed to be associated with females, were more likely to be incomplete. This would pose a problem for making valid conclusions from certain types of analysis, such as multivariate statistical analysis, which have a limited capability for dealing with incomplete data sets (see below). I worked on the quantification of bone preservation with a statistician using cranial measurements as an example of how this problem, which came to be known as the 'crumble factor',[33] could be assessed.

All the bones that were used in the investigation were described by a series of measurements and observations. The accuracy of each measurement was dependent on the completeness of the bone and the ease of location of specific landmarks. To quantify this, a four-point scoring system of confidence, or V-score, was assigned, based on that employed by Howells for cranial measurements. The value of the use of V-scores can be demonstrated from an inspection of the three-dimensional graphs for the V-scores of each of the cranial measurements. These are standard measurements that are used to describe the dimensions and shape of the skull.[34] The three-dimensional graphs display the frequency distribution of each measurement in the sample, along with the associated degree of confidence.

Certain measurements, such as glabello-occipital length (Figure 5.4),[35] the frontal chord[36] and parietal chord,[37] were found to be highly reliable, whereas measurements like maximum cranial breadth[38] and maximum frontal breadth[39] (Figure 5.5) were demonstrably less accurate. Bizygomatic breadth (Figure 5.6)[40] produced few results that were better than guesses.

It is also apparent that for the majority of measurements, for example, glabello-occipital length, nasio-occipital length[41] and maximum cranial breadth, there is no appreciable bias towards robust bones in relation to the

guesswork or observations on a limited number of cases. This is because access to skeletal material, of known individuals is limited by ethical considerations. Occasionally, it is possible to test hypotheses with well-documented archaeological material, as in the case of the large sample of eighteenth- and nineteenth-century skeletons with coffin plate and other documentary information that were excavated from the crypt of Christ Church, Spitalfields in London. Comparison between the skeletal evidence and biographic and genealogical data indicated that there was no correlation between childbearing and pitting in the areas where ligaments attach on the dorsal surface of the pubic symphysis and preauricular area. Instead, there was a significant correlation between pelvic size and pitting. It was concluded that these changes were more commonly observed on females than males because they tend to have a larger pelvic area.[32]

In terms of the determination of sex for the Pompeian pelvic sample, the reasons for the appearance of these features is not as important as the fact that they tend to be correlated with females rather than males, though it is important to be mindful that presence of these features does not necessarily provide incontrovertible evidence for a female attribution.

Initially, both right and left pelvic bones were used for sexing as the results of the early stages of sorting suggested that there were a greater number of right than left bones. I decided that it would be useful to look at both sides to establish whether the sex ratios were the same. A quick visual assessment suggested the proportion of males to females was roughly equivalent on both sides. When the bones were finally sorted and broken pelves reconstructed, it was found that there was minimal difference between the numbers of innominates representing each side and I only recorded the left bones in detail.

Bones were originally defined as adult only when epiphyseal fusion was complete (see Chapter 7). This definition, however, excluded certain bones where there was evidence of changes normally associated with female skeletons, such as a pre-auricular groove. The definition was cautiously altered to include bones where fusion was complete, except at the iliac crest and the tuberosity of the ischium. Fusion in these regions is often not completed until the third decade by which time the hormone changes to initiate sexual dimorphism have occurred and reproduction has been possible for some time.[33] It is notable that certain scholars[34] define innominates where fusion at the iliac crest has commenced as young adult rather than sub-adult. Sexual attributions based on innominate bones of individuals who had not yet attained complete maturity were noted separately.

Sex determination was based on a combination of ten observations and three measurements from a sample of 158 left adult and older adolescent innominate bones, mostly from the Sarno Baths.[35] This sample represents all the material that was available from the Pompeian collection.

Some of these features, such as the ventral arc, are known to be more useful discriminators than others. The range of features were chosen because they involved different parts of the bone, so that no matter how incomplete the specimen it would be possible to include it in the study. The more reliable indicators were employed as a baseline to enable population norms to be established for the pelves in the Pompeian sample.

As expected, the pelvis proved to be the most useful sex indicator of the samples of individual bones that were examined and should be used as a baseline for the interpretation of the other bones. It is notable, though not surprising, that the non-metric observations produced far better separation than the metric data. Since the morphology of the pelvis is based on biological function, the non-metric features were considered more reliable.

Both univariate and multivariate descriptive statistics produced similar results for the non-metric data (as typified by Figures. 6.1 and 6.2). Three main conclusions could be drawn with regard to the individual features. The first is that the best pelvic features for sex separation from the Pompeian material are the ventral arc, sub-pubic concavity and the sub-pubic angle, closely followed by the medial aspect of the ischio-pubic ramus and the obdurator foramen. The pre-auricular sulcus, sciatic notch and pubic tuber-cule are also good indicators but do not appear to separate the sample as well. The second is that the auricular area does not display any degree of bimodality (Figure 6.3) and, unlike the other features, is skewed towards the more female end of the range. It is clearly not a good sex separator but may perhaps be useful as a population descriptor. The third is that this research supported the assertion that dorsal pitting may not be specifically linked to parturition as it was also observed on pelves that were apparently male.

No matter how the data were treated in terms of statistical analysis, the pelvic observations, with the exception of the auricular area, consistently separated the sample into a higher proportion of males than females. This is at odds with the popular view that it was the women who were more likely to have become victims. The issue of sex determination from the pelvis, however, is complex and the results for individual non-pubic features do not necessarily reflect the actual ratio of males to females. Further consideration is required for the interpretation of the results.

It has been observed that female pelves tend to display more mid-range traits than males.[36] This certainly appeared to be the case for the Pompeian sample. Many of the pelves where the pubic region had not survived were rather androgynous in appearance and were difficult to classify. This phenomenon has been observed for other skeletal samples from central Southern Italy.[37] It is notable that Bisel considered the pelves in the Herculaneum skeletal sample to be highly dimorphic, though she probably had more complete bones in her sample (see below).[38] A number of pelves that were unequivocally female from examination of the os pubis, displayed either mid-range or male features, especially for the sciatic notch. In addition, it

and 'male' range of scores with a frequency of 40.6 : 59.3 'females' to 'males'. The other three components did not separate the sample.

Even though the skull has been traditionally used as one of the major sex indicators, it was only possible to have limited confidence in the results for sex determination from the skull for the Pompeian sample. Part of the problem could perhaps be related to the sample, which was not very dimorphic. This was recognized as a problem by D'Amore et al.[63] who expressed concern about the accuracy of the results they obtained on almost the same sample as the one used for the current study. They attributed the much higher frequency of males to females they identified in the sample to an artefact of the misdiagnosis of robust females. It is worth noting that my analysis produced a completely different set of results with a higher incidence of skulls with female attributes. A number of explanations can be used to account for this. First, they included juveniles in their sample, though one would have expected this to skew the results to the female range. Second, they used different criteria, such as cranial capacity, for sex determination. Finally, the sample appears to reflect a population that is somewhat androgynous and difficult to sex with consistency. It is significant that D'Amore et al. had problems with the determination of sex from this sample (see below), especially as D'Amore has had considerable experience with material from the Campanian region.[64] This suggests that the Pompeian sample may differ from other Campanian samples. In contrast, Bisel[65] considered the male and female skulls from Herculaneum easy to differentiate by sex, though she had the advantage of complete skeletons for comparison (see below).

The problem of the determination of sex from visual criteria on skulls is not confined to the material from Pompeii. Howells[66] included a lengthy discussion of the problems he encountered in attempting to determine sex from the skulls of the various populations he used in his craniometric analyses in his publications. He documented the problem of lack of concordance between observers. He also noted a possible tendency to favour female attribution. This is consistent with the results from the Pompeian sample. It is notable that Howells relied on morphological appearance rather than measurements to assess sex from the skull.

Measurements

Choice of skull measurements for this study was determined by the constraints of preservation. The cranial vault tended to have much higher survival rates than the facial region for the majority of the sample and was able to provide the largest, most complete data set. Measurements were also chosen that could be used for comparisons with the work of other scholars. Twelve skull measurements were used to establish whether it would be possible to separate the adult skulls from the Forum Bath collection by sex based on a metric analysis. Standard definitions were used for these measurements.[67]

Discriminant function analysis has traditionally been used for the determination of sex from skulls.[68] Discriminant function analyses are based on the extrapolation of parameters for sexual dimorphism from a known population onto unknown individuals to identify their sex. Interpopulation variation is significant enough to require the development of population-specific sets of equations.[69] As the Pompeian skeletal material derives from an unknown population, the use of a modern reference sample is likely to produce sex separations that do not reflect the actual sex ratio of the Pompeian victims. This analysis was not considered appropriate for the Pompeian sample.

The metric data proved to be more problematic for the determination of sex from the Pompeian skull sample than that based on inspection of non-metric features.[70] No results that could be used with confidence were obtained from the metric study of sex separation. The variables were too weakly correlated to produce a successful principal components analysis. It could be argued that the lack of success in sex identification is a reflection of underlying heterogeneity of the Pompeian sample. This problem, however, is not restricted to heterogeneous material and can be illustrated by the following example.

A series of 25 head and facial measurements was made on a relatively homogeneous sample of 900 Swiss soldiers of the same age in order to design a few standard gas masks that would be suitable for a number of 'typical' faces. Principal components analysis was employed in an attempt to establish these 'typical' faces by reducing all the variables to a few principal components. The aim of the exercise was to rank all the individuals on the basis of the first principal component. The main proviso for the success of such an exercise was that the first principal component be well defined and account for a considerable portion of the total variance. The principal components analysis was ultimately based on ten of the measurements. The first principal component was found to account for only 43 per cent of the total variance and could not be used as an approximation of the sample. This was considered a surprising result given that the first principal component often accounts for more than 80 per cent of variance in morphometric studies. The conclusion drawn from this study was that there are numerous ways in which skulls and faces, in particular, can vary and it is not possible to represent them by a few dimensions without a significant loss of information.[71]

Mandibles

Four features were observed on all the available adult mandibles from the Forum and Sarno Bath collections.[72] These features were chosen as they are based on relative robusticity and gracility and are generally accepted as good sex discriminators.[73] This appeared to be the case for the Pompeian sample. The first principal component accounted for 87 per cent of the variance and provided such good separation it could probably be used as a sex index

females from the metric information. Perhaps the most interesting result from this exploration of Nicolucci's data is revealed from an examination using cluster analysis. The fact that the data could not be forced into two groups suggests that the sample Nicolucci used was not comparable to that stored in the Forum Baths. The way the data split into specific groups perhaps implies that his sample was not random but was specially selected to include unusual specimens. It is notable that the alleged 'negro' skull he singled out formed a single cluster, implying that it really was significantly different from the other crania in his study.

The work of D'Amore *et al.* on the skulls housed in the Forum baths produced slightly different results to those obtained in the current study.[82] They poured millet into the skulls and then ordered them by increasing cranial capacity. The cranial index was also calculated so that the two features could be compared. These measurements were chosen for sex attribution because, according to Krogman,[83] female cranial capacity is generally about 200 cc less than that of males, and females have a relatively higher cranial index because their skulls are more rounded. These two elements formed the basis of their classification. They also employed other, perhaps more traditional, indicators of dimorphism, such as the presence of frontal bosses, sharp orbital margins, smaller zygomas and palates, and smaller muscle attachments to identify females.[84] They classified 43 skulls as female and 80 as male. These figures were calculated as percentages, namely 35 per cent and 65 per cent respectively as compared to Nicolucci's breakdown of 45 per cent females to 55 per cent males.[85]

The choice of cranial capacity and cranial index as the major sex indicators for this study requires some comment. These features are not commonly employed for sex segregation in current studies of archaeological skeletal material and are generally not recommended as criteria for sexing in physical anthropological texts.[86] Further, it has been asserted that the most useful sex indicators on the skull are to be found in the region of the face rather than in the area that houses the brain.[87] While it can be claimed that there is a slight difference between the average cranial indices of men and women in a population, the veracity of the assumption that males have greater cranial capacity than females has been questioned. Though there is some correlation between brain and body size, it is not certain what the extent of overlap is for the range of cranial capacity. It has been suggested that in the past, undue emphasis was placed on size differences for the determination of sex from skulls.[88] It has been further asserted that data may have been manipulated in the past, either consciously or unconsciously, to confirm preconceived ideas, namely that greater cranial capacity in males was a reflection of male superiority.[89]

D'Amore *et al.* were concerned about the results they obtained. Though it was not explicitly stated, this was possibly because they expected their evidence to support the notion that women were more likely to have been victims than men. They conceded that they did not know how many people were able to escape from the eruption or who they were. In their opinion, only a modest number of bodies had been recovered from Pompeii because the majority of skeletons were either lost or not collected during the course of excavation. They argued, therefore, that the higher male to female sex ratio they calculated was not necessarily an accurate reflection of the population of Pompeian victims. A comparison of their findings with the sex ratios obtained by other scholars, including Nicolucci, who worked on ancient and recent Italian skeletal material, led them to conclude that the number of males always exceeded the number of females in Italian samples. They explained this phenomenon as the result of a high incidence of robust females in these samples.[90]

It is possible that this explanation is correct, though the argument presented by D'Amore et al. to support this claim can be criticized. It is worth noting that the source for all their comparative data was compiled in 1904.[91] The methods for determining sex from skeletal material were improved considerably over the course of the twentieth century and it is possible that some of the sex attributions of these earlier works could be questioned. In addition, the documented tendency for a systematic bias towards male attributions from skeletal evidence[92] is unlikely to have been recognized, let alone corrected for, by nineteenth- and early twentieth-century anthropologists. Another possibility that D'Amore et al. do not appear to have considered is that the scholars whose work they cited may not have based their studies on random samples. Nicolucci certainly did not state the criteria he used for selecting his sample. It is probably reasonable to assume that he chose the more complete skulls available to him for measurement, along with those that he found interesting, such as the supposedly 'negroid' skull. The former may well have led to a bias towards the more robust skulls, which may explain the slightly higher number of males than females in his sample.

D'Amore et al. also explored the possibility of misdiagnosis as another reason for the higher frequency of males in their sample. They expressed reservations about the accuracy of their sex attributions as a result of the problems of sex determination based solely from the skull. Nonetheless, they apparently made no effort to compare their results with post-cranial bones from the Pompeian collection. They merely cited examples from the skeletal literature, which reinforced the view that sexual diagnosis from the skull was difficult and potentially inaccurate. The problems of sex determination from skulls were considered to result from the lack of unequivocal sex specific characteristics and variation between populations.[93]

D'Amore et al. concluded that there was probably considerable overlap between the sexes for the features that they chose for sex separation in their sample of Pompeian skulls. This diminished their confidence in the results that they obtained. They suggested that the Pompeian skeletal series was more robust than they expected and that skulls which they classified as males may well have belonged to females.[94]

Recent re-examination of the skulls, mandibles and pelves of essentially the same material used in my study confirmed the results reported in this chapter. Sex attribution based on the pelvis and mandible yielded a higher incidence of males to females, while examination of the skulls suggested more females than males.[95]

Herculaneum

Attribution of sex for the Herculaneum sample differed from that of Pompeii as individuals were represented by articulated, often complete, skeletons so there was no incentive to establish which bones were better indicators of dimorphism in the sample. As a result, comparisons of results for individual skeletal elements cannot easily be made between the two sites.

Of the 139 skeletons she studied, Bisel[96] determined 51 to be male and 49 to be female, the remaining 39 being juvenile and difficult to sex (see above). It is important to realize that these skeletons are included in all of the samples used by subsequent researchers.

Luigi Capasso established sex for 144 of the 162 skeletons available to him. He identified 83 as male and 61 as female. It is notable that he made sex attributions for juvenile skeletons, though he did acknowledge that there were problems with the technique he employed. He excluded a foetal skeleton that he sexed as female from these figures. He calculated the ratio of males : females as 1.38 : 1.[97]

More recently, a sample of 215 Herculanean skeletons were studied by Petrone *et al.*[98] They did not attempt to establish sex from young juvenile bones but did make attributions for individuals aged from mid teen years. They also obtained slightly higher numbers of males than females, with 37.4 per cent of the total sample sexed as male and 31.8 per cent as female.

Sex and population affinities

It is important to recognize that features associated with sex can be population specific. The determination of the sex of an individual is inextricably linked with their population affinities.[99] A number of features that were considered to be possible sex indicators, like the auricular area, are probably more useful as descriptors of the population. This is true for other features for different populations, such as the shape of the chin, brow ridges and septal apertures of the humerus.[100] The fact that there are not many diagnostic features for the separation of the Pompeians into male and female categories can also be interpreted as a population feature.

Skulls, in particular, have long held a fascination for scholars (see Chapter 3) and have often been the primary bone used for analysis. This study indicates that, at least for the Pompeian sample, they are of limited value. In addition, the inability of the metric data to provide information on intrapopulation data in the form of sex separation does not augur well for their value as population discriminators for the Pompeian victims.

Conclusion

The assumption that the sample of Pompeian victims was skewed towards females is not supported by the skeletal evidence, which suggests that, if anything, the sample has more of a male bias. No explanation can be offered for such a bias, especially because it is difficult to interpret whether or not it is significant owing to the problem of overlap.

It is notable that different bones provided different sex ratios. The pelvic non-metric observations yielded a considerably higher incidence of males in the sample, whilst the humeral and skull measurements along with the mandible observations, suggested almost equal separation with a slightly higher frequency of males. In contrast, the results from the femur measurements implied a greater number of more gracile, presumably female, individuals in the sample. Similarly, the pelvic measurements and the non-metric skull observations suggest that the sample was composed of more females than males.

Interpretation of these results is dependent on the establishment of which bones and traits are the most useful indicators of sex for the Pompeian sample. The results from the femur can be questioned on the basis of sample bias as a number of the bones were removed from the Pompeian stores for secondary usage as hinges (see Chapter 5). From the results, it appears that the bones that are most useful features for sex separation for this sample are the non-metric pelvic traits, followed by the non-metric mandible traits and the humerus measurements.

The association between sex and population is well documented with sexual dimorphism varying between populations. It appears as if the Pompeian sample shows a tendency towards androgyny for certain features, especially in the pelvis and skull. This study indicates that the skull, and the craniometric data in particular, is not very useful as a sex indicator for the Pompeian sample and, by implication, cranial measurements are of limited value for the determination of population affinities for this sample. This is because they did not indicate any real separation into well-defined groups. This could be explained if the sample were heterogeneous, though other evidence that has been collected does not support this view. The results of this research suggest that these cranial measurements are not a good indicator for either sex or population affinities for the Pompeian sample.

7

DETERMINATION OF
AGE-AT-DEATH

Estimation of age-at-death is more difficult than the attribution of sex from skeletal material as there are only two options for sex, whilst ageing is a continuous process. This means that it is virtually impossible to age individuals, especially adults, with a great deal of precision. A further problem for the estimation of age-at-death is that an individual's biological age may not reflect their chronological or actual age. This is because the relationship between the degree of skeletal development or degeneration and the actual age of an individual is not linear.[1]

Juvenile skeletons generally produce the most reliable results. Criteria for age determination of immature individuals are relatively straightforward as they are based on growth and development. While there is some variation between individuals and populations in timing, these factors tend to be relatively consistent and predictable. Juvenile age-at-death is generally determined by extrapolation from standards that have been derived from data obtained from children of known age from modern populations. A number of variables may influence this, such as illness and nutrition. Ideally, it is preferable to avoid the use of ageing criteria that are likely to be affected by such variables. An example of this can be seen in the size of bones, which tends to be a good indicator of foetal age. Apparently, poor maternal nutrition is less likely to affect foetal bone length than malnutrition after birth. Bone length of a growing child is subject to too many external influences to be a really useful indicator of age. The incomplete nature of most archaeological remains, however, makes it impossible to discard any evidence, even if it is problematic.

Teeth develop from the crown to the roots, with root formation continuing to completion after the tooth has erupted. Dental development tends to be complete by the beginning of the third decade of life, though the last tooth to erupt, the third molar, or wisdom tooth, is the most variable. While there is some variation between individuals, teeth tend to be reliable indicators of the age of sub-adults, as their development appears to be less influenced by environmental factors. This would also suggest that the modern standards for tooth formation and eruption are applicable to ancient populations. This theory was tested, using 63 named and well-documented skeletons of children from the Spitalfields crypt. Though they only date back as far as the eighteenth and nineteenth centuries, it is notable that there was a high correlation between documented age and the results obtained from a number of standard dental ageing techniques. The ages obtained from the dental standards minimally, but consistently, under-aged the Spitalfields children. It has been suggested that this is a reflection of the effects of poor nutrition on dental development.[2]

After teeth, skeletal development provides the best indicator of juvenile age-at-death. Growing long bones are made up of three parts: the shaft or diaphysis and the ends, which articulate with other bones, which are known as the epiphyses. The epiphyses are separated from the shaft by growth cartilage, which is where growth occurs. When the growth period ends, the cartilage ossifies and the epiphyses are fused with the shaft. The majority of other bones also have epiphyses. Epiphyseal fusion occurs in an orderly fashion in the period between adolescence and early adulthood. The actual age at which epiphyseal fusion occurs for different bones can vary between individuals, sexes and populations. Epiphyses tend to fuse earlier in the bones of females, whose period of growth is generally shorter than that of males. The last epiphysis to fuse is that of the medial clavicle or collarbone. The age of fusion for this epiphysis can vary between 21 and 30 years of age, though generally all bones have fused by about 28 years of age in modern populations.

The determination of adult age-at-death is fraught with problems. After the completion of development, the only changes that occur are essentially degenerative and individuals do not degenerate at the same rate. This is readily apparent on living people. Some people's hair, for example, goes grey when they are in their early twenties, whilst others can naturally retain their colour into old age. Differential degeneration is a biological fact that cannot be accounted for by any ageing technique. The sequence of changes after maturity is attained is variable and tends to be influenced by environmental factors; for example, the degree of tooth wear or attrition observed on an individual is determined by diet and lifestyle. Even with entire skeletons, it is difficult to establish the age-at-death of an adult. The addition of further complicating factors, such as a disarticulated unknown population, exacerbates the existing problems.[3]

Choice of age-at-death indicators for the Pompeian skeletal sample

As with the determination of sex, age-at-death can be more confidently assessed with complete skeletons. The constraints of the Pompeian skeletal sample limited the use of certain ageing techniques; for example, it was virtually impossible to employ a standard multiple trait assessment based on the examination of the entire skeleton.[4] Due to limitations of time and budget, emphasis was placed on the techniques that were deemed most useful at the time. The choice of the pelvis, skull and teeth as the indicators of age-at-death in the Pompeian sample was based on their well-documented potential to provide age information from birth to relative old age.[5] Criteria that were used to give an indication of adult age included changes to the surface of the pubic symphysis, ectocranial suture closure and tooth wear. Assessment based on dental attrition was of limited value for this sample, as most of the skulls can no longer be articulated with mandibles due to the manner in which they were stored. This meant it was not always clear whether wear related to occlusal problems or dietary behaviour. Consideration was also given to a number of cranial features, which could be used to separate adults from juveniles, such as fusion of the basi-sphenoid and development of the frontal sinuses. Though less reliable, features like endocranial suture closure were also recorded, especially when only limited material representing an individual was available.

Age-related pathology, such as hyperostosis frontalis interna (Chapter 8 and see below), was employed to give an indication of the relative longevity of the Pompeians. The range of bony indicators generally associated with advancing years that could be used for this purpose was determined by the disarticulated nature of the sample. For example, it was not possible to do more than note most cases of osteophytic change, as age-related arthropathy cannot necessarily be distinguished from trauma-related changes when examination is based on a single bone. Some scholars have argued the possibility that certain disorders associated with old age in a modern Western population occurred at comparatively earlier ages in an ancient population. It was therefore necessary for their association with elderly people to be corroborated by other skeletal age indicators.

There was relatively little advantage to be gained from an examination of all the samples of specific bones in the disarticulated Pompeian collection to establish age-at-death. Since the times of epiphyseal closure vary between bones in an individual, a study of the degree of epiphyseal union in all these samples would do little more than separate adults from juveniles.[6] For this reason only one post-cranial bone, the pelvis, was chosen to represent the entire sample. The degree of epiphyseal union was routinely recorded for juvenile bones that were included in non-metric trait scoring for long bones.

One of the constraints of this project was that it was not possible at the time of examination to obtain permission to perform destructive tests on Pompeian skeletal material. This precluded the use of various established methods, including bone cortex remodelling and root dentine transparency in teeth.[7] It is notable that research by the Victorian Institute of Forensic Pathology at Monash University has produced results that question the reliability of the former method.[8] Access to radiographic techniques, such as those suggested by Iscan and Loth,[9] was also not possible due to financial constraints. This meant that the determination of age-at-death in this study was limited to macroscopic observations.

Assignment of specific ages

It is misleading to ascribe exact ages to archaeological skeletal material from an unknown population for two reasons. First, the actual ages for epiphyseal fusion, dental eruption and subsequent degenerative bony changes associated with ageing are variable. Variation for all these changes can occur within and between individuals and populations. In addition, it can be correlated with sex.[10] As a result of these variations tolerances in age estimation can vary considerably. For example, those produced from the Suchey–Brooks technique of ageing from the pubic symphysis have tolerances (95 per cent) of between ± 5 years for phase 1 to well over ± 20 years for the later phases (see Table 7.1).[11]

Second, age estimates that have been established for skeletal material have been determined from modern Western samples. There is a standard seven-point scoring scheme to estimate relative age.[12] Two additional scores were included in this work to deal with some of the vagaries encountered with the establishment of adult age-at-death (Table 7.2). This system roughly classifies age in ten-year increments, as the order of accuracy of most available techniques is very poor. It must be remembered that these age ranges are artificial as age-related changes are continuous.[13] It is also important to understand that the classification of the last phase as relating to the sixth decade or older is purely a reflection of the upper limit of the techniques. It in no way is meant to indicate a shorter lifespan.

Age estimation based on the pelvis

Juvenile age

Juvenile and sub-adult pelves were scored in relation to the degree of fusion and the maximum width of the innominate bone.[14]

Table 7.1 Mean ages associated with the phases of the Suchey–Brooks ageing system from the pubic symphysis

Phase	Female mean	Female standard deviation	Female 95% range	Male mean	Male standard deviation	Male 95% range
I	19.4	2.6	15–24	18.5	2.1	15–23
II	25.0	4.9	19–40	23.4	3.6	19–34
III	30.7	8.1	21–53	28.7	6.5	21–46
IV	38.2	10.9	26–70	35.2	9.4	23–57
V	48.1	14.6	25–83	45.6	10.4	27–66
VI	60.0	12.4	42–87	61.2	12.2	34–86

Source: Adapted from Brooks and Suchey, 1990, 233.

141

Table 7.2 Modified standard scoring scheme for the attribution of relative age-at-death

Nine-point scoring scheme for the attribution of relative age-at-death

1. Foetal	This term applies to any time prior to birth.
2. Infant	The period from birth to three years of age. The choice of age 3 as a cut-off point was based on the tendency for the completion of eruption of the deciduous dentition by this age.
3. Juvenile	Consistent in age with between about 3 and 12 years of age in a modern population.
4. Adolescent	Consistent with ages between about 12 and 20 years of age in a modern western population.
5. Indeterminate	Cases where not enough evidence remains to distinguish between sub-adult and adult.
6. Young adult	Consistent with an age attribution in the third (20–35 years of age) decade in a modern western population.
7. Adult	Consistent with an age attribution in the fourth decade in a modern western population.
8. Mature adult	Consistent with an age attribution in the fifth decade in a modern western population.
9. Older adult	Consistent with an age attribution in the sixth decade or older in a modern western population.

Source: Modified from standard scoring schemes, like that of Buikstra and Ubelaker, 1994, 9.

The juvenile innominate bone is composed of three separate bones, the ilium, the ischium and the pubis. In a modern Western population the rami of the pubis and the ischium generally fuse in about the seventh or eighth year of life, though fusion can occur any time between the ages of five and eight. In about the twelfth year of life the cartilaginous strip that has separated the three bones begins to ossify. It can take up until the eighteenth year for ossification to be completed at this point. Epiphyses appear at the iliac crest, the anterior inferior iliac spine, the pubis and the ischial tuberosity at about puberty and fusion is usually completed by the twenty-sixth year. It should be noted that fusion occurs at an earlier age in females. In the case of the ilium, ischium and pubis, fusion occurs between the ages of 11 to 15 in females and 14 to 17 in males in modern Western populations. Various factors can influence the time of fusion including health, diet and the state of the endocrine system. In addition, there may be differences between populations.[15]

Correlation has been observed between maximum iliac breadth and juvenile age. The data that have been collected from a North American Indian population have been tabulated as a series of means, standard deviations and ranges of deviations for different age ranges and presented for comparison with other populations. It is important to note that comparative studies of growth rates between different populations have demonstrated that there is interpopulation variation in the rate of bone growth, e.g. the rate of growth of Americans of European heritage has been found to be greater than that of

American Indians, which in turn has been shown to be faster than that of Inuit. This suggests that though these data were most appropriately applied to other American Indian populations, they could be used with caution to obtain a general estimate of juvenile age-at-death for other populations. Even greater caution is required as some of these age-at-death estimates have been based on extremely small sample sizes, e.g. estimates for juveniles between 10.5 and 11.5 years of age were based on a sample of one bone.[16]

The use of North American Indian material for comparison with the Pompeian sample is far from ideal but no other data were available at the time of study. It did not enable exact ages to be assigned to individual bones but it did enable the juvenile pelvic remains to be seriated.

Out of 196 left innominate bones available for examination in the Pompeian collection, 6.1 per cent were completely unfused. Comparison of the maximum width of the eleven bones in this category that could be measured with the mean ages established for North American Indian populations from maximum iliac width, indicated that the younger immature individuals in the Pompeian sample fell within the juvenile category with ages consistent with a range in modern Western populations of between about three and twelve years. Bearing in mind the problems of extrapolation between populations, rough age estimates are presented here purely to give some indication of the range of development of the juvenile pelvic bones in the Pompeian sample. In summary, approximately 11 per cent of the sample presented as juvenile, reflecting an age range consistent with 2.5 to 15.5 years. A roughly even distribution of juveniles for each of the ages in this range was observed.

Since it was not possible to relate clavicles to pelves in the Pompeian collection, only epiphyseal fusion of the iliac crest was recorded. The value of these observations is that, in theory, they give some indication of the age of adolescents and individuals in the early years of adulthood. In the current study, fusion of the anterior iliac crest was only used to distinguish between adolescents and adults. In modern Western populations, the anterior and posterior epiphyses fuse to form a single cap for the crest and then commence fusion with the pelvis from 15–18 years in females and 17 to 20 years in males. Fusion tends to be complete by 23 years of age.[17]

There were 15 cases, or 7.65 per cent of the sample, which exhibited partial union of the epiphysis at the anterior iliac crest. It was possible to measure two of these cases. The widths of both bones were found to be significantly larger than the North American Indian comparative data for older adolescents.

Adult age

The pubic symphysis is the joint where the left and right pubic bones almost meet. They are separated by a fibro-cartilaginous disc. The underlying bone

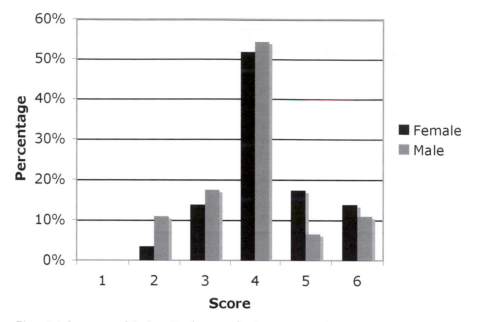

Figure 7.1 Sex separated Suchey–Brooks scores for the Pompeian adult sample

sinuses and the fusion of the basilar bone, could only be used to discriminate between adults and juveniles. Like the pelvic age indicators, the cranial ageing criteria suggested a much higher proportion of adults than juveniles in the Pompeian sample.

Cranial suture closure

The foetal skull is composed of a number of bones. The bones of the cranium are separate to enable some movement so that the skull can pass through the birth canal without damaging the brain. The cranial bones are separated by sutures. Growth of the skull occurs along these margins, which then fuse after growth has ceased. Age determination based on the order and degree of cranial suture closure was popular in the late nineteenth and early twentieth centuries, but fell from favour when studies revealed that these were unpredictably variable.[20] Since then endocranial, or inner table, suture closure has only been employed as a last resort in the absence of other skeletal remains.

Cranial suture closure was reassessed in the 1980s by Meindl and Lovejoy. Instead of using endocranial suture closure, which had previously been considered more reliable, they examined the ectocranial sutures, which are those that can be seen on the external surface of the cranium. They argued that these would be more useful for the calculation of age for older individuals as the ectocranial sutures close after the endocranial sutures. The authors stressed, however, that this technique should be used in conjunction with other ageing methods to produce an age based on a number of factors as there is no one reliable diagnostic feature for adult age-at-death.[21]

The endocranial sutures were open in only 15.4 per cent of the sample of 123 skulls. Thirty-six cases or 29.3 per cent of the sample exhibited partially fused endocranial sutures and the remaining 68 cases or 55.3 per cent of the skulls had endocranial sutures that had substantially fused.

The ectocranial suture scores give some indication of the actual age of the adult sample. From the histogram (Figure 7.2) of the ectocranial lateral-anterior suture closure scores (EctsutA), it is apparent that the majority of the sample (69.4 per cent) was aged between the 'adult' and 'older adult' age range. These scores are consistent with ages in a modern Western population of between the fourth and sixth decade or older. This technique does not provide information about individuals that have not yet reached the fourth decade of life. There were 34 skulls or 30.6 per cent of the sample that exhibited no sign of ectocranial suture closure and which, according to this system, could only be classified as being of indeterminate age.

The ectocranial vault suture closure (EctsutB) scores yield slightly different results, which is a reflection of the difference between the two scoring systems. Generally, more observations could be made using this method as it

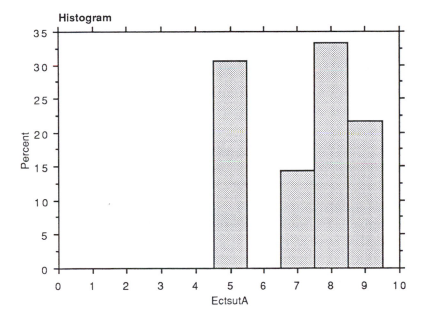

Figure 7.2 Estimated adult age-at-death based on ectocranial lateral-anterior suture closure scores (EctsutA)

Mandibular teeth compared with maxillary teeth

The evidence provided by the teeth of all the available mandibles and maxillae from the Forum and Sarno Bath collections confirmed the results of the pelvic and skull samples. There was no significant difference between the mandibles and maxillae for tooth eruption (Table 7.5). It is notable that neither series had any cases that could be classified as foetal or infants. Just under 24 per cent of maxillae and 22.2 per cent of mandibles were classified as being of indeterminate age. This was because they were either too incomplete to assess or required x-rays to determine whether the third molars had yet to erupt or had been lost ante mortem.

The majority of cases for both types of attrition assessment were identified as consistent with individuals in their third decade of life. As expected, the frequency of cases scored in this category was higher for Att A, as Att B covers a wider age range which enables the older cases to be distinguished (see Tables 7.6 and 7.7). It is evident from the tables that there was greater *in situ* preservation of mandibular than maxillary teeth. It is possible that differences in the way that crania and mandibles were stored could account for the higher post mortem retention of mandibular teeth (also see Chapter 8). It is important to note that many of the mandibles and maxillae did not have sufficient ante and post mortem dental survival to enable assessment, which is why the

Table 7.5 Age determination based on eruption of dentition

	Foetal/ infant	Juvenile	Adolescent	Adult	Indeterminate
Maxillary teeth	0%	3% (n = 3)	6.2% (n = 5)	67.7% (n = 65)	24% (n = 23)
Mandibular teeth	0%	6.2% (n = 5)	5.2% (n = 5)	65.4% (n = 53)	22.2% (n = 18)

Table 7.6 Age determination by AttA

	Adolescent	Adult	Mature adult	Old	Indeterminate
Maxillary teeth	2.1% (n = 1)	8.3% (n = 4)	12.5% (n = 6)	0%	8.4% (n = 4)
Mandibular teeth	7.1% (n = 5)	18.6% (n = 13)	8.6% (n = 6)	0%	8.5% (n = 6)

Table 7.7 Age determination by AttB

	Adolescent	Adult	Mature adult	Old	Indeterminate
Maxillary teeth	10.7% (n = 6)	8.3% (n = 4)	19.6% (n = 11)	1.3% (n = 1)	10.5% (n = 5)
Mandibular teeth	6.7% (n = 5)	22.7% (n = 17)	18.7% (n = 14)	0%	9.9% (n = 7)

percentages do not add up to 100. This should be borne in mind when assessing the results of attrition as an indicator of age for the Pompeian sample.

Age-related pathology

Pathological changes that are generally associated with advancing years have been observed on a number of the bones of the Pompeian sample (see Chapter 8). Because of the problems of diagnosis of disarticulated material, only two disorders were identified with certainty. These were diffuse idiopathic skeletal hyperostosis (DISH), which is more commonly found in older males and presents as fusion, especially of the right side of the thoracic vertebrae, and hyperostosis frontalis interna (HFI), a syndrome associated with an endocrine disorder that is highly correlated with post-menopausal women.

Contrary to expectations based on the assumption that the elderly were more likely to have become victims of Mt Vesuvius, the results of the age assessment of the Pompeian skeletal remains suggest that the proportion of older individuals in the sample was relatively low. In view of the acknowledged tendency for macroscopic ageing techniques based on morphological examination to underestimate adult age-at-death, especially in the older range, it was considered that the presence of age-related pathology might prove a more useful indicator.

As a result of serendipity, one age-related disorder was discovered with a frequency that enabled comments to be made about age and longevity in the Pompeian sample. This pathology presents unequivocally on the inner table of the frontal bone and is known as hyperostosis frontalis interna. It is a syndrome of unknown aetiology related to an endocrine disturbance and is reported to occur almost exclusively in older, usually post menopausal, females. It has an incidence of, at least, 11.1 per cent in the Pompeian sample, which is equivalent to the upper end of the range of the frequency for this disorder in a modern Western population. Only a limited number of cases, both temporally and geographically separated from Pompeii, have been reported in the archaeological literature (Chapter 8). It has been suggested that the reason this disorder has not been found frequently in archaeological contexts is because the average lifespan was much lower in antiquity.[29] The incidence of HFI in the Pompeian sample does not support this assertion. Since the frequency in this sample is comparable to the expected incidence in a modern population, it could be argued that the Pompeian skeletal collections reflect a normally distributed sample with a comparable lifespan to that of a modern community. If this were the case then further doubt could be cast on the presumption that the Pompeian sample was skewed towards the elderly as a result of their inability to escape the AD 79 eruption. The frequency of HFI in the Pompeian sample also suggests that a number of women were surviving to older ages. This is at variance with the assumption that women in ancient Roman society tended to have shorter life expectancies as a result of death during labour. It is perhaps worth noting that ancient authors suggested that women who survived childbirth tended to outlive males.[30]

The only other age-related disorder that could be diagnosed with relative certainty was diffuse idiopathic skeletal hyperostosis (DISH). This is an abnormality that is most apparent in the thoracic vertebrae and is specifically associated with older, usually male, individuals (Chapter 8). Only two cases were observed in the Pompeian collections, which does not allow for much comment beyond the statement that, at least a few individuals were living long enough to exhibit these bony changes. It is possible that this pathology is underrepresented in the Pompeian collections because vertebrae, which generally have not been preserved, are required for its diagnosis. A higher incidence of DISH has been observed in other ancient populations.

From a survey of a sample of 134 adult Nubian skeletons from Semma South in northern Sudan, 18 cases of DISH were identified, which meant that it occurred in the sample with a frequency of 13.4 per cent. This sample covered the period from 350 BC to AD 350. The frequency of this pathology has been determined to be about 10 per cent in people over the age of 70 in a modern Finnish population and 25 per cent in males over the age of 65 in the Todd skeletal collection. This led the researchers to conclude that the ancient Nubians did not have the short lifespans generally attributed to ancient populations.[31]

Similarly, Molleson reported a high proportion of cases of Paget's disease from the medieval Cathedral Green excavations at Winchester. This pathology is also highly correlated with old age and is recognizable by gross thickening of the long bones and skulls of affected individuals. Molleson documented these cases even though she generally subscribed to the view that ancient lifespans, especially those of the Romano-British populations she studied, were much shorter than those of modern populations. She used this example to promulgate the possibility that ancient skeletal material may have been underaged.[32]

This is a moot point. The demonstrated tendency for a number of ageing techniques to underage skeletal material can be used to confirm preconceived ideas about ancient populations. For example, palaeodemographic studies based on Roman skeletal material of the later Empire have presented the average age-at-death at about 24 to 25 years, with few individuals surviving into the fourth decade. Various reasons have been invoked to explain this phenomenon, such as poor sanitation and inadequate medical attention for the urban poor.[33]

So strong is the presumption of premature death in antiquity that the discovery of pathology associated with old age is often explained away by the suggestion that such diseases occurred at earlier ages in ancient populations. Anderson,[34] for example, considered that the occurrence of a case of HFI in an Anglo-Saxon skeleton was possibly a reflection of the earlier onset of menopause. Because of the vagaries of the available ageing techniques, especially in the identification of older individuals, it can be difficult to corroborate old age from skeletal remains. This makes it impossible to refute the argument of earlier onset of certain disorders, which means that interpretation can become a self-fulfilling prophecy.

There is no basis for the assumption that there have been significant changes in mortality over time and space. Similarly there is no compelling evidence to suggest that various stages in the life histories of earlier populations, like the onset of menopause, occurred at earlier ages than in current populations.[35]

Historical sources for old age in the Roman World

The literary sources do not resolve the issue of longevity in the Roman world, though they are instructive.

Parkin has made a detailed study of the concept of old age in the Roman world.[36] He noted that there is no consensus amongst ancient authors about the time of onset of old age. It was not uncommon for writers in the classical world to use blanket terms for different age classes that were not bound to numerical age, such as infant, adolescent and old. Some ancient writers do, however, provide information about when old age was said to commence. For example, in the different Hippocratic texts, the seventh stage of life or old age is said to commence at the ages of 42, 56 and 63 years of age. Censorinus, writing in the third century AD, suggested five stages, each being 15 years long, based on Varro's description of the first century BC. Other examples provided for the onset of old age include Galen, who gave an age of 49 and Isodorus who indicated an age of 70.[37]

Suetonius usually included the age of death of Roman Emperors in his lives of the Caesars. Augustus died just before his 76th birthday,[38] Claudius expired in his 64th year[39] and Vespasian died at the age of 69.[40] Tiberius was about 77 years of age when his life ended. It is notable that despite his venerable age, there was some suggestion that he did not die of natural causes but was perhaps slowly poisoned.[41] This suggests that such an age was not considered so remarkable, at least amongst those of the higher social strata. Similarly, Galba was murdered at the age of 73.[42] One could perhaps argue that the upper classes would be expected to have longer lifespans as a result of better diet, standard of hygiene and access to medical assistance.

Information about the rest of the population is incomplete. Almost none of the census information for Roman Italy has survived and ancient medical sources are filled with generalizations. Evidence from tombstones has been employed to determine longevity, though it has been argued that the interpretation of such evidence has often been simplistic.[43]

It would appear reasonable to assume that the census data that survive could provide information about the age range of ancient Romans. To highlight the problems associated with census information, Parkin cites the case of the AD 73–74 census instigated by Vespasian and Titus. Both Pliny the Elder, who wrote his account a few years after this event and Phlegon, who wrote in the time of Hadrian, record results of this census in relation to the number of centenarians in the region between the Po and the Apennines. It is clear that Phlegon is not merely repeating Pliny's report as his is much more detailed. Pliny reported ninety individuals who were one hundred years of age or older while Phlegon only mentions seventy. Some individuals are recorded as being up to 150 years of age. Apart from the inconsistency in the numbers presented by the two writers and the unlikely number of centenarians in that region, some of the ages that are reported just do not seem biologically possible. Parkin argues that rather than being an accurate reflection of actual age, these figures represent the high status associated with achieving a phenomenal age and that this example should serve as a warning against blind acceptance of other Roman census figures.[44]

The evidence from tombstones also shows a tendency to exaggerate lifespan. There are vast numbers of tomb inscriptions, which include large numbers of adolescents and elderly individuals with relatively few cases of people in the fourth and fifth decades. Dyson[45] presented an argument to explain this phenomenon. It is based on the likelihood that tombstone inscriptions explain more about Roman attitudes to premature death and what was considered a proper lifespan than the actual age composition of Roman communities. The inclusion of information about the length of life of individuals who survived into old age has been presented as a reflection of a fascination with the defiance of mortality in a society where extreme old age was perhaps desired but not common. This reasoning has been supported by the apparent interest of ancient writers, such as Pliny the Elder and Pliny the Younger, in examples of longevity in individuals or communities.[46] Further, it appears that some of these tombstone inscriptions record an unlikely frequency of extremely elderly individuals, such as the large number of centenarians on Roman African tombstones. This is probably more related to geographical variation in the method of commemoration of the dead than differential longevity in various regions of the ancient world.[47]

These cases suggest that, at least on occasion, ages were exaggerated. Parkin[48] noted that there were no bureaucratic implications associated with the degree of accuracy of ages ascribed to individuals on tombstones. As a result there was no reason to prevent the use of guesstimates when age was not known or for desired, rather than real age, to be recorded.

It has also been noted that the figures on tombstones have been rounded up or down to make them multiples of five. One possible explanation for this is that multiples of five are shorter in Roman numerals and therefore more economical to use if one has to pay for an inscription to be engraved. Other possible explanations for this phenomenon are illiteracy and ignorance of the exact age of the deceased. Parkin suggested that knowledge of the precise age of an individual was not important to the daily life of most ancient Romans.[49]

Examination of the various forms of evidence available led Parkin to conclude that there were no methods to reliably calculate or verify age in Roman Italy. Even though there were well-defined rules of age, for example, males came of legal age at the age of 25, these apparently relied on the statement of age provided by an individual rather than objective evidence.[50]

No compensation can be made for the bias generated by creative documentation and attempts to determine average lifespan from this class of evidence are of questionable value. Other forms of literary evidence, such as mummy labels, legal texts and tax receipts, have similar shortcomings and it has been suggested that, like the skeletal evidence, ancient written sources alone are not very reliable for the reconstruction of age-at-death information for the ancient Roman world.[51] Nonetheless, the evidence that does exist does not indicate that the potential lifespan of the ancient Romans was significantly different from that of a modern population.

Life tables and palaeodemography

It is appropriate to consider palaeodemography and the use of life tables at this point as they have been employed by scholars like Henneberg and Henneberg and Capasso,[52] but eschewed by Bisel[53] and myself, to describe the ancient populations of Pompeii and Herculaneum.

Palaeodemography is concerned with the reconstruction of ancient populations from archaeological skeletal material. The value of palaeodemographic studies has been debated for some decades.[54] The key problem that had to be addressed was the description of populations using sexing and, more particularly, ageing techniques for skeletal identification, with their attendant problems. Various methods have been developed in an attempt to address the issues associated with demographic reconstructions.[55] A series of assumptions were developed and justified to enable palaeodemographic studies to be considered useful. One of the most important, which allowed the construction of life tables from records of mortality, was population stability. A stable population is not affected by immigration or emigration, meaning that they balance each other out or that the population is closed to migration. The sex and age distribution will therefore be a function of the population's actual fertility and mortality. A stationary population is a stable population where birth and death rates are equal.[56]

Life tables are used to demonstrate mortality and survivorship. They were initially devised in the seventeenth century by Edmund Halley for the purpose of computing annuities for life insurance. The original models were derived from known populations, which meant that the data were relatively accurate.[57] Life tables have been applied to archaeological material to provide overall population profiles. Modern models are used but the level of accuracy of such models decreases when extrapolated onto ancient populations due to the number of assumptions that must be drawn.

Bisel argued that the victims of the AD 79 eruption represent a cross-section of a living population and that it would be meaningless to undertake a mortality study at Herculaneum as such studies are only valid for cemetery populations.[58] There certainly is a real difference between the make-up of a cemetery population and a sample of victims from a disaster. Survival of such an event would appear to be random and it is difficult to be certain that the victims reflect the actual AD 79 population.

Possibly even more problematic is the likelihood that the Pompeian and Herculaneum populations were not stable in the last 17 years of occupation as the available evidence suggests that they were in a state of flux as a result of the AD 62 earthquake and subsequent seismic activity. It is also possible that the population was seasonal and the make-up of the population of victims would have been determined by the season in which the disaster occurred. Further, Pompeii as a port town might be expected to have a variable population (see Chapter 4 and below).

These factors indicate that the use of life tables is inappropriate for the Pompeian and Herculaneum material. The models that are used rely on certain assumptions to deal with missing data. Their application in this case is likely to produce highly speculative results. It is important to note that this does not mean that the data should not be explored to describe the victims of the eruption. I would argue that the use of this technique may result in misleading information with this particular material and that it is better studied without the use of demographic modelling.

Estimation of age-at-death in Pompeii and Herculaneum

The most obvious results of the determination of age-at-death for the Pompeian sample are the high proportion of adults to children and the lack of neonatal and infant bones. The low recovery rate of the bones of neonates and very young juveniles from archaeological sites in general has been documented (Chapter 5). These bones do not tend to survive as well as the more robust bones of adults for various reasons. The Pompeian skeletal remains that were available for this study were not excavated by people with anatomical knowledge. It is quite possible that workers on the site have not recognized the bones of neonatals and infants as those of humans. In addition, the recovery of human remains, with the exception of the casts, was not a high priority in Pompeii until the latter part of the twentieth century. Another major factor that could account for the bias towards the survival of adult rather than juvenile bones in the sample is the method of storage.

The suggestion that this problem is related to recovery and storage rather than a real absence of young juveniles amongst the Pompeian victims is supported by the comparative frequency of juvenile bones in collections of skeletons that have been left *in situ* for display purposes, such as those observed in the *Casa del Menandro* (I, x, 4) and the number of children represented in the cast collection. For example, in 1960–61 the forms of thirteen individuals were cast in what is now known as the Garden of the Fugitives (I, xxi, 2). Six of these were clearly children, the youngest of which have been very roughly aged at about four of five years on the basis of visual inspection. While age estimates based solely on visual inspection can hardly be considered reliable, it is clear that these individuals were very young. Another example is a cast of young child that was found in the *Casa del Bracciale d'Oro* in the *Insula Occidentalis* (VI, xvii, 42), Figure 10.1.[59]

Other studies of age-at-death from the Pompeian skeletal sample

Nicolucci chose to study a sample of 100 skulls for his 1882 work. He considered that the entire range of ages was represented in his sample, with the majority being between the ages of 60 and 90. His age determinations were based on suture closure and examination of the teeth.[60] It should be noted that while the criteria he used to establish age-at-death were absolutely reasonable for nineteenth-century scholarship, they would no longer be considered reliable. Nicolucci unfortunately neglected to mention the criteria he used for his dental examination so it is difficult to assess the ages he established. It is probably reasonable to assume that he based his age determinations on attrition and tooth evulsion. It is quite possible that Nicolucci obtained such high ages for his sample as a result of extrapolation from his experience of contemporary Italian tooth wear and loss. Since his main interest was in the determination of 'racial' typology, he was not particularly concerned with establishing the actual proportions of age groups in the sample of victims.

The research done by D'Amore *et al.* in the latter part of the twentieth century had similar aims to that of Nicolucci, which meant that they also did not attempt to use their study to understand age groupings. Instead, they concentrated on a sample of 123 skulls, which were mostly adult, though they did include a few older juveniles to determine their 'racial' affiliations. Their determination of age-at-death involved a four-part classification system based on the work of Vallois: juvenile, covering the ages from about 12 or 13 to 21 years of age; adult, which incorporated individuals ranging in age from 21 to 40 years; mature, covering people from 40 to 59; and senile, which included those of 60 or more years.[61] They also applied this system to Nicolucci's series for comparative purposes and tabulated the results.[62] In their sample, 56 per cent of males were classified as mature and 58 per cent of the females as adult as compared to Nicolucci's classification of the majority of both genders as senile, viz. 71 per cent of males and 41 per cent of the females.[63]

D'Amore *et al.* did not supply details of the actual criteria they used to place each individual into this classification system and one can only conclude that those of Vallois were employed. Juvenile age-at-death was determined by tooth eruption and adult ages were based on cranial suture closure. Vallois considered tooth attrition to be too dependent on general health and diet to be of value for the study of ancient, unknown populations.[64]

Vallois' criteria for 'juvenile' age determination, namely from the end of the eruption of the second molar to the almost complete closure of the spheno-occipitalis synchondrosis and the first appearance of vault closures,[65] are quite reasonable, with the possible exception of the final criterion. Suture closure of the cranial vault, which was also the single component for Vallois' 'adult', 'mature' and 'senile' categories, using the skull,[66] as mentioned above, has been found to be of questionable value in the determination of age-at-death because of its high variability.

It is remarkable that Vallois' method for adult age classification was apparently employed so uncritically, despite the fact that the validity of suture closure as an age indicator had been challenged both by authors like Krogman, whose work D'Amore et al. referred to for sex attribution and by the other participants in the conference at which Vallois contributed this paper.[67] Indeed, it is notable that after having devoted so much space to a discussion of the problems associated with sex identification, D'Amore et al. gave minimal consideration to issues related to the determination of age-at-death. Their age estimates can be seen in Table 7.8. These results were compared with those obtained by Nicolucci (Table 7.9).

It is notable that D'Amore et al. did not consider the possibility that the consistently older ages identified by Nicolucci may have resulted from a lack of experience with teeth from ancient populations, which were more likely to demonstrate a greater degree of attrition as a result of consuming stone-

Table 7.8 Age-at-death determination from skulls examined by D'Amore et al.

Age-at-death	Number of individuals	Percentage
Juvenile	2	1.62
Adult	49	39.84
Mature adult	62	50.4
Senile	10	8.3

Source: Adapted from D'Amore et al., 1979, 306.

Table 7.9 Age-at-death determination from the skull sample studied by Nicolucci

Age-at-death	Number of individuals	Percentage
Juvenile	7	7.07
Adult	12	12.12
Mature adult	23	23.23
Senile	57	57.58

Source: Nicolucci, 1882, 10.

ground grain. D'Amore *et al.* concluded that they had made an empirical comparison between the breakdown of age-at-death in their sample and that of Nicolucci. They suggested that the difference between their results and those of Nicolucci could be explained by different samples or perhaps by a different system of classification.[68]

More recently, the Pompeian skeletal material has been re-examined by Henneberg and Henneberg. They based their estimates of age-at-death on essentially the same sample of material that was used for this publication. They used 364 skulls and 186 right-hip bones. The ageing criteria that were employed were the obliteration of the cranial sutures, the state of dentition and changes to the pubic symphysis and auricular surfaces (Table 7.10).[69] The results they obtained were not dissimilar from those obtained by the author.

The key difference between the two works can be seen in the interpretation of the available data, with possible variation resulting from differing expectations. According to the assessment by Henneberg and Henneberg, the majority of the sample comprised young adults, with an estimated age at death of between 20 and 40 years. They observed very few children and relatively few people in the very old age bracket. They explain the lack of young juveniles in the sample, with the same arguments mentioned above about survival and recognition of the bones of young individuals in the archaeological record. They argue that the age distribution of adults in the Pompeian sample does not vary significantly from that observed at ancient South Italian burial grounds, most notably those of Paestum, dating from the sixth to the fourth centuries BC and Patanello, which dates from the sixth to the third centuries BC. They also point out that the age distribution of the Pompeian adults is quite comparable with data from death records of pre-industrial Central European populations. This led them to conclude that the age structure of the Pompeian skeletal sample could be considered normal for a living ancient population. They use the lack of variation from ancient

Table 7.10 Age at death estimates by Henneberg and Henneberg

Age-at-death	Percentage
0–5	2.9
5–10	1.4
10–15	2.8
15–20	5.4
20–30	27.1
30–40	25.6
40–50	12.8
50–60	8.7
60+	13.7

Source: After Henneberg and Henneberg, 2002, 173. (Henneberg and Henneberg do not provide the sample size for this data.)

cemetery samples to argue that the Pompeian population was stationary and therefore appropriate to subject to demographic techniques. This can be questioned, as there is evidence to suggest that the population at Pompeii was probably not stationary during the last 17 years of occupation (Chapters 4 and 9).[70]

The age profiles that have been produced from these two works also need some consideration. The incomplete nature of some of the sample meant that there were a number of adult individuals whose age could not be identified with certainty. These cases were assigned an indeterminate score. It is difficult to assess this difference in result without access to all their raw data but it is possible that the use of the auricular surface by Henneberg and Henneberg provided them with fewer equivocal cases, though it is unlikely that the use of this technique would have completely resolved the problem. The net result is a greater sense of certainty in the results presented by Henneberg and Henneberg.[71]

While the overall results for age-at-death distribution are quite comparable, it is important to reiterate that the limitations of the available ageing techniques that were used for both studies means that it is likely that a number of the adults in the Pompeian sample have been underaged. The interpretation of age-at-death from the Pompeian skeletal sample should be tempered by other evidence, such as age-related pathology. The frequency with which HFI appears, indicates that there probably were more older people in the sample than the available skeletal ageing techniques could reasonably establish. This is at variance with the suggestion by Henneberg and Henneberg that the Pompeians had relatively short lives.[72]

Estimations of age-at-death from the Herculaneum skeletal sample

It is notable that more techniques could be used for the establishment of age at death from the Herculaneum sample as the skeletons were articulated and, in general, better preserved than the Pompeian skeletal sample. Also, combinations of techniques could be used for individual skeletons, which means that the ages obtained for the Herculaneum sample are potentially more accurate than those obtained from the samples of individual bones in the Pompeian sample.

Bisel determined age-at-death of the Herculaneum skeletal sample from an examination of epiphyseal fusion, tooth eruption, changes in the faces of the pubic symphysis, skull suture closure and the general appearance of the bone, including age-related pathological change.[73] Like Henneberg and Henneberg, she produced an age distribution, with a five-year range for each group, which could only be described as optimistic as the margin of error for adult age-at-death based on macroscopic examination substantially exceeds that figure (Table 7.11).

Table 7.11 Age distribution of the Herculaneum skeletal sample studied by Bisel

Age-at-death estimate in years	Number of individuals	Per cent
< 1	5	3.65
1–5	13	9.49
6–10	10	7.30
11–15	12	8.76
16–20	6	4.38
21–25	6	4.38
26–30	20	14.60
31–35	11	8.03
36–40	11	8.03
41–45	19	13.87
46–50	19	13.87
51–55	4	2.92
55+	1	0.73

Source: Adapted from Bisel and Bisel, 2002, 474.

It is significant that Bisel[74] reported a lower than expected incidence of juveniles in the Herculaneum sample she examined. This sample was excavated in the 1980s under the guidance of Bisel and it is highly unlikely that any remains were missed. Out of 139 skeletons, five (3.6 per cent) were aged at less than one year, 23 (16.5 per cent) covered the span of one to ten years and 12 (8.6 per cent) were interpreted as between ten and 16. Bisel considered that the proportion of sub-adult bones should have been much higher to ensure that the population could be sustained. Initially, she dismissed the possibility that a disproportionate number of juveniles were able to escape or that they sought shelter in a chamber that has not yet been excavated, though in more recent work by Bisel and Bisel, consideration was given to sample bias.[75] One argument presented by Bisel for the comparatively small number of children she observed was that it was a reflection of decreased parity amongst the Herculanean women, as a result of the ingestion of lead or other causes. The issues associated with this suggestion are discussed in Chapter 8.

Capasso used a raft of macroscopic and microscopic methods to establish the age-at-death of the Herculaneum sample, including: tooth eruption and attrition, epiphyseal fusion, ectocranial and endocranial suture closure, changes to the surface of the pubic symphysis, the auricular surface of the ilium and the sternal extremity of the ribs, accumulation of osteons in cortical bone and radiological examination of bone to establish degree of thinning of bone cortex.[76] Only 143 of the 163 skeletons that were examined by Capasso were sufficiently preserved to enable age at death to be determined. He excluded two foetal skeletons from his palaedemographic study.[77] The ages that Capasso obtained can be viewed in Table 7.12.

with the Suchey–Brooks technique can be as high as 14.6 years for females and 12.2 years for males. Further, it is difficult to modify these techniques to account for the acknowledged interpopulation differences for pubic symphyseal age changes. This is a particular problem for archaeological samples. In addition, it has been demonstrated that there is a tendency to underage older individuals with this and other ageing methods.[82]

Because of human variability for age changes it is unlikely that an accurate, objective test can be developed. The use of histological techniques, such as dentine root transparency and cemental annulations, appear to be the most promising for the future, though they are destructive and costly to perform. Jackes, in her review of current methods of age determination from skeletal remains, suggested that a complex system based on a number of techniques involving dentition may ultimately be able to produce results with a relatively high correlation to 'real age'. She did, however, concede that it is impossible to extrapolate ages with any degree of certainty onto ancient unknown samples as it would be impossible to account for environmental variables.[83]

Despite the increased potential for more reliable age estimates from the Herculaneum sample it should be noted that the tendency to apply ages within five-year intervals suggests greater accuracy than the methods that were employed in these studies can provide.

The disparity between the conclusions of this Pompeian study and that of Henneberg and Henneberg about the presence of a significant number of older individuals in the sample can be seen as a reflection of the inability of the available techniques for the determination of age-at-death to discriminate between adult ages from the skeletal record. In contrast with the conclusions of Henneberg and Henneberg about the demographic makeup of the Pompeian sample, the Herculaneum studies all suggest that, at least at Herculaneum, there was not a stable population. It could be argued that had the earthquake of AD 62 had such a devastating impact on the population of Herculaneum, it would be likely to have had a similar effect on the Pompeian population. It is therefore possible that the sample bias against very young individuals in the Pompeian skeletal collection may not entirely be due to failure to recognize infant bones in excavation and poor storage.

8

GENERAL HEALTH AND LIFESTYLE INDICATORS

Determination of health from skeletal evidence is fraught with difficulties, as many disorders that involve soft tissue do not present on bone. Most pathological changes to the skeleton reflect chronic ailments. Conversely, acute disorders, apart from trauma, are not likely to leave any trace on the skeleton. Further, bone can only respond to insult in a very limited number of ways; it can be lost or resorbed, new bone can be deposited or a combination of the two can occur. As a result, a number of diseases leave a similar appearance on the skeleton. It is preferable to base diagnoses on an examination of the entire skeleton as some pathology can be distinguished by the pattern of changes that can be observed on different bones.[1] The disarticulated nature of the Pompeian sample limited the study to disorders that could be diagnosed with confidence from gross inspection of a single bone, like healed trauma. In addition, the lack of access to x-ray facilities and destructive techniques, like sampling for histological analysis, constrained the kinds of questions that could be asked of the evidence.

While the Pompeian skeletal record only provides a very limited view, all signs of pathology reveal clues about the general health of the sample of victims. The presence of certain pathology and other indicators, like stature, act as health markers and assist in constructing a picture, albeit a rather indistinct one, of the general well-being of individuals and the sample as a whole. Apart from elucidating oral health and diet, dental data can provide some indication of underlying health problems as bacteria associated with dental and other pathology of the oral cavity have been implicated in some soft-tissue disease, like heart-valve problems. Stature is, in part, a reflection of health and nutrition during the growing years. Similarly, bone alterations, such as flattening of the proximal shaft of the tibia and femur, have been interpreted as indicators of stress during the period of skeletal development. Healed injuries, infections and other diseases yield information about the status of the immune system, while age-related disorders are a valuable gauge of health, as they do not manifest until an individual has achieved a certain age.

The main issues to be considered were whether there was any skewing towards individuals with signs of infirmity in the Pompeian sample and if the observed pathology was likely to have impeded escape from the eruption. Another issue that was considered was whether it was possible to detect any evidence of surgical or dental intervention. Comparisons could then be made with the bones that have been excavated from Herculaneum. The Herculaneum material should provide more information as complete skeletons were available for investigation, which not only provided more reliable diagnostic opportunities, but also increased the range of pathology that could be studied. In addition, researchers in Herculaneum have had access to radiography and funding to employ various destructive techniques to facilitate diagnosis.

The skeletal record has also been invoked as a valuable guide to professional activities and other aspects of life that can be reflected in changes to bones and teeth as a result of habitual activity. Brief consideration is given to the actual potential of the Pompeian and Herculaneum skeletal record to indicate ancient lifestyles.

Oral health

The difficulty of attempting to gain some insight into the general health of the Pompeian victims without the benefit of soft tissue may be partly mitigated by a study of oral health. An association has been found between poor oral health, infections and various systemic conditions. Micro-organisms in the oral cavity can be responsible for infections in a number of locations in the body. These are known as focal oral infections and they result from the introduction of oral micro-organisms or toxins from oral pathology into the bloodstream or the lymphatic system. Focal oral infections are exacerbated in elderly people and individuals with compromised immune systems. The bacteria associated with the formation of dental plaque have developed special mechanisms to ensure their adhesion to hard and soft oral tissues, as well as other oral bacteria. These bacteria, when transported in the bloodstream, can reach the heart and are well suited to adhere to damaged heart valves and can cause infective endocarditis. This is a disease that involves inflammation and infection of the inner surface of the heart. Correlation has also been found, between dental pathology, particularly periodontitis, and other cardiovascular disease, pre-term low birth rate, diabetes, aspiration pneumonia and abscesses of the lung. In addition, the bacterium associated with gastric ulcers, *Heliobacter pylori*, has been identified in samples of saliva and dental plaque.[2]

An examination of the maxillae and mandibles of the Pompeian sample provides some indication of the oral health and diet of the population. The state of the teeth and the alveolar region was assessed to establish the level of oral hygiene, whether there was any evidence of dental intervention and the general health of individuals during childhood. Dietary factors, such as the impact of the milling process of flour on the teeth, were also considered.[3]

Ninety-seven maxillae and 80 mandibles were examined. These represent all the mandibles and maxillae from the Forum and Sarno Bath collections that were available at the time of this study. Before one could assess the dental health of the population it was necessary to establish the number of teeth that remained *in situ* and the degree of post mortem tooth loss. The incidence of tooth retention determined the potential value of the survey of frequency of carious or decayed teeth, alveolar bone loss, calculus or calcified plaque deposits and enamel hypoplasia in the sample. There were very few cases where the mandible and maxilla of an individual could be rearticulated. This meant that for the majority of cases it was not possible to assess occlusion or bite.

Number of teeth in situ

Only one of the 97 available maxillae retained a full complement of teeth. Most of the maxillary teeth had suffered either ante or post mortem loss. No teeth at all survived in 42.3 per cent of the maxillae. Only 14 maxillae, or 14.4 per cent of the sample, retained eight or more teeth. A higher proportion of mandibular teeth were still *in situ*. No full sets of teeth were preserved. Only three mandibles were completely devoid of teeth. Twenty-three, or 19.8 per cent, of the 81 mandibles contained eight or more teeth. The high incidence of post mortem tooth loss means that the cases of caries and the degree of calculus and linear enamel hypoplasia can only be interpreted as their minimum expression in the Pompeian sample.

Ante mortem loss

Ante mortem tooth loss can be distinguished from post mortem loss as the process of healing, which involves the closing of the socket hole in the mandible or maxilla, usually takes about six months. The principal function of the alveolar bone is to support and maintain teeth in position so that they can function properly. It is gradually resorbed when deprived of this function as a result of tooth loss. It is possible to determine whether ante mortem loss occurred some time before death by the degree of remodelling of the socket and subsequent alveolar bone loss. The only ambiguity that cannot be accounted for is perimortem loss as it is impossible to differentiate teeth lost just prior to or after death from the skeletal record. In addition, it is not possible to establish whether teeth that were lost ante mortem were purposely extracted.[4] Ante mortem loss was scored as the number of teeth that were unequivocally lost before death, namely, in cases where some degree of bone remodelling had occurred.

At least one tooth had been lost prior to death in 69 per cent of the maxillae (n = 79) and 48 per cent of the mandibles (n = 56) in the Pompeian sample. The highest number of teeth lost from an individual mandible in the sample was 5 as compared to 14 for a single maxilla.

A strong association has been recorded between ante mortem tooth loss and advancing age for American Indian sites. The Pompeian results are not that conclusive, though a number of the mandibles and maxillae that have been inter-preted as belonging to older individuals who had lost teeth prior to death.[5]

There are some problems in comparing the Pompeian dental data with those from the Herculaneum sample as different scholars presented their findings in various ways. Further, comparison between the results of scholars who have worked on the Herculaneum skeletons is hampered by the differ-ent methods that they have used to record their results. Bisel, for example, described her results in terms of mouths, as she had the advantage of access to articulated jaws and did not see the need for separate discussion of the upper and lower dentition. By comparison, Capasso presented his data in terms of numbers of individual teeth and related these to the quantity of affected individuals, as did Torino and Fornaciari and Petrone et al.[6] These problems are exacerbated by the fact that none of the various data sets have been published in a standard format.

Bisel calculated a mean ante mortem tooth loss per mouth of 1.79 for males and 2.07 for females. As Bisel did not present her raw data it is not really possible to compare her results with those of the Pompeian sample.

Capasso presented data on the numbers and types of teeth that were lost prior to death. He noted that 37.4 per cent of a sample of 139 individuals lost, at least, one tooth prior to death. In most cases, only one tooth was lost, though there were three individuals who respectively lost 10, 12 and 30 teeth.[7]

Attrition

The degree of attrition or tooth wear can give some indication of dietary behaviour and methods of food processing. Alternatively, it can provide clues about habitual behaviour, such as tooth grinding or bruxism, or the indus-trial usage of teeth as tools.[8] It is often used as an indicator of age-at-death in archaeological samples (see Chapter 6). If attrition is very severe it can result in the use of the roots as an occlusal surface. The pulp cavity may then be exposed, leaving the tooth liable to bacterial infection. Resultant abscesses were potentially lethal in antiquity.

The frequencies of the different degrees of attrition were comparable for both mandibular and maxillary teeth, with the exception of those cases where the teeth were worn down to the roots, which had a mandibular incidence that was three times higher than for maxillae. This may just be a reflection of the greater likelihood of roots surviving in situ in mandibles, as they were generally stored with the teeth facing upwards, whereas maxillae were usually stored with the teeth facing down. However, a study of the dentition of a Roman skeletal sample from Quadrella, Molise, also revealed a higher frequency of wear on mandibular teeth.[9]

For the purposes of this study, attrition was generally scored to indicate relative adult age-at-death. Severe attrition was probably the result of dietary intake of stone as a result of the milling process.[10] The flour the Pompeians used for baking was ground in large basalt mills (Figure 7.6), which led to small particles of stone becoming incorporated into bread. No apparent evidence was observed for industrial usage of teeth but such wear is not precluded because it was not possible to fully assess the majority of mouths due to the high incidence of post mortem tooth loss. The loss was especially evident for the anterior teeth, which are most commonly employed as tools.[11] It is notable that Bisel observed what she interpreted to be industrial wear on the right maxillary incisors of one individual from Herculaneum.[12] Capasso also recorded evidence of industrial wear, most notably on anterior teeth, of 18 individuals in the Herculaneum sample. Apart from attrition as a result of tool use, he noted severe tooth wear in five per cent of the 2966 teeth that he examined.[13]

The tooth wear patterns observed in Pompeii are consistent with those observed on other ancient populations that apparently had constantly masticated abrasive substances in their food. For example, the tooth wear patterns from a series of small Pueblo sites in north-eastern Arizona were similarly interpreted as age-related and resultant from constant mastication of abrasive substances in food, rather than other factors. Conversely, little heavy wear was observed on the Roman dental sample from Quadrella. This was interpreted either as a reflection of a diet that was low in hard fibrous foods which required vigorous chewing, or care with cleaning and food preparation to soften the final product and to minimize the presence of abrasive material.[14]

Caries

The presence of caries cavities gives an indication of diet and oral hygiene. This pathology is directly related to the presence of dental plaque and a dietary intake of fermentable carbohydrates. It involves the progressive decalcification of enamel or dentine. Several bacterial organisms are associated with dental caries, though the main one is *Streptococcus mutans*. The position of caries can provide dietary information about the afflicted individual.[15] For the purposes of this study the survey of caries in the Pompeian sample was limited to the number of caries observed in each mouth and the degree of destruction. Scoring was based on the largest carious lesion in the mandible or maxilla under investigation. This study was based on direct visual inspection of the teeth with the aid of a dental probe.[16] It was not possible to undertake x-ray analysis, which would have produced more reliable results, especially for the size of carious lesions.

Of the 314 surviving maxillary teeth, 50, or nearly 16 per cent, were carious. Forty-three, or 9.7 per cent, of the 444 mandibular teeth that were still *in situ* had carious lesions. Because it was impossible to assess cases where teeth had been lost, the sample was limited to 27 mandibles and 27 maxillae. As a result of the lack of complete dentition for virtually all the maxillae and mandibles, it is impossible to determine the number of carious lesions per mouth. The data merely provides the minimum number of caries cavities per mouth. The degree of carious involvement was substantially greater for a higher proportion of maxillary than mandibular teeth. Nearly half of the caries in the maxillary teeth were described as advanced or gross as compared to just under a quarter for the mandibular teeth.

The Pompeian data set was too incomplete to draw firm conclusions about the relationship between the degree of carious lesions and advancing age, though it is not uncommon to observe a considerable involvement of the crowns of teeth with caries cavities in the mandibles and maxillae of individuals interpreted as older on the basis of attrition.[17] These results suggest that fermentable carbohydrates formed a significant part of the diet and that oral hygiene was not widely practised.

Bisel recorded an average of 0.92 caries per mouth for males and 0.68 for females in the Herculaneum sample.[18] The Pompeian material, which could only be used to assess the minimum number of caries, does not give an indication of the number of caries per mouth.

Bisel attributed the apparently low number of lesions in the mouths that she examined to a lack of sugar in the Herculanean diet. Honey was known to the Romans but was not used as extensively as sugar is used in a modern Western diet. In addition, Bisel suggested that a less processed diet would have been advantageous in that caries would have been worn away before they could develop. Hillson reasoned that low sugar consumption would provide a more likely explanation than attrition for the low incidence of caries in ancient populations as attrition would have to be very rapid to remove active deep fissure caries before the pulp cavity was penetrated.[19]

Torino and Fornaciari undertook a preliminary study of 87 victims, 64 of whom were adults and 23 juveniles. They documented 58 carious teeth in a sample of 2,020 teeth. Four of these were deciduous, while the remainder were permanent dentition. These reflected 1.8 per cent of the deciduous sample of 222 teeth and 3 per cent of the 1,798 permanent teeth. They considered that rate of caries in the sample was extremely low by both modern and ancient standards. They partially attributed this finding to the consumption of water and food with high fluorine levels, as attested to by the presence of cases of fluorosis in the sample.[20]

Like Torino and Fornaciari, Capasso recorded the presence of caries in relation to the total number of teeth he studied, rather than per mouth. He recorded 135 cases in 3,236 teeth, which is a 4.17 per cent incidence of teeth with carious lesions. Nine of these teeth were deciduous and they reflected 3.33 per cent of the sub group of 270 deciduous teeth in the sample. In contrast, Petrone et al. observed that 78.6 per cent of the 56 mouths that they examined had carious teeth, with 20 per cent of the 1,358 permanent teeth displaying evidence of tooth decay. Even though there is considerable variation in size between samples, it is difficult to account for the different results obtained by different researchers from the Herculaneum sample.[21]

Interdental alveolar resorption

Periodontal tissues, including jaw bone, gingivae or gums, cementum and the periodontal ligament, surround and support the tooth. Interdental alveolar resorption is generally the result of periodontal disease. On a living person, periodontal disease is marked by inflammation. The first stages only involve the soft tissue, notably the gingivae. All the periodontal tissues are involved in the most advanced stage, which is known as periodontitis. The most common form in modern Western populations is mostly seen in adults over thirty years of age. It can occur as a result of a lack of dental hygiene, advanced attrition or poor diet and causes the alveolar bone to recede. As bone loss increases, the teeth become loose and, if left unchecked, can ultimately be lost. It is generally marked by a ridge-like change to the labial side of the alveolus. The degree of recession can be recorded if the teeth are still present. Though more difficult to score, alveolar loss can be observed in mouths where no teeth are *in situ* but teeth have been lost some time prior to death and considerable remodelling and subsequent loss of bone has occurred.[22]

Alveolar loss was difficult to assess in cases where teeth had not survived. Most of the cases that could be scored for both mandibles and maxillae showed some degree of interdental alveolar resorption. There were relatively few examples of considerable alveolar loss.

Bisel found that about 75 per cent of the Herculaneum sample exhibited some degree of alveolar resorption. Of these, 60 per cent had only slight resorption and 9 per cent displayed a moderate to marked degree of periodontal disease. Because of the post mortem loss of so many teeth it was not possible to adequately assess the degree of alveolar recession in the Pompeian sample. Nonetheless, the data that could be collected suggested the incidence and degree of alveolar resorption was comparable with that of the Herculaneum sample.[23]

Dental abscess

Abscesses are the result of the build-up of dental infections that can be causally related to caries, excessive, rapid attrition, trauma and periodontal disease. These can generally be detected as a clearly defined circular cavity in the alveolus near the root of the affected tooth. These cavities function as drains for the pus produced by the abscess. Bony changes to the alveolus that could be attributed to dental abscesses were recorded for each maxilla and mandible. It should be noted that deep pockets from advanced periodontal disease are virtually impossible to distinguish from abscesses.[24]

There was a higher frequency of abscesses in the maxillae than the mandibles in the Pompeian sample, with at least one abscess in almost 43 per cent of the maxillae and just under 19 per cent of the mandibles. This is consistent with observations from other archaeological sites. A strong association was observed between advancing age and the presence and degree of abscesses in the skeletal series from Pueblo sites in Northeastern Arizona that were studied by Martin *et al.*[25] The Pompeian data was difficult to assess in this respect as it was not possible to estimate age-at-death in a number of cases where teeth and other age indicators had not survived. In the cases where assessment was possible, there did appear to be some correlation between age and the presence of dental abscesses, especially severe abscesses, which were almost always associated with older individuals (for example, Figure 8.1).[26]

Bisel recorded a mean of 0.73 abscesses per male mouth and 0.66 per female mouth in the Herculanean sample. This is a higher frequency than that for the Pompeian sample. Capasso observed a total of 52 abscesses in 23 individuals in his sample, 51 of which were periapical. Nine of these individuals had only one abscess, eight had two, one had three, two individuals presented with four and two had five, while one individual had a total of eight oral abscesses. Capasso suggested that these abscesses were associated with the development of carious lesions and severe tooth attrition, which involved exposure of the pulp cavity.[27]

Calculus

Calculus is mineralized plaque. It is attached to the surface of the tooth. The mineral, though deposited from plaque fluid, derives from saliva. As a result the greatest amount of calculus formation occurs at sites on teeth that are nearest to the salivary glands. The reasons for plaque mineralization are not fully known, though it is thought that bacteria are involved. The presence and degree of calculus observed in the Pompeian sample was recorded.[28]

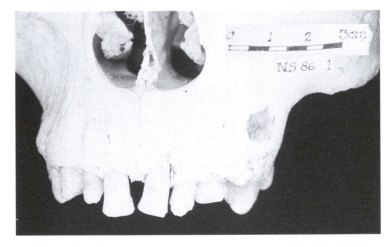

Figure 8.1 Large sinus for abscess drainage (TF NS 86: 1). This abscess formed as a result of severe attrition (7.4), where tooth wear was so great that the pulp cavity was exposed to the air, making it susceptible to bacterial infection

Most of the surviving teeth of the Pompeian sample had, at least, a slight calculus deposit. It is important to note that it was only possible to score minimal expression as the storage conditions were not conducive to the preservation of larger deposits. The degree of calculus deposited on approximately half of the teeth for both mandibles and maxillae was recorded as slight. Only 19.5 per cent of the available maxillary and 11.1 per cent of the mandibular teeth displayed no evidence of calculus. This suggests that oral hygiene, as it is known to modern Western communities, was not a high priority.

Bisel did not present data on the presence of calculus on the Herculaneum teeth, whereas Capasso commented that there was a particularly high frequency of calculus deposits in the sample he studied. Forty-two, or 39 per cent, of the 139 mouths he studied showed some degree of calculus deposition. Twenty-eight individuals displayed slight; ten, medium; and four had considerable deposits of calculus.[29]

Linear enamel hypoplasia

The presence of linear enamel hypoplasia is the direct result of the failure of the enamel to properly form in the developing tooth. It can result from a variety of factors, such as nutritional stress, infection, poisoning or trauma to the tooth or pulp of a deciduous tooth lying over a growing permanent tooth. Enamel hypoplasia often presents as transverse line of indented enamel on the sides of the tooth crown, though it can also present as pits and grooves. They can only form during the period of crown development, which means that if all the dentition is examined, presence of hypoplasia can potentially reflect the health and nutrition of an individual between approximately the second and fourteenth year of life. The position of the line gives some indication of the age of the individual when such periods of stress occurred. It should be noted, however, that absence of hypoplasia does not necessarily infer that there were no periods of stress in the years of crown formation. While the presence of enamel disruption suggests insult, its absence cannot automatically be interpreted as evidence of a healthy and well-nourished person. Modern individuals with a history of lengthy and major illness in early childhood do not always display enamel hypoplasia.[30]

Goodman and Armelagos discovered that anterior teeth were more susceptible to hypoplasias than posterior teeth because their developmental timing can be easily disrupted. Individuals exposed to the same environmental stressors may exhibit varying degrees of enamel hypoplasia. Martin *et al.* suggested that it was only really useful to record linear enamel hypoplasia in the case of anterior teeth.[31]

Equipment was not available for making accurate readings for the distance between lines in the Pompeian sample, so no attempt was made to determine the period in juvenile tooth growth when the disruption occurred.

Instead, the presence or absence of these lines was noted and a score was allocated with respect to the number of lines and degree of disruption to the enamel surface. Some degree of linear enamel hypoplasia was observed on 19 of the 33 maxillary teeth and 36 of the 45 mandibular teeth.

The Pompeian sample exhibited both a higher incidence and a greater degree of linear enamel hypoplasia on mandibular teeth. Nonetheless, most of the recorded cases of hypoplasia for the sample were slight. It is not reasonable to extrapolate interpretations from the small Pompeian sample onto the population at large, beyond the observation that a number of individuals experienced episodes of stress, possibly as a result of illness, during the period of crown formation.

In the posthumous publication of Bisel's work, the frequency of linear enamel hypoplasia is recorded at about 50 per cent. Her earlier publications indicate lower levels, with observations of some degree of linear enamel hypoplasia on about 25 per cent of the male and 16 per cent of the female Herculanean sample. Capasso observed some degree of enamel hypoplasia in the teeth of 71 individuals in the sample he studied. Of these, 42 were male and 29 were identified as female, which meant a male to female ratio of approximately 3 : 2. Petrone *et al.* examined the mouths of 51 individuals and recorded a frequency of enamel hypoplasia in 96.1 per cent, with some degree of expression in 36 males and 15 females.[32]

Evidence of dental intervention

No unequivocal evidence of dental intervention was observed in the available Pompeian sample. It is possible that teeth were extracted ante mortem, though it is impossible to distinguish intentional from unintentional ante mortem tooth loss from the skeletal evidence. There is some indication that tooth extraction was not practised even when removal might have alleviated a problem. A good example of this can be seen in the maxilla of a skull in the Forum Baths collection (see Figures 8.2 and 8.3).[33]

Only two teeth are still *in situ*, the right second molar and the left first molar. The former tooth is marked by a very thick deposit of calculus over the entire tooth, with the exception of a small polished facet on the mesial side of the crown. This wear facet is not on the normal occlusal surface. Considerable alveolar loss is apparent, with the exposure of more than half the roots of the remaining molar. The left first molar displays no sign of calculus. The degree of alveolar loss is comparable to that on the right side of the maxilla.

The excessive build-up of calculus on the right molar suggested that this individual was avoiding the use of this side of the mouth for mastication. The apparent reason for this was a large abscess associated with the palatal root of the adjacent first molar. This involved most of the lingual alveolar surface as evidenced by the marked resorption of the palatal process of the alveolar region. There is also a small sinus from an abscess associated with the distal buccal root of this tooth (Figure 8.2). It appears that this molar

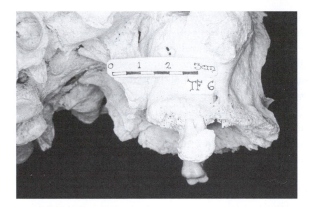

Figure 8.2 Lateral view of skull showing excessive build-up of calculus on tooth adjacent to an abscessed tooth (TF 6)

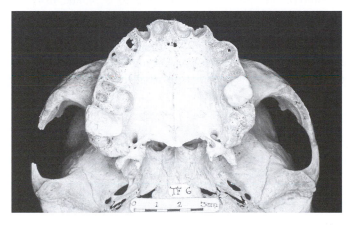

Figure 8.3 View of maxilla from below showing excessive build-up of calculus on tooth adjacent to an abscessed tooth (TF 6)

was lost post mortem. Tooth extraction would have provided an effective means of draining pus from chronic abscesses.[34]

Non-dental evidence for dental practice

It is likely that, at least, some of the observed ante mortem tooth loss was the result of deliberate extraction, even though no tooth forceps have been found amongst the repertoire of medical instruments discovered in Pompeii. General bone forceps may have been substituted for this purpose. Other examples of tooth forceps found in Roman archaeological contexts were made of iron and it is remotely possible that this material did not survive burial in Pompeii.[35]

There were specialists in extraction in the Roman world as can be seen in the case of a shop built into the podium of the Temple of Castor and Pollux in the Roman Forum, where dental procedures were undertaken, along with the sale of pharmaceutical and cosmetic goods. It was suggested that a combined dental and pharmaceutical practice would have been valuable as related problems could have been treated simultaneously. A total of 86 decayed teeth, including two molars from children, were found during excavation. There is evidence that they were removed by skilled practitioners as great care had been taken to ensure that the entire tooth was excised and that no portion of the roots remained in the sockets. In one case, a portion of alveolar bone was extracted with the tooth so that the extremely decayed crown did not break from the root. The dangers of leaving dental fragments in the jaw were discussed by Celsus in the sections on dentistry in his treatise, *De Medicina*, which he wrote in Italy in the early part of the first century AD. It is notable that he considered extraction to be a last resort, after the failure of other measures, like treatment of the gums. He also recommended the use of gold wire to bind teeth that had been loosened, by an accident or a blow, to firm teeth in order to stabilize them.[36]

Ante mortem tooth loss was clearly not uncommon in ancient Italy as dental prostheses have been found, dating from Etruscan times, and dentures are mentioned in some of the epigrams of Martial. In addition, one of the laws of the *Twelve Tables* at Rome expressly forbade the burial of gold with a corpse unless it was fastened to the teeth of the deceased, which indicates its use for ligatures and dentures.[37]

The dental evidence from the Pompeian sample provides no indication that oral hygiene was practised, though other sources from antiquity suggest that some of the associated health and social benefits were appreciated. Writers like Pliny the Elder and Scribonius Largus provide recipes for dentrifices. Some of these contained substances like rabbit's skull mixed with mouse head ashes, while others just prescribed the use of salt water. The charcoal from burnt bones in these recipes would have acted as a cleaning agent. Pumice was also employed for the same purpose. The use of toothpicks was also mentioned in the ancient literature as were 'chew sticks', which were used in place of toothbrushes, along with bare fingers.[38]

It would be reasonable to conclude from the number and degree of carious lesions, abscesses, ante mortem tooth loss and the degree of alveolar resorption and calculus deposition, that oral hygiene, as it is known in modern Western societies, was not practised. In addition, there appeared to be no evidence of dental intervention, with the possible exception of tooth extraction. While not enough evidence exists to draw firm conclusions from the results of an examination of the oral health of the Pompeian sample of victims, it still provides some insight into their general health. The high frequency of calculus and other dental problems indicates the potential presence of a number of systemic conditions, such as cardiovascular disease, diabetes, and gastric and respiratory disorders. Further, the presence of some degree of linear enamel hypoplasia on a number of the anterior teeth suggests that a proportion of the sample was exposed to stress, such as serious or chronic illness, during the period of crown development.

Due to the high frequency of post mortem tooth loss, the data set is too incomplete to determine with certainty whether the degree of dental pathology is correlated with age. The available evidence is consistent with such a conclusion.

Stature

Bone inheritance is multifactorial, which means that the ultimate height an individual attains is a compromise between their genetic potential and environmental factors, especially health and nutrition, during the years of bone growth. Information about the stature of earlier populations can provide insight into the health status of individuals in a sample.

The height of a human body is directly correlated with limb bone length. Regression formulae have been developed over time by a number of scholars to estimate the stature of individuals from long bone measurements.[39] Trotter and Gleser's formulae for white males and females have generally been favoured by physical anthropologists for height reconstruction for skeletal material from ancient European populations.[40] It should be noted that reconstructions from these formulae only provide a rough guide to the actual height of individuals from an unknown population as they were primarily devised for modern American forensic use. Even when applied to known modern populations, they only produce an estimate of stature with a margin of error of several centimetres. A brief consideration of the background of stature estimation and the establishment and application of techniques, particularly for archaeological material from Central and Southern Italy, highlights the problems associated with the interpretation of data that has been collected to date. The Pompeian material requires detailed attention as the disarticulation of this skeletal sample creates further difficulties for stature estimation.

Trotter and Gleser developed their regression formulae for stature reconstruction from the bones of European and African American soldiers who died in World War II and the Korean war, along with data from the Terry skeletal collection. Separate regression formulae were calculated for females.[41] It should also be recognized that the proportions of long bones relative to body length vary between populations; for example, Japanese people generally have proportionately shorter lower limb bones than Europeans, whilst those of black Africans are proportionately longer.[42] The proportions of long bone length to height can also vary within a single population. It has been recognized that as people age, their height diminishes and modifications have been made to the formulae for their application to the bones of older individuals to accommodate these changes.[43] Unfortunately, they could not be applied to the Pompeian sample as it was not possible to estimate age from individual adult femora.

Given the difficulties associated with height reconstruction, it has been suggested that long bone length alone would provide a more reliable indicator of the general health of archaeological populations. This would dispense with the problem of attempting to compare results between scholars who have used different techniques to estimate height.[44] As already stated, stature reconstruction, particularly using formulae that weren't designed to accommodate unknown populations is, at best, only an approximation. Nonetheless, until standardized data sets of long bone length are available for comparison, it is necessary to compare with the published material, which is based on stature estimation.

Measurements of skeletons from archaeological contexts *in situ*, prior to excavation, provide an indication of actual height and can be used as a basis for choosing the most appropriate regression formulae for stature estimation. Scholars working on Central and South Italian skeletal samples reported that the most reliable estimates were obtained from the application of the 1952 Trotter and Gleser formulae for the group they describe as 'American Negroes'.[45]

Unfortunately, the majority of scholars who estimated stature from Campanian skeletal samples have not specified which formulae were applied, though it is likely that they used those devised for 'American Whites' as these have been traditionally thought to be most appropriate. Both 'American Negro' and 'American White' sets of formulae were applied to the data collected from the Pompeian sample, the former as an acknowledgement of the results of recent research on South Italian material and the latter to facilitate comparison with other skeletal studies of victims of the AD 79 eruption.

The average heights of both males and females in the Pompeian sample were calculated from the maximum length of 148 left femora. Ideally, height reconstruction should be based on a combination of bones.[46] As it was not possible to do this for the disarticulated Pompeian sample, the femur was chosen because it is considered to be the most useful single bone for the reconstruction of height. Further, it has been observed that lower limbs are apparently more sensitive to environmental stressors than upper limbs, which means that they are better health indicators of a population.[47]

Apart from the problems associated with the application of formulae derived from modern populations onto an ancient unknown sample, one of the major difficulties in obtaining height estimates from the Pompeian femora was the need to separate them by sex (see Chapter 6). It is generally assumed that an individual whose stature is to be determined is of known sex so that the appropriate height reconstruction formula can be used. This was not possible for the ancient Pompeians as the sample of femora, though apparently dimorphic, exhibited considerable overlap. The femur measurement which showed the most bimodality was maximum length. As a result, it was considered to be reasonable to use the frequency distribution of maximum length to obtain height guesstimates for the Pompeian sample.

The use of the frequency histogram of maximum length measurements (Figure 6.5) for this purpose was based on several assumptions: first, that the histogram is, in fact, bimodal and that the separation is by sex, and second, some degree of normal distribution would be expected for each component curve for a random normal biological sample. The appearance of the histogram is consistent with what would be expected, based on these assumptions.

The degree of overlap between male and female curves differs between populations. This was illustrated by Pheasant, who presented curves of the range for male and female stature for a number of different human groups.[48] Populations that are very dimorphic with minimal overlap between the sexes have well-separated curves with two distinct peaks. The Dinka Nilotes from the southern Sudan provide an example of such a population. By contrast, Efe and Basua pygmies display very little dimorphism; with so much overlap it is difficult to separate the peaks of the two curves. It is notable that the Dinka are amongst the tallest people in the world and the Efe and Basua among the shortest. The frequency histogram for the Pompeians most closely resembles that of the British, the only European population presented by Pheasant.[49] The degree of overlap for this population is between that observed for the two extremes of the Dinka and the Efe and Basua.

The closeness of the mean of the curve to the sex mean of the sample is dependent on the degree of separation between the peaks of the curves. The further apart the peaks, the nearer the estimate to the mean of the peak, because overlap decreases with distance. A very rough guide to the mean stature of the 'male' and 'female' peaks could be obtained by applying the female formula to the mean of the left peak and the male for that of the right. This provides a rough guide to the Pompeian male and female mean stature.

It would be preferable if the numbers of males and females were roughly equivalent. The results of sex separation for the femora were inconclusive but suggest that the sample may have been skewed towards the more gracile bones (see Chapters 5 and 6).

The estimated mean for the right or 'male' peak was about 44 cm and approximately 40.75 cm for the left or 'female' peak. The results for height estimation using the various sets of regression formulae are presented in Table 8.1. The 'American Negro' mean heights are a few centimetres less than those calculated using the formulae devised for 'American Whites', though the margin of error means that there is considerable overlap.

It cannot be stressed too highly that the stature means for the Pompeian sample are rough estimates and need to be confirmed by results from complete skeletons, which can be more reliably sexed. These data may either come from skeletons revealed by new excavations at Pompeii or from x-rays of the sample of casts.

181

Table 8.1 Stature estimates based on Pompeian femora

Trotter and Gleser 'American Whites' male height (1958)	167.60 ± 3.94 cm
Trotter and Gleser 'American Whites' female height (1958)	154.75 ± 3.72 cm
Trotter 'American Whites' male height (1970)	166.13 ± 3.27 cm
Trotter 'American Whites' female height (1970)	154.75 ± 3.72 cm
Trotter and Gleser 'American Negroes' male height (1952, 1977)	163.19 ± 3.94 cm
Trotter and Gleser 'American Negroes' female height (1952, 1977)	152.67 ± 3.41 cm

Subsequent stature estimates have been made, based on the maximum length of the right femur and humerus from the disarticulated Pompeian sample. A number of regression formulae and estimates of proportional relationships between limb and body length have been applied to these data, though it is not clear whether those established for European or other populations were applied. The results that were obtained are consistent with those obtained from this study from the application of 'American White' formulae to the left femora.[50]

Possibly of greater significance than the calculated mean heights is the difference between them. Depending on the formulae that are applied, the difference between male and female stature varies from almost 11 cm to just under 13 cm, which is comparable to the difference between the means of modern North American males and females from a civilian sample.[51] If the observed difference in the Pompeian sample is not an artefact of the disarticulated sample, it indicates that the population was not exposed to many environmental stressors during the period of growth. It has been argued that males are affected more by stress, such as inadequate nutrition or disease, than females. This is manifested in diminished stature as a result of failure to achieve genetic potential for height. If this theory is correct it would follow that the greater the observed sexual dimorphism for stature in a population, the more likely its members were healthy and well nourished during the years of skeletal development.[52]

Stature reconstructions for the Herculaneum sample would be expected to be more reliable because the sexing of individuals was based on entire skeletons. It is notable that Capasso obtained slightly lower values than Bisel for mean height from what was essentially the same sample (see Table 8.2). He found it difficult to account for the difference between his results and Bisel's as he claimed that she did not provide details of the methodology for her calculations, though Bisel recorded that she employed Trotter and Gleser's 1958 height reconstruction formulae. These are the same formulae that Capasso used for his later study.[53] Capasso was in turn criticized for failing to state whether he applied Trotter and Gleser's formulae based on American 'Whites' or 'Negroes'.[54] As a result of the lack of methodological documentation, it is difficult to compare these results with those obtained from the Pompeian femora. Those obtained using the 'American White' are

Table 8.2 Stature estimates for the Herculaneum skeletal sample and a modern Neapolitan sample

Herculaneum males	169.1 cm
(Bisel and Bisel 2002 – using Trotter and Gleser 1958)	
Herculaneum females	155.2 cm
(Bisel and Bisel 2002 – using Trotter and Gleser 1958)	
Herculaneum males	163.8 cm
(Capasso 2001 – using Trotter and Gleser 1958)	
Herculaneum females	151.7 cm
(Capasso 2001 – using Trotter and Gleser 1958)	
Modern Neapolitan males	164 cm
(D'Amore *et al*. 1964)	
Modern Neapolitan females	152.6 cm
(D'Amore *et al*. 1964)	

comparable to those obtained by Bisel for the Herculaneum skeletal sample as they fall within the same range when the margin of error is considered. Similarly, the results based on the 'American Black' formulae are more comparable to those recorded by Capasso.

The reconstruction of height from long bones in the Pompeian sample enables comparison with modern Neapolitan average stature for both sexes, based on a study of living people that was published in 1964.[55] If the mean statures were observed to be comparable with those of the modern population, an argument could be constructed for regional continuity. Smaller average heights than those of the modern Neapolitans could imply that the ancient population had a lower standard of health and nutrition or constituted a different population. Higher means in the ancient sample could be interpreted as either a higher standard of health and diet or as a population that was not related to that of modern Naples.

It is noteworthy that when the 'American White' formulae are applied, both the Pompeian and Bisel's Herculaneum samples have comparable but slightly higher mean stature than a modern Neapolitan sample (see Tables 8.1 and 8.2).[56] The height estimates obtained from the Pompeian sample using the 'American Negro' formulae are closer to those of the modern Neapolitans. Regardless of the formulae that are applied, the heights mostly do not diverge by more than a few centimetres and the range of errors show considerable overlap. It is therefore possible to mount an argument for regional continuity, which may reflect a relationship between the ancient populations in the region and the modern Campanians.

While it is clear that stature is a useful health indicator, some scholars push the evidence to relate stature to social class and have incorporated data from height studies into social and economic histories.[57] There needs to be a word of caution about the extent to which stature reconstruction data can be interpreted. It has been claimed that as taller populations or tall subsets of a population are apparently the result of better health and nutrition, they reflect individuals or groups of higher status or social classes. It should be recognized that higher status is no guarantee of a more nourishing diet during the growing years, as can be demonstrated by the consumption of more processed food by wealthier English people between the Industrial Revolution and World War II (see Chapter 1).

As a result of the disarticulation of the sample, it was only possible to roughly estimate the mean Pompeian male and female stature. The results are consistent with the potentially more reliable mean heights that have been obtained from the recently excavated Herculaneum sample. There is a need, however, to apply the formulae for stature estimation that have been found to be most appropriate for Central and South Italian archaeological skeletal remains to all the AD 79 victims. The lack of clear documentation of techniques employed impedes comparison between skeletal samples and makes it difficult to draw conclusions. Despite these problems, the data that have been collected suggest regional continuity for height and that the ancient Campanians had adequate diets and were in relatively good health during the period of bone growth.

Platymeria and platycnemia

Flattening of the proximal end of the shaft of the femur is known as platymeria and platycnemia when it occurs in the tibia. Like stature, the presence of platymeria and platycnemia have been interpreted as indicators of general health as they are considered to be stress related, either biomechanical, or as a result of nutritional deficiencies. Platymeria and platycnemia are expressed as an index using the antero-posterior and transverse diameters of the proximal part of the shaft.[58]

A sample of 156 left femora from the Forum Bath collection were examined for platymeria. The mean index was 80.9 ± 0.65, which is well within the platymeric range. The Pompeian sample is apparently slightly more platymeric than that of the Herculaneum sample, which according to Bisel had a platymeric index of 83.1 for females and 81.9 for males. Capasso calculated combined indices for left and right femora of 84.2 for males and 85.1 for females. Bisel calculated an average Herculanean platymeric index of 82.4 as compared to Capasso's combined left and right index of 84.6. There is no apparent reason for the differences in the results of Bisel and Capasso, though they may just be a reflection of the larger sample available for the latter study. It was not possible to sex segregate the Pompeian sample for platymeria but it should be noted that the greater degree of platymeria in the Herculaneans was observed in femora of individuals interpreted as male which is not consistent with the view that this trait is more commonly observed in females.[59]

Fifty left and 51 right tibiae were examined for the presence of platycnemia. The mean index for the sample of left and right bones was 70.3 ± 0.61 which is beyond the range for platycnemia and is described as eurycnemia. Only 2.3 per cent of the left and 12.8 per cent of the right tibiae were platycnemic. No bimodality was observed, which implies that there is no sex separation for these measurements. There was no appreciable difference between the left and right samples. This means that both the left and right tibiae probably reflect the same population and can reasonably be compared.

The averaged Herculanean sample, like the Pompeian sample, is eurycnemic. This implies no significant flattening and suggests a sample more consistent with a modern population, such as that of the modern French, which has a cnemic index range of 71 to 74.[60]

It should be noted that there is no universal agreement as to the cause of proximal shaft flattening of the lower limbs. This is partly because of the difficulty in obtaining information on the causes of bony changes for human bones due to the ethical problems involved in human experimentation. It has been suggested that certain pathologies, such as osteoarthritis and osteoperiostosis may be associated with platymeria. Another possible cause for platymeria could be excessive strain on femora during childhood. The causes of platycnemia are also debated. Pathological factors have been cited. It has also been suggested that it is caused by constant squatting. Various pathological factors, including treponemal diseases and rickets, have been implicated for the production of long bone bowing.[61] It is reasonable to assume that no single factor is fully responsible for these changes and that interpretations must be based on an examination of whole skeletons in the context of their population, rather than of individual bones.

There is no significant difference between the Pompeian and Herculanean samples for these features. As it is difficult to isolate the cause or causes for the flattening of the proximal shafts of long bones, it is not really possible to interpret these results beyond stating that both the Pompeian and Herculanean populations may have had lifestyles that involved the application of greater stresses to the femora than the tibiae.

Pelvic brim index

Bisel argued that bone softening due to poor nutrition would result in a certain degree of flattening of the pelvis as it bears a great deal of the weight of the body above it. This could be expressed as an index of the pelvic brim. The Herculaneum sample displayed a mean figure of 83.9, which she compared to a mean of 93.3 for modern Americans. She interpreted this as a reflection of the better level of nourishment in the latter population.[62] This is not a commonly used skeletal marker and it is, therefore, difficult to assess its usefulness.

Pathological change: trauma

Trauma includes various bone injuries, caused by cutting or piercing of the bone by sharp implements or crushing by blunt objects. It includes fracture. Trauma also includes certain types of surgical intervention, such as amputation, trepanation or trephination. Trauma is the second most common cause of pathological change to bones after degenerative changes.[63]

Observations were made on all the bones stored in the Forum and Sarno Baths as well as the skeletal material in the *Casa del Fabbro* (I, x, 7) and the *Casa del Menandro* (I, x, 4). No obvious signs of trauma were discerned on bones other than skulls and long bones in the available sample. At least 350 skulls, 500 right and left femora, 400 right and left tibiae, 150 left and right fibulae, 400 right and left humeri, 200 right and left radii and 200 right and left ulnae were inspected for signs of trauma or surgical intervention.[64]

Only one case presented with an injury that was consistent with having occurred at or around the time of death. The fracture pattern suggested a perimortem blow to a skull, which may reflect a tephra-related injury (see Chapter 4).[65] All the other cases of trauma that were observed in the sample were either healed or healing.

No evidence of trauma was apparent on the bones from the Houses of the Fabbro or the Menander. Gross inspection of the 1,800 or so bones that were stored in the Forum and Sarno Baths yielded a total of seven unequivocal fractures and one unequivocal case of surgical intervention. There was also one case of a healed injury on a skull. Six of these fractures involved long bones. Three of these had healed with no bone displacement and three had healed with malalignment. The seventh was a depressed fracture of a skull. All the bones were identified as adult and all of these fractures had healed some time prior to death.

Fractures naturally commence the healing process shortly after the trauma occurs. The fracture causes blood vessels in the bone to rupture. Blood then flows into the area of the fracture and forms a bloody mass or haematoma, which then stimulates new bone formation, ultimately leading to the development of a hard callus. The callus acts as a natural splint and will remodel as the fracture heals. If the fracture ends are in line and the bone is immobilized during the period of healing, it can be difficult to detect evidence of the fracture in the remodelled bone, except in radiographs.[66]

The three bones that had healed with no bone displacement were identifiable by callus formation around the fracture site. They were a right ulna, a left radius and a right tibia.[67]

The right ulna and the left radius exhibited callus formation on the proximal third of the shaft, whilst the right tibia displayed similar pathological alteration to the distal third of the shaft. No signs of secondary infection were apparent. There is no reason to assume that there had been any medical intervention in these three cases as these all occurred in paired bones. If only one bone had been broken the other could have acted as a splint.

The three bones, which displayed compound fractures with some malalignment were a right femur and a right tibia and fibula from the same individual.[68]

The fracture of the right femur involved the proximal third of the bone (Figure 8.4). This was a compound fracture with associated secondary infection. Compound fractures are open to the external environment and therefore at risk of bacterial infection, which is what appears to have occurred in this case. Bone infection is described as osteomyelitis, which involves bone destruction and the formation of pus. In this case there are osteomyelitic lesions in the form of sinuses or cloacae, which would have initially formed inside the bone interior as abscesses containing pus. These abscesses eventually penetrated the compact bone wall to enable the pus to drain from the bone to the surface of the leg.[69] The broken sections of bone were malaligned, which meant that the femur healed with some angulation. This resulted in the shortening of the bone.

The right tibia and fibula[70] (Figure 8.5) are among the few cases in the stored Pompeian skeletal collection in the Sarno Bath complex where an individual is clearly represented by more than one bone. The remains were stored in a basket. They are fragmentary, but include a mandible and a maxilla,[71] a right and left tibia and two portions of the right fibula. The features of the maxilla are consistent with a male sex attribution.

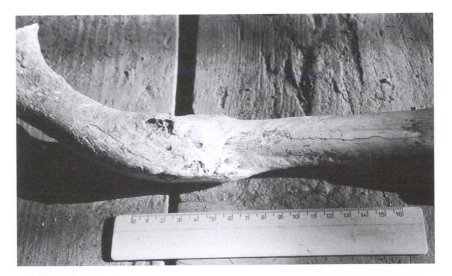

Figure 8.4 Healed fracture of a right femur (TdS R 11) with associated osteomyelitic lesions in the form of sinuses on the bone surface

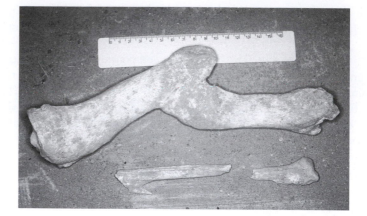

Figure 8.5 Right tibia and fibula from one individual (TdS #28.1) with healed compound
fractures exhibiting pronounced displacement and override at the midshaft of the
bone

The tibia and fibula display healed compound fractures. The tibia exhibited an oblique fracture with pronounced displacement and override at the
midshaft of the bone. This injury has resulted in considerable shortening of
the leg. The maximum length of the right tibia is 264 mm as compared to
the left tibia, which has a maximum length of 323 mm. There is no sign of
secondary infection on the tibia or the remains of the fibula. It is difficult to
assess the damage to the fibula as it is fragmentary but it is clear that it
suffered a compound fracture with apparent displacement as a result of the
same event that caused the fracture of the tibia.

A healed depressed fracture was observed on the remains of a skull in the
Sarno Baths (Figures 8.6 and 8.7).[72] The occipital bone and parietals are
essentially all that has survived of this skull. As a result, it lacks most of the
diagnostic features for sex determination. What remains appears rather
robust. An age-at-death estimate based on an examination of the ectocranial
suture closure on the remaining sutures suggested an age consistent with an
individual in, at least, the fifth decade at the time of death. The injury is
located on the left parietal bone superior to the anterior articulation for the
squamous portion of the temporal bone and just posterior to the lateral portion of the coronal suture. It is roughly circular in shape and covers an area
of 34 x 30 mm. Both the inner and outer tables are involved. The wound
presents on the inner table as a hemisphere about 23 x 30 mm in area and
protrudes about 10 mm from the normal surface of the bone. It was interpreted as a healed depressed fracture without comminution, or splintering of
the bone, consistent with a wound made by a blunt implement. The fracture
appeared to be fully healed, as evidenced by the rounded and remodelled
edges of the site of injury. There was no sign of infection.

Figure 8.6 Healed depressed fracture of a skull (TdS 199), displaying involvement of both the inner and outer tables. View of the outer table

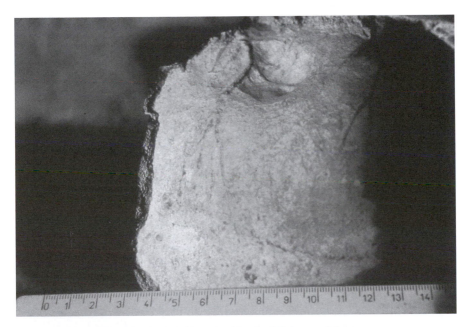

Figure 8.7 Inner table of a skull (TdS 199) with a healed depressed fracture

A healed injury was also observed on the right parietal bone of a skull stored in the Forum Baths.[73] It is approximately oval in shape and covers an area of 30 x 10 mm. The affected area presents as an oval region of granulated healing bone, which is ringed by a scar-like bony ridge. It is about 50 mm to the right of the sagittal suture. The outer table and inner tables are both involved though it is only just visible on the inner table. The injury has healed completely with no sign of secondary infection. It has been interpreted as being consistent with a wound resulting from a blow to the head.[74]

Apart from these cases there were two left femora that displayed pathological changes that were consistent with trauma, but interpretation required confirmation from histological and/or x-ray analysis. Two[75] appeared to exhibit healed fractures, one[76] of which was consistent with a bending fracture on the proximal third of the shaft.[77]

Another left femur[78] exhibited major changes to the femoral head and a shortening of the neck, which could variously be interpreted as a slipped femoral capital epiphysis as a result of a stress fracture, though the most likely interpretation is hip displacement, Perthes' disease or osteoarthritis to the head with extensive remodelling and shortening of the neck. Osteoarthritic changes could have been the result of displacement or dislocation as the articular cartilage would have been compromised and would not have been nourished by the synovial fluid, which in turn would have caused the cartilage to break down and the commencement of osteophytic change to the bone.[79]

A number of bones show evidence of osteophytic change (see below). Interpretation of such changes usually requires an examination of the entire skeleton to establish whether they were the result of arthropathy or trauma. It is possible that some of the osteophytic change, such as the presence of lipping and eburnation on the distal condyles of 11 of the sample of about 320 left and right femora in the Forum Bath collection, may reflect trauma. This interpretation may be supported by the fact that most of these cases display no signs of osteophytic change at the femoral head. It is possible that the local roads, with their deep gutters and unevenly worn stone blocks, ridged with ruts from carriage wheels, could have contributed to such injuries.

Effect of these injuries on survival potential

The perimortem skull fracture[80] is likely to have been the cause of death of this individual. The radius, ulna and tibia that had healed without displacement[81] would probably not have had an appreciable effect on the individuals associated with them and certainly would not have prevented their departure from Pompeii. While having a shorter leg would not have been an asset, it would probably not have impeded the escape of these individuals associated with the healed compound leg fractures[82] in the considerable period of time[83] associated with the first phase of the eruption.

190

The impact of the depressed fracture[84] requires further consideration. A fracture of this magnitude, with its involvement of both the tables, is likely to have resulted in some damage to the brain. The area involved corresponds with Broca's area of the brain, which is concerned with the production of speech. It is notable that for most humans the location of the main language centre is in the left hemisphere of the brain. This is almost independent of handedness, which means that language was probably the function that was affected in this individual regardless of which hand they favoured. The person who sustained these injuries would have had a problem with syntax, especially in relation to the generation of sentences. It is possible that another portion of the brain may have taken over this function over time. It is unlikely that this injury would have hampered the escape of an individual from the erupting volcano.[85]

Surgical intervention

Only one unequivocal case of surgical intervention was observed in the sample. This took the form of a trephination on a skull,[86] which from the degree of healing, had been performed a considerable time prior to death (Figure 8.8). The perforation associated with the surgery is surrounded by an almost circular region of granulated healing bone which, in turn, is ringed by a scar-like bony ridge. Both tables are involved, though the surface of the inner table is not raised. This suggests that the injury is not a depressed

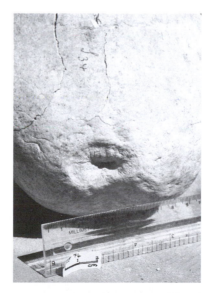

Figure 8.8 Healing trauma, interpreted as a trephination on the skull of individual (TF 74) with hyperostosis frontalis interna

191

fracture. The bone defect is about 4 x 1 mm. It is in the middle of a depression about 2.5 mm below the normal surface of the surrounding parietal bone. This depression is two stepped and oval in shape. The outer ring measures about 35 x 25 mm. The inner ring is more circular in shape and covers an area of 20 x 20 mm. Elongated growths of healing bone do not quite bridge the defect. There is no sign of secondary infection. The changes observed on this bone are all consistent with a healing trephination.

Trephination, or trepanation, is a surgical procedure that involves incision of the scalp, followed by cutting the skull, often into a circular shape to make a hole and the excision of bone. While most scholars use the terms interchangeably, the distinction between trepanation and trephination is that the former is more general and refers to an opening of the cranium made by any instrument or procedure, whilst the latter specifically relates to the surgical removal of a disk of bone. There is evidence in the skeletal record that this operation has been performed, often successfully, over a wide geographical area for many millennia. It is a very dangerous procedure as it ultimately involves exposure of the cranial cavity to the external environment, though before the problem of potential infection is faced, the surgeon has to avoid damage to the dura mater, which, if perforated, would result in fatal leakage of the cerebrospinal fluid in which the brain floats. The meninges, brain and blood vessels also have to be avoided for the patient to survive the operation.

From the degree of healing, it can be established that the trephination was performed a considerable time before death. The long-term survival of this individual with no sign of osteomyelitis is not uncommon for archaeological cases of trephination. It has been suggested that one of the reasons for the high success rate was the high vascularity of the soft tissue that overlies the cranial vault, which would have decreased the likelihood of secondary infection. The lack of observed infection also indicates the use of clean instruments for this procedure. It is notable that the operation was performed on the left parietal bone. No satisfactory explanation has been established for the observation that most archaeological cases of trephination involve the left frontal or parietal bones.[87]

Non-skeletal evidence for medical intervention

While there is minimal evidence of surgical intervention in the Pompeian skeletal sample, discoveries of other classes of archaeological material, like medical implements, indicate that it was practised more widely in the Campanian settlements. In Pompeii alone, medical instruments have been identified with certainty at 21 sites and equivocal examples at a further 6. In addition, finds of small collections of about ten tools have been interpreted as home medical kits used for the treatment of minor injuries and ailments.

The range of instruments discovered is impressive and includes scalpels, specula, catheters, tweezers, probes and implements for cauterizing. Identification of these instruments has largely been based on the considerable documentary evidence for the use of surgical procedures in the Roman Empire in the form of medical texts. The most useful for the Pompeian material is the *De Medicina* of Celsus, which was written in Italy during the reign of Tiberius. In addition, much medical equipment remained virtually unchanged in form until the first part of the twentieth century and function was easily established by medical practitioners in the late nineteenth and early twentieth centuries.[88]

Some of the instruments that have been found in excavations of the Vesuvian sites would have specifically been used to treat bones. For example, two bone elevators were identified in the collection that is now housed in the Naples museum, and records suggest that another one or two were discovered in Pompeii prior to 1826 but have subsequently been lost. Like most of the medical implements found in Pompeii, these were made of copper alloy and had a handle with an arched rectangular plate at each end. The plates were smooth on the outside and serrated on the inner surface to assist with grip. A bone elevator, or *vectis*, was used to lever fractured bones into position so that they could heal without distortion. Bone elevators could also be used to raise depressed bone and it has been suggested that they may have been used to facilitate tooth extraction. As there is no clear evidence that bone files have been discovered at the site, it has been argued that the serrated edges of the bone levers could also have been used for this function.[89]

About ten implements found in the Campanian excavations have been interpreted as chisels. The exact provenance is not known for a number of these pieces and interpretation is hampered by the fact that they tend to be represented by the bronze handles, rather than the blades, which would have been made of iron or steel, and have not survived. The function of the bone chisel or *scalper* is largely known through ancient medical writers, like Celsus,[90] who describes their use for the removal of diseased or fractured bones, especially from the cranium. He also mentions their application for smoothing out projecting bone from compound fractures after it was filed or cut.[91] Apparently, this tool was also employed for the removal of additional digits. It is notable that the bone chisel was generally smaller than those used for carpentry but it was possible that carpenter's chisels could also be employed for surgical use.[92]

According to Bliquez,[93] the discovery of such tools suggests that surgeons in the Campanian region were equipped to treat severe fractures. In view of this, it is interesting to note that a number of instruments that might have been expected as part of the bone surgeon's tool kit, such as gouges, bone files, drills and saws, have, so far, not been discovered at Pompeii. It is possible that these tools did not survive as they were made of materials that were not durable in an archaeological context, such as steel, though Bliquez is doubtful that this provides a sufficient explanation. It is possible that the full repertoire of tools has just not yet been excavated.[94]

Though drills, trephines and saws have not been discovered in Pompeii, Roman methods of trephination deserve a brief consideration in relation to the interpretation of the healing surgical procedure on the skull described above.[95] Bow-drills were often used for treatment of diseases or injuries to the skull. They were made of a straight steel or bronze rod with a rotating handle at the upper end and a steel augur or circular saw at the lower end. A piece of cord was attached and passed tightly around the drill. The augur or saw was placed against the bone and was rapidly rotated by the movement of the bow drill, which enabled rapid perforation of the bone. For the removal of small circular pieces of bone, the augur was replaced by a crown trephine or *modiolus*, which was a short steel tube with teeth at the lower end. After a disc of bone was excised, the edges of the hole were cut back with the chisel until healthy bone was revealed. Celsus[96] writes about the use of an instrument to protect the membrane that surrounds the brain during this type of surgery. It is possible that this was a version of a double blunt hook. The instrument was pushed under the bone that was to be removed as a guard to prevent the chisel penetrating the membrane.[97]

In view of the documentary and archaeological evidence for medical knowledge and practice in the Roman era, it perhaps seems remarkable that there was no apparent attempt to set the compound fractures of the femur and tibia and fibula.[98] There are a number of possible explanations for this. One is that these injuries might have been sustained in a geographical region where medical attention was not available. Another is that these individuals may not have had access to medical practitioners for financial or social reasons.

Frequency of trauma in the Pompeian and other samples

The frequency of trauma in the entire bone sample that could be identified from gross inspection was about 0.6 per cent. If the 11 cases of osteophytic change to the distal articular surface of the femur could be demonstrated to have resulted from trauma, the percentage would rise to 1.2 per cent. The rate of observed trauma in the radius and ulna was 0.5 per cent. For the tibia and fibula it was also 0.5 per cent and 0.8 per cent for the femur. If the additional eleven equivocal cases were added the frequency for trauma to the femur would rise to 3 per cent.

Bisel documented the cases of trauma that she observed in the Herculaneum sample that was available to her, though she did not distinguish between fractures, dislocations and inflammatory responses. This makes it difficult to compare her results with the Pompeian data. She reported that 32 per cent of the male sample and 11.4 per cent of the female sample displayed evidence of trauma, with a population average of 22.7 per cent. She did not consider that these figures indicated bias towards injury in the Herculaneum sample.[99]

Capasso recorded cases of fractures separately from evidence of other types of trauma. He reported 31 fractures in 17, or about 10.5 per cent, of the 162 individuals that he studied. Like Bisel, he found the majority of cases involved males, with a ratio of 4.7: 1. He attributed the higher incidence of fractures in males to gender-related division of labour. Four of the fractures involved the frontal bone of the skull, one the temporal bone, one the nasal region and one mandible. There were three fractures of the radius, four of the ulna, one of the humerus and one of the femur. It is notable that Capasso had access to x-ray technology for his study.[100]

It could be misleading to compare the Pompeian figures for the frequency of fractures with those obtained from other archaeological sites and modern populations as many of these studies would have utilized x-ray technology, and in the case of modern living populations, there is the advantage that all the skeleton is available for investigation. Bearing this in mind, it is instructive to make a brief survey of fracture rates in archaeological samples for comparison with the Pompeian results as they seem rather low compared to those from Herculaneum.

A fracture rate of between 1.0 and 3.6 per cent was reported for Greek and Turkish skeletal samples, dating from the seventh millennium to the second century AD. A 1.8 per cent rate of bone fracture was observed for a prehistoric central Californian population, the skeletons from the Libben site in Ohio had a 3 per cent fracture frequency and skeletal samples from various medieval British sites showed a range of between 0.3 to 6 per cent. Similarly, a visual survey of 6000 Egyptian skeletons revealed that about 3 per cent of the sample had sustained fractures. The bones most commonly affected are those of the arm, especially the forearm. Fractures to the femur tend to be fairly uncommon in most archaeological skeletal samples, as are fractures to the tibia and fibula.[101]

The Pompeian figures are a little lower than most of the above-mentioned populations, but still within the range that has been observed for numerous archaeological sites, whilst the figures from Herculaneum are somewhat higher. It is possible that the survival of complete skeletons and the use of radiography has contributed more to the disparity in observed frequency than possible skewing towards disability. Fifteen of the fractures observed in the Herculaneum sample involve ribs, carpals, metacarpals, tarsals and metatarsals, bones which generally did not survive in the disarticulated Pompeian sample. The possibility of sample bias must also be considered. Ciprotti, for example, mentions the removal to the museum in Naples in the nineteenth century of a femur that demonstrated pathological changes and while it is likely that there were other cases, this activity probably would not have had a significant effect on the post-cranial sample.[102] Attention was usually focused on crania in the nineteenth century and they were more likely to be collected. The use of femora for hinge manufacture (see Chapter 5) is unlikely to have contributed to the loss of bones affected by trauma as

Based on unselected samples in hospitals, the frequency of hyperostosis frontalis interna in modern European populations is generally thought to vary between 5 per cent and 12 per cent, though some scholars suggest the incidence might be as high as 15 per cent.[143] The frequency of HFI in the Pompeii sample, at between 11.1 per cent and 11.9 per cent, is consistent with this range.

Surveys of the incidence of HFI in modern Western populations indicate that HFI is most commonly associated with females.[144] It has been, perhaps rather extravagantly, suggested that the correlation between the occurrence of HFI and women is so high that its presence alone should be sufficient as a basis for sex attribution from archaeological skeletal material.[145]

It is most frequently observed on post-menopausal women, with a reported incidence of 40–62 per cent amongst this group in modern populations, and has been associated with adiposity and male-type hair growth patterns, though the three features do not always occur together. Various other signs and symptoms can accompany HFI, the most common being headaches. HFI-associated headaches apparently are hormonally induced and not related to excess bony development. The degree of bony change to the inner table of the frontal bone does not necessarily reflect the degree of development of other signs and symptoms, though it has been suggested that the severity, like the frequency, appears to be age dependent.[146] Nonetheless, it probably would not be reasonable to draw specific conclusions for the variation in expression observed in the Pompeian sample.

There is some suggestion that there may be a genetic component in the manifestation of this disorder. It has been detected in four generations of one family, and in individuals from archaeological contexts who possibly were related but, as yet, there have been no definitive inheritance studies.[147]

The Pompeian skulls diagnosed with HFI were examined to determine whether the presence of this syndrome had any bearing on the survival prospects of affected individuals in the AD 79 eruption or whether these cases just reflect the normal incidence of HFI in the ancient Pompeian community.

Attribution of sex and estimation of age-at-death

Since HFI is both sex and age-related, it was necessary to establish both for the sample, but there can only be limited confidence in sex and age-at-death attributions based solely on skulls, especially ones that are not well preserved.

The majority of the skulls[148] exhibited more female than male characteristics, which is consistent with the greater female prevalence of this disorder that has been observed in modern populations. One skull was completely mid-range, five skulls appeared to be more male than female and one skull presented as male. Another skull was so incomplete that no diagnostic features were retained and no sex attribution could be made.[149] It is possible that some of the six skulls, which display predominantly masculine traits, may be female. Virilism, in the form of the development of masculine facial features, has been associated with HFI and such changes could be detectable on the skull. In addition, it is not uncommon for the skulls of normal older females to develop male traits.[150] It should also be reiterated that the confidence levels for sex determination solely from skulls in the general Pompeian sample were not very high (see Chapter 6).

Though the skulls were generally too incomplete to enable a full set of observations to be made, it was still possible to see general trends in terms of relative age-at-death. The majority[151] could be identified as adult, with most of the individuals tending towards older ages. Two skulls lacked sufficient diagnostic features to establish age-at-death but did not appear to be juvenile. Six skulls could be identified with certainty as adult but they were too incomplete to enable further assessment. Seven skulls presented as consistent with an age estimation of, at least, the third decade, ten the fourth decade or older, the minimum ages of a further 14 were consistent with the fifth decade and four individuals with, at minimum, the sixth decade.[152]

It must be remembered that the ages attributed to nearly all of these cases reflect minimum ages-at-death as it was not possible to build up a complete score due to the poor preservation of the skeletal remains. It is therefore likely that most of the individuals in this sample were chronologically older than their estimated ages. Further, age-at-death attributions are notoriously unreliable for adult skeletons, especially when based solely on features of the skull. At best, the age markers that were employed could be used to seriate the sample. The results certainly demonstrate skewing towards the older age range, which would be expected for a sample of individuals with hyperostosis frontalis interna.

As for sex, the correlation between maturity and HFI is so high that it has been suggested that adult age can be reliably estimated for archaeological skulls that display some degree of HFI.[153] With some qualifications, the results obtained from the Pompeian sample for sex and age are consistent with a diagnosis of HFI.

Alternative diagnosis

Differential diagnoses have been considered for the archaeological cases of bony lesions that have been interpreted as hyperostosis frontalis interna.[154] The features that have been described for at least 40 of the cases of hyperostosis in the Pompeian sample are characteristic of HFI with clear boundaries, which limit overgrowth to the inner table of the frontal bone, an unaffected midline and overall bilateral symmetry. Other disorders that are associated with additional cranial bony growth, such as Paget's disease, senile hyperostoses, Leontiasis ossea and acromegaly, are easily distinguished from HFI as they do not tend to be confined to the frontal bone and they involve

been attempted on samples from both Pompeii and Herculaneum, but the results to date have been disappointing. The high temperatures to which the bodies were exposed at the time of death have been invoked to explain the poor preservation of nucleic acids in samples from the Herculaneum skeletons. Human skeletal remains from Pompeii have also yielded limited information due to poor DNA preservation. Nonetheless, these preliminary studies indicate that, at least in some cases, there is sufficient endogenous DNA to enable amplification and analysis.[3]

Cranial evidence

The main material used for this research was the cranial collection stored in the Forum Baths, as it appeared to reflect a random sample of adults that tended to be more complete than the skulls housed in the Sarno Baths (Chapter 5). Population studies are usually confined to adult material as the results obtained from skulls where growth is not yet complete would be misleading.

Metric evidence

Population studies have traditionally been based on measurements of skulls (Chapter 3). It was appropriate to commence the study of the Pompeian sample in a similar fashion as the data collected could be compared with those published in the earlier work of Nicolucci well as Bisel's measurements of the Herculaneum sample. Unfortunately, D'Amore *et al.* did not publish their raw data. Capasso only took minimal cranial measurements, enabling him to calculate a series of indices, which he considered to be most useful descriptors of the Herculaneum heads. Astonishingly, these included the now largely abandoned horizontal or cephalic index (Chapter 3). While he did present the indices for the sample, he did not include the raw data.[4]

Bisel restricted her study to adult male skulls[5] and made 11 measurements on 50 skulls. These were compared with an early study of Howells, which was used to develop standards based on Irish monastery burials. Bisel calculated the cumulative standard deviation for her sample and found it to be greater than the norm for the Howells data. Bisel suggested that the considerable variability of the cranial metric data from the Herculaneum sample was a reflection of a heterogeneous population with the implied benefits of hybrid vigour which would have been 'manifested in great energy and creativity'. While a large standard deviation does imply variability, recent work suggests that an isolated sample can also exhibit considerable variation. Howells, for example, demonstrated this in his later studies using Berg data, which represents a population that was geographically isolated over a number of generations.[6] It is apparent that the standard deviation alone does not provide information about the composition of a population.

The fact that many of the Pompeian skulls were incomplete hampered the collection of cranial metric data. A series of 12 measurements were made on 117 adult male and female skulls. The analysis of these data was compared with similar analyses based on the raw craniometric data published by Nicolucci in 1882 to establish whether there was consistency between samples. The 12 cranial measurements were then compared with data collected by Howells from a variety of European and African populations, the Pompeian skeletal sample studied by Nicolucci and the data collected from the Herculaneum material by Bisel to gain some understanding of the Pompeian sample in relation to other populations.[7]

Metric evidence from the skull sample provided insufficient evidence to establish whether the Pompeian and Herculaneum samples reflect homogeneous or heterogeneous populations. Comparison with other samples from European and African contexts tended to confirm the European affinities of the sample. As expected, the data from the current Pompeian sample was closest to Nicolucci's earlier sample and Bisel's Herculaneum sample, though there were exceptions for some measurements.

It should be noted that a large proportion of the observed craniometric differences in the Pompeian sample appear to be intrapopulational rather than interpopulational and probably reflect variation between male and female skulls. Even though differences could be observed between the sexes in the Pompeian sample, the results of my study indicate that the skull, and the craniometric data in particular, do not provide a very useful sex indicator for the Pompeian skeletons (Chapter 6). By implication, these cranial measurements are of limited value for the determination of population affinities for this sample as they did not indicate any real separation into well-defined groups.

Non-metric studies

Non-metric traits are anomalous skeletal variants, which are generally non-pathological. On the whole, these present as innocuous features on the bone. It is unlikely that individuals would ever notice that they had such traits. They are mostly of interest to physical anthropologists as they are easily observed and counted. They are also known as epigenetic traits and occur with varying frequency in all populations. A study of the pattern of cranial and post cranial anomalies can provide information about population variability.

Because skeletal inheritance is multifactorial, the genetic and environmental components of non-metric traits cannot easily be distinguished. Human and mouse pedigree studies have established a genetic component for a number of traits, though a genetic basis is not essential for a non-metric trait to be a useful population descriptor. The acquisition of traits as a result of shared environmental factors, especially during the period of growth and development, can also reveal information about a population. The potential

Table 9.1 Presence of palatine torus in various populations

Population	Sample size	Frequency (%)
Pompeii AD 79	52	96.2
Pompeii AD 79 (trace cases excluded)	52	73.1
Herculaneum AD 79	159	1.9
Pontecagnano (Campania) (7th–6th century BC)	32	21.9
Sala Consilina (Campania) (9th–6th century BC)	9	0
Termoli (Molise) (7th century BC)	9	100
Ardea (Latium) (8th– 6th century BC)	19	0
Romans (Latium) (6th–5th century BC)	167	14.9
Alfedena (Abruzzo) (6th century BC)	69	34.8
Campovalano (Abruzzo) (7th–6th century BC)	95	32.7
Perdasdefogu (Sardinia) (9th century BC)	17	0
Etruscans 1 (Central Etruria) (6th–5th century BC)	56	0
Etruscans 2 (Southern Etruria) (6th–5th century BC)	84	0
San Vincenzo al Volturno	153	23.7
Cefalu (17th century BC)	13	7.7
Plemmyrion (16th–14th century BC)	33	3
Castiglione (17th century BC)	11	18.2
Castiglione (8th– 6th century BC)	6	33.3
Thapsos (16th–14th century BC)	41	2.4
Lentini (5th– 4th century BC)	6	33.3
Siracusa (8th century BC)	29	6.9
Siracusa (3rd century BC)	109	11.9
Piscitello (5th – 4th century BC)	27	0
Carlentini (5th– 4th century BC)	11	0
Modern Roman sample	285	7.4
Undated Sardinian population	245	7.3
African sample (Mali) (1st millennium BC)	145	0
Nubian (historic)	33	3

Sources: Adapted from Capasso, 2001, 982; Hauser and De Stefano, 1989, 178–79; V. Higgins (University of Notre Dame, Rome) to E. Lazer, 1989–1990, personal communication; Lazer, 1995, 297; Rubini *et al.*, 1999, 10; Rubini *et al.*, 2007, 124.

Table 9.2 Frequency of palatine torus from Scandinavian archaeological samples

Population	Sample size	Frequency (%)
Medieval Norway (male)	48	70.8
Medieval Norway (female)	50	90.0
Medieval Iceland (male)	20	75.0
Medieval Iceland (female)	34	91.2
Eastern Early Greenland (male)	20	80.0
Eastern Early Greenland (female)	11	90.9
Eastern Middle–Late Greenland (male)	11	90.9
Eastern Middle–Late Greenland (female)	17	100
Western Greenland (male)	7	100
Western Greenland (female)	27	100

Source: Adapted from Halffman *et al.*, 1992, 151.

as absent.[27] Trace expression only accounts for 12 cases or 23.1 per cent of the Pompeian sample. Removal of all cases with a trace score still leaves an unequivocal 73.1 per cent with palatine torus. Since Capasso used the same standard scoring system as the Pompeii study, the lower frequency reported for the Herculanuem sample cannot be attributed to differences in recording. Nonetheless, it would be valuable for other ancient and contemporary skulls from the Vesuvian region to be examined for palatine torus to establish if this is a feature that is specific to ancient Pompeii or whether there are other populations in the region where the incidence of expression is high.

It does appear that the high frequency of this trait in the Pompeian sample is not an artefact. As already mentioned, the aetiology of this trait is not well understood. It appears that both environmental and genetic components contribute to the expression of palatine torus. Whatever the mechanism for the formation of the palatine torus, it has the potential to be a useful population descriptor for ancient Pompeians. It could be argued that the almost total presence of the trait in the sample might suggest a type of homogeneity that was not necessarily based on similarity of genotype but perhaps a shared environment during the period of osseous development. Dietary factors should be considered, though it would be hard to explain why there is such a low prevalence of this trait in the nearby settlement of Herculaneum, which has been argued to have relied heavily on marine protein (Chapter 8).

Double-rooted canines

The roots of canines in the mandible or lower jaw are occasionally divided into two parts: labial (facing the lips) and lingual (facing toward the tongue). The degree of division can vary and be either partial or complete. It is most uncommon to find a bifurcated root on an upper or maxillary canine.[28] This characteristic can be a useful population marker. During the course of research, loose canines were routinely removed from their sockets to facilitate measurement and a number of double-rooted canines were observed. Observations were also made of the sockets of canines that had been lost post-mortem. This is only useful for the identification of this trait when the roots are well divided. Scoring was limited to unequivocal cases. Only mandibular occurrence of this trait was observed by these means. Six of the 21 mandibles from which it was possible to make observations had teeth with roots that were divided. It is perhaps misleading to use percentages for such a small sample size, but for the purposes of comparison, the prevalence of double-rooted canines was about 28.6 per cent.

There is minimal comparative data for this trait in the literature. Maxillary canines of 13 Central Southern Italian Iron Age populations from either side of the Apennine Mountains and dating from the ninth to the second centuries BC were examined for the presence of bifurcated roots. Not surprisingly, no cases were observed in the 1,114 individuals, which included three

Campanian samples from the region to the south of Naples (Coppa *et al.* 1998: 375). The mandibular canines were not examined for this trait. Scott and Turner observed double-rooted canines in varying frequencies in a diverse sample of populations. Table 9.3 demonstrates that this trait is extremely rare in Asiatic, Oceanic and African populations. Turner found double-rooted canines to occur more frequently in European populations.[29]

Because of the small sample size and the lack of appropriate comparative data, it is not reasonable to draw too many conclusions from the presence of double-rooted canines in the Pompeian sample. The frequency appears to be considerably higher for Pompeians than for any other recorded population. This finding does appear to be remarkable and should be investigated further. The entire Pompeian skeletal sample should be subject to more detailed examination, with x-ray analysis of the jaws which still had teeth in-situ that could not be removed for inspection, as well as the cast collection. The Herculaneum skeletal collection should also be inspected for this trait, which, as yet, has not been recorded in the sample, as well as other ancient and modern samples from Campania and the rest of Italy to establish whether this feature is unique to the site of Pompeii or whether it has a high regional occurrence.

Table 9.3 Frequencies of mandibular double-rooted canines in various regions

Region	Sample size	Frequency (%)
Pompeii AD 79	21	28.6
Western Europe	314	0.057
Northern Europe	214	0.061
North Africa	347	0.023
West Africa	33	0.00
South Africa	192	0.00
Khoisan	14	0.00
China–Mongolia	401	0.00
Jomon	203	0.010
Recent Japan	335	0.012
Northeast Siberia	206	0.00

Sources: Adapted from Scott and Turner, 1997, 322 and Lazer, 1995, 314–15.

Metopic suture

Metopism is a hypostotic trait. Hypostotic traits involve the retention of forms that are usually visible in the embryonic or early infant state, such as metopic sutures or inca bones. They involve arrested development or incomplete ossification. At birth, the frontal bone is made up of two halves separated by a suture. This suture functions as an area where growth can occur and also enables the two frontal halves to move relative to each other during birth. If this suture persists after the first two to three years of life, it is scored as present. Studies of mice and macaques as well as x-ray examination of families suggest that there is a genetic component to metopism. It has been suggested that this trait occurs with a higher frequency in females.[30]

Observations for metopic suture were made on 121 Pompeian skulls. Twelve cases or 9.9 per cent of the sample retained complete metopic sutures, 13.2 per cent of the sample exhibited some degree of metopism. One case displayed partial persistence at the parietal end of the suture and there were three cases of partial persistence at both ends of the suture. It is notable that Nicolucci reported a frequency of 11 per cent in the Pompeian sample he studied; a figure he considered to be high. Capasso recorded seven cases in the Herculaneum sample which reflected a frequency of 4.4 per cent in the sample he examined. Six of the cases were complete and one was an incomplete superior metopic suture. The frequencies observed in Pompeii and Herculaneum can be compared with those found in other populations (Table 9.4). Much of the comparative material was scored using the method of Berry and Berry but their definition is not clear about whether partial persistence would be scored as present.[31] If one assumes that only total persistence was scored then the frequency of metopism in the Pompeian sample would be only 9.9 per cent.

The results of this study are relatively consistent with those of Nicolucci. The Pompeian incidence of this trait sits within the range reported for other Italian populations and is higher than the reported African samples. Possibly the most interesting observation is the fact that its frequency is more than double that of the Herculaneum sample, regardless of whether partial presence is included.

Inca bone

In the foetus, the inferior and superior squama of the occipital bone are separated by a suture that runs from asterion to asterion. This suture generally closes prior to birth, but if it persists into adult life it is classified as an inca bone. If the foetal sutures on the superior squama fail to unite, bipartite, tripartite or inca bones divided into four parts can result.[32] It is important to note that inca bones were treated as a separate entity from ossicle at lambda in this study as the latter tend to be fontanelle bones and result from a different cause (see below). It is possible to distinguish inca bone variants from sutural bones by morphological features but there is considerable ambiguity in recording in the literature.[33]

Six cases of inca bone variants were observed in a sample of 116 Pompeian skulls, which means that this trait occurred with a frequency of 5.2 per cent. Only one case, or 0.9 per cent of the sample, exhibited full expression of this trait. Nicolucci observed one case of an inca bone on a skull he interpreted as female in his sample of 100 Pompeian skulls.[34] In most populations this trait has been observed more frequently in males than females,[35] though no relationship between this trait and gender could be ascertained for the

Table 9.4 Frequency of metopic suture in various populations

Population	Sample size	Frequency (%)
Pompeii AD 79 (Lazer 1995)	121	13.2
Pompeii AD 79 (Lazer 1995)	121	9.9 (complete expression only)
Pompeii AD 79 (Nicolucci 1882)	100	11
Herculaneum AD 79	159	4.4
Pontecagnano (Campania) (7th– 6th century AD)	38	10.5
Sala Consilina (Campania) (9th– 6th century BC)	17	23.5
Termoli (Molise) (7th century BC)	50	16
Ardea (Latium) (8th– 6th century BC)	17	0
Romans (Latium) (6th– 5th century BC)	153	0.6
Alfedena (Abruzzo) (6th century BC)	64	17.2
Campovalano (Abruzzo) (7th– 6th century BC)	62	9.7
Perdasdefogu (Sardinia) (9th century BC)	17	29.4
Etruscans 1 (Central Etruria) (6th– 5th century BC)	35	5.7
Etruscans 2 (Southern Etruria) (6th– 5th century BC)	55	0
San Vincenzo al Volturno	153	7.2
Cefalu (17th century BC)	26	0
Plemmyrion (16th–14th century BC)	60	5
Castiglione (17th century BC)	52	5.8
Castiglione (8th–6th century BC)	52	19.2
Thapsos (16th –14th century BC)	48	6.25
Lentini (5th– 4th century BC)	7	0
Siracusa (8th century BC)	29	0
Siracusa (3rd century BC)	121	16.5
Piscitello (5th–4th century BC)	28	3.6
Carlentini (5th–4th century BC)	20	0
Modern Roman sample	300	10.7
Undated Sardinian population	260	8.1
African sample (Mali) (1st millennium BC)	156	3.8
Nubian (historic)	67	0

Sources: Adapted from Capasso, 2001, 982; Hauser and De Stefano, 1989, 42–43; Higgins, 1989–1990; Lazer, 1995, 293; Nicolucci, 1882: 10; Rubini *et al.*, 2007, 124.

Pompeian sample. This is in no small part due to the difficulty in establishing sex from the skulls in this sample. As a result of this problem, there was usually no attempt to establish sex association for cranial non-metric traits in the disarticulated Pompeian sample.

Capasso recorded five cases of inca bone variants in the Herculaneum crania. He is not clear about the size of the sample upon which this study was based. Based on the frequencies he documented for other cranial non-metric traits, he apparently examined 159 individuals, which means that the incidence of inca bones was 3.3 per cent. He observed that one case was a rare bipartite inca bone variant.[36]

It was extremely difficult to obtain appropriate comparative material for this trait (Table 9.5), which is testimony to its rarity. Non-metric studies of other Italian populations tended to only record ossicle at lambda, which may include inca bone variants, though the scoring system that was employed suggests that only fontanelle bones were recorded.[37]

Comparison of this trait with other samples is complicated by inconsistencies of scoring between scholars. The comparative data presented by Hauser and De Stefano gives a range of 3.7 per cent to 18 per cent for various European populations dating from the 1st–2nd millennium BC to the medieval period. Interpretation of these data, however, requires some consideration of the definitions for inca bone for each sample. For example, a medieval French sample was recorded as having an incidence of 11.6 per cent based on the definition of Berry and Berry, which is very vague and does not distinguish between the ossicle at lambda, the preinterparietal bone, an inca bone variant that should be scored separately, and the inca bone. Similarly, the definitions for the medieval Bohemians and Alamannes also pooled these three variants. If, for comparative purposes, the preinterparietal bones were pooled with the inca bones in the Pompeian sample, the incidence would increase to 6.9 per cent. Inclusion of the ossicle at lambda as well would raise the Pompeian incidence to 25 per cent. Only inca bone variants were scored for prehistoric Ukrainians and first to second millennium BC Lithuanians. The European and North African male and female samples and the Italian sample were all recorded in a consistent manner with the Pompeian sample.[38] The Pompeian and Herculaneum incidence is higher than the Italian and European frequencies recorded for these samples.

Table 9.5 Frequency of inca bones in various populations

Population	Sample size	Frequency(%)
Pompeii AD 79 (Lazer 1995)	116	5.2
Pompeii AD 79 (Nicolucci 1882)	100	1
Herculaneum AD 79	159 (?)	3.1 (?)
Italy (Frosinone, Rome, Sicily, Otranto, Abruzzo, recent soldiers)	202	1.5
European male	651	1.8
European female	176	1.1
North African male	537	3.2
North African female	345	2.0
Medieval French	69	11.6
Bohemian (8th–10th century AD)	555	18
Alamannes (6th– 8th century AD)	265	12.1
Lithuanian (1st– 2nd century BC)	2292	3.7
Prehistoric Ukrainian	153	4.6
Nigerian undated	40	15

Sources: Adapted from Capasso, 2001, 982; Higgins, 1989–1990; Hanihara and Ishida, 2001a, 141–43; Hauser and De Stefano, 1989, 102–103; Lazer, 1995, 305; Nicolucci, 1882, 10.

Wormian and fontanelle bones

Wormian bones are sutural bones or ossicles in the cranial vault. An ossicle is defined as any bone completely surrounded by a suture. They can be found, for example, in the coronal, sagittal and lambdoid sutures. Sutures permit very slight movement of the skull bones during birth to facilitate delivery. They also function as areas where postnatal bone growth can occur and contribute to the final shape and size of the skull. The embryology associated with the development of ossicles and fontanelle bones was discussed by Hauser and De Stefano. There is no satisfactory explanation for the function of ossicles, though there has been considerable discussion as to whether stress or pathology contributes to their presence.[39]

The practice of cranial deformation is apparently correlated with an increased frequency of lambdoid ossicles, as well as frequency changes in a range of other non-metric traits. It has been argued that this has little impact on the determination of biological distance between populations. El-Najjar and Dawson examined a sample of American Indian skulls with particular reference to the number of ossicles per side. They observed wormian bones on skulls that had not been subjected to cranial deformation but noted that in the cases of asymmetrical deformation, the number of wormian bones was higher on the side of deformation. There also was a positive correlation between an increased number of lambdoid wormian bones and the pressure associated with deformation. No significant side differences were observed in undeformed crania. It was concluded that cranial deformation could influence the development of lambdoid sutural bones but was not the sole factor that determined their presence. Ossicles are often found in undeformed skulls. In addition, skulls that have been intentionally deformed do not always contain wormian bones.[40]

There is an undoubted association between ossicles and the presence of some pathologies; for example they are almost invariably present and numerous in skulls of hydrocephalous individuals. It has been suggested that there is a link between the size, number and configuration of wormian bones and the presence of specific disorders. Similarly, this can be the case where there is delayed closure of sutures or fontanelle bones. A radiographic study of 81 skulls of individuals with osteogenesis imperfecta yielded a strong correlation between large numbers of wormian bones of a so-called 'significant' size, which are defined as more than ten bones of at least 6 mm by 4 mm which were arranged in a mosaic pattern.[41]

'Significant' numbers of wormian bones have also been found in relation to a host of other disorders including cretinism, familial osteoarthropathy, kinky-hair syndrome and hypogonadism. Infantile-type osteoporosis, Down syndrome and rickets have been found in association with large sutural bones that do not necessarily occur in a particular pattern or number. It has been claimed that the presence of wormian bones is the result of developmental malfunctions, possibly with a genetic component. Cremin et al. suggested that the occurrence of more than ten 'significant' wormian bones may reflect an underlying environmental or genetic problem that has affected skull growth in the early developmental stages. Pedigree studies in humans suggest that wormian bone expression has a genetic component. Mouse studies appear to confirm that this trait is subjected to normal population variability.[42]

Fontanelle bones can be found at the bregma, lambda and the asterion. There can also be fontanelle bones in the anterior lateral fontanelles. It has been suggested that the purpose of ossicles at bregma is to protect the brain in late foetal and early natal life. No similar explanation has been advanced to explain the presence of other fontanelle bones.[43]

Ossicles are age-related in that sutures tend to be obliterated with advancing years.[44] When scoring skulls with partially fused sutures in the Pompeian sample, ossicles were only counted as present when it was certain that they could not be artefacts of other phenomena, such as complex suture patterns.

Pardoe found a positive correlation between the six wormian bone traits he used in his study of Australian Aboriginal skeletal populations, from which he concluded that the presence of one sutural bone on a skull would increase the probability of there being further sutural bones on that skull. This correlation has also been reported by other scholars. A correlation has also been observed between the presence of lambdoid ossicles and inca bones. Sutural bone intercorrelation has also been reported by other scholars.[45]

The choice of which sutural bones would be studied was based on which bones could be identified without ambiguity and which were more likely to have survived, in order to provide the largest possible sample size. Squamo-parietal wormian bones were excluded as they were difficult to differentiate with certainty from post mortem damage. Additionally, the squamous portion of the temporal bone often had 'sprung', thus diminishing the possible number of observations.[46]

OSSICLE AT LAMBDA

The ossicle at lambda was present in 20.2 per cent of the 116 Pompeian skulls that were scored for this trait. More than half of the cases, about 11.4 per cent, involved single or multiple large ossicles. Two of these cases were classified as interparietal bones. Capasso did not report any cases of ossicle at lambda in his sample.[47] The observed frequency of this trait in the Pompeian crania is within the upper end of the range of the Italian and African populations that have been recorded and lower than some of the second millennium Sicilian populations (Table 9.6). Most notable is the absence of the trait in the Herculaneum sample.

LAMBDOID OSSICLES

Lambdoid ossicles were observed more frequently on the right than the left side in the 112 observations that could be made for each side of the

Pompeian cranial sample. They were scored as present to some degree in 34.8 per cent of cases for the left and 39.3 per cent for the right.[48] Capasso recorded 22 cases or 13.8 per cent cranial incidence in the Herculaneum sample, though he did not score them in any further detail than presence or absence. He reported an even division between the sexes. Nicolucci only observed eight cases of lambdoid ossicles in his sample, involving four males and four females.[49]

It is important to distinguish between cranial and side index for this bilaterally expressed trait. Tables 9.7 and 9.8 show the side and cranial frequencies that have been recorded for this trait for different populations. To calculate side incidence for bilateral traits, some scholars[50] pool the number of observations for both sides, which means that these can represent a figure greater than the number of crania that were examined. This is important to bear in mind when examining Table 9.7 as the column labelled *sample size*,

Table 9.6 Presence of ossicle at lambda in various populations

Population	Sample size	Frequency (%)
Pompeii AD 79	116	20.2
Herculaneum AD 79	159	0
Pontecagnano (Campania) (7th– 6th century BC)	42	19
Sala Consilina (Campania) (9th– 6th century BC)	16	25
Termoli (Molise) (7th century BC)	50	10
Ardea (Latium) (8th– 6th century BC)	17	5.9
Romans (Latium) (6th–5th century BC)	153	22.2
Alfedena (Abruzzo) (6th century BC)	83	19.2
Campovalano (Abruzzo) (7th– 6th century BC)	40	22.5
Perdasdefogu (Sardinia) (9th century BC)	17	11.8
Etruscans 1 (Central Etruria) (6th–5th century BC)	35	22.8
Etruscans 2 (Southern Etruria) (6th–5th century BC)	55	18.1
San Vincenzo al Volturno	153	18.6
Cefalu (17th century BC)	12	25
Plemmyrion (16th–14th century BC)	50	34
Castiglione (17th century BC)	42	33.3
Castiglione (8th– 6th century BC)	40	30
Thapsos (16th –14th century BC)	50	2
Lentini (5th– 4th century BC)	7	0
Siracusa (8th century BC)	29	13.8
Siracusa (3rd century BC)	131	13
Piscitello (5th– 4th century BC)	29	3.4
Carlentini (5th– 4th century BC)	22	0
Modern Roman sample	255	25.1
Undated Sardinian population	238	14.3
African sample (Mali) (1st millennium BC)	154	20
Nubian (historic)	67	10.4

Sources: Adapted from Capasso, 2001, 982–83; Hauser and De Stefano, 1989, 178–79; Higgins, 1989–1990; Lazer, 1995, 294; Rubini *et al.*, 1999, 10; Rubini *et al.*, 2007, 124.

as for all the other non-metric data presented in this chapter, refers to the total number of observations upon which scoring was based.

Lambdoid ossicles, like other sutural bones, have been found to be correlated with the presence of other wormian bones. The only statistically significant correlation for the Pompeian sample was between the left lambdoid ossicle and the ossicle at lambda.

Comparison between the different samples is complicated by the way that the material is presented with some scholars only calculating cranial frequency and others just side incidence. The majority of Italian and other populations presented in Table 9.7 have a higher side incidence of lambdoid ossicles than the Pompeian sample, with only three other populations displaying a similar frequency, and two a lower incidence. The cranial incidence for this trait in the Pompeian sample is lower than that for other Italian populations documented in Table 9.8, though it is substantially higher than that recorded for the Herculaneum sample. It is difficult to account for the huge discrepancy with the very low incidence recorded by Nicolucci.

Table 9.7 Side incidence of lambdoid ossicles in various populations

Population	Number of observations	Frequency (%)
Pompeii AD 79 (Lazer 1995)	224	37.1
Pontecagnano (Campania) (7th – 6th century BC)	78	56.4
Sala Consilina (Campania) (9th– 6th century BC)	29	72.3
Termoli (Molise) (7th century BC)	100	24
Ardea (Latium) (8th – 6th century BC)	34	35.3
Romans (Latium) (6th–5th century BC)	306	49.3
Alfedena (Abruzzo) (6th century BC)	169	32
Campovalano (Abruzzo) (7th– 6th century BC)	72	37.5
Perdasdefogu (Sardinia) (9th century BC)	32	56.2
Etruscans 1 (Central Etruria) (6th–5th century BC)	70	51.4
Etruscans 2 (Southern Etruria) (6th–5th century BC)	110	52.7
San Vincenzo al Volturno	153	55.8
Modern Roman sample	516	58.3
Undated Sardinian population	220	67.3
African sample (Mali) (1st millennium BC)	296	46.3
Nubian (historic)	134	25.4

Sources: Adapted from Hauser and De Stefano, 1989, 178–79; Higgins, 1991; Lazer, 1995, 294; Rubini et al., 1999, 10; Rubini, et al., 2007, 124.

CORONAL OSSICLES

Of the 111 left and 117 right side observations for coronal ossicles, there was only one medium ossicle observed on the left side of a skull. This means that there is a cranial incidence of 0.9 per cent and a side incidence of 0.4 per cent. Nicolucci also recorded one case of a coronal ossicle in the sample that he studied, which translates into a cranial index of 1 per cent. Similarly, Capasso recorded one case in his sample, which is a cranial index of 0.63 per cent.[51]

The Pompeian side incidence of coronal ossicles is considerably lower than that recorded for the majority of the populations shown in Table 9.9. Similarly, the cranial incidence (Table 9.10) is much lower than that of the other recorded Italian populations, with the exception of the Herculaneum sample. The cranial incidence for this trait in the Pompeian sample is consistent with that obtained by Nicolucci and only minimally higher than that of the Herculaneum sample.

OSSICLE AT BREGMA

Only one strongly expressed ossicle at bregma was observed in the entire sample of 116 skulls, which meant that there was a cranial index of just under 0.9 per cent. Capasso did not record any cases of this trait. Inspection of Table 9.11 demonstrates that the frequency of this trait in the Pompeian sample is within the range observed for other Italian samples, though it should be noted that the sample sizes for a number of these populations are rather small.

SAGITTAL OSSICLES

Sagittal ossicles were observed in the Pompeian sample with a frequency of 7.8 per cent in the sample of 116 skulls that could be scored. Of these, 6.9 per cent were of medium expression or greater. Nicolucci only recorded one instance of this case in his sample of 100 skulls. Capasso recorded two cases of this trait, which means that there was a cranial incidence of 1.3 per cent. There was minimal appropriate comparative material for this trait (Table 9.12).[52]

Given the paucity of comparative material, interpretation of the incidence of sagittal ossicles is difficult, though it is notable that the Pompeian frequency is significantly lower than that recorded for the Sardinian sample but does seem to be at the upper end of the range of frequencies for a disparate

Table 9.8 Cranial incidence of lambdoid ossicles in various populations

Population	Sample size	Frequency (%)
Pompeii AD 79 (Lazer 1995)	112	50
Pompeii AD 79 (Nicolucci 1882)	100	8
Herculaneum AD 79	159	13.8
San Vincenzo al Volturno	153	55.8
Undated Sardinian population	220	67.3

Sources: Adapted from Hauser and De Stefano, 1989, 178–79; Higgins, 1989–1991; Lazer, 1995, 294; Nicolucci, 1882, 11; Rubini *et al.*, 1999, 10; Rubini *et al.*, 2007, 124.

Table 9.9 Side incidence of coronal ossicles in various populations

Population	Sample size	Frequency (%)
Pompeii AD 79	228	0.4
Pontecagnano (Campania) (7th – 6th century BC)	64	3.1
Sala Consilina (Campania) (9th– 6th century BC)	21	4.8
Termoli (Molise) (7th century BC)	91	1
Ardea (Latium) (8th– 6th century BC)	34	11.8
Romans (Latium) (6th–5th century BC)	306	12
Alfedena (Abruzzo) (6th century BC)	135	3
Campovalano (Abruzzo) (7th– 6th century BC)	50	10
Perdasdefogu (Sardinia) (9th century BC)	34	0
Etruscans 1 (Central Etruria) (6th–5th century BC)	70	18.5
Etruscans 2 (Southern Etruria) (6th–5th century BC)	110	9
African sample (Mali) (1st millennium BC)	287	1.5
Nubian (historic)	134	13.5

Sources: Adapted from Hauser and De Stefano, 1989, 178–79; Higgins, 1989–1990; Rubini *et al.*, 1999, 10; Lazer, 1995, 294; Rubini *et al.*, 2007, 124.

Table 9.10 Cranial incidence of coronal ossicles in various populations

Population	Sample size	Frequency (%)
Pompeii AD 79 (Lazer 1995)	117	0.9
Pompeii AD 79 (Nicolucci 1882)	100	1
Herculaneum AD 79	159	0.63
San Vincenzo al Volturno	153	26.8
Modern Roman sample	300	41.7
Undated Sardinian population	260	3.5

Sources: Adapted from Capasso, 2001, 982; Hauser and De Stefano, 1989, 178–79; Higgins, 1989–1990; Lazer, 1995, 294; Nicolucci, 1882, 11; Rubini *et al.*, 1999, 10; Rubini *et al.*, 2007, 124.

collection of European populations. Again, it is difficult to account for the much lower incidence of this trait in Nicolucci's sample. It is possible that he did not take too much interest in these traits, except when they were strongly expressed, as they were only mentioned as a side issue in his article. Perhaps the most significant finding is the much higher frequency for the Pompeian sample than for that from Herculaneum.

OSSICLE AT THE ASTERION

Ossicles at the asterion were slightly more frequent on the right side than the left in the 101 observations that were possible for each side. There was an 8.9 per cent presence on the left side and a presence of 10.9 per cent on the right. Only one case involved a large ossicle, the rest were classified as small or medium. Capasso recorded just one case of ossicle at the asterion,

Table 9.11 Frequency of ossicle at bregma in various populations

Population	Number of observations	Frequency (%)
Pompeii AD 79 (Lazer 1995)	116	0.9
Herculaneum AD 79	159	0
Pontecagnano (Campania) (7th–6th century BC)	37	0
Sala Consilina (Campania) (9th–6th century BC)	18	0
Termoli (Molise) (7th century BC)	48	2
Ardea (Latium) (8th–6th century BC)	17	0
Romans (Latium) (6th–5th century BC)	153	2.6
Alfedena (Abruzzo) (6th century BC)	73	1.4
Campovalano (Abruzzo) (7th–6th century BC)	51	3.9
Perdasdefogu (Sardinia) (9th century BC)	17	0
Etruscans 1 (Central Etruria) (6th–5th century BC)	35	0
Etruscans 2 (Southern Etruria) (6th–5th century BC)	55	1.8
San Vincenzo al Volturno	153	0
Modern Roman sample	296	1
Undated Sardinian population	243	2.5
African sample (Mali) (1st millennium BC)	153	0
Nubian (historic)	67	0

Sources: adapted from Capasso, 2001, 982–83; Hauser and De Stefano, 1989, 178–79; Higgins, 1990, Table 4; Lazer, 1995, 294; Rubini *et al.*, 1999, 10, Rubini *et al.*, 2007, 124.

Table 9.12 Presence of sagittal ossicles in various populations

Population	Sample size	Frequency (%)
Pompeii AD 79 (Lazer 1995)	116	7.8
Pompeii AD 79 (Nicolucci 1882)	100	1
Herculaneum AD 79	159	1.3
Undated Sardinian population	174	23.6
Lithuanians (1st–2nd millennium BC)	2681	5.4
Bohemians (8th–10th century AD)	557	3.8
Alamannes (6th– 8th century AD)	243	1.6
Prehistoric Ukrainians	112	7.8

Sources: Adapted from Capasso, 2001, 982–83; Hauser and De Stefano, 1989, 94–95; Lazer, 1995, 303, Nicolucci, 1882, 110.

which reflects a cranial incidence of 0.63 per cent. This individual also displayed lambdoid ossicles.[53]

Table 9.13 indicates that the Pompeian side incidence for this feature was in the mid range for Italian populations, though it again should be noted that a number of these populations are represented by very small sample sizes. It was considerably lower than the frequencies observed for a modern Roman sample and two African populations. The cranial incidence documented for San Vincenzo al Volturno (Table 9.14) is about double that of Pompeii. Again, it is notable that the cranial frequency for this trait is much higher for the Pompeian than the Herculaneum sample.

Table 9.13 Side incidence of ossicle at asterion in various populations

Population	Sample size	Frequency (%)
Pompeii AD 79	202	9.9
Pontecagnano (Campania) (7ᵗʰ – 6ᵗʰ century BC)	48	6
Sala Consilina (Campania) (9ᵗʰ– 6ᵗʰ century BC)	16	6.2
Termoli (Molise) (7ᵗʰ century BC)	43	0
Ardea (Latium) (8ᵗʰ– 6ᵗʰ century BC)	34	8.8
Romans (Latium) (6ᵗʰ–5ᵗʰ century BC)	306	7.8
Alfedena (Abruzzo) (6ᵗʰ century BC)	142	8.5
Campovalano (Abruzzo) (7ᵗʰ–6ᵗʰ century BC)	73	9.6
Perdasdefogu (Sardinia) (9ᵗʰ century BC)	32	15.6
Etruscans 1 (Central Etruria) (6ᵗʰ–5ᵗʰ century BC)	70	17.4
Etruscans 2 (Southern Etruria) (6ᵗʰ–5ᵗʰ century BC)	110	15
Modern Roman sample	553	20.3
Undated Sardinian population	500	6
African sample (Mali) (1ˢᵗ millennium BC)	315	12.7
Nubian (historic)	134	18.6

Sources: Adapted from Hauser and De Stefano, 1989, 198–99; Lazer, 1995, 305; Rubini *et al.*, 2007, 124.

Table 9.14 Cranial incidence of ossicle at asterion in various populations

Population	Sample size	Frequency (%)
Pompeii AD 79	101	13.9
Herculaneum AD 79	159	0.63
San Vincenzo al Volturno	153	20.6

Sources: Adapted from Capasso, 2001, 982; Higgins, 1989–1990; Lazer, 1995, 305.

Post-cranial evidence

Ten post-cranial non-metric traits were scored for the Pompeian sample.[54] In addition to recording many of these traits, Capasso was able to examine the Herculaneum sample for numerous post-cranial non-metric features that did not survive in the incomplete, disarticulated Pompeian collection, such as anomalies of the vertebrae.[55] He also had the advantage of being able to associate bilaterally expressed traits and different non-metric features on the same individuals. Comparison between the results obtained from the two sites was hampered by the limitations associated with the Pompeian material. While there are some apparent differences in the observed frequencies for two of the femoral non-metric traits,[56] for the purposes of this study, only one post-cranial non-metric trait – lateral squatting facets on the tibia – will be presented in detail. This trait was singled out as it appears to be most useful as a population marker for the Pompeian sample of victims.

While Nicolucci reported similar frequencies for metopic suture and coronal ossicles, he recorded significantly fewer cases of other ossicles in the sample he studied. The discrepancies between the results obtained for the current study and that of Nicolucci for the incidence of inca bones, lambdoid ossicles and sagittal ossicles can possibly be explained by the fact that the observation of non-metric traits was more of passing interest than a major research consideration. Nicolucci's primary research objective involved a craniometric analysis of the Pompeian skulls and he may not have either noticed or recorded cases that were not strongly expressed.

Perhaps the most remarkable results of this study are the huge differences in frequency between Pompeii and Herculaneum for a number of cranial and post-cranial non-metric traits. It is difficult to establish exactly what the non-metric results mean as their aetiology is not well understood. These results may imply that there were either significant genetic differences between the two samples of victims or that they experienced substantially different environments during the growing years. It would be instructive to reassess all the available Pompeian and Herculaneum material for as many non-metric traits as possible to establish whether the differences are real and not the result of interobserver error. It would also be extremely valuable to score these traits on other Italian skeletal material, especially in the Campanian region. Calculation of the frequency of these traits over time and space should aid in the determination of whether they are regional features or if they are specific to Pompeii.

10

THE CASTS

The first casts of humans

A remarkable phenomenon was revealed in 1772, during the excavation of victims in the so-called Villa of Diomedes. Preserved in the hardened ash around some of the twenty-odd skeletons[1] that were found collapsed on top of one another in the *cryptoporticus* corridor were the negative forms of human bodies. Though the eruption sequence was not fully understood at the time, there was an appreciation of the fact that a unique set of circumstances had contributed to the production of fossils at this site. The fine ash that covered Pompeii in the lethal fourth and subsequent surges had hardened and sealed organic material. Over time, these remains decomposed and were drained through the porous layers of ash and pumice on which they lay. This left what were essentially moulds of the shapes of organic remains as they had appeared at the time of the destruction.[2]

An attempt was made to preserve the forms of victims found in the Villa of Diomedes but only the impression of the draped bosom and arms of a woman could be properly salvaged. They were first transported to the *Real Gabinetto di Portici*, and eventually were moved to the *Palazzo degli Studi* in Naples. These remains provided an image of a young woman, apparently in the last moment of her existence. The responses of those who viewed the ash image tended to be rather melodramatic and are best captured in Gautier's short story *Arria Marcella*, which was published in 1852.[3]

The excavators of the Villa of Diomedes also recognized the forms of non-human organic material that had decomposed over time in the hardened ash.[4] A technique was developed in the nineteenth century to reveal the shapes of wooden furniture by pouring plaster of Paris into cavities in the ash and removing the ash when the plaster dried. A door was cast in this manner in 1856.[5] Seven years later, Giuseppe Fiorelli revolutionized the way human remains from Pompeii were regarded when he and his assistant Andrea Fraia applied this method to Pompeian victims whose forms had been preserved in the fine ash of the second phase of the eruption. The first casts were made of four victims in the so-called Street of the Skeletons on 5 February 1863.[6] It

247

has been suggested that there had been earlier but ultimately unsuccessful attempts to cast human victims, first of a presumed female from the House of the Faun in 1831 and again in 1861 when a victim was found with a clear impression of clothing and a jewellery box in the surrounding ash.[7]

The type of preservation that enabled victims to be cast is unique to the region around Pompeii and cannot be seen at Herculaneum. The variation in preservation across Campania is in no way related to the eruption processes or the cause of death, as the majority of victims died as a result of surges in the second phase of the eruption. The differential preservation between these sites has been attributed to differences in the groundwater table. The Herculaneum victims are buried below the level of the post-eruption groundwater table and their skeletons have been encased in relatively soft and wet volcanic ash. These conditions coupled with the pressure of 20 or so metres of debris deposited above the bodies and other organic material, ensured that the forms of victims were not preserved.

In contrast, the individuals who were killed by the fourth and possibly later surges in Pompeii rest on 2.5 to 2.8 metres of porous ash and pumice that is well above the level of the groundwater table, and which has facilitated the drainage of decomposing soft tissue. The fine ash associated with the surges hardened quickly around the bodies and other organic material before there was time for them to decay. In the right circumstances, the fine-grained surge deposit preserved phenomenal detail, including the impression of facial features and clothing. The potential for the preservation of forms of organic material was enhanced by there being only about two metres of overburden above the material preserved in the S4 layer in Pompeii.[8]

The casts of the human victims from Pompeii and its immediate environs are both compelling and confronting. This is because they present victims as they appeared at or around the time of death. In a number of cases, the features that identified victims as individuals have been well preserved. Not only could faces be discerned but also their apparent expressions, as well as the clothes they wore and the objects that they carried. It is also possible to see how people died in the context of the environment in which they had lived.

While there are many cases of well-preserved bodies from around the world, the casts of the forms of the Pompeian victims are remarkable in that they represent individuals who do not come from a burial context. These people were victims of a mass disaster who, along with their culture, were preserved in the destruction layers. Not only is the viewer acutely aware of their untimely deaths, they are also exposed to the smallest details associated with the daily life of the victims. Despite the fact that the flesh has not survived, it is probably easier to relate to these casts than preserved bodies from tombs that have been subjected to unfamiliar death rituals.

The impact of the casts on nineteenth-century visitors is exemplified by this description by Marc Monnier:

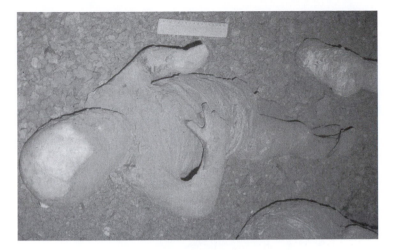

Figure 10.1 Cast of a very young victim from the *Casa del Bracciale d'Oro* (VI, xvii, 42), which was found with three other victims between 3 and 6 June 1974. It displays a high degree of preservation of the facial features and clothing details

Any one can see them now, in the museum at Naples; nothing could be more striking than the spectacle. They are not statues, but corpses, moulded by Vesuvius; the skeletons are still there, in those casings of plaster which reproduce what time would have destroyed, and what the damp ashes have preserved – the clothing and the flesh, I might almost say the life. The bones peep through here and there, in certain places which the plaster did not reach. Nowhere else is there anything like this to be seen. The Egyptian mummies are naked, blackened, hideous; they no longer have anything in common with us; they are laid out for their eternal sleep in the consecrated attitude. But the exhumed Pompeians are human beings whom one sees in the agonies of death.[9]

The Last Days of Pompeii and the interpretation of casts

Bulwer-Lytton's influence on the interpretation of Pompeian human remains was already well established when the first human forms were cast in 1863. Because of the survival of considerable personal detail, the casts could be employed as even more eloquent props than skeletons to illustrate the terrible fate of the victims of the eruption. Circumstantial evidence, in the form of associated artefacts, was combined with the attitude and perceived expression on the faces of the casts to establish their final moments. It is notable that one of the contemporary accounts of the first body forms that were revealed by Fiorelli included the statement that they 'would have

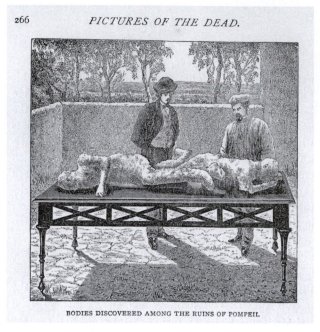

266   *PICTURES OF THE DEAD.*

BODIES DISCOVERED AMONG THE RUINS OF POMPEII.

Figure 10.2 Two of the first bodies successfully cast in 1863 (from Adams, 1868, 266)

furnished a thrilling episode to the accomplished author of the "Last Days of Pompeii"'.[10]

The groundbreaking application of the casting technique to humans captured the imagination of visitors to the site and numerous accounts were published in a variety of languages in the latter part of the nineteenth century.[11] These pieces owe much to Bulwer-Lytton, with their sense of melodrama and interpretations based solely on superficial visual inspection of the casts and their accoutrements.

In one version, dating from 1864,[12] two of the first group of bodies that were cast were described as possibly being a mother and daughter. The elder was considered to be of humble birth on the basis of the size of her ears and, perhaps less remarkably, because she was wearing an iron ring. Her stretched out raised left leg was proffered as evidence of her suffering. The younger female was assigned an age of less than 15. The impression of the drapery of her clothing was described in detail, as was a reconstruction of how she met her end. The writer, Marc Monnier, claimed that she raised her robe over her head in terror and subsequently fell while running. Unable to rise again, she had supported her 'young and feeble head' on one arm. He considered that she did not endure any lengthy period of pain. In front of these individuals was a victim described as female and assumed to be noble as she was found near a substantial sum of money, jewels, a key and two silver vases. Her attitude is described in some detail and from this the author was able to conclude that she had struggled for a considerable period of time in agony as he considered that pose reflected suffering rather than death. He was of the opinion that her anguish had been greater than that of the woman that fell behind her as the poor 'lose less in dying'. The fourth victim is identified as a giant of a man who had 'flung himself on his back to die bravely'.

The interpretation in another nineteenth-century account, published in the *Quarterly Review*,[13] is so similar to that described above, it seems likely that both were derived from a common source. There is general agreement about the sex and age attributions, as well as the social status of these victims. This author was also concerned with the level of suffering of the victims. From the poses it was deduced that the supposedly wealthy woman battled for her life and that the man had chosen to lie down to 'meet death like a brave man'. The young girl also fought hard before dying, while the cast that was presumed to be that of her mother had died without a struggle. The cast flesh of females was of particular interest to the writer. The skin of the girl, which was revealed where her garments had torn, was described as 'smooth young skin' that appeared like 'polished marble'. Similarly, the exposed leg of the wealthy woman was said to be rather shapely and could well have been cast from 'an exquisite work of Greek art'.

The tendency to accord special attention to females that were considered attractive can be seen in a number of works, like that of Gusman. He described a cast interpreted as that of a young girl, as 'a graceful creature with a delicate neck, a slender figure and well-shaped legs' and another as having 'rounded thighs and delicately modelled knees and ankles'.[14] Mostly this was used as a device to make the death of an individual more poignant. The casts were perceived as a valuable resource for illustrating the human loss in this disaster. This attitude is perhaps best summarized in the *Quarterly Review* article:

> And more ghastly and painful, yet deeply interesting and touching objects, it is difficult to conceive. We have death itself moulded and cast – the very last struggle and final agony brought before us. They tell their story with a horrible dramatic truth that no sculptor could ever reach.[15]

The tradition of using the casts for Bulwer-Lytton style storytelling has continued right into the twenty-first century. Emphasis has been placed on a few specific casts or groups of casts and stories based on their interpretation dominate both the academic and popular literature. A few key examples will suffice.

A cast found outside the Nucerian Gate has commonly been interpreted as a male beggar because it was carrying a sack, presumably for alms.

Man with Sandals (Museum of Pompei)

Figure 10.3 Cast of a man with sandals, generally assumed to be a beggar (Gusman, 1900, 16)

The impression of sandals can be seen on the feet. They appear to be of high quality and it has been assumed that they would have been much too good for a beggar. They have been explained away as a donation from a public charity.[16] Another cast is that of a squatting figure that was found near the remains of a donkey. This person is generally assumed to have been male and to have worked as a muleteer (Figure 10.4).[17] Several of the casts have been interpreted as pregnant women, including a cast found in the Via Stabiana (Figures 10.7 and 10.8) and one of the group of casts made in about 1989 in Region I, Insula 22. Though these assumed pregnancies have been solely based on the shape of the belly, some writers have even reported the age of the foetus.[18]

A number of groups of casts, such as the nine casts made in the grounds of the *Casa del Criptoportico* (I, vi, 2) in 1914 and the 13 that were produced from bodies found in the *Orto dei Fuggiaschi* (I, xxi, 2) in 1961, have provided the basis for elaborate stories very much in the style of those associated with the first casts that were made in 1863. Etienne, for example, described casts made in 1961 as having comprised people from three families who had taken shelter under a roof. A woman had tried to filter the foul air through a cloth pressed to her mouth. Despite the lack of evidence, he concluded that 'her husband must have watched her die, still holding the hand of their child before finally succumbing himself'.[19] Maiuri presented a similar reconstruction of the relationships of the victims and their terrible death from the gardens of the *Casa del Criptoportico* (I, vi, 2). He described them as a 'pitiful' group, including what he interpreted as a mother and daughter locked in a 'tragic embrace'.[20]

These casts still elicit strong emotions and are commonly described in these terms in the more recent literature.[21] The melodramatic narrative approach has been so pervasive it has even entered the scientific literature on preserved bodies.[22]

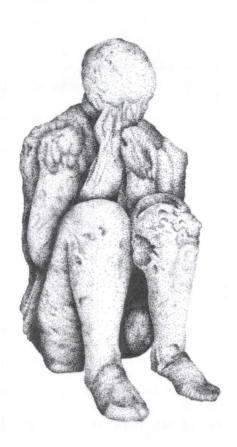

Figure 10.4 Cast of a fugitive found near the latrine of the large palaestra (II, 7), commonly
interpreted as a muleteer

It is a remarkable testimony of the power of the legacy of *The Last Days of
Pompeii* that superficial inspection of the casts, flimsy circumstantial evidence
and dollops of imagination have driven the interpretation of forms of the
victims. Even though the bones survived, there was no attempt to use the
skeletal record to test any of the assumptions about the identification of
individuals that were made from visual inspection until the end of the
twentieth century (see below). It should also be noted that there is differential preservation across the site. While incredible detail is preserved on
some of the casts, on many only a crude form is discernible, like a partially
realized image. The ambiguity of details has not been an impediment to
personal identification for many writers, as in the case of the rough form of
the so-called muleteer, which has been confidently identified as a male.

253

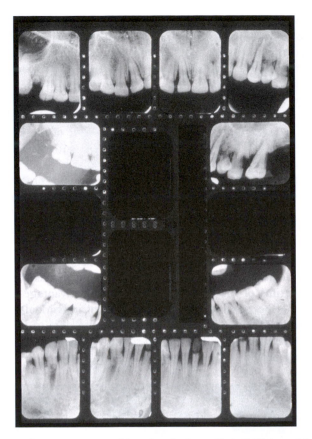

Figure 10.14 Dental x-rays (courtesy of Associate Professor Chris Griffiths and Ian White)

The human casts provide one of the most compelling series of finds from Pompeii. Initially, they merely served as a narrative device to illustrate the devastation of the site. While their scientific potential has since been recognized, very little such work has been undertaken. One reason for this is probably that the majority of the forms were cast in plaster of Paris, which is more difficult to x-ray successfully than translucent resin. Another is that they tend to be fragile and are difficult to transport without causing damage. Recent developments in digital imaging, along with increased accessibility of portable equipment, may provide solutions to these problems. The possibilities of the casts as a resource that can provide information about the life and death of the Pompeians are yet to be fully realized.

11

MAKING SENSE

Interpretation of the human skeletal remains from Pompeii and Herculaneum has been dominated by a storytelling approach, which originated from
the culture of bodies that developed in Pompeii in the eighteenth century.
Initially, this involved the use of human skeletal finds as props to produce vignettes for visiting dignitaries. A mythology was created, mostly
based on finds from the eighteenth century, such as the human remains
discovered in the so-called Villa of Diomedes and the alleged well-heeled
woman found in the gladiator's barracks (VII, vii, 16–17). The next and
probably most enduring influence was that of Edward Bulwer-Lytton's 1834
novel *The Last Days of Pompeii*, which combined circumstantial evidence from
associated artefacts with the context of skeletons found in Pompeii to weave
a story about the lives and deaths of the victims. The legacy of the Bulwer-
Lytton approach can be clearly observed in both academic and popular works
about the human victims in Pompeii and Herculaneum. It is easy to understand why this approach persists as it is very attractive to invest the victims
with personalities and names, which facilitate empathy. Epigraphic evidence
is often invoked for this purpose, despite the fact that there is little
likelihood that names found, for example, on inscriptions, could be related to specific individuals. By continuing this trend we do a disservice to
the victims of the event. The lives that are recreated almost certainly tell us
more about the scholars who write the work than about the individuals
who continue to act as props for these scenarios. The tales tend to obscure
rather than reveal information and there is always the risk that evidence may
be sacrificed for the sake of a good narrative. This problem is exacerbated
when it is presented with a veneer of science, as it is difficult for the lay
reader to establish what is reasonable and what is pure creation. Another
key problem in applying a storytelling approach is that there is the
expectation that everything will be resolved with a neat ending, which
belies the nature of archaeology, a subject that deals in probabilities rather
than certainty.

   The astonishing wealth of finds associated with the Vesuvian destruction
layer has added to the problem as it has, on occasion, lured normally sensible

scholars into the false notion that they should somehow be able to know everything about the site and reconstruct it into nice history or diorama.

A further complication is that physical anthropologists appear to be reticent to divulge the limitations of their field. This can partially be explained by the fact that they generally write for their peers, who understand the constraints of the discipline. Another contributing factor to this problem is the way that the discipline is funded. Grants are unlikely to be bestowed on conservative projects that deal with vague probabilities. Certainty and the grand statement are much more likely to be rewarded. This encourages scholars to push the evidence to make conclusions that cannot be supported. Archaeology and ancient history have become increasingly multidisciplinary in their approach, though it is nearly impossible to become proficient in all the disciplines that are encompassed. One of the aims of this work is to arm the lay reader with enough information to be able to critically assess the literature associated with physical anthropology.

Pompeii and Herculaneum have been in the grip of the Bulwer-Lytton approach for far too long and it is timely to explore new ways of making the findings accessible without pushing the evidence beyond what is reasonable. The human skeletal remains from Pompeii present a particularly problematic data set because they have been compromised, mostly as a result of post-excavation treatment of the bones. Perhaps it has required more than a little coaxing but it has been possible to tease out enough information to provide tantalizing glimpses into the lives and deaths of these victims.

The context of the human finds revealed that, as expected, the majority of the Pompeian victims were killed by the lethal second phase, though a substantial number appear to have died as a result of roof and wall collapse due to the build up of ash and pumice in the first phase of the eruption. Human remains that have been studied *in situ*, the casts in particular, confirm the current interpretation of the AD 79 event, as the victims that survived to the second phase of the eruption for the most part appear to have died quickly and were exposed to high temperatures at or about the time of death.

Analysis of the skeletal remains enabled commonly held views about the population to be tested. The assertion that young, healthy males were most likely to survive was not supported by the skeletal evidence. It appeared that there were roughly even numbers of each sex represented in the sample of victims at both Pompeii and Herculaneum. If the Pompeian sample were at all skewed, it was slightly towards those skeletons that had male attributes. Similarly, the skeletal evidence did not confirm the notion that the sample would be biased toward those that were old or extremely young. While establishing age-at-death is much more difficult than sex determination for adults, it appeared that a full range of ages was represented with the exception of very young individuals. Poor storage and the inability of untrained excavators to recognize infant bones as human may not fully account for the lack of babies and young children in the Pompeian collection as the well-excavated Herculaneum sample yielded a similar bias. One possible explanation is that the AD 79 populations at these two sites were not stable. It is important to note that the Pompeian and Herculaneum samples cannot be used to comment about infant mortality because victims of mass disasters do not provide evidence that pertains to such issues.

While there are many disorders that do not present on bone, the skeletal record for both Pompeii and Herculaneum displays no apparent skewing towards individuals with pathology. It is possible to gain a little insight into the general health of the Pompeian victims from the skeletal evidence. Regional continuity in stature and the height difference between males and females indicates that the majority of victims were not exposed to major illness and had access to reasonable nutrition in their growing years. The number of healed and healing injuries reflects a certain robusticity in their immune systems, though the dental data suggest that there may have been some underlying health problems. The poor state of oral hygiene in many mouths possibly provides indirect evidence for systemic infections or more serious soft-tissue pathology.

The presence of age-related disorders, like hyperostosis frontalis interna (HFI) and diffuse idiopathic skeletal hyperostosis (DISH) suggests that individuals were surviving into old age. This challenges the view that is often presented by scholars, including physical anthropologists, that ancient people were shorter lived than their modern counterparts. The discovery of a significant number of cases of HFI was of particular importance because the incidence of its occurrence in the sample is comparable to that in a modern Western population. This indicates that the sample was not only random and normally distributed but also that the Pompeian lifespan was similar to that of a modern Western population. It is notable that minimal evidence for the presence of this disorder was recorded for the Herculaneum sample.

The most useful population indicators for the Pompeian sample proved to be non-metric traits. The extremely high incidence of certain traits in relation to other populations, like palatine torus, double-rooted canines and squatting facets of the tibia suggests a certain level of homogeneity, either as a result of shared genes or a common environment during the years of growth and development. This discovery is at odds with the traditional view that the Pompeian population was heterogeneous. It is possible that the various populations described by ancient writers, like Strabo and Pliny the Elder, which were said to have inhabited the region, were not genetically distinct but were separated by culture and language. The apparent homogeneity of the Pompeian sample could also be accounted for by a possible alteration to the composition of the population by some sections of the community moving from the settlement, either as a direct result of the AD 62 earthquake or as a result of disruptions caused by continuing seismic activity in the last 17 years of occupation. There could be other reasons for change to the population, as would be expected in any dynamic community with a long occupation history. The time of the year that the eruption occurred could also have influenced the composition of the victims. It now appears unlikely that the event occurred in the summer of AD 79, which means that seasonal occupants would have returned to their main residences in Rome.

Perhaps the most interesting and unexpected discovery involves the large differences in the reported frequency of both cranial and post-cranial non-metric traits between the Pompeian and Herculaneum samples. If these results are correct, they suggest that there were either significant genetic distinctions between the samples of victims at the two sites or that they were exposed to different environments during the period of growth and development. Consideration should be given to the possibility that variation in the way the eruption was experienced at Pompeii and Herculaneum may have had an impact on who became victims at each location.

The recorded divergence between the Pompeian and Herculaneum samples for pathology and non-metric traits requires some attention. It is important to establish that these differences are real and not an artefact of variations in recording standards between scholars. To rule out interobserver error, it would be valuable to have a collaborative overarching study of the human remains from both sites, using standardized techniques. It would also be instructive to establish whether the features and pathology recorded in the Pompeian sample are distinctly associated with this site or whether there is evidence for them in other Campanian sites and if they persist over time.

When I first commenced work on this material, other scholars considered that my study was virtuous but not of any real value. The Pompeian skeletal finds had been all but written off as they had been superseded by the carefully excavated, articulated Herculaneum skeletons, which were clearly capable of providing much more information. The apparent differences between the Pompeian and Herculaneum samples underline the importance of not jettisoning evidence, regardless of how compromised it may be as a result of poor post-excavation treatment. They also indicate that, regardless of their proximity, contemporaneity and death as a result of the same event, the victims from these two sites cannot be treated as interchangeable.

The potential to cast the forms of the victims that have left their impressions in the hardened ash in the layers associated with the second phase of the eruption is unique to the region around Pompeii. Like the skeletal evidence, they have primarily served as poignant reminders of the catastrophe and evocative tools for elaborate storytelling. The x-ray and CT analysis of the resin cast from Oplontis demonstrates that the casts are an extremely valuable scientific resource. Not only do their poses provide some information about cause of death but they also provide a source of articulated skeletons that can be analyzed to test the results obtained from the disarticulated sample.

This baseline study of the human skeletal remains from Pompeii involved measurements and observations to obtain information that would describe the population in terms of sex, age-at-death, population affinities and pathology. The results of this research challenge assumptions that had been made about the people who became victims from both Pompeii and Herculaneum and can be tested by future studies on the casts and any new skeletons that are revealed in forthcoming excavations. It provides the groundwork for further studies at the macroscopic, microscopic and, if the technology becomes available, molecular level.

It would be remiss to neglect to mention the ethical considerations associated with the study and display of human remains from this archaeological context. Ideally, this section should appear at the beginning of a volume but I have specifically chosen to put it at the end in this case as, to date, these issues have not been high on the agenda for Pompeii and Herculaneum. Nonetheless, it is essential to be a bit introspective about undertaking a study that involves human skeletal material.

As a scholar coming from an Australian perspective, it is not possible to contemplate studying any human remains without some thought about the ethical issues. Archaeologists have been forced to consider the sensibilities of Indigenous people in Australia as a result of a history of collection and study of bones without consent, often for nefarious purposes, to maintain the *status quo* of 'racial' inequality. From the latter part of the twentieth century, Indigenous people in North America and Australia began to lobby for the return of the remains of individuals that they identified as ancestors. Laws have now been enacted to facilitate this process.[1] Further, codes of ethics have been devised to ensure that research is appropriately carried out with the consent of stakeholders.[2] There has been a flow-on effect as a result of the need to address the concerns of traditional communities. It is possible to discern increasing interest in the treatment of the remains of humans in a more sensitive manner, from cultures that have not previously been concerned about the study and display of their ancestors, including those from a modern Western context. One form in which this has been manifested is the development of a series of guidelines for dealing with European remains and cemetery excavations. Australia has been a leader in this field. In 2005, English Heritage and the Church of England produced guidelines for the excavation, study and reburial of Christian remains from archaeological contexts.[3] This is significant as it is possible that there may ultimately be a knock-on effect that will have an impact on the treatment of archaeological human remains in Europe.

It should, however, be noted that there is a long tradition of displaying human anatomical images in Europe, often in an extremely theatrical manner. The major work of the sixteenth-century anatomist Andreas Vesalius of Brussels, *De Humani Corpus Fabrica*, includes detailed woodcuts of humans divesting themselves of layers of their anatomy, often within the setting of a romantic landscape (see Frontispiece).[4] The exhibitions of plastinated bodies devised by Gunther von Hagens, while considered highly offensive by some people, clearly operate within this tradition. It is possible that some of the public outrage about Von Hagen's exhibitions of posed humans reflects a shift in attitude.

Italy may be slightly more immune from changing global attitudes, as there is a tradition dating back to medieval times of public exhibition of human remains for religious purposes. Natural mummification of deceased individuals who had been placed in crypts, for example, was considered to be the result of divine intervention, as a failure to putrefy was seen as suspension of the laws of nature, and such bodies were usually displayed. Similarly, monks and lay supporters of the Capuchin monastery at Palermo, who were either naturally or artificially mummified between the sixteenth and turn of the twentieth centuries, are on view in subterranean chambers of the building.[5] Sometimes bodies have been exhibited to emphasize views about the Resurrection and the separation of body and soul, like the disarticulated remains of approximately 4,000 Capuchin brothers and other individuals who died between 1528 and 1870. These bones have been used to form elaborate patterns, such as a clock made from vertebrae and other skeletal elements, which decorate the crypt of Santa Maria della Concezione in Rome.[6]

To date, there has been no controversy about the ethical considerations associated with the study of human remains in either Pompeii or Herculaneum and, while there is evidence that human skeletal elements have been souvenired from Pompeii, there has been no call for their repatriation. Human remains have been on view to the public in Pompeii since the eighteenth century and this is unlikely to change in the foreseeable future. Still, ethical issues are dynamic and it is possible that attitudes could eventually alter.

Human skeletal remains in Herculaneum have, until recently, been on display. Some of the more recent finds were cast in latex prior to their removal for analysis, which allows skeletons to be observed as they were found in their original locations. This is probably more the result of pragmatic considerations, rather than the desire to deal with sensibilities about seeing real skeletons *in situ*. Ongoing problems with groundwater provide an imperative for the removal of bones, particularly those on the ancient beachfront.

Discussion with members of the Herculaneum Conservation Project revealed that the local community identify as stakeholders and maintain a continued interest in being able to view the remains of the victims, preferably *in situ*.[7] They have expressed disappointment when told that the human remains can no longer be viewed on site. There have been suggestions from foreign visitors, mostly North Americans and Australians, that the human remains should not be displayed as they might upset visitors to the site.

It is perhaps rather chauvinistic for people from other cultures to extrapolate their values onto site management. Ultimately, the decisions that are made are the responsibility of the stakeholders, though it could be argued that these sites are of world significance and that we could all be described as stakeholders.

The most essential and pleasurable part of the morning ritual to gain access to the Sarno and Forum bath skeletal collections was to share coffee and a chat with the custodians responsible for the keys to these buildings.

Their main interest in my Antipodean background was the wildlife – mostly its potential as cuisine. One of the custodians was a touch on the corpulent side and another rather thin. One morning the thin one was giving his rounder colleague a hard time about the quantity of food he ate. The subject of kangaroos came up and the better fed of the two quipped that this was just the kind of meat that his more slender counterpart would eat as it was lean and hard. He concluded that regardless of the fact that his colleague never ate any fat, he was going to die just the same. Sadly, he was correct and both of them are no longer alive. We cannot stave off death, no matter what we do. A mass disaster does not discriminate and has left us with what appears to be a random sample that reflects a living population. While the victims did not choose their fate, their rediscovery and subsequent subjection to analysis has bestowed upon them a modicum of immortality.

GLOSSARY[1]

Abscess An abscess is a localized collection of pus in a cavity that is formed by the disintegration of tissue. In the case of dental abscess, they often occur within the alveolar bone near the apex of the root of a tooth.

Acetabulum This is the portion of the hip joint formed by the coxa. It is the socket, which articulates with the head of the femur.

Aetiology The study of the origins, causes and reasons for diseases and the way in which they operate. When a disorder is described as being of unknown aetiology, it means that the cause is not known.

Alveolar Derived from the Latin, *alveolus*, meaning little holes. The term refers to tooth sockets.

Alveolar resorption The removal of alveolar bone.

Amphitheatre A type of structure with no Greek antecedents. Oval in plan, its primary purpose was to seat the spectators of gladiatorial fights and other spectacles. The earliest surviving amphitheatre is in Pompeii and dates to about 80 BC.

Anatomic position The standard for anatomical descriptions. It involves an erect posture with the arms at the side and the palms facing forward.

Ankylosis An abnormal consolidation of a joint, which immobilizes it.

Anomaly Unlike the usual form.

Ante mortem Prior to death.

Anthropometric The measurement of the human form.

Anthropometry Measurement of the human body.

Aperture An opening.

Apex The most superior point of the skull, directly superior to the porion.

Apical Towards the apex or tip of the root of a tooth.

Apodyterium The equivalent of a cloak room or changing room in a bath complex. It was also thought to serve as a waiting room for slaves and attendants.

Appendicular skeleton The bones of the limbs, the shoulder and pelvic girdles, but not the sacrum.

Apposition To fit together.

Arthritis The inflammation of a joint.

Arthropathy Any disease that affects the joints.

Articulation A normal point of contact between two adjacent bones.

Ash Fragmentary or pulverized volcanic materials.

Asterion The external point where the lambdoid and temporoparietal sutures intersect.

Asterionic bone An extra-sutural or wormian bone. It tends to be triangular in shape and occurs at the junction of the lambdoid and temporoparietal suture. The boundaries for this bone are the parietal, temporal and occipital bones.

Atrium The central hall of a traditional house of Italic design.

Atrophy Wasting away and reduction in size.

Attrition In the context of skeletal biology, this term refers to the wearing down of a structure from abrasion as a result of use; usually applied to tooth wear.

Auricular Earlike. In the human skeleton, the auricular surface refers to the articular surface between the sacrum and the ilium, which is vaguely shaped like an ear.

Axial skeleton The skull, vertebrae, ribs, sternum and sacrum.

Basicranium The bones of the base of the cranium.

Basilar Base (of the skull). This term is also used to describe the suture on the base of the skull between the occipital and the sphenoid.

Basion A landmark situated at the midpoint of the anterior margin of the foramen magnum.

Bicuspid A premolar tooth is also known as a bicuspid as it generally has two cusps.

Bifid Cleft into two parts.

Bimodal A frequency distribution of numerical data that has two peaks or modes.

Biological age This term is used as an acknowledgement of the fact that there is not a linear relationship between growth and actual or chronological age. Biological age provides an indication of where an individual can be placed on the continuum of the ageing process.

Bitumen Any natural hydrocarbon. It is also known as mineral pitch.

Bombs Fist sized or larger lumps of rock that are ejected during an eruption.

Bony exostosis An additional, often abnormal, overgrowth of bone in a localized area.

Boss A protuberance or rounded eminence.

Brachy Short. For example, brachydactyly means short fingers.

Brachycephalic Interchangeable with brachycranic. Short-headed. It is defined by having a cephalic index above 80.

Bregma Derived from a Greek word, meaning moist. In anatomy, it refers to the site of the anterior fontanelle (or little fountain), which is at the junction of the coronal and sagittal sutures in the midline of the skull. The brain can be felt pulsating at this point in early infancy. It is located at the midline at the point of intersection between the coronal and sagittal sutures.

Bruxism Generally unconscious tooth grinding, which is usually associated with greater forces on the teeth than chewing and can result in significant tooth wear.

Calcaneus Derived from the Latin, *calx*, refers to the bone of the heel.

Calculus Dental calculus is mineralized plaque. It is also called tartar.

Caldarium Hot room in a bath complex.

Caldera A broad depression, generally circular in form and volcanic in origin. It characteristically has a diameter that is greater than one kilometre and sub-vertical walls. A caldera is created when a section that overlies the magma chamber collapses and the chamber empties out in a violent eruption.

Calliper In this context a calliper is a device used to measure bones. It can have either spreading or sliding arms.

Callus. An unorganized network of woven bone that forms at the site of a bone fracture. It is normally replaced as the bone heals.

Calvarium (pl. Calvaria) The portion of the skull containing the brain, namely, the cranium. This term refers to the area above the supraorbital ridge and the superior nuchal line and does not include the facial skeleton.

Canal A tunnel or channel.

Cancellous Derived from the Latin, *cancelli*, meaning grating or lattice. Refers to spongy bone with a lattice-like structure. It is porous and lightweight and is found under protuberances and where tendons attach, in the vertebral bodies, the ends of long bones, short bones and is sandwiched within flat bones. It is also known as trabecular bone.

Canine tooth Single-rooted tooth between the lateral incisor and the first premolar.

Capsule From the Latin *capsa*, or box.

Caries Decay, resulting in the softening, discolouration and destruction of a tooth. It involves the decalcification of enamel or dentine.

Carpus Wrist. Carpals are bones of the wrist.

Cartilage Specialized fibrous connective tissue. Its key characteristics are that it is not mineralized and that it is tough and elastic.

Cartilaginous joint A joint where the articulating bones are united by cartilage, which restricts movement.

Cementum Bony tissue that covers the roots of the teeth.

Cervical This term relates to the neck. The vertebrae of the neck are known as the cervical vertebrae. This word is also used to describe the margin between the root and crown of a tooth (also known as the cervicoenamel line or junction (CEJ)).

Chondral Relating to cartilage.

Chronological age The actual age of an individual.

Clavicle The collarbone. This bone articulates medially with the sternum and laterally with the scapula.

Closed population This is a population that does not experience either immigration or emigration of people.

Collagen A supportive protein substance that is a major organic component of cartilage and bone.

Colles' fracture This is a transverse fracture at the distal end of a radius. It often results from falling on an outstretched arm.

Comminute This refers to breakage into small pieces. A comminuted fracture is one in which the bone splinters.

Commingled Bone assemblages that contain a number of individuals. These assemblages are often incomplete and fragmentary.

Compact bone Dense, solid bone that makes up the walls of bone shafts and external bone surfaces. It is also known as cortical bone.

Compound fracture This term is used for a fracture where the broken bone perforates the skin.

Condyle Derived from the Greek kondylos or knuckle. A condyle is a rounded eminence. This term is often used to describe rounded articular surfaces, such as those on the mandible and the femur.

Congenital A condition that is present at birth. Such conditions are acquired during development and are not genetic.

Cord This term is used to describe a straight line that joins two points on a curve.

Coronal suture This suture separates the frontal from the parietal bones.

Corpus Body.

Cortex The outer, more dense portions of bone.

Costal Ribs.

Coxa Another term for the hip or innominate bone. It is formed by the fusion of the ischium, pubis and ilium.

Cranial Towards the head.

Cranial sutures These are fibrous joints of the skull.

Cranium The skull without the mandible or hyoid bone.

Crater A sub-circular depression, which is usually located at the summit or along the sides of the volcanic edifice, above the volcanic conduit. The volcanic material is emitted through the crater.

Cribra orbitalia Lesions that present as bilateral pitting that can be observed in the orbital part of the frontal bone.

Cryptoporticus A subterranean covered portico.

Cusp A conical projection of the crown of a tooth.

Cuspid An elevation in a tooth that is smaller than a cusp.

CT scans Computed (axial) tomography (CT) scans were developed by Hounsfield in 1972. This technique enables computerized image reconstruction from a series of cross-sectional x-ray scans.

Cyst An abnormal sac that contains solid or liquid material.

Deciduous To shed. Deciduous dentition refers to the primary or milk teeth, which are shed and replaced with the permanent teeth.

Dehiscence This means to burst open or to split and refers to the presence of extra slits in a bone.

Demography The study of population statistics.

Dentin The major constituent of a tooth, also known as ivory.

Diagenesis Physical, chemical and biological changes to bone over time. It includes the uptake of elements from the surrounding soil or leaching of elements into the surrounding soil. Apparently the outer compact layer of bone is less susceptible to diagenesis than the trabecular bone, which provides less reliable data.

Diaphysis The shaft of a long bone. It is also the primary ossification centre of a long bone.

Diploë The spongy tissue between the inner and outer tables of the cranial bones.

Dimorphism See sexual dimorphism.

Disarticulate Separate.

Dolichocephalic Interchangeable with dolicocranic. Long-headed. It is defined by a cephalic index below 75.

DNA or deoxyribonucleic acid A class of complex molecules called nucleic acids. DNA is found in the nucleus of virtually all living cells. It contains the genetic code that is required for a cell to produce the proteins needed to perform its function.

Dysplasia An abnormality of development.

Eburnation The polished surface of bone that is produced over time after the destruction of articular cartilage, as a result of contact between adjacent bones at the joint.

Ectocranial The external surface of the cranium.

Enamel The hard outer structure of the tooth.

Enamel hypoplasia Malformation of the crown of a tooth, including linear furrowing, a complete lack of enamel or pitting. These can occur as a result of periods of malnutrition or ill health during the period in infancy and childhood when the crown is being formed. It should be noted that periods of stress do not always result in enamel hypoplasia and a lack of enamel hypoplasia is not necessarily an indicator of good health and nutrition during the growing years.

Endemic A disease that is specific to a locality or region and reoccurs persistently in that population.

Endocranial Within the cranium.

Epicondyle An eminence at the articular end of a bone above a condyle.

Epidemic A disease that spreads rapidly and widely in a population and is difficult to control.

Epidemiology The study of causes and transmission of disease.

Epigenetic traits Anomalous skeletal variants, which are generally non-pathological. On the whole, these present as innocuous features on the bone.

Epigraphic Written evidence; it includes inscriptions and graffiti.

Epiphysis A secondary centre of ossification of a long bone. It is separated from the shaft of a bone by cartilage, also known as the epiphyseal plate, which ossifies when growth has been completed.

Eruption An explosion of fused solid or gaseous volcanic material from the crater after the rise of magma in the volcanic conduit.

Eversion To turn outward.

Evulsion To extract.

Exostosis An additional, often abnormal, overgrowth of bone in a localized area.

Facet A small, smooth area on a bone or tooth, which serves as a point of contact between bones or teeth. Tooth facets are often produced by wear.

Fallout The settling and deposition of particulate matter out of an eruption plume and onto the surface of the ground. This includes volcanic aerosols and tephra.

Falx Sickle-shaped structure. In the case of the frontal bone, it is a sickle-shaped structure in the midsection of the inner table.

Fecundity The biological potential for bearing children.

Femur Thigh bone.

Fibula The outer, or lateral, lower leg bone.

Fissure Deep grooves or cracks. It can also be used to describe a fault in a tooth surface, which can result from an imperfect union of two lobes or cusps.

Flexion Bending.

Fontanelle Areas of membrane between the ossification centres of infant cranial bones. It literally means a small spring or fountain.

Foramen A small opening or hole.

Foramen magnum Large opening at the base of the skull, through which the spinal cord passes. It is the largest opening of the skull.

Forensic Related to the law. Forensic medicine is legal medicine.

Forum A public area in a Roman town, which served numerous functions, including as a centre for business, judicial activities and as a marketplace.

Fossa A depression or pit.

Frigidarium Cool room and bath in a bath complex.

Frontal The frontal bone is the bone of the forehead.

Fuller Fullers dealt with the manufacture and cleaning of cloth

Fusion This is the term used to describe a union of two adjacent bones or parts of bone.

Gingivae In the jaws, the alveolar process is covered with a layer of soft tissue, which is known as the mucosa. It is gathered up in a cuff at the base of the crown of each tooth. The mucosa that actually forms the cuff is known as the gingivae.

Glabella The most anterior point of the forehead. This landmark is located in the midline at the level of the supraorbital ridges.

Gnathion This landmark is the most anterior inferior point of the mandible in the median sagittal plane.

Gonial angle This is the angle formed by the intersection of the horizontal body and ascending ramus of the mandible.

Gonion The most lateral external point of the gonial angle of the mandible. The lowest posterior and most outward point of the angle of the mandible.

Gracile From the Latin *gracilis*, which means slender.

Growth Progressive changes in size and morphology during the development of an individual. Growth tends to be positively correlated with age.

Growth plate region The site of formation of bone tissue in a long bone that is growing. The growth plate consists of rows of cartilage cells that are highly ordered. The row that is furthest removed from the bony shaft is known as a germinative layer and it is responsible for cell replication and cartilage growth at the bone shaft. Eventually, the cartilage will be re-formed into true bone tissue.

Haematoma A mass or pocket of blood that is outside the circulatory system.

Head In an anatomical context, a head is a rounded smooth eminence that articulates with another bone.

Heterogeneous Mixed.

Histology Investigation of the microscopic structure of tissues.

Homogeneous Of the same kind or alike.

Homologous Derived from common ancestry.

Humerus The upper arm bone.

Hyaline cartilage The translucent cartilage that covers the articular surface of a bone.

Hyperostosis An abnormal growth of bone tissue. It usually results in the development of bone tissue that projects from the normal surface of the bone.

Hyperostotic trait Associated with excessive ossification into structures that are usually made up of cartilage or dura.

Hyperplasia An abnormal increase of cells in a structure.

Hyperthermia When the body temperature is elevated to a temperature that is significantly higher than normal.

Hypoplasia This is an incomplete or defective development of tissue. This term is usually applied to problems with the development of dental enamel.

Hypostotic traits These traits reflect neotony in that they involve the retention of forms that are usually visible in the embryonic or early infant state, such as metopic sutures or inca bones.

Ilium Dorsal part of the innominate bone.

Inca bone This epigenetic trait results from a failure of the suture that runs from asterion to asterion to unite. The occipital bone is separated into two or more parts by a transverse suture, the upper part of which is defined as an inca bone.

Incisal Cutting or biting edge of the incisor teeth.

Incisor The first two front, or anterior, teeth on each side of the mandible and the maxilla.

Innominate bone The hip bone or pelvis. Also known as the os coxa.

Insula Derived from the Latin word for island and is used to describe an ancient city block.

Intercondylar Between condyles.

Interpopulation Between populations. Interpopulation differences are variations between populations.

Intrapopulation Within a population. Intrapopulation variation refers to differences within a population.

Isis This Egyptian goddess is best known as the sister and wife of Osiris, as well as the mother of Horus and the protector of Imseti.

Lambda The midline point of intersection of the sagittal and lambdoid sutures.

Lapilli Volcanic fragments, ranging from 2 to 64 mm in size that are ejected during an explosive eruption. Also used to describe pumice stones.

Lararium Household shrine. These shrines were dedicated to the household gods, the *lares*.

Lava Rock formed by the cooling of magma after it has been ejected from a volcano. The term is also used to describe the magma when it is being ejected.

Life tables These are mathematical devices that are designed to measure the duration of certain phenomena. In demography, life tables usually measure the duration of life.

Magma Material that is derived from the fusion of rock at high temperatures. These can range from 900 to 1200° C. Magma is siliceous in composition.

Magmatic chamber The zone where magma accumulates beneath the surface of the earth. Magma can remain still for long periods of time before rising through the volcanic conduit and reaching the surface, thus creating an eruption.

Mastoid process A large protuberance of the skull behind and below the external ear. This is the point of attachment for the sternomastoid muscle.

Menarche The time of the first menstrual period.

Menopause This is the sudden or gradual end of the menstrual cycle, which happens as a result of the loss of ovarian function.

Metopic suture A midline fibrous joint between the two bones that make up the frontal bone. It is generally obliterated by the growth and fusion of the two bones by 8 years of age.

Metric analysis is that based on measurements as compared to non-metric, which is based on observations rather than measurements.

Mofeta Term employed by the eighteenth-century excavators to describe the noxious gases, notably carbon monoxide, that were trapped in the volcanic debris that covered the Vesuvian sites.

Morphology The study of shape and form.

Multifactorial inheritance This term applies to bone as the features of a bone result from a combination of genes and the environment.

Mummy Mummies are preserved corpses of humans or other animals. In ancient Egypt this was done intentionally. The word mummy is derived from the Persian *múmiyá*, which means bitumen.

Nasion This is a landmark in the midline at the root of the nose, where it joins the forehead.

Neonate A newborn infant under 28 days of age.

Neotony The retention of infantile or juvenile traits into adulthood.

Non-metric Observations made directly from bone where no measurement is involved.

Nulliparous Women who have not had a pregnancy come to term.

Occiput The occiput is the back of the skull.

Occlusion Dental occlusion refers to the way teeth fit together within and between the jaws. Normal occlusion is a standard, based on a young adult with complete dentition with all the teeth arranged in a regular and symmetrical fashion.

Pacchionian depressions Small pits or depressions that can be seen on the sides of the superior margin of the parietal bone.

Palaestra An open space that was used for sport and exercise. It was generally enclosed by colonnades.

Palaeoepidemiology The study of disease in an ancient community.

Palaeopathology In 1892, R.W. Schufeldt, a German scholar, introduced the term palaeopathology to describe the study of the illnesses of ancient human remains. Palaeopathology can be defined as the study of diseases in ancient populations, based on examination of skeletal remains and preserved soft tissues.

Parturition Childbirth; the process of giving birth.

Perimortem Occurring at or around the time of death.

Peristyle An internal courtyard, which is generally flanked by a colonnade.

Perthes disease This pathology generally has a distinctive appearance that is described as a 'mushroom shaped' femoral head. A disorder that results from an obstruction of the blood supply to the growing femoral head with resulting necrosis. It occurs four times as frequently in males than females and is most apparent on the femoral head, which appears deformed, flattened and widened. The femoral neck tends to be widened and is shorter than normal.[2]

Plaque Dental plaque is made up of a dense accumulation of micro-organisms on the surface of the tooth. Most of the diseases that affect erupted teeth are due in some measure to dental plaque.

Plastic The capacity of a biological material, like bone, to be modified by the environment, often during the period of growth and development. This can also occur as a result of disease or trauma.

Plinian eruption Named after the description of the AD 79 eruption of Mt Vesuvius by Pliny the Younger in his letters to Tacitus. These are major explosive eruptions, which produce very high columns of ash and pumice that can rise tens of kilometres above the volcano and which result in considerable fallout.

Postmortem Occurring after death.

Prognathism A forward projection of one or both jaws from their normal relationship.

Pumice A froth of volcanic glass that forms very vesicular and low-density bubble rich material. It is usually light grey in colour. It has been suggested that the word derives from the Greek *spuma*, which means foam. Pumice bombs are greater than 64 mm in size, pumice lapilli are between 2 and 64 mm and when it is less than 2 mm in diameter it is termed ash.

Pyroclastic flow A dense avalanche of concentrated particles of pumice, ash and gas. The direction of a pyroclastic flow is determined by topography. They characteristically have high temperatures and velocities and result from the collapse of the eruptive column.

Pyroclastic surge A dilute turbulent cloud of particles that are suspended in hot air and gas. Unlike pyroclastic flows, low-density, highly turbulent pyroclastic surges are not dependent on ground features. They are also associated with high temperatures and velocities. They are also known as base surges and are usually associated with phreatomagmatic eruptions.

Pyroclastites Volcanic rocks formed from pyroclasts.

Pyroclasts Also known as tephra. These consist of solid volcanic material, including ash, lapilli, sand and volcanic bombs, that are ejected during a volcanic eruption.

Qualitative data Information that describes character and attributes, without emphasis on numerical measurement.

Quantitative data Information that has been numerically measured.

Sexual dimorphism Observable differences between males and females of the same species.

Skeletal age and skeletal maturation A measure of biological maturation, as compared to chronological age, and based on skeletal development. An age-at-death assessment can only produce a biological age, which may differ from the actual age the individual was when they died.

Stable population A construct to enable demographic studies to be made. A stable population is closed to inward and outward migration. Constant birth and death rates over a period of time indicate that the population will eventually converge on a stable age structure, with population size increasing or decreasing at a constant rate. In a stable population the numbers of people in each age category will increase or decrease at the same rate as the entire population. It has been suggested that rapid changes in fertility and mortality rates associated with demographic transitions appear to be a recent historical phenomenon and that pre-industrial populations can approximate stable populations.[3]

Stationary population A special case of a stable population. In a stationary population, birth and death rates are roughly equal and population size is neither increasing nor decreasing.[4]

Sulcus A groove or fissure.

Superior Above.

Supernumerary Additional or extra elements, such as teeth.

Suture The fibrous joints between cranial bones. The word is derived from the Latin word *sutura* or seam.

Symphysis A joint where two bones are united by fibrocartilage. This generally refers to the median joints, such as the pubic symphysis.

Synchondrosis The union of two bones by cartilage.

Syndrome A pathology, which is characterized by a suite of signs and symptoms.

Syntosis This refers to the osseus union of adjacent bones.

Systemic Conditions that affect the body as a whole.

Tendon A band of connective tissue that binds muscle to bone or other tissue.

Tephra Collective term for solid particles of silicate glass, which result from the quenching of magma. They are transported in eruption plumes in the atmosphere. The particles can range in size from microns, known as volcanic dust, to a few centimetres. This term is generally applied to pumice and lithic fragments that are ejected from an explosive eruption.

Tepidarium Warm room in a bath complex.

Thalassemia A general term applied to several pathological conditions, characterized by a deficiency in the synthesis of haemoglobin.

Thermae Roman public-bathing establishment.

Thoracic Relates to the chest. It is also used to describe the vertebrae that support the ribs in the thorax.

Tibia The larger of the lower leg bones.

Tooth cusps These are major elevations of the biting or occlusal surfaces of the premolars and molars.

Torus A bony prominence.

Trabeculae Stress-bearing structures that can be found in the spongy marrow of bones.

Transverse Crosswise.

Transverse process A process that extends laterally and dorsally from the arch of a vertebra. The term also applies to the lateral crest of a sacrum.

Trepanation (or trephination) A surgical technique that involves making an artificial hole in the cranial vault of an individual. There are various different methods, including scraping away the bone with a sharp tool or drilling a series of holes.

Trochanter The two processes that can be observed below the neck of the femur. These are the greater and lesser trochanter. An unusually prominent gluteal tuberosity on the femur shaft is generally referred to as a third trochanter.

Trochlea This term refers to pulley-shaped structures on bones, as can be observed on the humerus.

Tubercle Derived from the Latin word *tuber*, which means swelling or lump. Tubercle is a diminutive of this and refers to a small, usually bony, prominence. This term is also used for a nodule or small eminence on a tooth.

Tuberosity Comes from the Latin word *tuberositas* and means lumpy. It refers to a robust elevation or protuberance.

Tuff Interchangeable with *tufa* and is synonymous with ash. It is usually used to describe consolidated volcanic ash deposits. These can be compressed to form a type of stone, known as tufa.

Ulna The medial lower arm bone.

Ventral Towards the front or anterior.

Vertebra A vertebra is a bone of the spinal column.

Volcanic ash Fine volcanic material that is less than 2 mm in size.

Wormian bones Extra-sutural bones. These additional bones can be observed in the suture line between the bones of the cranium.

Zygomatic bone Cheek bone. This term is derived from the Greek word *zygon*, or yoke, and refers to the bone that joins the frontal, maxillary, temporal and sphenoid bones.

APPENDIX 1

Historical overview of excavations in Campania[1]

It should be noted that there are slight discrepancies in the dates reported by various scholars.

Knowledge of the whereabouts of the Campanian towns and villas was lost some time after the eruption of AD 79. The town of Resina was later built above the site of Herculaneum. The name Civita was given to the region around Pompeii as a reflection of a dimly recollected ancient town in this area.

c. 1592	Construction of a conduit to supply water to Torre Annunziata involved tunnelling through the hill of Civita. Marble fragments and coins dating to the time of Nero were revealed in this excavation.
1637	Luc Holstenius suggested that Pompeii lay beneath Civita.
1689	Excavations undertaken in search of water uncovered a stone with an inscription that included the name of Pompeii on it. There followed considerable discussion but no consensus as to whether this meant that Pompeii was situated under Civita.
1709	A smallholder discovered part of the theatre at Herculaneum while sinking a shaft for a well. A report of the marbles associated with this structure reached the Prince d'Elbeuf, who was a cavalry officer in the Austrian imperial army, which controlled Naples. He bought the land and commenced excavation. This was essentially a mining operation to obtain artefacts, mostly sculptures, for the Austrian nobility in Naples. A number of these pieces found their way to their palaces in Vienna. The Pope issued a complaint about the removal of antiquities from Italy.
1738	Charles III of Spain, King of the Two Sicilies, appointed a surveying engineer, Joaquin de Alcubierre, director of the excavations. The main objective of this exercise was to provide precious artefacts for the Spanish nobility. Alcubierre sank a

series of shafts in Herculaneum which were refilled as soon as excavation was completed so as not to destabilize the modern Resina residences. On occasion, gunpowder was employed to speed up the process. Alcubierre was involved in the excavations until his death in 1780. La Vega was promoted to the position of director of excavations in Pompeii in 1765.

1748	Royal permission was granted for Civita to be excavated. The site was later positively identified as Pompeii (see below).
1750–64	Karl Weber was initially employed as Alcubierre's aide. He suggested that it would be beneficial to introduce systematic excavation of specific sections of Pompeii in place of the rather haphazard digging that had preceded his work. He put his idea into practice with the excavation of an area in the vicinity of the Herculanean Gate. His performance was so impressive that Alcubierre became jealous and attempted to sabotage his work.
1758, 1762	Winckelmann, the German scholar who established the principles of art-historical scholarship for the study of antiquities, was denied access to the archaeological excavations of Pompeii and Herculaneum. He was later granted permission to view the sites.
1763	Discovery of an inscription, which unequivocally proved that the ancient site of Pompeii was buried under Civita.
1764	Francesco la Vega, Weber's successor, discovered the Temple of Isis. La Vega established the first overall plan of the excavations in 1778. Even though this work was fairly rigorous, the primary aim was still to plunder precious objects from the site. In addition, excavation of a building only proceeded until its function was determined. Once a building had yielded both its treasures and its purpose, it was left. La Vega was also famous for organizing the re-excavation of finds for noble visitors.
1764–1800	William Hamilton, from 1767 English Ambassador to Naples, regularly observed the excavations at Pompeii.
1770	Caroline, the wife of Ferdinand I, King of the Two Sicilies, unlike her husband, showed considerable interest in the excavations and often visited Pompeii.
1787	Goethe visited the excavations at Pompeii.
1808–14	Murat and Caroline, the sister of Napoleon I, ascended the throne of Naples. They were interested in archaeology and personally financed some of the excavations. The documentation of this work was made under the supervision of Francois Mazois, a French architect.
1815–25	Antonio Bonucci appointed director of the excavations after the Bourbons reclaimed the throne in 1815, though he had also been a director in 1814 in the Napoleonic period.

1825   Francis I, brother of Ferdinand I, became King of the Two Sicilies.

1830   Ferdinand II succeeds Francis I. During his reign, the House of the Faun (*Casa del Fauno*) (VI, xii, 2) was uncovered in Pompeii and the 'Alexander Mosaic' was discovered.

1830   William Gell was appointed the resident corresponding member for the Society of Dilettanti in Naples.

1834   Edward Bulwer-Lytton published *The Last Days of Pompeii*.

1860   Garibaldi entered Naples, ending Spanish Bourbon rule. He gave the directorship of the excavations to Alexandre Dumas, author of *The Three Musketeers*, in gratitude for his support of his campaign. Dumas, as a foreigner, was not popular with the local population and was soon replaced.

1860–75   Italy was united under the leadership of Victor-Emmanuel II and Cavour. Giuseppe Fiorelli was appointed, first as inspector in1860, and then as director of the excavations in 1863. Although people associated with the site had previously attempted or suggested a more systematic approach to excavation, Fiorelli was the first person to actually implement a rigorous method of excavation and recording in Pompeii.

1875–93   Michele Ruggiero replaced Fiorelli as director in Pompeii. He was an architect by training and he continued the excavations, using the techniques established by Fiorelli.

1893–1901   Giulio de Petra, an epigrapher, assumed the directorship of the excavations. The House of the Vettii was unearthed from 1894–95.

1901–5   The historian, Ettore Pais, was responsible for the excavation of Pompeii. During this period (1902–5), the House of the Gilded Cupids was excavated.

1905–10   Antonio Sogliano's directorship of the site was marked by an increasing interest in the development of on-site conservation techniques.

1910–23   Vittorio Spinazzola continued and further developed the systematic traditions of Fiorelli. He concentrated his efforts on exposing the so-called Via dell'Abbondanza. Spinazzola's excavations differed from those of his predecessors in that he unearthed the site from the top down, rather than exposing structures from the side. This meant that the stratigraphic sequence of the eruption could be better understood. It also increased the chances of exposing and preserving the upper levels of buildings. He was more interested in revealing the town plan than in excavating individual houses and for this reason chose to only expose the fronts of buildings as he followed the line of the street. This approach had its problems, not the least of which was the need to protect the facades he uncovered from the weight of the ash and lapilli that remained behind them.

1924–61   Amedo Maiuri's directorship was marked by extensive systematic excavation and a policy of leaving objects in situ to give visitors an impression of how the site looked at the time of its destruction. He also undertook some excavations, for example in the region of the Temple of Apollo, to establish stratigraphic sequences. In addition, he studied the standing masonry structures in an attempt to determine the history of occupation at Pompeii. After a break in excavation during World War II, Maiuri resumed excavations at an unprecedented scale and pace. This meant that uncovering the site took priority over documentation and restoration.

1961–76   Alfonso de Franciscis was superintendent of archaeology for the provinces of Naples and Caserta.

1977–81   Fausto Zevi's period as superintendent of archaeology for the provinces of Naples and Caserta was notable as he chose to cease excavation of Pompeii in favour of restoration and photographic documentation of what had already been revealed.

1981–84   Giuseppina Cerulli Irelli was superintendent of Pompeii.

1984–95   Baldassare Conticello was superintendent of Pompeii.

1995–present The current superintendent of Pompeii is Pietro Giovanni Guzzo. Maiuri's successors have essentially taken a rigorous approach to excavation and management of sites in Campania. Emphasis has been placed on recording and consolidating structures that have already been exposed, rather than on large-scale excavation. A programme of weed clearing, restoration and re-roofing of houses was initiated in Pompeii in the mid-1980s. Where possible, traditional materials were used for the restorations as opposed to the unsympathetic and ultimately destructive use of reinforced concrete and steel in the 1950s. Photogrammetry was employed to accurately map the site. Management of Herculaneum lagged behind. A multidisciplinary and multinational conservation project for Herculaneum was devised and implemented in the first five years of the twenty-first century to address the deterioration of the site. In 1985 a project was commenced in conjunction with IBM Italia and Fiat Engineering to create a database of all the excavated artefacts and archival material associated with Pompeii. The photographic records made of painting and mosaics initiated by Fausto Zevi were included in an 11-volume publication, *Pompei pitture e mosaici*, which was published between 1990 and 2003. From the 1970s, international co-operative projects were undertaken to record, analyze and interpret individual houses, groups of houses and entire blocks or insulae. These projects have resulted in significant publications. Until the latter part of the twentieth century, site management was largely focused on the AD 79 levels. A number of projects, including Italian and international teams, have had the opportunity to dig below the AD 79 level at selected sites. In conjunction with this work, there has been a significant increase of interest in a multidisciplinary approach to the archaeology of the sites destroyed by the AD 79 eruption of Mt Vesuvius.

APPENDIX 2

Terms associated with anatomical orientation

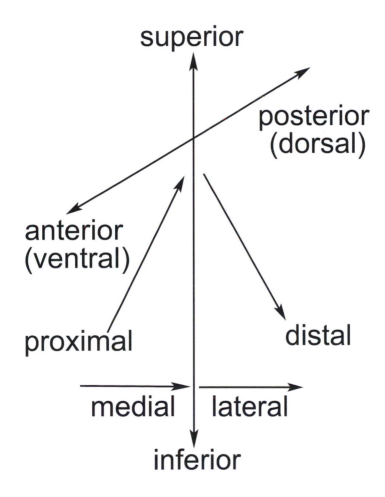

Figure A2.1 Anatomical orientation

Anterior Anatomical term meaning before or in front. This term is equivalent to ventral.

Buccal The cheek or the area near the cheek.

Coronal plane A plane that passes longitudinally through the body from side to side at right angles to the median plane. It bisects the body into anterior and posterior portions. It is also known as the frontal plane.

Cranial Towards the head.

Distal Away from the centre.

Dorsal Posterior or towards the back.

External Outside.

Frontal In front.

Frontal plane This is an alternate term for the coronal plane, which divides the body into anterior (front) and posterior (back) portions.

Inferior Anatomical descriptor meaning lower or below; for example, the mandible can also be described as the inferior maxilla.

Infra Below.

Internal Inside.

Lateral Away from the midline, to the side.

Labial Relating to the lips.

Lingual Relating to the tongue.

Medial Towards the midline.

Mesial Towards the midline.

Posterior Behind.

Proximal Nearest the centre.

Superficial Near the surface.

Superior Above.

Supra A prefix referring to an area or landmark above a landmark on a bone.

Transverse Crosswise.

Ventral In front.

APPENDIX 3

Diagrams

coronal suture

sagittal suture

lambdoid suture

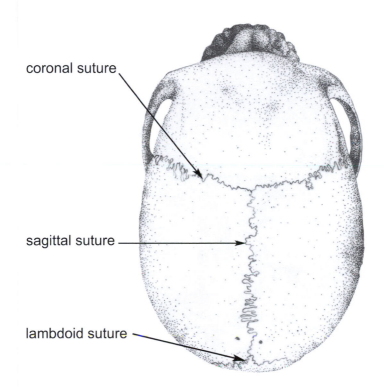

Figure A3.1 Superior view of the skull showing sutures (adapted from White and Folkens, 2005, 80)

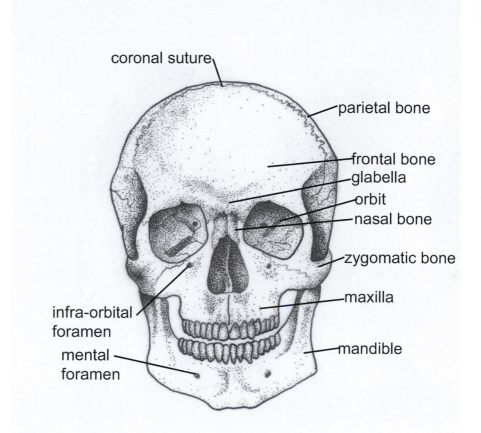

Figure A3.2 Frontal view of the skull (adapted from Comas, 1960, in Krogman, 1962, 316 and Brothwell, 1981, 94)

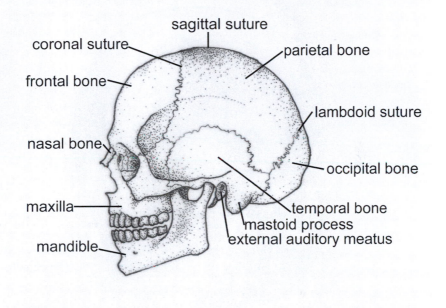

Figure A3.3 Lateral view of the skull (adapted from Comas, 1960, in Krogman, 1962, 317)

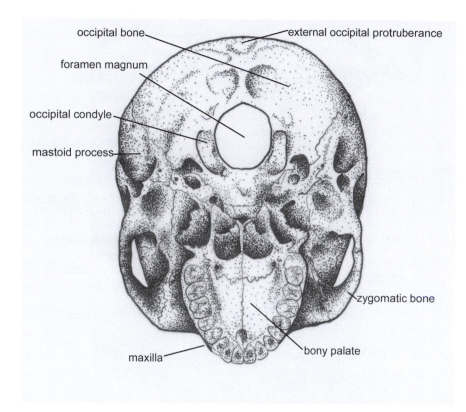

Figure A3.4 Basilar view of the skull (adapted from Comas, 1960, in Krogman, 1962, 318)

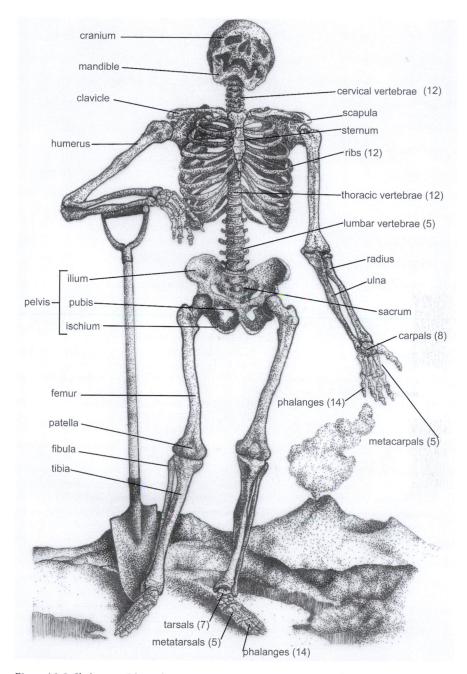

cranium

mandible

clavicle

humerus

cervical vertebrae (12)

scapula

sternum

ribs (12)

thoracic vertebrae (12)

lumbar vertebrae (5)

radius

ulna

ilium

pelvis

pubis

ischium

sacrum

carpals (8)

femur

patella

fibula

tibia

phalanges (14)

metacarpals (5)

tarsals (7)

metatarsals (5)

phalanges (14)

Figure A3.5 Skeleton, with apologies to Vesalius (adapted from Vesalius' first book of *De Humani Corporis Fabrica*, c. 1543. Reproduced in Saunders and O'Malley, 1982, 85)

NOTES

1 Skeletons as artefacts

1 House (VIII, ii, 39). This event is commemorated in an illustration by Mazois. E.C.C. Corti, *The Destruction and Resurrection of Pompeii and Herculaneum*. Translated by K. Smith and R.G. Smith. London: Routledge & Kegan Paul, 1951, 147–48; A. De Vos, and M. De Vos. *Pompei, Ercolano, Stabia*. Rome: Laterza, 1982, 59; R. Etienne, *Pompeii: The Day a City Died*. Translated by C. Palmer. London: Thames & Hudson, 1992, 22.

2 M. Brion, *Pompeii and Herculaneum: The Glory and the Grief*. London: Cardinal, 1973/1960. F.M. Bullard, *Volcanoes of the Earth*. Austin: University of Texas Press, 1984, 54; A.E. Cooley, *Pompeii*. London: Duckworth, 2003; 76; E. Lazer, 'Human skeletal remains in Pompeii: Vols I and II', unpublished PhD thesis, Department of Anatomy and Histology. Sydney: University of Sydney, 1995, 54; E. Lazer, 'The people of Pompeii', in *Pompeii Revisited: The Life and Death of a Roman Town*, ed. Harrison, D. Sydney: Meditarch, 1994, 144; E. Lazer, 'Resti umani scheletrici nella Casa del Menandro', in *Menander: La Casa del Menandro di Pompei*. Edited by G. Stefani. Milan: Electa, 2003, 65; W. Leppmann, *Pompeii in Fact and Fiction*. London: Elek, 1968, 86; R. Ling, *Pompeii: History, Life and Afterlife*. Stroud, Gloucestershire: Tempus, 2005, 163.

3 The history of the excavations at Pompeii and the nearby site of Herculaneum has been well documented, e.g. by J.W. Alexander, 'The impact of discoveries', in *The Buried Cities and the Eruption of Vesuvius: The 1900th Anniversary*. Edited by H.W. Benario and G.W. Lawall (Amherst: NECN & University of Massachusetts, 1979), 23–29; C. Amery and B. Curran, *The Lost World of Pompeii*. London: Frances Lincoln, 2002, 30–47; Brion, 1973/1960, op. cit., 42–72; E.C.C. Corti, *The Destruction and Resurrection of Pompeii and Herculaneum*. Translated by K. Smith, and R.G. Smith. London: Routledge & Kegan Paul, 1951, 92–213; R. Etienne, *Pompeii: The Day a City Died*. Translated by C. Palmer. London: Thames & Hudson, 1992, 16–41; P. Gusman, *Pompei: The City, its Life and Art*. Translated by F. Simmonds and M. Jourdain. London: Heinemann, 1900, 22–26; W. Leppmann, *Pompeii in Fact and Fiction*. London: Elek, 1968, 48–91; R. Ling, *Pompeii: History, Life and Afterlife*. Stroud, Gloucestershire: Tempus, 2005, 157–70; A. Mau, *Pompeii: Its Life and Art*. Translated by Kelsey, F.W. London: Macmillan, 1907, 25–30; C.C. Parslow, *Rediscovering Antiquity: Karl Weber and the Excavation of Herculaneum, Pompeii and Stabiae*. Cambridge: Cambridge University Press, 1995; R. Trevelyan, *The Shadow of Vesuvius: Pompeii AD 79*. London: Michael Joseph, 1976, 39–117. See Appendix for a chronology of the excavations.

4 Amery and Curran, 2002, op cit., 34–35; Cooley, 2003, op. cit., 69; A. De Simone, 'Archaeology and science', in *Rediscovering Pompeii: IBM Gallery of Science and Art*. Edited by Conticello, B. Rome: 'L'Erma' di Bretschneider, 1990, 71; J.W. Goethe, *Italian Journey (1786–1788)*, Translated by W.H. Auden and E. Mayer. Middlesex: Penguin, 1970, 211; Leppmann, 1968, op. cit., 59–60; Ling, 2005, op. cit., 160–61; Parslow, 1995, op. cit., 3–4; Trevelyan, 1976, op. cit., 44.

5 Cooley, 2003, op. cit., 69–70; Corti, 1951, op. cit., 113, 122; Leppmann, 1968, op. cit., 55–56; Trevelyan, 1976, op. cit., 45–48.

6 Corti, 1951, op. cit., 125–42; G.E. Daniel, *A Short History of Archaeology*, London: Thames & Hudson, 1981, 17; Etienne, 1992, op. cit., 18, 146–49; Leppmann, 1968, op. cit., 70–77; Ling, 2005, op. cit., 161; R. Lullies and W. Schiering, *Archäologenbildnisse: Porträts und Kurzbiograhien von Klassischen Archäologen Deutscher Sprache*. Zabern: Verlag, 1988, 5–7; Trevelyan, 1976, op. cit., 52–53.

7 A. De Vos, 'Casa dei quadretti teatrali', in *Pompei: Pitturi e Mosaici*. Rome: Istituto dell'Enciclopedia, 1990, 361–96; W. Ehrhardt, *Stilgeschichte Untersuchungen an Römischen Wandmalereien von der Späten Republik bis zur zeit Neros*, Mainz am Rhein: Philip von Zabern, 1987; K. Schefold, 'Die bedeutung der malerei Pompejis', in *Pompejanische Wandmalerei*. Edited by G. Cerulli Irelli, M. Aoyagi and D. Stefano. Zurich: Belser, 1990, 107–14.

8 Amery and Curran, 2002, op. cit., 155–60; F. Bologna, 'The rediscovery of Herculaneum and Pompeii in the artistic culture of Europe in the eighteenth century', in *Rediscovering Pompeii: IBM Gallery of Science and Art*. Edited by B. Conticello. Rome: 'L'Erma' di Bretschneider, 1990, 79; Etienne, 1992, op. cit., 16–18; Leppmann, 1968, op. cit., 61; Ling, 2005, op. cit., 161; Trevelyan, 1976, op. cit., 50, 55, 74.

9 Alexander, 1979, op. cit., 27–28; Bullard, 1984, op. cit., 209–10; Corti, 1951, op. cit., 138; P. Francis, *Volcanoes: A Planetary Perspective*, Oxford: Clarendon Press, 1993, 69; Goethe, 1970, op. cit., 315; W. Hamilton, *Observations on Mt Vesuvius, Mt Etna and Other Volcanoes in a Series of Letters Addressed To the Royal Society ... To Which Are Added Notes by the Author, Hitherto Unpublished*. London: Royal Society, 1774; Trevelyan, 1976, op. cit., 55–59.

10 See, e.g., Francis, 1993, op. cit., 69; Leppmann, 1968, op. cit., 55.

11 Goethe, 1970, op. cit., 203.

12 E. Clay and M. Fredericksen (eds), *Sir William Gell in Italy: Letters to the Society of Dilettanti, 1831–1835*, London: Hamilton, 1976, 1, 19; Daniel, 1981, op. cit., 15; Trevelyan, 1976, op. cit., 75.

13 Clay and Frederikson, 1976, op. cit. 3, 18, 21, 23, 29–30, 147; Trevelyan, 1976, op. cit., 127, n. 59.

14 T.H. Dyer, *Pompeii: Its History, Buildings and Antiquities*. 2nd edn. London: George Bell & Sons, 1883, 4–5.

15 For example, W. Gell, *Pompeiana: The Topography, Edifices and Ornaments of Pompeii: The Results of Excavations since 1819*. London: Jennings & Chaplin, 1832, 6, 44.

16 Bologna, 1990, op. cit., 89, 95; Brion, 1973, op. cit., 63–68; Cooley, 2003, op. cit., 92–95; Corti, 1951, op. cit., 189; Etienne, 1992, op. cit. 29–30; Ling, 2005, op. cit., 164–65; Trevelyan, 1976, op. cit. 85.

17 E. De Carolis, and G. Patricelli. *Vesuvius, AD 79: The Destruction of Pompeii and Herculaneum*. Translated by The J. Paul Getty Trust. Rome: 'L'Erma' di Bretschneider, 2003b, 111.

18 Lazer, 1995, op. cit., Appendix 2, 376–79.

19 For example, see W.F. Jashemski, 'Pompeii and Mt Vesuvius AD 79', in *Volcanic Activity and Human Ecology*. Edited by P.D. Sheets and D.K. Grayson. New York: Academic Press, 1979b, 587–622.

20 J.-P. Descœudres, *Pompeii Revisited: The Life and Death of a Roman Town*, Sydney: Meditarch, 1994, 152–68; Lullies and Schiering, 1988, op. cit., 78–79; Mau, 1907, op. cit., 446–60; J.B. Ward-Perkins and A. Claridge. *Pompeii AD79: Treasures from the National*

Archaeological Museum, Naples and the Pompeii Antiquarium, Italy, 2nd edn. Sydney: Australian Gallery Directors' Council, 1980, 59–64.

21 For example, F.L. Bastet and M. De Vos, *Proposta per una Classificazione del Terzo Stile Pompeiano*. Translated by De Vos, A. Vol. 4, Archeologische Studien van het Nederlands Instituut te Rome. s-Gravenhage: Staatsuitgeverij, 1979; M.G. Cerulli Irelli, 'Der letzten Pompejanische stil', in *Pompejianische Wandmalerei*. Edited by G. Cerulli Irelli, M. Aoyagi and D. Stefano. Zürich: Belser, 1990, 233–38; Ehrhardt, 1987, op. cit.

22 Corti, 1951, op. cit., 201–2; Etienne, 1992, op. cit., 38–41; Trevelyan, 1976, op. cit., 95–97,107. See Chapter 11 for consideration of this issue in relation to the casts.

23 G. Luongo *et al.*, 'Impact of the AD 79 explosive eruption on Pompeii, II: Causes of death of the inhabitants inferred by stratigraphic analysis and areal distribution of the human casualties', *Journal of Volcanology and Geothermal Research*, Vol. 126, Nos 3–4, 2003: 169–200; S.C. Nappo, 'Il rinvenimento delle vittime dell'eruzione del 79 d.C. nella Regio 1 insula 22', *Hydria*, Vol. 63, No. 19, 1992: 16–18.

24 See, for example, Cooley, 2003, op. cit., 80–96; A. De Simone, 'Archaeology and science', in *Rediscovering Pompeii: IBM Gallery of Science and Art*. Edited by B. Conticello. Rome: 'L'Erma' di Bretschneider, 1990, 62–77.

25 Corti, 1951, op. cit., 117; Machiarelli pers. comm.

26 As demonstrated in the works of Brion, 1973, op. cit., 40; Corti, 1951, 117, 148, 158, 170–71,182,197; Gell, 1832, op. cit., 6, 44, 150–51,177; M. Grant, *Cities of Vesuvius: Pompeii and Herculaneum*, Middlesex: Penguin, 1976, 36–37; Gusman, 1900, op. cit., 15–16; Trevelyan, 1976, op. cit., 16.

27 A version of this section was originally published in Italian; see Lazer, 2003, op. cit., 64–69.

28 Ling, R., 'La Casa del Menandro', in *Menander: La Casa del Menandro di Pompei*. Edited by G. Stefani. Milan: Electa, 2003, 11.

29 A. Maiuri, *La Casa del Menandro e il Suo Tesoro di Argenteria*. Roma: La Libreria dello Stato, 1933, 11–12.

30 Ibid., 12.

31 Ibid.

32 Ibid.

33 P.M. Allison, 'The Distribution of Pompeiian House Contents and Its Significance. Vols. I and II', unpublished PhD thesis, School of Archaeology, Classics and Ancient History. Sydney: The University of Sydney, 1992, 170.

34 Maiuri, 1933, op. cit., 14.

35 E. Lazer, 'Human skeletal remains in the Casa del Menandro: Appendix F', in *The Insula of the Menander at Pompeii*. Edited by R. Ling. Oxford: Clarendon Press, 1997, 342–43; Lazer, 2003, op. cit.

36 For example, F.P. Maulucci, *Pompeii*, Naples: Carcavallo, 1987, 177.

37 Lazer, 1997, op. cit., 343.

38 Maiuri, 1933, op. cit., 13, Fig. 5.

39 Ibid.

40 For a summary of the literary evidence for this claim, see E.M. Moorman, 'Literary evocations of ancient Pompeii', in *Tales from an Eruption: Pompeii, Herculaneum, Oplontis: Guide to the Exhibition*. Edited by P.G. Guzzo. Milan: Electa, 2003, 20–24.

41 E. Bulwer-Lytton, *The Last Days of Pompeii*. New York: Putnam, 1897, 374–75.

42 Ibid.

43 E. Prettejohn, 'Recreating Rome: Catalogue II', in *Imagining Rome: British Artists and Rome in the Nineteenth Century*. Edited by M.J.H. Liversidge and C. Edwards. London: Merrell Holberton, 1996a, 126–28, illustrated on 126.

44 Cooley, 2003, op. cit., 85.

45 Dyer, 1883, 531.

46 Moormann, 2003, op. cit., 23–25.

47 For example, De Carolis and Patricelli, 2003b, op. cit., 113–14.

48 Civale in *Tales from an eruption* 2003: 95; De Carolis and Patricelli Vesuvius, 2003, op. cit., 115–17; Grant, 1976, op. cit., 36.

49 Bulwer-Lytton 1897, op. cit., 371–74.

50 A. Civale, 'Pompeii: The Temple of Isis', in *Tales from an Eruption: Pompeii, Herculaneum, Oplontis: Guide to the Exhibition*, ed. Guzzo, P.G. (Milan: Electa, 2003), p. 95.

51 Brion, 1973, op. cit., 38; De Carolis and Patricelli, 2003, op. cit., 114–15; Grant, 1976, op. cit., 37; Leppmann, 1968, op. cit., 75; Trevelyan, 1976, op. cit., 13; T. Rocco, 'The Quadriporticus of the theatres (VIII, 7, 16–17)', in *Storie da un'Eruzione: Pompei, Ercolano, Oplontis: Guida alla Mostra*. Edited by A. d'Ambrosio, P.G. Guzzo and M. Mastroroberto. Milano: Electa, 2003b, 99.

52 Rocco, 2003b, op. cit., 99.

53 This has been reviewed by various scholars, for example: Leppmann, 1968, op. cit., 129–54 and Moormann, 2003, op. cit., 14–33. Literary works that were based on human finds from Pompeii are discussed by Leppmann, 1968, op. cit., 129–54; Moormann, 2003, op. cit., and De Carolis and Patricelli 2003, op. cit., 110–11.

54 L. Alma Tadema, 1867, Cleveland Museum of Art, USA, Catalogue No. 1977.128.

55 C. Edwards, 'The roads to Rome', in *Imagining Rome: British Artists and Rome in the Nineteenth Century*, ed. M.J.H. Liversidge, and C. Edwards (London: Merrell Holberton, 1996), 14; Prettejohn, 1996, op. cit., 65, 127; M.J.H. Liversidge, 'Representing Rome: Catalogue I', in *Imagining Rome: British Artists and Rome in the Nineteenth Century*, ed. Liversidge, M.J.H. and C. Edwards. London: Merrell Holberton, 1996, 116–17.

56 F. Pesando, 'Shadows of light: Cinema, peplum and Pompeii', in *Tales from an Eruption: Pompeii, Herculaneum, Oplontis: Guide to the Exhibition*, ed. P.G. Guzzo. Milan: Electa, 2003, 35–42.

57 Bulwer-Lytton is particularly famous for the astonishing prose of his 1830 novel *Paul Clifford*, which starts with the words: 'It was a dark and stormy night; the rain fell in torrents – except at occasional intervals, when it was checked by a violent gust of wind which swept up the streets (for it is in London that our scene lies), rattling along the housetops, and fiercely agitating the scanty flame of the lamps that struggled against the darkness.' E. Bulwer-Lytton, *Paul Clifford*. London: Routledge, 1875, 1.

58 Bulwer-Lytton, 1897, op. cit., 95.

59 Bulwer-Lytton, 1897, op. cit., iii, v.

60 Ibid., 300; Leppmann, 1968, op. cit., 136.

61 S.J. Gould, *The Mismeasure of Man*. Middlesex: Pelican, 1984, 92; Bulwer-Lytton, 1897, op. cit., 300.

62 Ibid., 392; T. Rocco, 'The Villa of Diomedes', in *Tales from an Eruption: Pompeii, Herculaneum, Oplontis: Guide to the Exhibition*. Edited by P.G. Guzzo. Milan: Electa, 2003a, 92.

63 Moormann, 2003, op. cit., 15.

64 T. Gautier, *Arria Marcella: A Souvenir of Pompeii*. Translated by De Sumichrast, F.C. New York: C.T. Brainard, 1901, 316.

65 Ibid., 328.

66 Ibid., 334.

67 Ibid., 335.

68 Ibid., 340–43.

69 Ibid., 355.

70 Ibid., 356.

71 Ibid., 361–62.

72 Ibid., 363–64.

73 Ibid., 366.

74 Leppmann, 1968, op. cit., 135–36; Rocco, 2003a, op. cit., 92.

75 Various claims have been made for the number of bodies in this house. Depending on the publication, the number generally ranges between 11 and 22 bodies. Though Corti (1951,

op. cit., 73) claimed that 34 people and one goat met their deaths in this villa the larger figure is probably more accurate. See Moormann, 2003, op. cit., 25 and Rocco, 2003a, op. cit., 92.

76 Ibid.

77 Bulwer-Lytton, 1897, op. cit., xi.

78 Bulwer-Lytton, 1897, op. cit., 304 n. V (a).

79 J.L. Campbell, *Edward Bulwer-Lytton*. Boston: Twayne, 1986, 4–5, 21, 72, 132; Leppmann, 1968, op. cit., 132, 136.

80 Clay and Frederikson, 1976, op. cit., 155. Bulwer-Lytton's novel inspired works in a number of media, including painting, opera, pyrodramas and films (See M. Wyke, *Projecting the Past: Ancient Rome, Cinema, and History*. London: Routledge, 1997, 147–82.) That *The Last Days of Pompeii* has continued to exert an influence on the popular imagination can be seen in the fact that the most recent film version was made at Pompeii in 1985, starring major actors including Franco Nero and Laurence Olivier.

81 Anonymous quoted in Dyer, 1883, op. cit., 477.

82 Corti, 1951, op. cit., 69–78.

83 P. Ciprotti, 'Der letzte tag von Pompeji', *Altertum,* Vol. 10, 1964, 47–48, 51, 53, 54.

84 S.C. Bisel and J.F. Bisel, 'Health and nutrition at Herculaneum: An examination of human skeletal remains', in *The Natural History of Pompeii*. Edited by W.F. Jashemski, and F.G. Meyer. Cambridge: Cambridge University Press, 2002, 451; S.C. Bisel *et al.*, *The Secrets of Vesuvius*. Toronto: Madison Press, 1990, 10–11.

85 For example, Bisel and Bisel, 2002, op. cit.

86 Bisel *et al.*, 1990, op. cit.

87 Bisel *et al.*, 1990, op. cit., 14, 43; Bulwer-Lytton, 1897, op. cit., 155, 285–86.

88 R. Gore, 'After 2000 years of silence: The dead do tell tales at Vesuvius', *National Geographic,* Vol. 165, No. 5, 1984, 556–613; G.M. Grosvenor, 'An exciting year of discovery', *National Geographic,* Vol. 162, No. 6, 1982, 820–21; J. Judge, 'On the slope of Vesuvius a buried town gives up its dead', *National Geographic,* Vol. 162, No. 6, 1982: 686–93.

89 J.J. Deiss, *Herculaneum: Italy's Buried Treasure*. 2nd edn. New York: Harper & Row, 1985, 194; Gore, 1984, op. cit., 572–73, 588–89, 600, 604–5.

90 Gore, 1984, op. cit., 597–600.

91 Suetonius, *The Twelve Caesars*. Translated by R. Graves. Middlesex: Penguin, 1957, Augustus, 79.

92 D.R. Brothwell, *The Bog Man and the Archaeology of People*. London: British Museum Publications, 1986, 110; J. Hay, *Ancient China*. London: Bodley Head, 1973, 94–99; T. H.G. Oettlé (former Director of the New South Wales Forensic Institute, Sydney) to E. Lazer, 1983, personal communication.

93 C. Renfrew and P. Bahn, *Archaeology: Theory, Methods and Practice*. London: Thames & Hudson, 1991, 175–76.

94 Bisel *et al.*, 1990, op. cit., 23.

95 A.L. Zihlman, *The Human Evolution Colouring Book*. New York: Barnes & Noble, 1982, 105.

96 S.C. Bisel to E. Lazer 1988c, Physical anthropologist, Herculaneum.

97 Deiss, 1985, op. cit., 189–96.

98 Maiuri in Deiss, 1985, op. cit., xii.

99 S.C. Bisel, 'The skeletons of Herculaneum, Italy', in *Wet Site Archaeology: Proceedings of the International Conference on Wet Site Archaeology, Gainesville, Florida, December 12–14, 1986; sponsored by the National Endowment for the Humanities and University of Florida*. Edited by B. A. Purdy. Caldwell, New Jersey: Telford Press, 1988b, 209.

100 Bisel, 1988b, op. cit. 209–10; Bisel and Bisel, 2002, op. cit., 468, (Erc 26).

101 S.C. Bisel, 'Human bones at Herculaneum', *Rivista di Studi Pompeiani*, Vol. 1, 1987, 127–28; S.C. Bisel, 'The human skeletons of Herculaneum', *International Journal of Anthropology,* Vol. 6, No. 1, 1991, 14, 16.

102 Bisel, 1987, op. cit., 127.

103 Bisel, 1988b, op. cit., 65.

104 Bisel and Bisel, 2002, op. cit.

105 As can be seen, for example, in C. Pellegrino, *Ghosts of Vesuvius: A New Look at the Last Days of Pompeii, How Towers Fall and Other Strange Connections*. New York: William Morrow, 2004, 219–28.

106 P. Wilkinson, *Pompeii: The Last Day*. London: BBC Books, 2003, 158–59.

107 Wilkinson, 2003, op. cit., 159.

108 A. Butterworth and A. Laurence. *Pompeii: The Living City*. London: Weidenfeld & Nicolson, 2005, 304–6.

109 A. Civale, 'Pompeii: The house of Julius Polybius (IX, 13, 1–3)', in *Tales from an Eruption: Pompeii, Herculaneum, Oplontis: Guide to the Exhibition*. Edited by P.G. Guzzo. Milan: Electa, 2003e, 163.

110 Ibid.

111 G. Di Bernardo *et al.*, 'Analisi dei reperti ossei della Casa Grado di conservazione ed amplificazione del DNA antico', in *La Casa di Giulio Polibio: Studi Interdisciplinari*. Edited by A. Ciarollo and E. De Carolis. Pompeo: Centro Studi arti Figurative, Università di Tokio, 2001, 79–91; M. Henneberg, and R. Henneberg, 'Skeletal material from the house of C. Iulius Polybius in Pompei, 79 AD', in *La Casa di Giulio Polibio: Studi Interdisciplinari*. Edited by A. Ciarallo and E. De Carolas. Pompei: Centro Studi arti Figurative, Università di Tokio, 2001, 79–92; P. Oriente *et al.*, 'Studio della densità minerale ossea negli scheletri di età Romana rinvenuti in Pompei nella Casa di Polibio', in *La Casa di Giulio Polibio: Studi Interdisciplinari*. Edited by A. Ciarallo and E. De Carolas. Pompei: Centro Studi arti Figurative, Università di Tokio, 2001, 107–10; M. Torino and G. Fornaciari, 'Paleopatologia degli individui nella Casa di Giulio Polibio', in *La Casa di Giulio Polibio: Studi Interdisciplinari*. Edited by A. Ciarallo and E. De Carolis. Pompei: Centro Studi arti Figurative, Università di Tokio, 2001, 93–106.

112 Bernardo *et al.*, 2001, op. cit.; M. Cipollaro *et al.*, 'Histological analysis and ancient DNA amplification of human bone remains found in Caius Iulius Polybius House in Pompeii', *Croatian Medical Journal*, Vol. 40, No. 3, 1999a: 392–97.

113 Henneberg and Henneberg, 2001, op. cit., 80–85.

114 Henneberg and Henneberg, 2001, op. cit., 81–82, 84.

115 A.C. Aufderheide and C. Rodriguez-Martin. *The Cambridge Encyclopaedia of Human Palaeopathology*. Cambridge: Cambridge University Press, 1998, 61–62; C. Roberts, and K. Manchester. *The Archaeology of Disease*. 2nd edn. Ithaca, New York: Cornell University Press, 1995, 36; T.W. Sadler, *Langman's Medical Embryology*. 10th edn. Philadelphia: Lippincott Williams & Wilkins, 2006, 293–94.

116 Henneberg and Henneberg, 2001, op. cit., 84.

117 This assumption has been used by various scholars to reconstruct the number of pregnancies that had come to term in Pompeii and Herculaneum. See, for example, Bisel and Bisel, 2002, op. cit., 461, 467, 472; L. Capasso, *I Fuggiaschi di Ercolano: Paleobiologia delle Vittime dell'Eruzione Vesuviana del 79 d.C.* Roma: 'L'Erma' di Bretschneider, 2001, 973–78; M. Henneberg *et al.*, 'Skeletal material from the house of C. Iulius Polybius in Pompeii, 79 AD', *Human Evolution,* Vol. 11, No. 3, 1996: 255.

118 M.A. Kelley, 'Parturition and pelvic changes', *American Journal of Physical Anthropology*, Vol. 51, 1979, 545.

119 Butterworth and Laurence, 2005, op. cit., 297.

120 Butterworth and Laurence, 2005, op. cit., 305.

2 An Egyptian interlude

1 A.C. Aufderheide, *The Scientific Study of Mummies*. Cambridge: Cambridge University Press, 2003, 515–18; A. Cockburn *et al.* (eds), *Mummies, Disease and Ancient Cultures.*

22 A. Busignani, *Botticelli: The Life and Work of the Artist*. London: Thames & Hudson, 1968, pl 26–32; M. Rosci, *Leonardo*. New York: Mayflower Books, 1981, 129, 148.

23 Hartman 1876 in Nicolucci, 1882, op. cit., 23; Nicolucci, 1882, op. cit., 21–22; Retzius 1864 in Nicolucci, 1882, op. cit., 23.

24 See, for example, Gould, 1984, op. cit., 24–26, 35, 74.

25 A.M. Brues, *People and Races*. New York: Macmillan, 1977, 232; S.J. Gould, 'Morton's ranking of races by cranial capacity: Unconscious manipulation of data may be a scientific norm', *Science*, Vol. 200, No. 43, 41, 1978, 503; Gould, 1984, op. cit., 89–112; Morton, S.G. *Crania Aegyptiaca; or Observations on Egyptian Ethnography Derived from Anatomy, History and the Monuments*. Philadelphia: John Pennington, 1844.

26 Gould, 1978, op. cit., 505; Gould, 1984, op. cit., 53–54.

27 J.L. Angel, 'A racial analysis of the ancient Greeks: An essay on the use of morphological types', *American Journal of Physical Anthropology*, Vol. 2, 1944, 329–76; Angel, 1945, op. cit., 279–363; J.L. Angel, 'Skeletal change in ancient Greece', *American Journal of Physical Anthropology*, Vol. 4, 1946, 69–97; M.F. Ashley Montagu, *Man's Most Dangerous Myth: The Fallacy of Race*. 3rd edn. New York: Harper & Brothers, 1952, 34; C.M. Fürst, 'Zur anthropologie der prähistorischen Griechen in Argolis', *Lunds Arsskrift*, Vol. 26, No. 8, 1930, 130; C.M. Fürst, 'Zur Kenntniss der anthropologie prähistorischen bevölkerung der Insel Cypern', *Lunds Arsskrift*, Vol. 29, No. 6, 1933, 1–106; S.J. Gould, 'The geometer of race,' *Discover*, Vol. 15, No. 11, 1994, 65, 67; Nicolucci, 1882, op. cit., 12; S.R. Saunders, 'Nonmetric skeletal variation', in *Reconstruction of Life from the Skeleton* ed. M.Y. Iscan and K.A.R. Kennedy. New York: Alan R. Liss, 1989, 95–96.

28 Ashley Montagu, 1952, op. cit., 34; D.C. Cook, 'The old physical anthropology and the New World: A look at the accomplishments of an antiquated paradigm', in *Bioarchaeology: The Contextual Analysis of Human Remains*, ed. J.E. Buikstra and L.A. Beck. Amsterdam: Academic Press, 2006, 29–34; J. Diamond, 'Race without colour', *Discover*, Vol. 15, No. 11, 1994, 82–89; J. Ferguson, 'The laboratory of racism', *New Scientist*, Vol. 103, 1984, 18; Gould, 1984, op. cit., 50–69; S.G. Morton, *Crania Americana or, a Comparative View of the Skulls of Various Aboriginal Nations of North and South America*. Philadelphia: John Pennington, 1839.

29 F. Boas, 'Changes in bodily form of descendants of immigrants (reprint of 1912 article)', in *Frontiers of Anthropology*, ed. M.F. Ashley Montagu. New York: Capricorn Books, 1974, 321–32; Ferguson, 1984, op. cit. Subsequent studies in different parts of the world have confirmed the plasticity of certain traits as a result of altered environment for example Ashley Montagu, 1952, op. cit., 4; P.M. Buzarbaruah, 'Changes in anthropometric measurements due to migration and environment: A preliminary observation', *Anthropologie*, Vol. 30, No. 2, 1992: 189–95; C.C. Gravlee *et al.*, 'Boas's changes in bodily form: The immigrant study, cranial plasticity, and Boas's physical anthropology', *American Anthropologist*, Vol. 105, No. 2, 2003, 326–32; C.U.A. Kappers, and L.W. Parr, *An Introduction to the Anthropology of the Near East in Ancient and Recent Times*. Amsterdam: Noord–Hollandsche uitgeversmaatschappij, 1934, 5; A.L. Kroeber, 1948, op. cit., 167–68.

30 L.E. St Hoyme and M.Y. Iscan, 'Determination of sex and race: Accuracy and assumptions' in *Reconstruction of Life from the Skeleton*, ed. M.Y. Iscan and K.A.R. Kennedy. New York: Alan R. Liss, 1989, 56. For the validity of European racial classification, especially for the so-called European races compare with W.Z. Ripley, *The Races of Europe: A Sociological Study*. London: Kegan Paul, 1899. This issue is discussed at length by Ashley Montagu, 1952, op. cit., M.F. Ashley Montagu (ed.), *The Concept of Race*. New York: Free Press, 1964; W.C. Boyd, *Genetics and the Races of Man*. Boston: Little, Brown & Co., 1950, 3–26; C.S. Coon, *The Origin of Races*. London: Jonathan Cape, 1963; C.S. Coon, and E.E. Hunt (eds), *The Living Races of Man*. (London: Jonathan Cape, 1965; C. D'Amore *et al.*, 'Primi risultati degli studi sull'antropologia Pompeiana del 79 d.C.', in *La Regione Sotterrata dal Vesuvio: Studi e Prospettive, Atti del Convegno Internazionale 11–15 Novembre 1979*. Napoli: Università degli Studi, 1982, 927–43.

31 T.D. White and P.A. Folkens, *The Human Bone Manual*. Boston: Academic Press, 2005, 400–403; also for discussion of the 'race concept' and its impact on physical anthropology, see M. Cartmill, and K. Brown, 'Surveying the race concept: A reply to Lieberman, Kirk, and Littlefield', *American Anthropologist*, Vol. 105, No. 1, 2003, 114–15; R. Caspari, 'From types to populations: A century of race, physical anthropology, and the American Anthropological Association', *American Anthropologist*, Vol. 105, No. 1, 2003, 65–76; K.A. Kaszycka, and J. Strziko. '"Race" – Still an issue for physical anthropology? Results of Polish studies seen in the light of the US findings', *American Anthropologist*, Vol. 105, No. 1, 2003, 116–24; L. Lieberman, *et al.*, 'Exchange across difference: The status of the race concept – Perishing paradigm: Race – 1931–99', *American Anthropologist*, Vol. 105, No. 1, 2003, 110–13.

32 N.A. Barnicot and D.R. Brothwell, 'The evaluation of metrical data in the comparison of ancient and modern bones', in *CIBA Foundation Symposium on Medical Biology and Etruscan Origins*, ed. G.E.W. Wolstenholme and C.M. O'Connor. London: J. & A. Churchill, 1959, 131–48.

33 Barnicott and Brothwell, 1959, op. cit., 136, 138.

34 C. D'Amore *et al.*, 'Antropologia pompeiana del 79 d.C.: Sesso ed età di morte', *Archivio per l'Antropologia e la Etnologia*, Vol. 109, 1979, 298, 300–301, 304; D'Amore *et al.*, 1982, op. cit., 928. For a short discussion on the importance of the skull as a basis of most physical anthropological studies until the latter part of the twentieth century see W.M. Krogman, *The Human Skeleton in Forensic Medicine*. Springfield, Illinois: Charles C. Thomas, 1962, 114.

35 D'Amore *et al.*, 1982, op. cit., 927.

36 D'Amore *et al.*, 1979, op. cit., 300–301; D'Amore *et al.*, 1982, op. cit., 928.

37 D'Amore *et al.*, 1979, op. cit., 297–308; D'Amore, *et al.*, 1982, op. cit., 929; Nicolucci, 1882, op. cit., 10.

38 D'Amore, *et al.*, 1982, op. cit., 927–38.

39 Ibid.

40 For example, M. Cipollaro *et al.*, 'Ancient DNA in human bone remains from Pompeii archaeological site,' *Biochemical and Biophysical Research Communications,* Vol. 247, 1999b, 901–4; G. Di Bernardo *et al.*, 'Analisi dei reperti ossei della Casa Grado di conservazione ed amplificazione del DNA antico', in *La Casa di Giulio Polibio: Studi Interdisciplinari*, ed. A. Ciarollo and E. De Carolis. Pompeo: Centro Studi arti Figurative, Università di Tokio, 2001, 79–91; H. Etani *et al.*, 'La campagna di scavo del Japan Institute of Palaeological Studies di Kyoto del 2002', *Opuscula Pompeiana*, Vol. 12, 2004, 125–37; F.M. Guarino *et al.*, 'Bone preservation in human remains from the Terme del Sarno at Pompeii using light microscopy and scanning electron microscopy', *Journal of Archaeological Science,* Vol. 33, 2006: 513–20; M. Henneberg, and R. Henneberg, 'Skeletal material from the house of C. Iulius Polybius in Pompei, 79 AD', in *La Casa di Giulio Polibio: Studi Interdisciplinari*, ed. A. Ciarallo and E. De Carolis. Pompei: Centro Studi arti Figurative, Università di Tokio, 2001, 79–92; M. Henneberg and R.J. Henneberg, 'Reconstructing medical knowledge in ancient Pompeii from the hard evidence of bones and teeth', presented at a conference at Deutsches Museum, Munich 21–22 March 2000, in *Homo Faber: Studies in Nature, Technology and Science at the Time of Pompeii*, ed. Renn, J. and G. Castagnetti. Roma: L'Erma di Bretschneider, 2002, 169–87; M. Henneberg *et al.*, 'Skeletal material from the house of C. Iulius Polybius in Pompeii, 79 AD', *Human Evolution*, Vol. 11, No. 3, 1996, 249–59; P. Oriente *et al.*, 'Studio della densità minerale ossea negli scheletri di età Romana rinvenuti in Pompei nella Casa di Polibio,' in *La Casa di Giulio Polibio: Studi Interdisciplinari*, ed. A. Ciarallo and E. De Carolas. Pompei: Centro Studi arti Figurative, Università di Tokio, 2001, 107–10; M. Torino and G. Fornaciari, 'Paleopatologia degli individui nella Casa di Giulio Polibio', in *La Casa di Giulio Polibio: Studi Interdisciplinari*, ed. Ciarallo, A. and E. De Carolis. Pompei: Centro Studi arti Figurative, Università di Tokio, 2001, 93–106.

41 S.C. Bisel, 'The Herculaneum Project: Preliminary Report', *Palaeopathology Newsletter*, Vol. 41, 1983, 6–7; S.C. Bisel, 'Human bones at Herculaneum', *Rivista di Studi Pompeiani*, Vol. 1 1987, 123–31; S.C. Bisel, 'The human skeletons of Herculaneum,' *International Journal of Anthropology*, Vol. 6, No. 1, 1991, 1–20; S.C. Bisel, 'Nutrition in first century Herculaneum', *Anthropologie*, Vol. 26 1988a: 61–66; S.C. Bisel, 'The people of Herculaneum', *Helmartica*, Vol. 37, 1986, 11–23; S.C. Bisel, 'The skeletons of Herculaneum, Italy', in *Wet Site Archaeology: Proceedings of the International Conference on Wet Site Archaeology, Gainesville, Florida, December 12–14, 1986; sponsored by the National Endowment for the Humanities and University of Florida*, ed. Purdy, B.A. Caldwell, New Jersey: Telford Press, 1988b; S.C. Bisel and J.F. Bisel, 'Health and nutrition at Herculaneum: An examination of human skeletal remains', in *The Natural History of Pompeii*, ed. W.F. Jashemski and F.G. Meyer. Cambridge: Cambridge University Press, 2002, 451–75; L. Capasso, *I Fuggiaschi di Ercolano: Paleobiologia delle Vittime dell'Eruzione Vesuviana del 79 d.C.* Roma: "L'Erma" di Bretschneider, 2001, 11; M. Pagano, 'L'antica Ercolano,' in *Vesuvio 79 AD: Vita e Morte ad Ercolano*, ed. Petrone, P.P. and F. Fedele. Naples: Fredericiana Editrice Universitaria, 2002, 55–66; P.P. Petrone *et al.*, 'La popolazione di Ercolano', in *Vesuvio 79 AD: Vita e Morte ad Ercolano*, ed. P.P. Petrone and F. Fedele. Naples: Fredericiana Editrice Universitaria, 2002, 70; P.P. Petrone, 'Le vittime dell'eruzione del 79 AD', in *Storie da un'eruzione. In margine alla mostra, Atti della Tavola Rotonda, Napoli, 2003, Associazione Internazionale Amici di Pompei, Dipartimento di Discipline Storiche, Università degli Studi di Napoli Federico II*, ed. P.G. Guzzo. Pompei: Litografia Sicignano, 2005, 31; Sigurdsson, 1985, op. cit., 364.
42 D.C. Cook and M.L. Powell, 'The evolution of American paleopathology,' in *Bioarchaeology: The Contextual Analysis of Human Remains*, ed. J.E. Buikstra and L.A. Beck. Amsterdam: Academic Press, 2006, 300. See also Chapter 8.
43 S.C. Bisel (Physical anthropologist, Herculaneum) to E. Lazer., 1988c, personal communication.
44 Bisel and Bisel, 2002, op. cit., 451.
45 Capasso, 2001, op. cit.
46 For example, see Torino and Fornaciari, 2000, op. cit., 60–63.
47 Capasso, 2001, op. cit., 7–8.
48 For example, L. Capasso, 'Indoor pollution and respiratory diseases in ancient Rome', *The Lancet*, Vol. 356, No. 9243, 2000b, 1774; L. Capasso and G. Di Tota, 'Tuberculosis in Herculaneum (AD 79)', in *Tuberculosis Past and Present*, ed. G. Pálfi, O. Dutour, J. Deák and I. Hutás. Budapest: Golden Books & Tuberculosis Foundation, 1999, 463–67; L. Capasso, 'Infectious diseases and eating habits at Herculaneum (1st century AD, Southern Italy),' *International Journal of Osteoarchaeology*, Vol. 17, No. 4, 2007, 350–57.
49 P.P. Petrone *et al.*, 'La popolazione di Ercolano,' in *Vesuvio 79 AD: Vita e Morte ad Ercolano*, ed. Petrone, P.P. and F. Fedele. Naples: Fredericiana Editrice Universitaria, 2002, 67–73; P.P. Petrone, L. Fattore and V. Monetti, 'Alimentazione e malattie ad Ercolano', in *Vesuvio79 AD: Vita e Morte ad Ercolano*, ed. P.P. Petrone and F. Fedele. Naples: Fredericiana Editrice Universitaria, 2002, 75–83.
50 P.P. Petrone to E. Lazer, 2008, personal communication.

4 Context of a mass disaster

1 R. Ascher, 'Analogy in archaeological interpretation', *SouthWestern Journal of Anthropology*, Vol. 17, 1961, 324; L.R. Binford, 'Behavioural archaeology and the "Pompeii Premise" in archaeology', *Journal of Anthropological Research*, Vol. 37, 1981: 195–208; but also see M.B. Schiffer, *Formation Processes of the Archaeological Record*. Albuquerque, New Mexico: University of New Mexico, 1987, 237; M.B. Schiffer, 'Is there a "Pompeii Premise" in archaeology?', *Journal of Anthropological Research*, Vol. 41, 1985, 18–41. The concept of the 'Pompeii Premise' can be traced back to Ascher, an archaeologist who had never worked

on the sites destroyed by the AD 79 eruption and did not appreciate their complexity and who apparently only had limited contact with the academic literature on Pompeii. This is also the case for the other proponents of the Pompeii Premise. This is suggested by the bibliographies of Binford, 1981, op. cit., 207–8; and Schiffer, 1985, op. cit. 39–41.

2 This skeleton was found on 19 April 1748. E.C.C. Corti, *The Destruction and Resurrection of Pompeii and Herculaneum*. Translated by K. Smith and R.G. Smith. London: Routledge & Kegan Paul, 1951, 117.

3 E.C.C. Corti, *The Destruction and Resurrection of Pompeii and Herculaneum*. Trans. K. Smith and R.G. Smith. London: Routledge & Kegan Paul, 1951, 135–36; M. Grant, *Cities of Vesuvius: Pompeii and Herculaneum*. Middlesex: Penguin, 1976, 31.

4 In one passage she describes the site as a reflection of the last moments of the town. De Staël in W. Leppmann, *Pompeii in Fact and Fiction*. London: Elek, 1968, 106.

5 For example, P.M. Allison, 'Artefact assemblages: Not the "Pompeii Premise"', in *Papers of the Fourth Conference of Italian Archaeology, University of London, 1990*, ed. E. Herring, R. Whitehouse and J. Wilkins. London: Accordia Research Centre, 1992a, 49; P.M. Allison, *Pompeian Households: An Analysis of the Material Culture*, Monograph 42. Los Angeles: Cotsen Institute for Archaeology, University of California, 2004, 4; A.E. Cooley, *Pompeii*. London: Duckworth, 2003, 13.

6 For example, J.W. Alexander, 'The impact of discoveries', in *The Buried Cities and the Eruption of Vesuvius: The 1900th Anniversary*, ed. H.W. Benario and G.W. Lawall. Amherst: NECN & University of Massachusetts, 1979, 26; W. Jongman, P.W. De Neeve and H.W. Pleket (eds), *The Economy and Society of Pompeii*. Vol. 4, Dutch Monographs on Ancient History and Archaeology. Amsterdam: J.C. Gieber, 1988, 55–56.

7 J.-P. Descœudres, 'Rome and Roman art', in *The Enduring Past: Archaeology of the Ancient World for Australians*, ed. A. Cremin. Sydney: NSW University Press, 1987, 174.

8 Seneca, 'Naturales Quaestiones', in *Loeb Classical Library*. Cambridge, Massachusetts: Harvard University Press, 1972, VI, 1.1–3, 10; VI.27.1,VI.31.

9 Tacitus, 'Annals of Imperial Rome'. Trans. B. Radice and R. Baldick. Middlesex: Penguin, 1971, 22.

10 P.M. Allison, 'The Distribution of Pompeiian House Contents and its Significance. Vols. I and II', unpublished PhD thesis, School of Archaeology, Classics and Ancient History. Sydney: University of Sydney, 1992b, 5; P.M. Allison, *Pompeian Households: An Analysis of the Material Culture*, Monograph 42. Los Angeles: Cotsen Institute for Archaeology, University of California, 2004, 17–18; J. Andreau, 'Il terremoto del 62', in *Pompei 79: Raccolta di Studi per il Decimonono Centenario dell'Eruzione Vesuviana*, ed. F. Zevi. Napoli: Gaetano Macchiaroli, 1979, 40; H.W. Benario, 'The land, the cities, the event', in *The Buried Cities and the Eruption of Vesuvius: The 1900th Anniversary*, ed. Benario, H.W. and G.W. Lawall, *Lectures presented at Emory University on May 7, 1979 in a symposium sponsored by the Dept. of Modern Languages and Classics, Alpha Sigma chapter of Eta Sigma Phi, and the Atlanta Society of the Archaeological Institute of America*. Amherst: NECN & University of Massachusetts, 1979, 3; A.E. Cooley, *Pompeii*. London: Duckworth, 2003, 127, note 4; L. Richardson, *Pompeii: An Architectural History*. Baltimore: Johns Hopkins University Press, 1988, xxi, 18. The discrepancy is the result of the different consular dates given by Seneca, op. cit., 6, 1, 2; and Tacitus, op. cit., 15, 22. The event was dated to AD 63 by Seneca and AD 62 by Tacitus. The AD 62 date is now most commonly accepted by scholars.

11 Allison, op. cit. 1992b, 8–9; Andreau, 1979, op. cit., 40–44; M. Brion, *Pompeii and Herculaneum: The Glory and the Grief*. London: Cardinal, 1973/1960, 21–24; Corti, 1951, op. cit., 44–45, 48; Corti, 1951, op. cit., 44–45, 48; J.-P. Descœudres, 'A brief history of Pompeii', in *Pompeii Revisited: The Life and Death of a Roman Town*, ed. D. Harrison. Sydney: Meditarch, 1994a, 34–37; L. Richardson, 'Life as it appeared when Vesuvius engulfed Pompeii', *Smithsonian*, Vol. 9, No. 1, 1978, 84, 86; L. Richardson, *Pompeii: An Architectural History*. Baltimore: Johns Hopkins University Press, 1988, xxi–xxii, 18–22.

12 CIL X 846 = ILS 6367. For the full inscription see A.E. Cooley and M.G.L. Cooley. *Pompeii: A Sourcebook*. London: Routledge, 2004, 31.

13 For an illustration, see Cooley and Cooley, 2004. op. cit., 30.

14 Allison, 1992b, 86–97; P.M. Allison, 'On-going seismic activity and its effects on the living conditions in Pompeii in the last decades', in *La Regione Vesuviana dal 62 al 79 d. C.: Problemi Archeologici e Sismologici*, ed. Frölich, T. and L. Jacobelli. Munich: 1995, 162–69; Allison, 2004, op. cit., 17–19; Cooley, 2003, op. cit., 23; E. De Carolis, and G. Patricelli. *Vesuvius, AD 79: The Destruction of Pompeii and Herculaneum*. Translated by The J. Paul Getty Trust. Rome: 'L'Erma' di Bretschneider, 2003b, 71–76; J.-P. Descœudres, 'Did some Pompeians return to their city after the eruption of Mt. Vesuvius in AD 79? Observations in the house of the coloured capitals,' in *Ercolano 1738–1988: 250 Anni di Ricerca Archeologica*, ed. L.F. Dell'Orto. Rome: 'L'Erma' di Bretschneider, 1993, 173; Descoeudres, op. cit., 1994a, 35.

15 For example by Allison, 1992a, op. cit., Allison, 1995, op. cit.

16 Seneca, op. cit., VI,12.

17 Suetonius, 'The Twelve Caesars.' Middlesex: Penguin, 1957, Nero, 20.

18 Seneca, op. cit., XV, 34:1.

19 Pliny the Younger, 'Letters and Panegyrics', in *Loeb Classical Library*. Cambridge, Massachusetts: Harvard University Press, 1969, VI, 20.

20 See, for example, Allison, 2004, op. cit., 17–19; Cooley, 2003, op. cit., 23–25.

21 For example R.J. Blong, *Volcanic Hazards: A Sourcebook on the Effects of Eruptions*. Sydney: Academic Press, 1984, 189; F.M. Bullard, *Volcanoes of the Earth*. Austin: University of Texas Press, 1984, 190; P. Francis, *Volcanoes: A Planetary Perspective*. Oxford: Clarendon Press, 1993, 65, 67; H. Sigurdsson, and S.N. Carey, 'The eruption of Vesuvius in AD 79', in *The Natural History of Pompeii*, ed. W.F. Jashemski, and F.G. Meyer. Cambridge: Cambridge University Press, 2002, 33–34.

22 Allison, 1992b, op. cit., 10; Allison, 2004, op. cit., 17; K. Schefold, *Die Wände Pompejis*. Berlin: Topographisches Verzeichnis der Bildemotive, 1957, 152.

23 Allison, 1992b, op. cit., 86–97; Allison, 1995, op. cit., 162–69; Allison, 2004, op. cit., 16–19. Other studies that provide convincing evidence of repairs resulting from continued seismic events between AD 62 and 79 are summarized by Cooley, 2003, op. cit., 23.

24 De Carolis and Patricelli, 2003b, op. cit., 75–76 also conclude that the archaeological record supports the notion of a series of earthquakes between AD 62 and 79.

25 Allison, 1992b, op. cit., 86, Allison, 1995, op. cit., 162; Allison, 2004, op. cit., 201–3.

26 D.K. Grayson and P.D. Sheets, 'Volcanic disasters and the archaeological record', in *Volcanic Activity and Human Ecology*, ed. P.D. Sheets and D.K. Grayson. New York: Academic Press, 1979, 626–27.

27 Though see Allison, 1992b, op. cit., 97; Allison, 2004, op. cit., 202–3.

28 M. Biddle, 'The archaeology of Winchester', *Scientific American*, Vol. 230, No. 5, 1974: 35–43.

29 Seneca, op. cit., VI, I, 10–12.

30 Leppmann, 1968, op. cit., 73.

31 Lippi and Tondi in P. Ciprotti, 'Der letzte tag von Pompeji', *Altertum*, Vol. 10, 1964, 40.

32 For example, Allison, 1992b, op. cit., 97; Allison, 2004, op. cit., 20; Corti, 1951, op. cit., 46–47; A. Maiuri, *La Casa del Menandro e il Suo Tesoro di Argenteria*. Roma: La Libreria dello Stato, 1933, 11–16.

33 For example, by Corti, 1951, op. cit., 82–83; Richardson, 1988, op. cit., 25–27.

34 For example, Allison, 1992b, op. cit., 97; Descœudres, 1993, op. cit., 173. Though for an alternative view see Cooley, 2003, op. cit., 34.

35 Maggi in R. Gore, 'After 2000 years of silence: The dead do tell tales at Vesuvius', *National Geographic*, Vol. 165, No. 5, 1984: 570.

36 Cooley, 2003, op. cit., 25–35; J.J. Dobbins, 'Problems of chronology, decoration and urban design in the forum at Pompeii', *American Journal of Archaeology*, Vol. 98, 1994,

629–94; J.J. Dobbins, 'The Pompeii Forum Project 1994–95', in *Sequence and Space in Pompeii*, ed. S.E. Bon and R. Jones. Oxford: Oxbow Monograph 77, 1997, 86. Though Allison, 2004, op. cit., 21 argues that the evidence is complex and conflicting and that further investigation is required before conclusions can be drawn.

37 De Carolis and Patricelli, 2003b, op. cit., 76.

38 For W. Engelmann, *New Guide to Pompeii*. Leipzig: Wilhelm Engelmann, 1925, 2; R. Etienne, *Pompeii: The Day a City Died*. Translated by C. Palmer. London: Thames & Hudson, 1992, 44.

39 Strabo, op. cit. (V, iv, 8).

40 P. Carafa, 'Recent work on early Pompeii', in *The World of Pompeii*, ed. J.J. Dobbins and P.W. Foss. London: Routledge, 2007, 63–72; W. Engelmann, *New Guide to Pompeii*. Leipzig: Wilhelm Engelmann, 1925, 2; W.F. Jashemski, *The Gardens of Pompeii, Herculaneum and the Villas Destroyed by Vesuvius*. New York: Caratzas Brothers, 1979a, 4; J.B. Ward-Perkins and A. Claridge. *Pompeii AD 79: Treasures from the National Archaeological Museum, Naples and the Pompeii Antiquarium, Italy*. 2nd edn. Sydney: Australian Gallery Directors' Council, 1980, 11.

41 J.A.K. De Waele, 'The "doric" temple in the Forum Triangulare', in *Pompeii, Opuscula Pompeiana, III* (1993), 112; Engelmann, 1925, op. cit., 2; Etienne, 1992, op. cit., 44; Grant, 1976, op. cit., 15, 17.

42 De Waele, 1993, op. cit., 108–13.

43 Brion, 1973, op. cit., 11–17; Cooley, 2003, op. cit., 17–19.; Cooley and Cooley, 2004, op. cit., 17; Engelmann, 1925, op. cit., 2–3; Etienne, 1992, op. cit., 44, 48–49; Grant, 1976, op. cit., 15, 17, 20, 22–23; Jashemski, 1979a, op. cit., 4; P. Wilkinson, *Pompeii: The Last Day*. London: BBC Books, 2003, 8–14.

44 For example, by A. Maiuri, *Pompeii: The New Excavations, the Villa dei Misteri, the Antiquarium*. Translated by Priestley, V. 7th ed. Roma: Istituto Poligrafico dello Stato, 1962, 17; A. Mau, *Pompeii: Its Life and Art*. Translated by F.W. Kelsey, 1907 edn. London: Macmillan, 1907, 16; G. Nicolucci, 'Crania Pompeiana: Descrizione de' crani umani rinvenuti fra le ruine dell' antica Pompei', *Atti della R. Accademia delle Scienze Fisiche e Matematiche,* Vol. 9, No. 10, 1882, 3–5,21–23.

45 C. Giordano, and I. Kahn. *The Jews in Pompeii, Herculaneum, Stabiae and in the Cities of Campania Felix*. Napoli: Procaccini, 1979, 44; Mau, 1907, op. cit., 16–18; Ward-Perkins and Claridge, 1980, op. cit., 15, 33.

46 For example, by Corti 1951, op. cit., 208.

47 Mau, 1907, op. cit., 18.

48 Naples Museum 73879 from house (VIII, vi, 6).

49 Giordano and Kahn, 1979, op. cit., 56–58, 60–70; Mau, 1907, op. cit., 17; V. Tran Tam Tinh, *Essai sur le Culte d'Isis à Pompei*. Paris: de Boccard, 1964; R.E. Witt, *Isis in the Graeco-Roman World*. London: Thames & Hudson, 1971.

50 Allison, 1992b, op. cit., 97; P.M. Allison, 'Recurring tremors: The continuing impact of the AD 79 eruption of Mt Vesuvius', in *Natural Disasters and Cultural Change*, ed. R. Torrence and J. Gratton. London: Routledge, 2002, 112; Corti, 1951, op. cit., 48, 204; Descœudres, 1994a, op. cit., 36; Maiuri, 1933, op. cit., 11–16.

51 Corti, 1951, op. cit., 52; M. Della Corte, *Casa ed Abitanti di Pompei*. 3rd edn. Napoli: Fausto Fiorentino, 1965, 67–71; Richardson, 1988, op. cit., 324; R. Trevelyan, *The Shadow of Vesuvius: Pompeii AD 79*. London: Michael Joseph, 1976, 17.

52 Cooley, 2003, op. cit., 27. For a detailed consideration of whether the site was abandoned by certain sections of the population, see Cooley, 2003, op. cit., 25–35.

53 Corti, 1951, op. cit., 54; Descœudres, 1994, op. cit., 36.

54 E. Lazer, 'Pompeii AD 79: A population in flux?', in *Sequence and Space in Pompeii*, ed. S.E. Bon and R. Jones. Oxford: Oxbow Monograph 77, 1997a, 102–20.

55 Jashemski, 1979a, op. cit., 343, n. 56; W. Jongman, P.W. De Neeve and H.W. Pleket, (eds), *The Economy and Society of Pompeii*. Vol. 4, Dutch Monographs on Ancient History

and Archaeology. Amsterdam: J.C. Gieber, 1988; 55, 108–12; J.C. Russell, *The Control of Late Ancient and Medieval Population*. Philadelphia: The American Philosophical Society, 1985, 1–4; A. Wallace-Hadrill, 'Houses and households: Sampling Pompeii and Herculaneum', in *Marriage, Divorce and Children in Ancient Rome*, ed. B. Rawson. Oxford: Oxford University Press, 1991, 191–202; A. Wallace-Hadrill, *Houses and Society in Pompeii and Herculaneum*. Princeton, New Jersey: Princeton University Press, 1994, 95–98.

56 G. Fiorelli, *Gli Scavi di Pompei dal 1861 al 1872*. Napoli: Tipografica nel Liceo V. Emmanuele, 1873, 14; E. La Rocca, M. De Vos and A. De Vos. *Guida Archeologica di Pompei*. 1st edn. Verona, Italy: Arnoldo Mondadori, 1976, 21; Russell, 1985, op. cit., 1.

57 Fiorelli, 1873, op. cit., App. 3, 14; S. Pheasant, *Bodyspace: Anthropology, Ergonomics and Design*. London: Taylor & Francis, 1986, 189; P. Tutt and D. Adler (eds), *New Metric Handbook*. London: Architectural Press, 1979, 221.

58 Dio Cassius, 'Dio's Roman history', in *Loeb Classical Library*. Cambridge, Massachusetts: Harvard University Press, 1914–27, LXVI, 24.

59 Tacitus, op. cit., xiv, 17; Corti, 1951, op. cit., 42–43; Engelmann, 1925, op. cit., 3; Russell, 1985, op. cit., 2; Trevelyan, 1976, op. cit., 11. This event is commemorated on a painting from the House of Anicetus (I, iii, 23); Naples Museum inv. 112222.

60 Fiorelli, 1873, op. cit., App. 3, 12–13; Jashemski, 1979a, op. cit., 343 n. 56; Russell, 1985, op. cit., 2; Wallace-Hadrill, 1991, op. cit., 201.

61 Nissen 1877 in Jongman, 1988, op. cit., 110 and Nissen 1877 in Mau, 1907, op. cit., 16. See also Jashemski, 1979a, op. cit., 343 n. 56; Wallace-Hadrill, 1991, op. cit., 201.

62 For example, with Bullard, 1984, op. cit., 200; Engelmann, 1925, op. cit., 4; P. Francis, *Volcanoes: A Planetary Perspective*. Oxford: Clarendon Press, 1993, 70; N. Hammond, 'Ancient cities', *Scientific American*, Vol. 5, No. 1: Special Issue, 1994, 8.

63 Mau, 1907, op. cit., 16; Maiuri, 1962, op. cit., 17.

64 Beloch 1898 in Jashemski, 1979a, op. cit., 343 n. 56; Jongman, 1988, op. cit., 108.

65 Cary and Scullard 1975 in Jashemski, 1979a, op. cit., 343 n. 56.

66 Jashemski 1979a, op. cit., 343 n. 56; Russell, 1985, op. cit., 3; Wallace-Hadrill, 1991, op. cit., 199.

67 H. Eschebach *et al.*, *Pompeji: Erlebte Antike Welt*. Leipzig: Seeman, VEB, 1978, 6; Jongman, 1988, op. cit., 110; Jashemski, 1979a, op. cit., 343 n. 56; La Rocca *et al.*, 1976, op. cit., 21.

68 Jashemski, 1979, op. cit., 24, 343 n. 56.

69 Jongman, 1988, op. cit., 108–12; Wallace-Hadrill, 1991, op. cit., 199–201; Wallace-Hadrill, 1994, op. cit., 93–96.

70 Jongman, ibid., 55, 110–12.

71 Wallace-Hadrill, 1991, op. cit., 200–203; Wallace-Hadrill, 1994, op. cit., 97–98.

72 Wallace-Hadrill, 1991, op. cit., 202.

73 Wallace-Hadrill, ibid., 203, 225; Wallace-Hadrill, 1994, op. cit., 98.

74 One issue that is seldom addressed is the definition of the extent of the site and whether estimates only relate to the area inside the walls of the town.

75 W. Gell, *Pompeiana: The Topography, Edifices and Ornaments of Pompeii: The Results of Excavations since 1819*. London: Jennings & Chaplin, 1832, xix.

76 E. Bulwer-Lytton, *The Last Days of Pompeii*. New York: Putnam, 1897, 304.

77 T.H. Dyer, *Pompeii: Its History, Buildings and Antiquities*. 2nd edn. London: George Bell & Sons, 1883, 46; Fiorelli, 1873, op. cit., 172; Russell, 1985, op. cit., 4.

78 For example, S.C. Bisel *et al.*, *The Secrets of Vesuvius*. Toronto: Madison Press, 1990, 31; Brion, 1973, op. cit., 34; Corti, 1951, op. cit., 81; Engelmann, 1925, op. cit., 4; Grant, 1976, op. cit., 34; Mau, 1907, op. cit., 23; Wilkinson, 2003, op. cit., 73.

79 For example, Bullard, 1984, op. cit., 201; Cerulli Irelli in Russell, 1985, op. cit., 5 n. 22; G. Perl, 'Pompeji-geschichte und untergang', in *Pompeji: 79–1979: Beiträge Zum Vesuvausbruch und seiner Nachwirkung*, ed. M. Kunze. Stendal: Beiträge der Winckelmann Gesellschaft, 1982, 22; H. Sigurdsson, S. Cashdollar, and S.R.J. Sparks. 'The Eruption of

Vesuvius in AD 79: Reconstruction from historical and volcanological evidence', *American Journal of Archaeology*, Vol. 86, 1982, 51.

80 For example P. Gusman, *Pompei: The City, its Life and Art*. Translated by F. Simmonds and M. Jourdain. London: Heinemann, 1900, 15.

81 Blong, 1984, op. cit., 79; Russell, 1985, op. cit., 5.

82 De Carolis and Patricelli, 2003b, op. cit., 111–12; E. Lazer, 'Human Skeletal Remains in Pompeii: Vols. I and II', unpublished PhD thesis, Department of Anatomy and Histology. Sydney: University of Sydney, 1995, 69–70; Lazer, 1997a, op. cit., 107.

83 Blong, 1984, op. cit., 79; D. Herbet and F. Bardossi. *Kilauea: Case History of a Volcano*. New York: Harper & Row, 1968, 12–13.

84 See Chapter 5 and S. De Caro (Ex–director, Superintendency of Pompeii) to E. Lazer., 1988, personal communication; De Carolis and Patricelli, 2003a, op. cit., 66–67.

85 De Carolis and Patricelli, 2003a, op. cit., 64–72; De Carolis and Patricelli, 2003b, 111–12; E. De Carolis, G. Patricelli and A. Ciarallo. 'Rinvenimenti di corpi umani nell'area urbana di Pompei', *Rivista di Studi Pompeiani*, Vol. 9, 1998, 75–123.

86 Francis, 1993, op. cit., 67; Sigurdsson *et al.*, 1982, op. cit., 47; Ward-Perkins and Claridge, 1980, op. cit., 13.

87 Strabo, 'The Geography', in *Loeb Classical Library*. Cambridge, Massachusetts: Harvard University Press, 1988, 5.4.8.

88 Pliny the Elder, op. cit., III, 62.

89 Sigurdsson, 2002, op. cit., 32; H. Sigurdsson, 'The environmental and geomorphological context of the volcano', in *The World of Pompeii*, ed. P.W. Foss and J.J. Dobbins. London: Routledge, 2007, 45.

90 For example, by Trevelyan, 1976, op. cit., 9; F.L. Sutherland, 'The volcanic fall of Pompeii', in *Pompeii Revisited: The Life and Death of a Roman Town*, ed. D. Harrison. Sydney: Meditarch, 1994, 74.

91 Pliny the Younger, op. cit., VI, 16; VI, 20.

92 Allison, 1992b, op. cit., 11; H.W. Benario, 'The land, the cities, the event', in *The Buried Cities and the Eruption of Vesuvius: The 1900th Anniversary*, ed. H.W. Benario and G.W. Lawall, *Lectures presented at Emory University on May 7, 1979 in a symposium sponsored by the Dept. of Modern Languages and Classics, Alpha Sigma chapter of Eta Sigma Phi, and the Atlanta Society of the Archaeological Institute of America*. Amherst: NECN & University of Massachusetts, 1979, 1–7; Ciprotti, 1964, op. cit., 44; Ciprotti, 2004, op. cit., 19–20; Descœudres, 1993, op. cit., 168,171–72; U. Eco, 'A portrait of the Elder as a Young Pliny: How to build fame', in *On Signs*, ed. M. Blonsky. Oxford: Blackwell, 1985, 289.

93 For example, by Bullard, 1984, op. cit., 195; E. De Carolis, and G. Patricelli, 'Le vittime dell'eruzione', in *Storie da un'Eruzione: Pompei, Ercolano, Oplontis: Guida alla Mostra*, ed. A. d'Ambrosio, P.G. Guzzo and M. Mastroroberto. Milano: Electa, 2003a, 56; Sigurdsson *et al.*, 1982, op. cit., 39–40; H. Sigurdsson *et al.*, 'The eruption of Vesuvius in AD 79,' *National Geographic Research*, Vol. 1, No. 3, 1985: 332–87; Sigurdsson, 2002, op. cit., 41.

94 Eco, 1985, op. cit., 290, 294–96, 301.

95 Anonymous. *The Etna Poem*. Translated by J.W. Duff and A.M. Duff. Revised edn. Vol. 1, Minor Latin Poets in Two Volumes. Cambridge, Massachusetts: Harvard University Press, 1982. The arguments for this claim have been summarized by Allison, 1992b, op. cit., 11; Allison, 2002, op. cit., 110; Allison, 2004, op. cit., 20.

96 Dio Cassius, *Dio's Roman history*. Translated by E. Carey. Loeb Classical Library. Cambridge, Massachusetts: Harvard University Press, 1914–27, LXVI, 21–23.

97 Suetonius, Titus, 8.

98 Allison, 2004, op. cit., 19.

99 For example, De Carolis and Patricelli, 2003a, op. cit., 56; De Carolis and Patricelli, 2003b, op. cit., 77; Descœudres, 1994, op. cit., 37; Perl, 1982, op. cit., 21; Sigurdsson *et al.*, 1982, op. cit., 39; Sigurdsson, 2004, op. cit., 44–50; Trevelyan, 1976, op. cit., 28;

Ward-Perkins and Claridge, 1980: 8. The arguments in favour of the 24 August date have been reviewed by Ciprotti, 1964, op. cit., 41–42.

100 Ward-Perkins and Claridge, 1980, op. cit., 9.

101 Strabo, op. cit., 5.4.8.

102 A. De Franciscis, *The Pompeian Wall Paintings in the Roman Villa of Oplontis*. Recklinghausen, Germany: Aurel Bongers, 1975, 14–15; Grant, 1976, op. cit., 74; Richardson, 1988, op. cit., xv; Trevelyan, 1976, op. cit., 25; Ward-Perkins and Claridge, 1980, op. cit., 9. For problems associated with the establishment of ownership of Pompeian houses on the basis of epigraphy, see P.M. Allison, 'Placing individuals: Pompeian epigraphy in context', *Journal of Mediterranean Archaeology*, Vol. 14, No. 1, 2001: 53–74.

103 Ciprotti, 1964, op. cit., 41.

104 Dio Cassius, op. cit., LXVI, 24.

105 For example, Mau, 1907, op. cit., 19.

106 For example, Ciprotti, 1964, op. cit., 42 makes a point of mentioning this event in his summary of the arguments for the different dates of the eruption.

107 U. Pappalardo, 'L'eruzione pliniana del Vesuvio nel 79 d.C.: Ercolano', in *Volcanology and Archaeology*, ed. C. Albore Livadie and F. Widerman. Strasburg: Council of Europe, 1900, 209–10. See also A.M. Ciarello and E. De Carolis. 'La data dell' eruzione', *Rivista di Studi Pompeiani*, Vol. 9, 1998: 63–73, for a discussion of the eruption date.

108 Pliny the Younger, op. cit., VI, 16.

109 Ciprotti, 1964, op. cit., 48.

110 G. Stefani, 'La Vera Data dell'Eruzione', *Archeo,* Vol. 260, No. 10, 2006: 10–13.

111 For example, F.M. Bullard, 'Volcanoes and their activity', in *Volcanic Activity and Human Ecology*, ed. P.D. Sheets and D.K. Grayson. New York: Academic Press, 1979, 31; Bullard, 1984, op. cit., 184, 200–201, A. Maiuri, 'Last moments of the Pompeians', *National Geographic,* Vol. 120 1961, 51–55. For a discussion of the different views about the form of the AD 79 eruption, see H. Sigurdsson and S.N. Carey, 'The eruption of Vesuvius in AD 79', in *The Natural History of Pompeii*, ed. W.F. Jashemski and F.G. Meyer. Cambridge: Cambridge University Press, 2002, 37.

112 Bullard, 1979, op. cit., Bullard, 1984, op. cit., 184.

113 Pliny the Younger, op. cit., VI, 16.

114 Bullard, 1984, op. cit., 195; Francis, 1993, op. cit., 69; Sigurdsson *et al.*, 1985, op. cit., 336.

115 P.J. Baxter, 'Medical effects of volcanic eruptions', *Bulletin of Volcanology*, Vol. 52, 1990, 532; Francis, 1993, op. cit., 208, 213, 236; W.E. Scott, 'Volcanic and related hazards', in *Volcanic Hazards*, ed. Tilling, R.I., *Short Course in Geology*. Washington, DC: American Geophysical Union, 1989, 11–14; Sigurdsson, 1985, op. cit., 337–38; Sigurdsson and Carey, 2002, op. cit., 44.

116 Baxter, 1990, op. cit., 539; M. Krafft, *Volcanoes: Fire from the Earth*. Translated by P.G. Bahn, London: Thames & Hudson, 1993, 118; L. Lirer *et al.*, 'Two Plinian pumice-fall deposits from Somma-Vesuvius, Italy', *Geological Society of America Bulletin*, Vol. 84, 1973, 759; Sigurdsson *et al.*, 1982, op. cit., 85–86; Sigurdsson and Carey, 2002, op. cit., 37; Trevelyan, 1976, op. cit., 24.

117 Francis, 1993, op. cit., 198–202, 241–44; Carey and Sigurdsson, 1987, 303–14; Sigurdsson *et al.*, 1982, op. cit., 47–50; Sigurdsson *et al.*, 1985, op. cit., 339–63; Sigurdsson and Carey, 2002, op. cit., 37–64; Sutherland, 1994: 72–75.

118 For example, Sigurdsson *et al.*, 1982, op. cit., 86; H. Sigurdsson, *Melting the Earth: The History of Ideas on Volcanic Eruptions*, Oxford: Oxford University Press, 1999, 67–68; Sigurdsson and Carey, 2002, op. cit., 38, 41, 44–50; Sigurdsson, 2007, op. cit., 51–52.

119 Sigurdsson, 1999, op. cit., 1.

120 For example, by Cooley, 2003, op. cit., 38–45; De Carolis and Patricelli, 2003a, op. cit., 56–59; De Carolis and Patricelli, 2003b, op. cit., 83–108.

121 De Carolis and Patricelli, 2003b, op. cit., 78.

122 Pliny the Younger, op. cit., VI, 16.

123 Pliny the Younger, op. cit., VI, 20.

124 M.S. Greenberg *et al.*, 'When believing is seeing: The effect of scripts on eyewitness memory', *Law and Human Behavior*, Vol. 22, No. 6, 1998: 685–86.

125 J.M. Brown, 'Eyewitness memory for arousing events: Putting things into context', *Applied Cognitive Psychology*, Vol. 17, No. 1, 2003, 104; B.L. Cutler *et al.*, 'The reliability of eyewitness identification', *Law and Human Behavior*, Vol. 11, No. 3, 1987, 233–58; Greenberg *et al.*, 1998, op. cit.

126 Bullard, 1979, op. cit., 31; Bullard, 1984, op. cit., 200–201. The interpretation of the letters of the Younger Pliny by Sigurdsson and his team has been used to demonstrate that he did describe these events; for example, see Sigurdsson and Carey, 2002, op. cit., 50.

127 Francis, 1993, op. cit., 186, 201–2; Sigurdsson *et al.*, 1982, op. cit., 48; Sigurdsson and Carey, 2002, op. cit., 47–48.

128 Sigurdsson *et al.*, 1982, op. cit., 48–49; Sigurdsson and Carey, 2002, op. cit., 48.

129 Baxter, 1990, op. cit., 540; Blong, 1984, op. cit, 79–80; Sigurdsson *et al.*, 1982, op. cit., 39; Sigurdsson and Carey, 2002, op. cit., 48.

130 De Carolis and Patricelli, 2003b, op. cit., 83–98; Sigurdsson *et al.*, 1982, op. cit., 42, 49; Sigurdsson *et al.*, 1985, op. cit., 351–52, 364; Sigurdsson and Carey 2002: 49–50, 53–54; Sigurdsson, 2007, op. cit., 51–54.

131 Bullard, 1979, op. cit., 200–201; Sigurdsson *et al.*, 1982, op. cit., 50.

132 For example, near the necropolis outside the Nocera Gate of Pompeii. Sigurdsson *et al.*, 1982, op. cit., Pl. 4, Fig. 2; Sigurdsson *et al.*, 1985, op. cit., 350.

133 De Carolis and Patricelli, 2003b, op. cit., 111–12; De Carolis and Patricelli, 1998, op. cit., 75–123; G. Luongo *et al.*, 'Impact of the AD 79 explosive eruption on Pompeii, II: Causes of death of the inhabitants inferred by stratigraphic analysis and areal distribution of the human casualties', *Journal of Volcanology and Geothermal Research*, Vol. 126, Nos 3–4, 2003b: 169–200.

134 Sigurdsson *et al.*, 1985, op. cit., 364–66; Sigurdsson and Carey, 2002, op. cit., 49.

135 J.W. Eisele *et al.*, 'Deaths during the May 18, 1980, eruption of Mt St Helens', *The New England Journal of Medicine*, Vol. 305, No. 16, 1981, 936.

136 P.J. Baxter *et al.*, 'Medical aspects of volcanic disasters: An outline of the hazards and emergency response measures', *Disasters*, Vol. 6, No. 4, 1982, 269; Baxter, 1990, op. cit., 533–34; Eisele *et al.*, 1981, op. cit., 933–35; Francis, 1993, op. cit., 98; Sigurdsson *et al.*, 1985, op. cit., 365; Sigurdsson and Carey, 2002, op. cit., 49.

137 Sigurdsson *et al.*, 1985, op. cit., 365; Sigurdsson and Carey, 2002, op. cit., 58.

138 De Carolis and Patricelli, 2003a, op. cit., 66–72; De Carolis and Patricelli, 2003b, op. cit., 111–12; De Carolis *et al.*, 1998, op. cit., 78–123; Luongo *et al.*, 2003b, 174–98.

139 Luongo *et al.*, 2003a, op. cit., 221–22; Luongo *et al.*, 2003b, op. cit., 178–80.

140 Luongo *et al.*, 2003b, op. cit., 180.

141 Blong, 1984, op. cit., 79; W. Hamilton, *Observations on Mt Vesuvius, Mt Etna and Other Volcanoes in a Series of Letters Addressed To the Royal Society … To Which Are Added Notes by the Author, Hitherto Unpublished*. London: Royal Society, 1774, 95.

142 Skull TF 111. This interpretation was confirmed by T.H.G. Oettlé (former Director of the New South Wales Forensic Institute, Sydney) to E. Lazer, 1983, personal communication.

143 Baxter, 1990, op. cit., 532; Scott, 1989, op. cit., 11–14; Sigurdsson *et al.*, 1982, op. cit., 49; Sigurdsson *et al.*, 1985, op. cit., 364–65; Sigurdsson, 2002, op. cit., 48–49.

144 S.C. Nappo, 'Il rinvenimento delle vittime dell'eruzione del 79 d.C. nella Regio 1 insula 22', *Hydria*, Vol. 63, No. 19, 1992: 16–18.

145 De Carolis and Patricelli, 2003a, op. cit., 66–72; De Carolis and Patricelli, 2003b, op. cit., 111–12; De Carolis *et al.*, 1998, op. cit., 78–123; Luongo *et al.*, 2003b, op. cit., 178.

146 Luongo *et al.*, 2003a, op. cit., 219–20; Luongo *et al.*, 2003b, op. cit., 181.

147 L. Giacomelli *et al.*, 'The eruption of Vesuvius of AD 79 and its impact on human environment in Pompeii', *Episodes,* Vol. 26, No. 3, 2003: 237–38.

148 Ibid.

149 Luongo *et al.*, 2003b, op. cit., 181.

150 Giacomelli *et al.*, 2003, op. cit., 238.

151 Baxter, 1990, op. cit., 539; Blong, 1984, op. cit., 95–103; D'Amore *et al.*, 'Antropologia pompeiana del 79 d.C.: Sesso ed età di morte', *Archivio per l'Antropologia e la Etnologia,* Vol. 109 1979, 300; Francis, 1993, op. cit., 70–71; Sigurdsson *et al.*, 1982, op. cit., 49–50.

152 Baxter, 1990, op. cit., 539.

153 Baxter, 1990, op. cit., 535–37, 539, 541; B. Knight, *Forensic Pathology*. 2nd edn. London: Arnold, 1996, 309–10; S. Cole (forensic dentist, New South Wales Institute of Forensic Medicine, Sydney) to E. Lazer, 2002, personal communication; C. Lawrence (former forensic pathologist, New South Wales Institute of Forensic Medicine, Sydney) to E. Lazer, 1994, personal communication; A. Middleton (forensic dentist, New South Wales Institute of Forensic Medicine, Sydney) to E. Lazer, 2002, personal communication; V.D. Plueckhahn, *Ethics, Legal Medicine and Forensic Pathology*. Carlton, Victoria: Melbourne University Press, 1983, 168.

154 Baxter, 1990, op. cit., 542; Knight, 1996, op. cit., 63–64.

155 Baxter, 1990, op. cit., 532; A.L. Hansell *et al.*, 'The health hazards of volcanoes and geothermal areas', *Occupational & Environmental Medicine*, Vol. 63, No. 2, 2006, 152; Sigurdsson *et al.*, 1985, op. cit., 365. Though it has been noted that post-eruption epidemic disease and famine actually account for more deaths than pyroclastic density currents. J.-C. Tanguy *et al.*, 'Victims from volcanic eruptions: A revised database', *Bulletin of Volcanology*, Vol. 60, No. 2, 1998, 137.

156 Baxter, 1990, op. cit., P.J. Baxter *et al.*, 'Physical modelling and human survival in pyroclastic flows', *Natural Hazards,* Vol. 17, No. 2, 1998: 166–68; Hansell *et al.*, 2006, op. cit., 153.

157 L. Gurioli *et al.*, 'Interaction of pyroclastic density currents with human settlements: Evidence from ancient Pompeii', *Geology,* Vol. 33, No. 6, 2005, 441–44.

158 Baxter, 1990, op. cit., 533, 540–41; Baxter *et al.*, 2005, op. cit., 310.

159 Baxter, 1998, op. cit., 166; Lawrence, op. cit.

160 De Carolis and Patricelli, 2003a, op. cit., 72; De Carolis and Patricelli, 2003b, op. cit., 101, P.P. Petrone, 'Le vittime dell'eruzione del 79 AD', in *Storie da un'eruzione. In margine alla mostra, Atti della Tavola Rotonda, Napoli, 2003, Associazione Internazionale Amici di Pompei, Dipartimento di Discipline Storiche, Università degli Studi di Napoli Federico II*, ed. P. G. Guzzo. Pompei: Litografia Sicignano, 2005, 31; Sigurdsson and Carey, 2002, op. cit., 55.

161 L. Capasso, 'Herculaneum victims of the volcanic eruptions of Vesuvius in 79 AD', *The Lancet*, Vol. 356, No. 9238, 2000a: 1344–46; L. Capasso, *I Fuggiaschi di Ercolano: Paleobiologia delle Vittime dell'Eruzione Vesuviana del 79 d.C.* Roma: 'L'Erma' di Bretschneider, 2001, 21–67, 1053–54.

162 G. Mastrolorenzo and P.P. Petrone, 'Nuove evidenze sugli effetti dell'eruzione del 79d.C. ad Ercolano da ricerche biogeoarcheologiche', *Forma Urbis*, Vol. 10, No. 3: Edizione speciale: La rinascita di Ercolano, 2005, 31–34; G. Mastrolorenzo *et al.*, 'Archaeology: Herculaneum victims of Vesuvius in AD 79', *Nature,* Vol. 410, No. 6830, 2001, 769–70; P.P. Petrone, 'Le vittime dell'eruzione del 79 AD', in *Storie da un'eruzione. In margine alla mostra, Atti della Tavola Rotonda, Napoli, 2003, Associazione Internazionale Amici di Pompei, Dipartimento di Discipline Storiche, Università degli Studi di Napoli Federico II*, ed. P.G. Guzzo. Pompei: Litografia Sicignano, 2005, 31–44.

163 Allison, 1992b, op. cit., 10–11; Allison, 2004, op. cit., 19.

164 Diodorus Siculus, 'Diodorus Siculus,' in *Loeb Classical Library*. Cambridge, Massachusetts: Harvard University Press, 1933–67, 4, 21, 5.

165 Suetonius, op. cit., Caligula, 51.

166 *The Etna Poem*, op. cit., Leppmann, 1968, op. cit., 25.

167 Strabo, op. cit., 5, 4, 8.

168 *The Etna Poem*, op. cit., 352–53, 431–32.

169 Allison, 1992b, op. cit., 10; Allison, 2004, op. cit., 19.

170 Pliny the Elder, op. cit., II, 200; Allison, 1992b, op. cit., 10–11; Sigurdsson, 1999, op. cit., 56.

171 Bullard, 1984, op. cit., 188–89

172 Plutarch, *Makers of Rome: Nine Lives*, Translated by Scott-Kilvert, I. Harmondsworth, England: Penguin, 1965, 2: 279.

173 Pliny the Younger, op. cit., IV, 16.

174 Especially Suetonius, op. cit., Titus 8 and Dio Cassius, op. cit., LXV, 24.

175 Luongo *et al.*, 2003b, op. cit., 179.

176 Francis, 1993, op. cit., 98.

177 Francis 1993, op. cit., 244; M.L. Nolan, 'Impact of paricutin on five communities', in *Volcanic Activity and Human Ecology*, ed. P.D. Sheets and D.K. Grayson. New York: Academic Press, 1979, 302–3; R.S. Punongbayan and R.I. Tilling, 'Some recent case histories', in *Volcanic Hazards*, ed. R.I. Tilling, *Short Course in Geology*. Washington, DC American Geophysical Union, 1989, 82– 83, 90–91, 93, 96–99.

178 Blong, 1984, op. cit., 72–73, 79–80; Grayson and Sheets, 1979, op. cit., 626–27; S. Manning (Department of Classics, University of Reading, UK) to E. Lazer, 1989, personal communication; Russell, 1985, op. cit., 7–8.

179 For example, Allison, 1992b, op. cit., 17–19; Cooley, 2003, op. cit., 51 ff.; Descœudres, 1993, op. cit., 165–78.

180 Brion, 1973, op. cit., 53; Gusman, 1900, op. cit., 19; Trevelyan, 1976, op. cit., 39.

181 Corti, 1951, op. cit., 134; Dyer, 1883, op. cit., 47; Jashemski, 1979b, op. cit., 612–15; Leppmann, 1968, op. cit., 74; Richardson, 1988, op. cit., 25–27; Russell, 1985, op. cit., 6; Ward-Perkins and Claridge, 1980, op. cit., 14.

182 For example by Bullard, 1984, op. cit., 202; M.G. Cerulli Irelli, 'Intorno al problema della rinascita di Pompei', in *Neue Forschungen in Pompeji*, ed. Andreae, B. and H. Kyrieleis. Recklinghausen: Aurel Bongers, 1975, 292; Corti, 1951, op. cit., 82; De Carolis and Patricelli, 2003b, op. cit., 106; Gusman, 1900, op. cit., 22; Jashemski, 1979b, op. cit., 612; and Ward-Perkins and Claridge, 1980, op. cit., 14.

183 Various scholars have suggested that the highest parts of some structures were still visible after Vesuvius erupted. For example, Bullard, 1984, op. cit., 202; Cerulli Irelli, 1975, op. cit., 292; Corti, 1951, op. cit., 82; Gusman, 1900, op. cit., 22; Jashemski, 1979b, op. cit., 612; and Ward-Perkins and Claridge, 1980, op. cit., 14. Descœudres examined the literature and concluded that there was insufficient evidence to support this view. Allison, 2004, op. cit., 23; Descœudres, 1993, op. cit., 167–69.

184 Corti, 1951, op. cit., 89; Leppmann, 1968, op. cit., 48; F.L. Sutherland, 'The volcanic fall of Pompeii', in *Pompeii Revisited: The Life and Death of a Roman Town*, ed. D. Harrison, D. Sydney: Meditarch, 1994, 72.

185 The same evidence has also been cited as indicative of post-earthquake abandonment. Allison, 1992b, op. cit., 18; Jashemski, 1979b, op. cit., 612; Parslow, 1995, op. cit., 113; Richardson, 1988, op. cit., 25–26; Ward-Perkins and Claridge, 1980, op. cit., 14.

186 Cooley, 2003, op. cit., 34.

187 Allison, 1992b, op. cit., 18; Allison, 2004, op. cit., 24; Grayson and Sheets, 1979; op. cit., 626; K. Neumann, *Rabaul: Yu Swit Moa Yet: Surviving the 1994 Volcanic Eruption*. Oxford: Oxford University Press, 1996, 79–88. However, Allison cites evidence of looting, mostly for necessities like food and shelter, as well as some household goods, after the 1994 Rabaul eruption. Allison, 1992b, op. cit., 17–19, 37–39, Cooley, 2003, op. cit., 53–55 and Descœudres, 1993, op. cit., 167–71, have also reviewed the evidence for post-eruption disturbances to the site.

188 For example, by Jashemski, 1979b, op. cit., 612 and Ward-Perkins and Claridge, 1980, op. cit., 14.

189 Allison, 1992b, op. cit., 18; Cerulli Irelli, 1975, op. cit., 295.

190 Cerulli Irelli, 1975, op. cit., 295; Cooley, 2003, op. cit., 55; Jashemski, 1979b, op. cit., 613.

191 Cerulli Irelli, 1975, op. cit., 295.

192 From the skeletons associated with Skull Numbers 4, 7, and 9. See Fig. 1.2. Lazer, 1995, op. cit., 54–58; E. Lazer, 'Resti umani scheletrici nella Casa del Menandro', in *Menander: La Casa del Menandro di Pompei*, ed. G. Stefani. Milan: Electa, 2003, 66–67.

193 Allison, 1992b, op. cit., 19, 171; Maiuri, 1933, op. cit., 12; Allison, 1992b, op. cit., 19, 171.

194 For example, Descœudres, 1993, op. cit., 169–70.

195 Richardson, 1988, op. cit., 26–27.

196 Allison, 1992b, op. cit., 38; Allison, 2002, op. cit., 114; Parslow, 1995, op. cit., 113.

5 The nature of the evidence

1 T.H. Dyer, *Pompeii: Its History, Buildings and Antiquities*. 2nd edn. London: George Bell & Sons, 1883, 479; G. Nicolucci, 'Crania Pompeiana: Descrizione de' crani umani rinvenuti fra le ruine dell' antica Pompei', *Atti della R. Accademia delle Scienze Fisiche e Matematiche*, Vol. 9, No. 10, 1882, 2.

2 A. Kosloski–Ostrow, *The Sarno Bath Complex: Architecture in Pompeii's Last Years*. Monographie 4, Ministero per i Beni Culturali ed Ambientali, Soprintendenza Archeologia di Pompei. Rome: 'L'Erma' di Bretschneider, 1990, 10–11.

3 A. De Vos. and M. De Vos, *Pompei, Ercolano, Stabia*. Rome: Laterza, 1982, 58.

4 C. D'Amore *et al.*, 'Primi risultati degli studi sull'antropologia Pompeiana del 79 d.C.', in *La Regione Sotterrata dal Vesuvio: Studi e Prospettive, Atti del Convegno Internazionale 11–15 Novembre 1979*. Napoli: Università degli Studi, 1982, 928.

5 S. De Caro (Ex–director, Superintendency of Pompeii) to E. Lazer, 1988, personal communication.

6 See, for example, S.C. Bisel (Physical anthropologist, Herculaneum) to E. Lazer, 1988c, personal communication.

7 D'Amore *et al.*, 1979, op. cit; C. D'Amore *et al.*, 'Primi risultati degli studi sull'antropologia Pompeiana del 79 d.C.', in *La Regione Sotterrata dal Vesuvio: Studi e Prospettive, Atti del Convegno Internazionale 11–15 Novembre 1979*. Napoli: Università degli Studi, 1982, 927–43.

8 The fact that there will be loss or bias in all classes of archaeological evidence is well documented, for example S. Mays, *The Archaeology of Human Bones*. London: Routledge, 1998, 13–25, discusses these problems in relation to skeletal evidence.

9 For example, Bisel, 1988c, op. cit.

10 D'Amore *et al.*, 1982, op. cit., 928.

11 M. Brion, *Pompeii and Herculaneum: The Glory and the Grief*. London: Cardinal, 1973/1960, 126.

12 D'Amore *et al.*, 1979, op. cit., 301.

13 The majority of the fieldwork for this project was carried out over five seasons, from 1986 to 1990, with additional field seasons in 1995 and 1996.

14 E. De Carolis and G. Patricelli. *Vesuvius, AD 79: The Destruction of Pompeii and Herculaneum*. Translated by The J. Paul Getty Trust. Rome: 'L'Erma' di Bretschneider, 2003b, 110.

15 W. Leppmann, *Pompeii in Fact and Fiction*. London: Elek, 1968, 136.

16 Hester Lynch Piozzi 1789 Observations and Reflections made in the Course of a Journey through France, Italy and Germany II, London in: E.M. Moorman, 'Literary evocations of ancient Pompeii', in *Tales from an Eruption: Pompeii, Herculaneum, Oplontis: Guide to the Exhibition*, ed. P.G. Guzzo. Milan: Electa, 2003, 27.

17 Quoted in De Carolis and Patricelli, 2003b, op. cit., 109.

18 This house is in the insula of the Menander.

19 De Caro, 1988, op. cit.

20 Ibid.

21 S.C. Bisel, 'The skeletons of Herculaneum, Italy', in *Wet Site Archaeology: Proceedings of the International Conference on Wet Site Archaeology, Gainesville, Florida, December 12–14, 1986; sponsored by the National Endowment for the Humanities and University of Florida*, ed. B.A. Purdy. Caldwell, New Jersey: Telford Press, 1988b, 208.

22 A.T. Chamberlain, *Demography in Archaeology*, Cambridge Manuals in Archaeology. Cambridge: Cambridge University Press, 2006, 70; P. Drackett, *The Book of Great Disasters*. Berkshire: Purnell, 1977, 115; G. Luongo *et al.*, 'Impact of the AD 79 explosive eruption on Pompeii, II: Causes of death of the inhabitants inferred by stratigraphic analysis and areal distribution of the human casualties', *Journal of Volcanology and Geothermal Research*, Vol. 126, Nos 3–4, 2003b: 169–200; G. Nicolucci, 'Crania Pompeiana: Descrizione de' crani umani rinvenuti fra le ruine dell' antica Pompei', *Atti della R. Accademia delle Scienze Fisiche e Matematiche*, Vol. 9, No. 10, 1882, 1.

23 Strabo. *The Geography*. Translated by H.R. Jones, Loeb Classical Library. Cambridge, Massachusetts: Harvard University Press, 1988, V, IV, 8; Pliny the Elder, 'Natural Histories', in *Loeb Classical Library*. Cambridge, Massachusetts: Harvard University Press, 1938/1962, 3.60–62.

24 A 5 cm thick layer of dust covered the floor of the Sarno Baths. As it was partially the result of wind-borne dust from the site, it could not be permanently cleared without sealing the structure. Since the building was damp, the dirt often hardened around the bones which meant that its removal could be time-consuming. The Forum Baths were partially sealed and the disarticulated bones were stored on shelves. Nonetheless, a certain quantity of fine dust was able to enter the building and settle on the bones between visits. In addition to the annual deposit of dust, there was a build-up of excreta from animals which inhabited these buildings.

25 D'Amore *et al.*, 1982, op. cit., 928.

26 Ibid.

27 D'Amore *et al.*, 1979, op. cit.; D'Amore *et al.*, 1982, op. cit.

28 The bones were arbitrarily marked with consecutive numbers. A prefix was assigned which denoted the building in which the bone was housed (TF = Terme Feminile del Foro; TdS = Terme del Sarno). Sometimes an extra prefix was added which referred to either an exact location (e.g. BQ = Basket Q) or a recently excavated skeleton of known provenance (NS 84 = Nuovo scavo 1984).

29 D'Amore *et al.*, 1982, op. cit., 928.

30 A.T. Chamberlain, *Demography in Archaeology*, Cambridge Manuals in Archaeology. Cambridge: Cambridge University Press, 2006, 89; T.I. Molleson, 'The archaeology and anthropology of death: What the bones tell us,' in *Mortality and Immortality: The Anthropology and Archaeology of Death*, ed. S.C. Humphreys and H. King. London: Academic Press, 1981, 20–21; H.V. Vallois, 'Vital statistics in prehistoric population as determined from archaeological data', in *The Application of Quantitative Methods in Archaeology*, ed. R.F. Heizer and S.F. Cook. Chicago: Quadrangle, 1960, 186.

31 Compare with D.R. Brothwell, *Digging up Bones: The Excavation, Treatment and Study of Human Skeletal Remains*. 3rd edn. London: British Museum (Natural History) & Oxford University Press, 1981/1965, 78, Fig. 4.1. Long bone and some pelvic measurements (maximum iliac breadth in juveniles) were made using an osteometric board based on the design in Brothwell (1981: 78). Vernier callipers were also used for some long bone measurements. Maximum circumference of long bone measurements were made with a 3–metre plastic tape measure that was cut into 25 cm strips. The strips were all calibrated to ensure there was no difference between them. Each strip was replaced as soon as evidence of stretching was observed. Skull measurements were made with a pair of spreading callipers. To ensure stability whilst it was being measured, the skull was placed on a bean bag.

32 J.E. Buikstra and D.H. Ubelaker (eds), *Standards for Data Collection from Human Skeletal Remains: Proceedings of a Seminar at the Field Museum of Natural History Organized by Jonathon Haas*. Fayetteville, Arkansas, 1994.

33 M. Smith (Department of Econometrics, University of Sydney) to E. Lazer, circa 1993, personal communication.

34 W.W. Howells, *Cranial Variation in Man: A Study by Multivariate Analysis of Patterns of Difference among Recent Populations*. Vol. 67, Papers of the Peabody Museum of Archaeology and Ethnology. Cambridge, Massachusetts: Harvard University, 1973, 34–35. See also E. Lazer, 'Human Skeletal Remains in Pompeii: Vols. I and II', unpublished PhD thesis, Department of Anatomy and Histology. Sydney: The University of Sydney, 1995, 94–102.

35 Lazer 1995, op. cit., GOL: Fig. 4.2, 96.

36 Ibid., FRC: Fig. 4.11, 100.

37 Ibid., PAC: Fig. 4.12, 101.

38 Ibid., XCB: Fig. 4.6, 98.

39 Ibid., XFB: Fig. 4.7, 98.

40 Ibid., ZYB: Fig. 4.8, 99.

41 Ibid., NOL: Fig. 4.3, 96.

42 Ibid., ASB: Fig. 4.10, 100.

43 Ibid., BNL: Fig. 4.4, 97.

44 Ibid., OCC: Fig. 4.13, 101.

45 Ibid., FRC: Fig. 4.11, 100.

46 Ibid., BBH: Fig. 4.5, 97.

47 Ibid., AUB: Fig. 4.9, 99.

48 Compare with C. Pardoe, 'Prehistoric Human Morphological Variation in Australia', unpublished PhD thesis. Canberra: Australian National University, 1984, 25.

49 Discriminant function analysis is based on the assumption that all groups have the same intrapopulation covariance matrix. In the case of sex, interpopulation variability is great enough to require the development of separate sets of equations for different populations for sex attribution. In addition, it relies on the use of data derived from known populations to place unknown individuals into 'correct' groups with a high probability, such as for sex. This highlights the questionable value of applying this technique to an unknown population, as it will probably produce results that are artefacts.

50 W. Haglund, 'Forensic "art" in human identification', in *Craniofacial Identification in Forensic Medicine*, ed. J.G. Clement and D.L. Ranson. London: Arnold, 1998, 235.

51 Haglund, 1998, op. cit., 237–40.

52 K.T. Taylor, *Forensic Art and Illustration*. Boca Raton, Florida: CRC Press, 2001, 85.

6 Attribution of sex

1 P. Drackett, *The Book of Great Disasters*. Berkshire: Purnell, 1977, 115; G. Nicolucci, 'Crania Pompeiana: Descrizione de' crani umani rinvenuti fra le ruine dell' antica Pompei', *Atti della R. Accademia delle Scienze Fisiche e Matematiche*, Vol. 9, No. 10, 1882, 1.

2 A. Massa, *The World of Pompeii*. London: Routledge, 1972, 135–36.

3 E. De Carolis *et al.*, 'Rinvenimenti di corpi umani nell'area urbana di Pompei', *Rivista di Studi Pompeiani*, Vol. 9, 1998, 79, 84, 113.

4 B.E. Anderson, 'Ventral arc of the os pubis: Anatomical and developmental considerations', *American Journal of Physical Anthropology*, Vol. 83, 1990, 454; M.Y. El-Najjar, and K.R. McWilliams, *Forensic Anthropology: The Structure, Morphology and Variation of Human Bone and Dentition*. Springfield, Illinois: Charles C. Thomas, 1978, 76; W.M. Krogman, and M.Y. Iscan, *The Human Skeleton in Forensic Medicine*. 2nd edn. Springfield, Illinois: Charles C. Thomas, 1986, 190; S. Mays, *The Archaeology of Human Bones*. London:

Routledge, 1998, 38–42; F.W. Rösing, 'Sexing immature human skeletons', *Journal of Human Evolution*, Vol. 12, 1983, 149; L. Scheuer and S. Black, *The Juvenile Skeleton*. Amsterdam: Elsevier, 2004, 19–21; L.E. St Hoyme and M.Y. Iscan, 'Determination of sex and race: Accuracy and assumptions', in *Reconstruction of Life from the Skeleton*, ed. M.Y. Iscan and K.A.R. Kennedy. New York: Alan R. Liss, 1989, 54.

5 S.M.C. Holcomb and L.W. Konigsberg, 'Statistical study of sexual dimorphism in the human foetal sciatic notch', *American Journal of Physical Anthropology*, Vol. 97, 1995, 113–25, Mays, 1998, op. cit., 39.

6 H. Schutkowski, 'Sex determination of infant and juvenile skeletons: 1. Morphognostic features', *American Journal of Physical Anthropology*, Vol. 90, 1993, 199–205.

7 K.M. Bowden, *Forensic Medicine*. 2nd edn. Brisbane: Jacaranda, 1965, 481; G. Gustafson, *Forensic Odontology*. London: Staples Press, 1966, 91; St Hoyme and Iscan, 1989, op. cit., 54, 69; D.H. Ubelaker, *Human Skeletal Remains: Excavation, Analysis, Interpretation*. 2nd edn. Vol. 2, Manuals on Archaeology. Washington: Taraxacum, 1989, 52.

8 Mays, 1998, op. cit., 39–42; Scheuer and Black, 2004, op. cit., 20.

9 D. Donlon, 'The Value of Postcranial Nonmetric Variation in Studies of Global Populations in Modern Homo Sapiens', unpublished PhD thesis. Armidale: University of New England, 1990, 109, 128; Scheuer and Black, 2004, op. cit., 20.

10 A.C. Stone *et al.*, 'Sex determination of ancient human skeletons using DNA', *American Journal of Physical Anthropology*, Vol. 99, 1996, 231–38.

11 To gain an appreciation of some of the problems, it is worth considering an example. An attempt was made to obtain samples of DNA from skeletons from an historic nineteenth–early-twentieth-century cemetery site at Cadia in Central Western NSW, Australia. Small samples were extracted from juvenile and adult dental material using techniques that were established for the skeletal study of the cemetery site at the Destitute Children's Asylum at the Prince of Wales Hospital, Randwick, Australia (Donlon *et al.*, 1997, op. cit., 7–178.) Genetic material can often be obtained from the pulp cavity of the tooth, especially in the case of adults when the root has fully formed and provides a seal against contamination. Genetic material is also bound with the dentine. Whilst it is still possible to obtain genetic material from juvenile teeth, they are less likely to provide a good yield of DNA. The material extracted from these skeletons appeared promising but ultimately did not yield any readable sequences of DNA. (E. Lazer, *Report on the Excavation of the Cadia Cemetery, Cadia Road, Cadia, NSW, 1997–98*. Vol. 4: Skeletal Report: Unpublished report for Cadia Holdings. Orange, NSW: Edward Higginbotham & Associates, 2001, 8, 20.)

12 Scheuer and Black, 2004, op. cit., 21.

13 D.R. Brothwell, *Digging up Bones: The Excavation, Treatment and Study of Human Skeletal Remains*. 3rd edn. London: British Museum (Natural History) & Oxford University Press, 1981/1965; Krogman and Iscan, 1986, op. cit., 195; Ubelaker, 1989, op. cit., 53; T.D. White, *Human Osteology*. 1st edn. San Diego, California: Academic Press, 1991, 320.

14 El-Najjar and McWilliams, 1978, op. cit., 76; St Hoyme and Iscan, 1989, op. cit., 54, 59.

15 V. Higgins, 'A model for assessing health patterns from skeletal remains', in *Burial Archaeology: Current Research, Methods and Developments*, ed. C.A. Robert, F. Lee and J. Bintliff, 211. Oxford: BAR, 1989, 182, 191–94; St Hoyme and Iscan, 1989, op. cit., 59.

16 S. Genovés, 'Sex determination in earlier man', in *Science in Archaeology: A Survey of Progress and Research*, ed. Brothwell, D. and E. Higgs. London: Thames & Hudson, 1969a, 431–32.

17 Higgins, 1989, op. cit, 194.

18 Brothwell, 1981, op. cit., 59; El-Najjar and McWilliams, 1978, op. cit., 75; St Hoyme and Iscan, 1989, op. cit., 59; White, 1991, op. cit., 322.

19 The standard scoring system takes into account the difficulties involved with the identification of sexual markers in biological material where there can be considerable overlap between males and females for particular features. In addition, there can be diversity within and between populations, respectively known as intrapopulation and interpopulation

variation. I modified the standard five point system with the addition of two further scores to include equivocal cases for which a sexual attribution could be inferred. Observations made on skulls and innominate bones were therefore scored in terms of a seven point scale which ranged from hyperfemale (1) to hypermale (7) See Table 6.1.

20 The data for each measurement and observation were visualized as a series of histograms to determine whether any individual measurement displayed significant bimodality (define bimodality), which could be used as an indicator of sex separation in the sample. Histograms using Z-scores, standardized about the mean, were employed to demonstrate whether there was any skewing. The pooled measurements were subjected to a k means cluster analysis. Principal components analysis was also employed as a descriptive technique. E. Lazer, 'Human Skeletal Remains in Pompeii: Vols. I and II', unpublished PhD thesis, Department of Anatomy and Histology. Sydney: The University of Sydney, 1995, 130.

21 Brothwell, 1981, op. cit., 62; El-Najjar and McWilliams, 1978, op. cit., 76; Krogman and Iscan, 1986, op. cit., 200; Ubelaker, 1989, op. cit., 53.

22 Anderson, 1990, op. cit., 453.

23 M.A. Kelley, 'Phenice's visual sexing technique for the os pubis: A critique', *American Journal of Physical Anthropology*, Vol. 48, 1978, 121–22; T.W. Phenice, 'A newly developed visual method of sexing the os pubis', *American Journal of Physical Anthropology*, Vol. 30, 1967, 297–301.

24 For these reasons the pubic index was not used. The measurement of this index has also been found to be very time-consuming. Brothwell, 1981, op. cit., 62–63; Phenice, 1969, op. cit., 297–98; White, 1991, op. cit., 325; was not used.

25 Krogman and Iscan, 1986, op. cit., 247; Ubelaker, 1989, op. cit., 55, 60.

26 Brothwell, 1981, op. cit., 62; El-Najjar and McWilliams, 1978, op. cit., 80–81; P. Houghton, 'The relationship of the pre-auricular groove of the ilium to pregnancy', *American Journal of Physical Anthropology*, Vol. 41, 1974, 381.

27 Genovés, 1969a, op. cit., 430.

28 S. Genovés, 'Estimation of age and mortality', in *Science in Archaeology: A Survey of Progress and Research*, ed. D. Brothwell and E. Higgs. London: Thames & Hudson, 1969b, 449; T. D. Stewart, 'Distortion of the pubic symphyseal surface in females and its effect on age determination', *American Journal of Physical Anthropology*, Vol. 15, 1957, 9–18.

29 A.T. Chamberlain, *Demography in Archaeology*, Cambridge Manuals in Archaeology. Cambridge: Cambridge University Press, 2006, 96; J.M. Suchey et al., 'Analysis of dorsal pitting in the os pubis in an extensive sample of modern American females', *American Journal of Physical Anthropology*, Vol. 51, 1979, 522; T.D. White, and P.A. Folkens, *The Human Bone Manual*. Boston: Academic Press, 2005, 380.

30 M.A. Kelley, 'Parturition and pelvic changes', *American Journal of Physical Anthropology*, Vol. 51, 1979, 541.

31 Tague 1988 in T.D. White, *Human Osteology*. 2nd ed. San Diego, California: Academic Press, 2000, 354–55.

32 M. Cox and A. Scott, 'Evaluation of the obstetric significance of some pelvic characters in an 18th century British sample of known parity status', *American Journal of Physical Anthropology*, Vol. 89, 1992, 431–40; T. Molleson et al., *The Spitalfields Project*. Vol. 2: The Anthropology: The Middling Sort, Council for British Archaeology Research Report 86. York, UK: Council for British Archaeology, 1993, 214.

33 Brothwell, 1981, op. cit., 66; D. Ferembach et al., 'Recommendations for age and sex diagnoses of skeletons (Workshop of European Anthropologists)', *Journal of Human Evolution*, Vol. 9, No. 7, 1980, 517–49.

34 For example, R.G. Tague, 'Bone resorption of the pubis and preauricular area in humans and nonhuman mammals', *American Journal of Physical Anthropology*, Vol. 76 1988, 255.

35 Lazer, 1995, op. cit., 114–17.

36 Kelley, 1978, op. cit., 121–22.

37 V. Higgins (University of Notre Dame, Rome) to E. Lazer, 1989–90, personal communication.

38 Ibid.

39 Molleson, 1981, op. cit., 20.

40 Lazer, 1995, op. cit., 119–21.

41 W.M. Bass, *Human Osteology: A Laboratory and Field Manual of the Human Skeleton*. 2nd edn. Columbia: Missouri Archaeological Society, 1984, 114–15; Brothwell, 1981, op. cit., 85; D.L. France, 'Osteometry at muscle origin and insertion in sex determination', *American Journal of Physical Anthropology*, Vol. 76, 1988, 517–20.

42 France, 1988, op. cit., 517.

43 J. Dittirick and J.M. Suchey, 'Sex determination of prehistoric central California skeletal remains using discriminant analysis of the femur and humerus', *American Journal of Physical Anthropology*, Vol. 70, 1986, 3.

44 Bass, 1984, op. cit., 114–15; Brothwell, 1981, op. cit., 85.

45 France, 1988, op. cit., 515–26; Dittrick and Suchey, 1986, op. cit., 3–9.

46 Dittrick and Suchey, 1986, op. cit., 8–9.

47 France, 1988, op. cit., 523.

48 France, 1988, op. cit., 523; Dittrick and Suchey, 1986, op. cit., 8.

49 France, 1988, op. cit., 523.

50 France, 1988, op. cit., 524.

51 Lazer, 1995, op. cit., 136–37.

52 Lazer, 1995, op. cit., 117–19

53 Dittrick and Suchey, 1986, op. cit., 8–9.

54 Lazer, 1995, op. cit., 121–24.

55 Brothwell, 1981, op. cit., 59–61; J.E. Buikstra *et al.* (eds), *Standards for Data Collection from Human Skeletal Remains: Proceedings of a Seminar at the Field Museum of Natural History Organized by Jonathon Haas*. Fayetteville, Arkansas, 1994, 19–20; Ferembach *et al.*, 1980, op. cit., 523–25; El-Najjar and McWilliams, 1978, op. cit., 83–84; Krogman and Iscan, 1986, op. cit., 192–93; White, 1991, op. cit., 322–23.

56 Ferembach *et al.*, 1980, op. cit., 523.

57 Compare with White, 1991, op. cit., 322.

58 These were supraorbital ridges, zygomatic processes and overall shape (Lazer, 1995, op. cit., 137, Figs. 5.31, 5.32 and 5.33).

59 For example, temporal line, glabella, mastoid process and nuchal crest (Lazer, 1995, op. cit., 137).

60 Features that were skewed towards female attribution were overall shape, degree of angling of the frontal bone, supraorbital ridges, glabella, orbital shape, orbital rims, parietal bosses, mastoid process, nuchal crest, external occipital protuberance, zygomatic bone and dental arch. Features that were apparently skewed towards male attribution were posterior root of the zygomatic process, frontal eminences and the temporal line. Only one feature, the zygomatic process, separated into equal numbers of each sex. Lazer, 1995, op. cit., 137.

61 Ferembach *et al.*, 1980, op. cit., 523.

62 Five factors were extracted from a principal components analysis of 12 of the skull observations. BZYG, ZYGP and DEN were excluded. Overall shape was also excluded because it appeared to operate more like a sex index than an individual feature. Lazer, 1995, op. cit., 139.

63 D'Amore et al., 1979, op. cit., 304.

64 For example, D'Amore *et al.,* 1964, op. cit.

65 S.C. Bisel (Physical anthropologist, Herculaneum) to E. Lazer, 1988c, personal communication.

66 W.W. Howells, *Cranial Variation in Man: A Study by Multivariate Analysis of Patterns of Difference among Recent Populations*. Vol. 67, Papers of the Peabody Museum of Archaeology and Ethnology. Cambridge, Massachusetts: Harvard University, 1973, 7–8; Howells, W. W. *Skull Shapes and the Map: Craniometric Analyses in the Dispersion of Modern Homo*. Vol. 79, Papers of the Peabody Museum of Archaeology and Ethnology. Cambridge, Massachusetts: Harvard University, 1989, 3.

67 Brothwell, 1981, op. cit., 83; Howells, op. cit., 1973, 174–76; Lazer, 1995, op. cit., 124–28.

68 Brothwell, 1981, op. cit., 61; Krogman and Iscan, 1986, op. cit., 193–98; Ubelaker, 1989, op. cit., 55.

69 Ubelaker, 1989, op. cit., 55.

70 Lazer, 1995, op. cit., 140–41.

71 B. Flury, and H. Riedwyl, *Multivariate Statistics: A Practical Approach*. London: Chapman & Hall, 1988, 218–28.

72 Lazer, 1995, op. cit., 128–29.

73 Brothwell, 1981, op. cit., 59–61; Buikstra and Ubelaker 1994: 19–20; El-Najjar and McWilliams, 1978, op. cit., 83–84; Ferembach *et al.*, 1980, op. cit., 523–25; Krogman and Iscan, 1986, op. cit., 192–93; White, 1991, op. cit., 322–23. Since a mandible board was not available, sex was assessed purely from visual inspection.

74 Brothwell, 1981, op. cit., 59; Ferembach *et al.*, 1980, op. cit., 525; S. Hillson, Teeth, Cambridge Manuals in Archaeology. Cambridge: Cambridge University Press, 1986, 240–41; Krogman and Iscan, 1986, op. cit., 193, 366–69; Lazer, 1995, op. cit., 129–30.

75 Compare with B.C.W. Barker, 'Concerning the possibility of estimating the original dimensions of worn Aboriginal teeth', *Australian Dental Journal*, Vol. 17, 1972, 448–53.

76 G. Nicolucci, 1882, op. cit., 10.

77 The measurements for my study were based on the definitions of Howells and Brothwell (see note 68 above). It is highly probable that Nicolucci's method of measurement for at least some of these measurements differed substantially from these definitions.

78 Such as the vertical index (INDVER), the alveolar index (INDALV), the nasal index (INDNAS), the orbital index (INDORB) and the cephalic index (CEFI).

79 Brothwell, 1981, op. cit., 87.

80 Brothwell, 1981, op. cit., 84.

81 Lazer, 1995, op. cit., 141.

82 D'Amore *et al.*, 1979, op. cit., 297–308.

83 W.M. Krogman, *The Human Skeleton in Forensic Medicine*. Springfield, Illinois: Charles C. Thomas, 1962, 114–22.

84 D'Amore *et al.*, 1979, op. cit., 301, 304.

85 D'Amore *et al.*, 1979, op. cit., 304; Nicolucci, 1882, op. cit., 10.

86 For example Brothwell, 1981, op. cit., 59–60; Ferembach *et al.*, 1980, op. cit., 523–25.

87 St Hoyme and Iscan, 1989, op. cit., 70.

88 St Hoyme and Iscan, 1989, op. cit., 70.

89 S.J. Gould, *The Mismeasure of Man*. Middlesex: Pelican, 1984, 26, 74.

90 D'Amore *et al.*, 1979, op. cit., 304.

91 D'Amore *et al.*, 1979, op. cit., 304.

92 K.M. Weiss, 'On the systematic bias in skeletal sexing,' *American Journal of Physical Anthropology*, Vol. 37 1972, 239–49.

93 D'Amore *et al.*, 1979, op. cit., 304–5.

94 D'Amore *et al.*, 1979, op. cit., 305.

95 The ratio of males to females from examination of the pelvis was 103 : 83, the mandible, 63 : 48 and the skull, 148 : 187. M. Henneberg, and R.J. Henneberg, 'Reconstructing medical knowledge in ancient Pompeii from the hard evidence of bones and teeth (Presented at a conference at Deutsches Museum, Munich 21–22 March 2000)', in *Homo Faber: Studies in Nature, Technology and Science at the Time of Pompeii*, ed. J. Renn and G. Castagnetti. Roma: L'Erma di Bretschneider, 2002, 173.

96 S.C. Bisel, 'The human skeletons of Herculaneum', *International Journal of Anthropology*, Vol. 6, No. 1, 1991, 2; S.C. Bisel, 'Nutrition in first century Herculaneum', *Anthropologie*, Vol. 26, 1988a, 61.

97 L. Capasso, *I Fuggiaschi di Ercolano: Paleobiologia delle Vittime dell'Eruzione Vesuviana del 79 d.C.* Roma: 'L'Erma' di Bretschneider, 2001, 73, 948–54, 956–57. He used standard morphological observations for adults and less accepted techniques for infants. For example, see H. Schutkowski, 'Sex determination of infant and juvenile skeletons: 1. Morphognostic features', *American Journal of Physical Anthropology*, Vol. 90, 1993: 199–205.

98 P.P. Petrone *et al.*, 'La popolazione di Ercolano', in *Vesuvio 79 AD: Vita e Morte ad Ercolano*, ed. P.P. Petrone and F. Fedele. Naples: Fredericiana Editrice Universitaria, 2002, 67–71.

99 St Hoyme and Iscan, 1989, op. cit.

100 St Hoyme and Iscan, 1989, op. cit., 53–54.

7 Determination of age-at-death

1 For issues associated with the relationship between biological and chronological age, see A. Kemkes-Grottenthaler, 'Aging through the ages: Historical perspectives on age indicator methods', in *Paleodemography: Age Distributions from Skeletal Samples*, ed. R.D. Hoppa and J.W. Vaupel, *Cambridge Studies in Biological and Evolutionary Anthropology*. Cambridge: Cambridge University Press, 2002, 48–50.

2 H.M. Liversidge, 'Accuracy of age estimation from developing teeth of a population of known age (0–5.4 years)', *International Journal of Osteoarchaeology*, Vol. 4,1994, 37–45; S. Mays, *The Archaeology of Human Bones*. London: Routledge, 1998, 42–49; T.D. White, *Human Osteology*. 2nd edn. San Diego, California: Academic Press, 2000, 340–42, 349.

3 D.R. Brothwell, *Digging up Bones: The Excavation, Treatment and Study of Human Skeletal Remains*. 3rd edn. London: British Museum (Natural History) & Oxford University Press, 1981/1965, 64–73; A.T. Chamberlain, *Demography in Archaeology*, Cambridge Manuals in Archaeology. Cambridge: Cambridge University Press, 2006, 105; Kemkes-Grottenthaler, 2002, op. cit., 48; D.H. Ubelaker, *Human Skeletal Remains: Excavation, Analysis, Interpretation*. 2nd edn. Vol. 2, Manuals on Archaeology. Washington: Taraxacum, 1989, 74; T.D. White, *Human Osteology*. 1st edn. San Diego, California: Academic Press, 1991, 308–9.

4 Kemkes-Grottenthaler, 2002, op. cit., 58–66. Also, the lack of survival of certain skeletal elements, like ribs, meant that many well established ageing techniques could not be employed.

5 Brothwell, 1981, op. cit., 64–72; Kemkes-Grottenthaler, 2002, op. cit., 57–58; Krogman and Iscan, 1986, op. cit., 129–30, 146–69; P. Shipman *et al.*, *The Human Skeleton*. Cambridge, Massachusetts: Harvard University Press, 1985, 255–70; White, 1991, op. cit., 308–27.

6 Kemkes-Grottenthaler, 2002, op. cit., 58–60, 62, 65–66; Krogman and Iscan, 1986, op. cit., 95, 97; C.O. Lovejoy *et al.*, 'Multifactorial determination of skeletal age at death: A method and blind tests of its accuracy', *American Journal of Physical Anthropology*, Vol. 68, 1985a, 1–14, Shipman *et al.*, 1985, op. cit., 264–65.

7 J. Ahlqvist, and D. Damsten, 'A modification of Kerley's method for the microscopic determination of age in human bone', *Journal of Forensic Sciences*, Vol. 14, 1969, 205–12; Chamberlain, 2006, op. cit., 111–12; M.Y. El-Najjar, and K.R. McWilliams, *Forensic Anthropology: The Structure, Morphology and Variation of Human Bone and Dentition*. Springfield, Illinois: Charles C. Thomas, 1978, 70–72; G. Gustafson, *Forensic Odontology*. London: Staples Press, 1966, 120–23; E.R. Kerley, 'The microscopic determination of age in human bone', *American Journal of Physical Anthropology*, Vol. 23, 1965, 149–64; Krogman and Iscan, 1986, op. cit., 180–84, 364–65; S. Pfeiffer, 'Comparison of adult age estimation techniques using an ossuary sample', *Canadian Review of Physical Anthropology*, Vol. 4, No. 1, 1985, 21–25.

8 J.G. Clement (Victorian Institute of Forensic Pathology, Melbourne) to E. Lazer, 1994, personal communication.

9 M.Y. Iscan and S.R. Loth, 'Osteological manifestations of age in the adult', in *Reconstruction of Life from the Skeleton*, ed. M.Y. Iscan and K.A.R. Kennedy. New York: Alan R. Liss, 1989, 31–34.

48 Parkin, 1992, op. cit., 14; Parkin, 2003, op. cit., 31–35.

49 Parkin notes that illiteracy and age rounding appear to have been linked. Apparently, age rounding was more prevalent outside the cities, among women and those of lower economic or social status and lower levels of education. Parkin, 2003, op. cit., 32–35.

50 Parkin, 2003, op. cit., 94, 189.

51 Dyson, 1992, op. cit., 15, 17, 19; Parkin, 1992, op. cit., 134; Parkin, 2003, op. cit., 36.

52 L. Capasso and L. Capasso. 'Mortality in Herculaneum before volcanic eruption in 79 AD', *The Lancet*, Vol. 354, No. 9192, 1999, 1826; 277–88; L. Capasso, *I Fuggiaschi di Ercolano: Paleobiologia delle Vittime dell'Eruzione Vesuviana del 79 d.C.* Roma: 'L'Erma' di Bretschneider, 2001, 947–72; M. Henneberg, and R.J. Henneberg, 'Reconstructing medical knowledge in ancient Pompeii from the hard evidence of bones and teeth. Presented at a conference at Deutsches Museum, Munich 21–22 March 2000', in *Homo Faber: Studies in Nature, Technology and Science at the Time of Pompeii*, ed. J. Renn and G. Castagnetti. Roma: L'Erma di Bretschneider, 2002, 169–87.

53 S.C. Bisel, 'Human bones at Herculaneum', *Rivista di Studi Pompeiani*, Vol. 1, 1987, 123; S.C. Bisel, 'Nutrition in first century Herculaneum', *Anthropologie*, Vol. 26, 1988a, 61; S. C. Bisel, 'The skeletons of Herculaneum, Italy', in *Wet Site Archaeology: Proceedings of the International Conference on Wet Site Archaeology, Gainesville, Florida, December 12–14, 1986; sponsored by the National Endowment for the Humanities and University of Florida*, ed. B.A. Purdy. Caldwell, New Jersey: Telford Press, 1988b, 209.

54 See for example, J.-P. Bocquet-Appel, and C. Masset. 'Farewell to paleodemography', *Journal of Human Evolution*, Vol. 11, 1982, 321–33, J.P. Bocquet-Appel and C. Masset. 'Paleodemography: Resurrection or Ghost?', *Journal of Human Evolution*, Vol. 14, No. 2, 1985, 107–11; Chamberlain, 2006, op. cit., 84–87.

55 Chamberlain, 2006, op. cit., 87–132.

56 Chamberlain, 2006, op. cit., 26–32, 88–89.

57 I.B. Cohen, *The Triumph of Numbers: How Counting Shaped Modern Life*. New York: WW Norton & Company, 2005, 47–48; Chamberlain, 2006, op. cit., 27–32.

58 Bisel, 1987, op. cit., 123; Bisel, 1988a, op. cit., 61; Bisel, 1988b, op. cit., 209.

59 W.F. Jashemski, *The Gardens of Pompeii, Herculaneum and the Villas Destroyed by Vesuvius*. New York: Caratzas Brothers, 1979a, 243.

60 G. Nicolucci, 'Crania Pompeiana: Descrizione de' crani umani rinvenuti fra le ruine dell' antica Pompei', *Atti della R. Accademia delle Scienze Fisiche e Matematiche*, Vol. 9, No. 10, 1882, 10.

61 C. D'Amore *et al.*, 'Antropologia pompeiana del 79 d.C.: Sesso ed età di morte', *Archivio per l'Antropologia e la Etnologia*, Vol. 109, 1979, 305; H.V. Vallois, 'Vital statistics in prehistoric population as determined from archaeological data', in *The Application of Quantitative Methods in Archaeology*, ed. R.F. Heizer and S.F. Cook. Chicago: Quadrangle, 1960, 194.

62 D'Amore *et al.*, 1979, op. cit., 305–6.

63 D'Amore *et al.*, 1979, op. cit., 304.

64 Vallois, 1960, op. cit., 187–93.

65 Vallois, 1960, op. cit., 194.

66 Ibid.

67 Krogman, 1962, op. cit., 76–89. Also, see the discussion that followed Vallois' paper. Vallois, 1960, op. cit., 205–22, especially 212–13.

68 D'Amore *et al.*, 1979, op. cit., 305.

69 Henneberg and Henneberg, 2002, op. cit., 172.

70 Also E. Lazer, 'Pompeii AD 79: A population in flux?', in *Sequence and Space in Pompeii*, ed. S.E. Bon and R. Jones. Oxford: Oxbow Monograph 77, 1997a, 102–20.

71 Henneberg and Henneberg, 2002, op. cit., 171–74.

72 Ibid., 185.

73 Bisel, 1988a, op. cit., 61; S.C. Bisel, 'The human skeletons of Herculaneum', *International Journal of Anthropology*, Vol. 6, No. 1, 1991, 2; S.C. Bisel and J.F. Bisel, 'Health and

nutrition at Herculaneum: An examination of human skeletal remains', in *The Natural History of Pompeii*, ed. W.F. Jashemski and F.G. Meyer. Cambridge: Cambridge University Press, 2002, 453–54.

74 Bisel, 1991, op. cit., 2–3; Bisel and Bisel, 2002, op. cit.

75 Bisel and Bisel, 2002, op. cit., 474.

76 Capasso, 2001, op. cit., 73–75; Chamberlain, 2006, op. cit., 110–11; Kerley, 1965, op. cit., 149–64.

77 Capasso, 2001, op. cit., 947; Capasso and Capasso, 1999, op. cit., 1826.

78 Capasso, 2001, op. cit., 956.

79 Capasso and Capasso, 1999, op. cit., 1826; Capasso, 2001, op. cit., 967–69.

80 P.P. Petrone *et al.*, 'La popolazione di Ercolano', in *Vesuvio 79 AD: Vita e Morte ad Ercolano*, ed. P.P. Petrone and F. Fedele. Naples: Fredericiana Editrice Universitaria, 2002a, 69.

81 Petrone *et al.*, 2002, op. cit., 71; Seneca. *Naturales Quaestiones*. Translated by T.H. Corcoran, Loeb Classical Library. Cambridge, Massachusetts: Harvard University Press, 1972, VI, 1, 26, 27, 31.

82 Chamberlain, 2006, op. cit., 82; Jackes, 1992, op. cit., 189–224; J.M. Suchey, and D. Katz, 'Skeletal age standards derived from an extensive multiracial sample of modern Americans (unpublished paper)', in *The Fifty-Fifth Annual Meeting of the American Association of Physical Anthropologists*. Albuquerque, New Mexico: 1986, J.M. Suchey, D.V. Wiseley and D. Katz, 'Evaluation of the Todd and McKern–Stewart methods for aging the male os pubis', in *Forensic Osteology: Advances in the Identification of Human Remains*, ed. K.J. Reichs. Springfield, Illinois: Charles. C Thomas, 1986, 33–67; J.M. Suchey, S.T. Brooks and D. Katz, *Instructions for the Use of the Suchey–Brooks System for Age Determination of the Female Os Pubis*, Instructional materials accompanying female pubic symphyseal models of the Suchey–Brooks System, 1988, 5.

83 Chamberlain, 2006, op. cit., 110–12; B. Grosskopf, 'Individualaltersbestimmung mit hilfe von zuwachsringen im zement bodengelagerter menschlicher zähne', *Zeitschrift für Rechtsmedizin,* Vol. 103, No. 5, 1990, 351–59; Jackes, 1992, op. cit., 199, 210, 218; V.K. Kayshap, and N.R. Koteswara Rao, 'A modified Gustafson method of age estimation from teeth', *Forensic Science International*, Vol. 47, No. 3, 1990, 237–47; M. Lorentsen, and T. Solheim. 'Age assessment based on translucent dentine', *Journal of Forensic Odontostomatology*, Vol. 7, No. 2, 1989, 3–9; A.E.W. Miles, 'Teeth as an indicator of age in man', in *Development, Function and Evolution of Teeth*, ed. P.M. Butler and K.A. Joysey. New York: Academic Press, 1978, 460–61.

8 General health and lifestyle indicators

1 T.D. White, *Human Osteology*. 2nd edn. San Diego, California: Academic Press, 2000, 383; T.D. White and P.A. Folkens, *The Human Bone Manual*. Boston: Academic Press, 2005, 309–11.

2 C.H. Cabell *et al.*, 'Bacterial endocarditis: The disease, treatment, and prevention', in *Circulation* (American Heart Association, 2003); R. Gendron *et al.*, 'The oral cavity as a reservoir of bacterial pathogens for focal infections', *Microbes and Infection*, Vol. 2, No. 8, 2000, 897–906; Meyer, D.H. and P.M. Fives-Taylor, 'Oral pathogens: from dental plaque to cardiac disease', *Current Opinion in Microbiology*, Vol. 1, No. 1, 1998, 88–95; J. Molloy *et al.*, 'The association of periodontal disease parameters with systemic medical conditions and tobacco use', *Journal of Clinical Periodontology*, Vol. 31, No. 8, 2004, 625–26, 631; P.G. O'Reilly and N.M. Claffey, 'A history of oral sepsis as a cause of disease', *Periodontology 2000*, Vol. 23, No. 1, 2000: 13, 16–18.

3 E. Lazer, 'Human Skeletal Remains in Pompeii: Vols. I and II', unpublished PhD thesis, Department of Anatomy and Histology. Sydney: University of Sydney, 1995, 210–13.

4 Odin Langsjoen in A.C. Aufderheide and C. Rodriguez-Martin, *The Cambridge Encyclopaedia of Human Palaeopathology*. Cambridge: Cambridge University Press, 1998, 397; K. Manchester, *The Archaeology of Disease*. Bradford: University of Bradford, 1983, 51.

5 S.C. Bisel, 'The human skeletons of Herculaneum', *International Journal of Anthropology*, Vol. 6, No. 1, 1991, 8; L.D. Martin *et al.*, *Black Mesa Anasazi Health: Reconstructing Life from Patterns of Death and Disease*. Vol. 14, Occasional Paper Carbonale, Illinois: Center for Archaeological Investigations: Southern Illinois University at Carbondale, 1991, 183–84; Lazer, 1995, op. cit., Appendix 3, 401–3.

6 S.C. Bisel and J.F. Bisel, 'Health and nutrition at Herculaneum: An examination of human skeletal remains', in *The Natural History of Pompeii*, ed. W.F. Jashemski and F.G. Meyer. Cambridge: Cambridge University Press, 2002, 451–75; M. Torino and G. Fornaciari, 'Gli Scheletri di Ercolani: Richerche paleopatologiche', in *Gli Antichi Ercolanesi: Antropologia, Società, Economia*, ed. M. Pagano. Napoli: Electa, 2000, 60–63; L. Capasso, *I Fuggiaschi di Ercolano: Paleobiologia delle Vittime dell'Eruzione Vesuviana del 79 d.C.* Roma: 'L'Erma' di Bretschneider, 2001. P.P. Petrone *et al.*, 'Alimentazione e malattie ad Ercolano', in *Vesuvio79 AD: Vita e Morte ad Ercolano*, ed. P.P. Petrone and F. Fedele. Naples: Fredericiana Editrice Universitaria, 2002b, 75–83.

7 Capasso, 2001, op. cit., 1047.

8 D.R. Williams and C.M. Woodhead, 'Attrition: A contemporary dental viewpoint', in *Teeth and Anthropology*, ed. E. Cruwys and R.A. Foley, 291. Oxford: British Anthropological Reports International, 1986, 109.

9 B. Bonfiglioli *et al.*, 'Dento-alveolar lesions and nutritional habits of a Roman Imperial age population (1st–4th C. AD): Quadrella. Molise, Italy', *Homo: Journal of Comparative Human Biology*, Vol. 54, No. 1, 2003, 40.

10 Such as that observed on TF NS 86: 1 (Figures 7.4 and 7.5).

11 Martin *et al.*, 1991, op. cit., 190.

12 S.C. Bisel, 'Human bones at Herculaneum', *Rivista di Studi Pompeiani*, Vol. 1 1987, 128.

13 Capasso, 2001, op. cit., 1040–42.

14 Bonfiglioli *et al.*, 2003, op. cit., 49; Martin *et al.*, 1991, op. cit., 174; White and Folkens, 2005, op. cit., 328–29.

15 S. Hillson, *Teeth*, Cambridge Manuals in Archaeology. Cambridge: Cambridge University Press, 1986, 287–95; S. Hillson, *Dental Anthropology*. Cambridge: Cambridge University Press, 1996, 269; Martin *et al.*, 1991, op. cit., 166–67; S. Mays, *The Archaeology of Human Bones*. London: Routledge, 1998, 148–52; D.J. Ortner, *Identification of Pathological Conditions in Human Skeletal Remains*. 2nd edn. San Diego: Academic Press, 2003, 590; C.G. Turner, II, *et al.*, 'Scoring procedures for key morphological traits of the permanent dentition: The Arizona State University Dental System', in *Advances in Dental Anthropology*, eds. M.A. Kelley and C.S. Larsen. New York: Wiley-Liss, 1991, 27; White and Folkens, 2005, op. cit., 329.

16 This approach is recommended for archaeological samples by scholars like Hillson, 1996, op. cit., 279.

17 For example TF 99, TF NS 86: 3, TF NS m 86: 3, TF 105, TF 17, TdS NS 84: 1.

18 Bisel, 1991, op. cit., 8.

19 S.C. Bisel, 'Nutrition in first century Herculaneum', *Anthropologie*, Vol. 26, 1988a, 63; Bisel, 1991, op. cit., 4; Hillson, 1986, op. cit., 299.

20 Torino and Fornaciari, 2000, op. cit., 60–62.

21 Capasso, 2001, op. cit., 1044–47; Petrone *et al.*, 2002b, op. cit., 75.

22 D.R. Brothwell, *Digging up Bones: The Excavation, Treatment and Study of Human Skeletal Remains*. 3rd edn. London: British Museum (Natural History) & Oxford University Press, 1981/1965, 154–55; Hillson, 1986, op. cit., 309–12; Hillson, 1996, op. cit., 260–63; Martin *et al.*, 1991, op. cit., 167–68; White and Folkens, 2005, op. cit, 330.

23 Bisel, 1991, op. cit., 4, 8; S.C. Bisel and J.F. Bisel, 'Health and nutrition at Hercula-neum: An examination of human skeletal remains', in *The Natural History of Pompeii*, ed. W.F. Jashemski and F.G. Meyer. Cambridge: Cambridge University Press, 2002, 455.

24 Brothwell, 1981, op. cit., 156–57; Manchester, 1983, op. cit., 51; Martin *et al.*, 1991, op. cit., 168; Turner, *et al.*, op. cit., 27; White and Folkens, 2005, op. cit, 330.

25 Martin *et al.*, 1991, op. cit., 180, 182,190.

26 For example, TF 105, TF 11, TdS m 39, TF NS 86:1. For the last case, see Plate 8.3.

27 Bisel, 1991, op. cit., 8; Capasso, 2001, op. cit., 1042–44.

28 Hillson, 1996, op. cit., 255–56; White and Folkens, 2005, op. cit, 330–31.

29 Capasso, 2001, op. cit., 1042.

30 Hillson, 1986, op. cit., 129–36; Martin *et al.*, 1991, op. cit., 99–100; Mays, 1998, op. cit., 156; Dr Alain Middleton pers. comm.; White and Folkens, 2005, op. cit, 329.

31 A.H. Goodman and G.J. Armelagos, 'Factors affecting the distribution of enamel hypo-plasias within the human permanent dentition', *American Journal of Physical Anthropology*, Vol. 68, 1985, 479; Martin *et al.*, 1991, op. cit., 101, 103; E.J. Neidburger, 'Enamel hypoplasias: Poor indicators of dietary stress', *American Journal of Physical Anthropology*, Vol. 82, 1990: 231–32.

32 Bisel 1988a, op. cit., 62–63; Bisel, 1991, op. cit., 4; Bisel and Bisel, 2002, op. cit., 455; Capasso, 2001, op. cit., 1035–38; Petrone *et al.*, 2002b, op. cit., 75–78.

33 TF 6.

34 G. Majno, *The Healing Hand: Man and Wound in the Ancient World*. 1991 edn. Cambridge, Massachusetts: Harvard University Press, 1975. 73.

35 L.J. Bliquez, *Roman Surgical Instruments and Other Minor Objects in the National Museum of Naples*. Mainz, Germany: Philipp von Zabern, 1994, 78.

36 Celsus, 'De Medicina', in *Loeb Classical Library*. Cambridge, Massachusetts: Harvard Uni-versity Press, 1938, Book 6, Ch 9–13, Book 7, Ch 12, Book 8, 12. B. Ginge *et al.*, 'Of Roman extraction', *Archaeology*, Vol. 42, No. 4, 1989, 34–37; B.W. Weinberger, *An Introduction to the History of Dentistry*, Vols I and II, St Louis, Missouri: Mosby, 1948, 133–35.

37 A. Hoffman, *A History of Dentistry*. Translated by H.M. Koehler. Chicago, Illinois: Quin-tessence Publishing Co, 1981, 68; Martial, 'Epigrammata: English and Latin Selections', London: Hart-Davis, MacGibbon, 1973, Epigrams V.43, XII.23 and XIV.56; Wein-berger, 1948, op. cit., 123–26; 130–31.

38 Weinberger, 1948, op. cit., 139–44.

39 W.M. Bass, *Human Osteology: A Laboratory and Field Manual of the Human Skeleton*. 2nd edn. Columbia: Missouri Archaeological Society, 1984, 175; Brothwell, 1981, op. cit., 100–102; Higgins, V., 'Rural Agricultural Communities of the Late Roman and Early Medieval Periods Including a Study of Two Skeletal Groups from San Vincenzo al Vol-turno', unpublished PhD thesis. Sheffield: University of Sheffield, 1990, 355–56; V. Higgins, 'A model for assessing health patterns from skeletal remains', in *Burial Archaeology: Current Research, Methods and Developments*, ed. C.A. Roberts, F. Lee and J. Bintliff, 211. Oxford: BAR, 1989, 182, 191; W.M. Krogman and M.Y. Iscan, *The Human Skeleton in Forensic Medicine*. 2nd edn. Springfield, Illinois: Charles C. Thomas, 1986, 302–12; M. Trotter and G.C. Gleser. 'A re-evaluation of estimation of stature based on measurements of stature taken during life and of long bones after death', *American Journal of Physical Anthropology*, Vol. 16, 1958, 79–123; D.H. Ubelaker, *Human Skeletal Remains: Excava-tion, Analysis, Interpretation*. 2nd edn. Vol. 2, Manuals on Archaeology. Washington: Tar-axacum, 1989, 60–63; White, 2000, op. cit., 369–72; White and Folkens, 2005, op. cit, 398–400.

40 Bisel, 1991, op. cit., 4; Brothwell, 1981, op. cit., 100–102; Molleson pers. comm.; Mays, 1998, op. cit., 70; Trotter and Gleser, 1958, op. cit., 79–123; M. Trotter, 'Estimation of stature from intact long bones', in *Personal Identification in Mass Disasters*, ed. T.D. Stewart. Washington, DC: Smithsonian Institution Press, 1970, 71–83.

41 Brothwell, 1981, op. cit., 101; Krogman and Iscan, 1986, op. cit., 304–9; Trotter and Gleser, 1958, op. cit., 79–123. The Terry skeletal collection is housed in the Department of Anthropology of the National Museum of Natural History of the Smithsonian Institution. It comprises 1,728 extensively documented human skeletons, which makes it a particularly valuable scientific resource.

42 Krogman and Iscan, 1986, op. cit., 305; S. Pheasant, *Bodyspace: Anthropology, Ergonomics and Design*. London: Taylor & Francis, 1986, 50; Trotter and Gleser, 1958, op. cit., 121.

43 Trotter, 1970, op. cit., 71–83; White, 2000, op. cit., 372; White and Folkens, 2005, op. cit., 398.

44 W. Jongman, 'Gibbon was right: The decline and fall of the Roman economy', in *Crises and the Roman Empire. Proceedings of the Seventh Workshop of the International Network Impact of Empire (Nijmegen, June 20–24, 2006)*, ed. O. Hekster, G. de Kleijn and D. Slootjes. Leiden: Brill, 2007, 194, Graph 7.

45 M.J. Becker, 'Calculating stature from in situ measurements of skeletons and from long bone lengths: An historical perspective leading to a test of Formicola's hypothesis at 5th century BCE Satricum, Lazio, Italy', *Rivista di Antrolopologia* Vol. 77 1999, 225–47; V. Formicola, 'Stature reconstruction from long bones in ancient population samples: An approach to the problem of its reliability', *American Journal of Physical Anthropology*, Vol. 90, No. 3, 1993, 351–58; M. Giannecchini and J. Moggi-Cecchi. 'Stature in archeological samples from Central Italy: Methodological issues and diachronic changes', *American Journal of Physical Anthropology*, Vol. 135, No. 3, 2008, 284–92; M. Trotter and G.C. Gleser. 'Estimation of stature from long bones of American Whites and Negroes', *American Journal of Physical Anthropology*, Vol. 10 1952, 463–514; M. Trotter, and G.C. Gleser. 'Corrigenda to "estimation of stature from long limb bones of American Whites and Negroes," *American Journal of Physical Anthropology* (1952), *American Journal of Physical Anthropology*, Vol. 47, No. 2, 1977, 355–56.

46 See, for example, Krogman and Iscan, 1986, op. cit., 310.

47 Giannecchini and Moggi-Cecchi, 2008, op. cit., 290; Krogman and Iscan, 1986, op. cit., 310–11.

48 Pheasant, 1986, op. cit., 43, Fig. 3.1.

49 Pheasant, 1986, op. cit., 42–43.

50 Henneberg and Henneberg used Pearson's regressions from 1899, Hrdlicka's 1939 proportions, Trotter and Gleser's 1952 and regression formulae, Dupertius and Hadden's 1951 proportions and Telka's 1950 regressions. M. Henneberg and R.J. Henneberg, 'Reconstructing medical knowledge in ancient Pompeii from the hard evidence of bones and teeth. Presented at a conference at Deutsches Museum, Munich 21–22 March 2000', in *Homo Faber: Studies in Nature, Technology and Science at the Time of Pompeii*, ed. J. Renn and G. Castagnetti. Roma: L'Erma di Bretschneider, 2002, 183. The height estimates that they obtained ranged from 163.1 to 169.4 cm for males and 151.6 to 155.8 cm for females. They estimated that the mean male height was about 166 cm and mean female height was around 154 cm.

51 Pheasant, 1986, op. cit., 45.

52 Higgins, 1989, op. cit., 193–94; Higgins, 1990, op. cit., 357.

53 Bisel, 1987, op. cit., 123–24; Bisel 1988a, op. cit., 64; Bisel, 1991, op. cit., 4; Bisel and Bisel, 2002, op. cit., 455; Capasso, 2001, op. cit., 925, 927.

54 Capasso stated that he employed Trotter and Gleser (1958). M.J. Becker, 'Review [untitled]', Rev. of I Fuggiaschi di Ercolano: Paleobiologia delle vittime dell'eruzione Vesuviana del 79 D.C. by L. Capasso. Rome: L'Erma di Bretschneider, 2001, *Journal of Roman Studies*, Vol. 93, 2003, 405; Capasso, 2001, op. cit., 927

55 C. D'Amore *et al.*, 'Definizione antropologica della popolazione adulta di un commune della provincia di Napoli', in *Rendiconto dell'Accademia delle Scienze, Fisiche e Matematiche della Societa Nazionale di Scienze, Lettere ed Arti in Napoli, Serie IV, XXXI*. Napoli: 1964.

56 D'Amore *et al.*, 1964, op. cit., 409.

57 See, for example, Becker, 1999, op. cit., 226–27 for an overview of such studies.
58 Brothwell, 1981, op. cit., 88; L. Capasso *et al.*, *Atlas of Occupational Markers on Human Remains*, Journal of Paleontology: Monographic Publication 3. Teramo: Journal of Paleontology & Edigrafital, 1999, 101.
59 Bisel 1988a, op. cit., 64; Bisel, 1991, op. cit., 6; Bisel and Bisel, 2002, op. cit., 455; Brothwell, 1981, op. cit., 89; Capasso, *et al.*, 1999, op. cit., 101; Capasso, 2001, op. cit., 936–37.
60 Bass, 1984, op. cit., 187; Bisel and Bisel, 2002, op. cit., 455; Capasso, 2001, op. cit., 937–38.
61 Brothwell, 1981, op. cit., 89; K.A.R. Kennedy, 'Skeletal markers of occupational stress', in *Reconstruction of Life from the Skeleton,* ed. M.Y. Iscan and K.A.R. Kennedy. New York: Alan R. Liss, 1989, 136–37.
62 S.C. Bisel, 'The Herculaneum Project: Preliminary Report', *Palaeopathology Newsletter,* Vol. 41, 1983, 6; Bisel, 1987, op. cit., 124; Bisel 1988a, op. cit., 62, 64; S.C. Bisel, 'The skeletons of Herculaneum, Italy', in *Wet Site Archaeology: Proceedings of the International Conference on Wet Site Archaeology, Gainesville, Florida, December 12–14, 1986; sponsored by the National Endowment for the Humanities and University of Florida*, ed. B.A. Purdy. Caldwell, New Jersey: Telford Press, 1988b, 210; Bisel, 1991, op. cit., 4, 8; Bisel and Bisel, 2002, op. cit., 455–56.
63 Brothwell, 1981, op. cit., 119–20; D.J. Ortner and W.G.J. Putschar, *Identification of Pathological Conditions in Human Skeletal Remains*. Vol. 28, Smithsonian Contributions to Anthropology. Washington: Smithsonian Institution Press, 1981, 55; R.T. Steinbock, *Paleopathological Diagnosis and Interpretation: Bone Diseases in Ancient Human Populations*. Springfield, Illinois: Charles C. Thomas, 1976, 17; White, 2000, op. cit., 383–84; White and Folkens, 2005, op. cit, 312.
64 Fractures were described in accordance with Merbs 1989: 161–66 and Roberts 1991: 232–35. Healed nasal fractures were noted but not included in this study as it is unlikely that they would have had any impact on survival prospects from the eruption.
65 Skull TF 111.
66 Aufderheide and Rodriguez–Martin, 1998, op. cit., 20–21; C. Roberts and K. Manchester, *The Archaeology of Disease*. 2nd edn. Ithaca, New York: Cornell University Press, 1995, 67–72; White and Folkens, 2005, op. cit, 48, 312–14.
67 Respectively TdS R 15, TdS L 21 and TdS R 42.
68 Respectively TdS R 11 and TdS # 28:1.
69 Aufderheide and Rodríguez-Martin, 1998, op. cit., 172; Roberts and Manchester, 1995, op. cit., 126–27; White and Folkens, 2005, op. cit, 318.
70 Associated with TdS # 28:1.
71 Lazer, 1995, op. cit., 233.
72 TdS 199.
73 TF 103.
74 Henneberg and Henneberg, 2002, op. cit., 177.
75 TF L 25, TF L 87.
76 TF L 25.
77 Compare with Ortner and Putschar, 1981, op. cit., 57–59, Fig. 50.
78 TF L 140.
79 Aufderheide and Rodríguez-Martin, 1998, op. cit., 84; Ortner and Putschar, 1981, op. cit., 239–42, Figs. 375–81; R.A. Tyson and E.S.D. Alcauskas (eds), *Catalogue of the Hrdlicka Paleopathology Collection*. San Diego, California: San Diego Museum of Man, 1980, 216–19; White and Folkens, 2005, op. cit, 314.
80 Associated with TF 111.
81 Associated with TdS R 15, TdS L 21 and TdS R 42.
82 TdS R 11 and the bones of TdS # 28:1.

83 Arguably estimated by Sigurdsson and Carey at about eighteen hours. H. Sigurdsson and
S.N. Carey, 'The eruption of Vesuvius in AD 79', in *The Natural History of Pompeii*, ed. W.
F. Jashemski and F.G. Meyer. Cambridge: Cambridge University Press, 2002, 59.

84 Associated with TdS 199.

85 A.R. Damasio and H. Damasio, 'Brain and language', *Scientific American*, Vol. 267, No. 3,
1992, 62–63; H. Gray, *Anatomy, Descriptive and Surgical*. Revised American from the 15th
English edn. New York: Bounty Books, 1977, 649.

86 TF 74.

87 Aufderheide and Rodríguez-Martin, 1998, op. cit., 31; F.P. Lisowski, 'Prehistoric and
early trepanation', in *Diseases in Antiquity: A Survey of the Diseases, Injuries and Surgery of
Early Populations*, ed. D.R. Brothwell and A.T. Sandison. Springfield, Illinois: Charles C.
Thomas, 1967, 651–70; E.L. Margetts, 'Trepanation of the skull by the medicine men of
primitive cultures, with particular reference to present-day native East African practice', in
Diseases in Antiquity: A Survey of the Diseases, Injuries and Surgery of Early Populations, ed. D.
R. Brothwell and A.T. Sandison. Springfield, Illinois: Charles C. Thomas, 1967, 673–94;
Ortner and Putschar, 1981, op. cit., 95–98; Figs. 112–14; Ortner, 2003, op. cit., 169–
74; Roberts and Manchester, 1995, op. cit., 91–94; Steinbock, 1976, op. cit.; Tyson and
Alcauskas (eds), 1980, op. cit., 74–89.

88 Bliquez, 1994, op. cit., 93–94; Celsus, op. cit.; J.J. Deiss, *Herculaneum: Italy's Buried
Treasure*. 2nd edn. New York: Harper & Row, 1985, 192; P. Gusman, *Pompei: The City, its
Life and Art*. Translated by F. Simmonds and M. Jourdain. London: Heinemann, 1900,
238; R. Jackson, 'Roman doctors and their instruments: Recent research into ancient
practice', *Journal of Roman Archaeology*, Vol. 3, 1990, 6; Majno, 1991, op. cit., 353–68.

89 Bliquez, 1994, op. cit., 43, 77; R. Caton, 'Notes on a group of medical and surgical
instruments found near Kolophon', *Journal of Hellenic Studies*, Vol. 34, 1914, 114–18.

90 Celsus, op. cit.; vii, 3.

91 Celsus, op. cit.; 10, 7.

92 Bliquez, 1994, op. cit., 44; Jackson and La Niece 1986: 143–45.

93 Bliquez, 1994, op. cit., 72.

94 Bliquez, 1994, op. cit., 78.

95 TF 74.

96 viii, 3, 8–9.

97 Caton, 1914, op. cit., 114–15; R. Jackson and S. La Niece, 'A set of Roman medical
instruments from Italy', *Britannia*, Vol. 17 1986, 143–44; Jackson, 1990, op. cit., 18,
Fig. 5; J. Kirkup, *The Evolution of Surgical Instruments: An Illustrated History from Ancient
Times to the Twentieth Century*. Novato, California: Norman Publishing, 2006, 71.

98 TdS R 11 and TdS # 28:1 respectively.

99 Bisel, 1987, op. cit., 124–25.

100 Capasso, 2001, op. cit., 998–1002.

101 Majno, 1991, op. cit., 84; Roberts and Manchester, 1995, op. cit., 74–75.

102 P. Ciprotti, 'Der letzte tag von Pompeji', *Altertum,* Vol. 10, 1964, 40–54.

103 TdS # 28:1.

104 Though compare with Henneberg and Henneberg, 2002, op. cit., 174–76.

105 L. Capasso and G. Di Tota, 'Lice buried under the ashes of Herculaneum', *The Lancet*,
Vol. 351, No. 9107, 1998, 992; L. Capasso, 'Indoor pollution and respiratory diseases in
ancient Rome', *The Lancet,* Vol. 356, No. 9243, 2000b, 1774; Capasso, 2001, op. cit.,
1000–1002; L. Capasso, 'Infectious diseases and eating habits at Herculaneum (1st century AD, Southern Italy)', *International Journal of Osteoarchaeology*, Vol. 17, No. 4, 2007,
353–54.

106 L. Capasso, and G. Di Tota, 'Tuberculosis in Herculaneum (79 AD)', in *Tuberculosis Past
and Present*, ed. G. Pálfi, O. Dutour, J. Deák and I. Hutás. Budapest: Golden Books &
Tuberculosis Foundation, 1999, 463–67; Capasso, 2007, op. cit., 354; T. Molleson *et al.*,

The Spitalfields Project. Vol. 2: The Anthropology: The Middling Sort, Council for British Archaeology Research Report 86. York: Council for British Archaeology, 1993, 83.

107 Aufderheide and Rodríguez–Martin, 1998, op. cit., 192–93; L. Capasso, 'Bacteria in two-millennia-old cheese, and related epizoonoses in Roman populations', *Journal of Infection*, Vol. 45, No. 2, 2002, 122–27; Capasso *et al.*, 1999, op. cit., Capasso 2002; op. cit., 122–26; Capasso, 2007, op. cit., 351; Ortner, 2003, op. cit., 215–21.

108 Capasso, 2007, op. cit., 350–57.

109 Brothwell, 1981, op. cit., 165; Martin *et al.*, 1991, op. cit., 149; D.M. Mittler and D.P. van Gerven, 'Developmental, diachronic, and demographic analysis of cribra orbitalia in the medieval Christian populations of Kulubnarti', *American Journal of Physical Anthropology*, Vol. 93, 1994, 287–88; T.I. Molleson, 'Urban bones: The skeletal evidence for environmental change', in *Actes des Troisièmes Journées Anthropologiques de Valbonne, Notes et Monographies Techniques.* Paris: Editions du CNRS, 1987, 145; Ortner and Putschar, 1981, op. cit., 258–63; Rothschild, B. 'Porotic hyperostosis as a marker of health and nutritional conditions', *American Journal of Human Biology*, Vol. 14, No. 4, 2002, 417; P. Shipman *et al.*, *The Human Skeleton.* Cambridge, Massachusetts: Harvard University Press, 1985, 299; Steinbock, 1976, op. cit., 239; P. Stuart-Macadam, 'Porotic hyperostosis: Changing interpretations', in *Human Palaeopathology: Current Syntheses and Future Options*, ed. D.J. Ortner and A.C. Aufderheide. Washington: Smithsonian Institution Press, 1991, 36–39; White, 2000, op. cit., 394–95; White and Folkens, 2005, op. cit, 320–22.

110 J.E. Buikstra, D.H. Ubelaker and D. Aftandilian (eds), *Standards for Data Collection from Human Skeletal Remains: Proceedings of a Seminar at the Field Museum of Natural History Organized by Jonathon Haas.* Fayetteville, Arkansas, 1994, 120–21; Mittler and Van Gerven, 1994, op. cit., 289; White and Folkens, 2005, op. cit, 320.

111 The scoring system that was used was based on the standards for data collection from human skeletal remains. J.E. Buikstra and D.H. Ubelaker (eds), 1994, op. cit., 121, 151–53; and P. Stuart-Macadam, 'Porotic hyperostosis: Representative of a childhood condition', *American Journal of Physical Anthropology*, Vol. 66 1985, 391–98.

112 Mittler and Van Gerven, 1994, op. cit., 289.

113 Stuart-Macadam, 1991, op. cit., 36–38; White and Folkens, 2005, op. cit, 322.

114 B.M. Rothschild *et al.*, *Relationship between porotic hyperostosis and cribra orbitalia?* (2004); from *PaleoBios*, http://anthropologie-et-paleopathologie.univ-lyon1.fr/ (accessed 4 April 2005); U. Wapler, 'Is cribra orbitalia synonymous with anemia? Analysis and interpretation of cranial pathology in Sudan', *American Journal of Physical Anthropology*, Vol. 123, No. 4, 2004, 333–39.

115 For example, see A. Cucina *et al.*, 'The Necropolis of Vallerano (Rome, 2nd–3rd Century AD): An anthropological perspective on the Ancient Romans in the Suburbium', *International Journal of Osteoarchaeology*, Vol. 16, No. 2, 2006, 113–14.

116 J.L. Angel, 'Porotic hyperostosis, anemias, malarias and marshes in the prehistoric Eastern Mediterranean', *Science,* Vol. 153, 1966, 760–63; J.L. Angel, 'The bases of palaeodemography', *American Journal of Physical Anthropology*, Vol. 30, 1969a, 427–37; A. Ascenzi, 'Physiological relationship and pathological interferences between bone tissue and marrow', in *The Biochemistry and Physiology of Bone*, ed. G.H. Bourne. New York: Academic Press, 1976, 429; A. Ascenzi, 'A problem in palaeopathology: The origin of thalassemia in Italy', *Virchows Archiv A: Pathological Anatomy and Histopathology*, Vol. 384, 1979, 128; Bisel, 1987, op. cit., 125; Bisel 1988a, op. cit., 64; Bisel 1988a, op. cit., 62; Bisel, 1988b, op. cit., 213; Bisel, 1991, op. cit., 14; Bisel and Bisel, 2002, op. cit., 458; D.C. Cook and M.L. Powell, 'The evolution of American paleopathology', in *Bioarchaeology: The Contextual Analysis of Human Remains*, ed. J.E. Buikstra and L.A. Beck. Amsterdam: Academic Press, 2006, 300; Martin *et al.*, 1991, op. cit., 147–52; Stuart-Macadam, 1991, op. cit., 36–39.

117 E28 Capasso, 2001, op. cit., 1012–15, 1055.

118 Brothwell, 1981, op. cit., 146; Manchester, 1983, op. cit., 65–70; Rogers and Manchester 1995; 105–6; J. Rogers, *et al.*, 'Arthropathies in palaeopathology: The basis of classification according to most probable cause', *Journal of Archaeological Science*, Vol. 14 1987, 179–93; Manchester, 1983, op. cit., 65, 68. White and Folkens, 2005, op. cit, 325, 424;

119 Rogers *et al.*, 1987, op. cit., 179.

120 Devised by Ubelaker, 1989, op. cit., 87.

121 Ubelaker's Type d osteophytic change was observed on TF L 46, 77, 78, 146, 147; TF R 15, 24, 32, 58, 92, 116. Ubelaker, 1989, op. cit., 87.

122 For example, TF L 147.

123 TF L 140.

124 Ubelaker's Type d was recorded for the following humeri TF L, 5, 10, 64, 86, 98, 46 and 59. Ubelaker, 1989, op. cit., 87.

125 TF L 27.

126 B.T. Arriaza, et al., 'Diffuse idiopathic skeletal hyperostosis in Meroitic Nubians from Semna South, Sudan', *American Journal of Physical Anthropology*, Vol. 92, 1993, 243–48; Aufderheide and Rodríguez–Martin, 1998, op. cit., 97–98; M. Cammisa et al., 'Diffuse idiopathic skeletal hyperostosis', *European Journal of Radiology*, Vol. 27, No. Supplement 1, 1998, 7; C. Kiss et al., 'The prevalence of diffuse idiopathic skeletal hyperostosis in a population-based study in Hungary', *Scandinavian Journal of Rheumatology*, Vol. 31, No. 4, 2002a, 226–29; C. Kiss et al., 'Risk factors for diffuse idiopathic skeletal hyperostosis: A case-control study', *Rheumatology*, Vol. 41, No. 1, 2002b, 27–30; Ortner, 2003, op. cit., 558–59; Roberts and Manchester, 1995, op. cit., 120–21; J. Rogers et al., 'Arthropathies in palaeopathology: The basis of classification according to most probable cause', *Journal of Archaeological Science*, Vol. 14, 1987, 186–88; R.M. Weinfeld et al., 'The prevalence of diffuse idiopathic skeletal hyperostosis (DISH) in two large American Midwest metropolitan hospital populations', *Skeletal Radiology*, Vol. 26, No. 4, 1997, 222–25.

127 TdS 1.

128 TF NS 86:1.

129 Aufderheide and Rodríguez-Martin, 1998, op. cit., 98; Roberts and Manchester, 1995, op. cit., 119, 121; Lazer, 1995, op. cit., Appendix 3.

130 Ubelaker Types b and c. Ubelaker, 1989, op. cit., 87.

131 Molleson, 1987, op. cit., 149; Rogers *et al.*, 1987, op. cit., 185.

132 Type d osteophytic change. Ubelaker, 1989, op. cit., 87.

133 Aufderheide and Rodríguez-Martin, 1998, op. cit., 98; Arriaza *et al.*, 1993, op. cit., 243–44; Ortner, 2003, op. cit., 558–59; Rogers *et al.*, 1987, op. cit., 187.

134 The case of DISH was observed in ERC 27, a male, rather specifically aged at 46 years, Bisel 1988a, op. cit., 63–64; Bisel 1988b, op. cit., 212; Bisel, 1991, op. cit., 14; Bisel and Bisel, 2002, op. cit., 468–69.

135 Capasso, 2001, op. cit., 1018–31; the cases of DISH were in E27, E61, E86, E117, E141A; Becker, 2003, op. cit., 405.

136 For the methods used in this study, see Lazer, 1995, op. cit., 244–49; E. Lazer, 'Revealing secrets of a lost city', *The Medical Journal of Australia*, Vol. 165, No. 11/12, 1996, 620–23.

137 Henschen and to a lesser extent on that of Moore, the latter proving less useful for this sample as it was based purely on x-rays rather than direct observation of gross appearance. F. Henschen, *Morgagni's Syndrome: Hyperostosis Frontalis Interna, Virilismus, Obesitas*. Edinburgh: Oliver & Boyd, 1949, 5; Moore, S. *Hyperostosis Cranii (Stewart–Morel Syndrome, Metabolic Craniopathy, Morgagni's Syndrome, Stewart–Morel–Moore Syndrome (Ritvo), le Syndrome de Morgagni–Morel)*. Springfield, Illinois: Charles C. Thomas, 1955, 18.

138 I. Hershkovitz *et al.*, 'Hyperostosis frontalis interna: An anthropological perspective', *American Journal of Physical Anthropology*, Vol. 109, 1999, 306. I developed a six-point scoring system (see Lazer, 1995, op. cit., 249) based on the studies that were available

when I did my fieldwork. I have since reassessed them using the system suggested by Hershkovitz *et al.*, as this makes my work more easily comparable with more recently published work – see next endnote.

139 Hershkovitz *et al.*, 1999, op. cit., 303–10; Ortner and Putschar, 1981, op. cit., 294; Ortner, 2003, op. cit., 416; J.J. Cocheton *et al.*, 'Le syndrome de Morgagni–Stewart–Morel: Mythe ou réalité?', *Semaine des Hôpitaux*, Vol. 50, 1974, 2946; A. Salmi *et al.*, 'Hyperostosis cranii in a normal population', *American Journal of Roentgenology, Radium Therapy & Nuclear Medicine*, Vol. 87, 1962, 1032; R.M. Stewart, 'Localized cranial hyperostosis in the insane', *The Journal of Neurology and Psychopathology*, Vol. 8, 1928, 321.

140 Translated into the Hershkovitz *et al.*, 1999, op. cit., 303–25; system (306), there were 26 cases or 67.4 per cent presented as the equivalent of Type A, 27.9 per cent as Type B, 2.3 per cent as Type C and 2.3 per cent as Type D. Lazer, 1995, op. cit., 392 contains a record of the range and frequency of pathology in this series of skulls.

141 Hershkovitz *et al.*, 1999, op. cit., 306.

142 Aufderheide and Rodríguez-Martin, 1998, op. cit., 419; F.J. Fernandez-Nogueras and V. J. Fernandez-Nogueras. 'The Stewart–Morel Syndrome in the differential diagnosis of patients with frontal headache', *Anales Ortorrinolaringologicos Ibero-Americanos*, Vol. 20, No. 4, 1993, 383–91; Henschen, 1949, op. cit.; Hershkovitz *et al.*, 1999, op. cit., 323; E. Kollin and T. Fehér, 'Androgens, bone mineral content and hyperostosis frontalis interna in pre-menopausal women', *Experimental Clinical Endocrinology*, Vol. 87, 1986, 211–14; Moore, 1955, op. cit., 180–81; Ortner, 2003, op. cit., 416; M. Pawlikowski and J. Komorowski, 'Hyperostosis frontalis interna and the Morgagni–Stewart–Morel Syndrome', *Lancet*, Vol. 1, No. 8322, 1983, 474; E.F. Talarico Jr *et al.*, 'A case of extensive hyperostosis frontalis interna in an 87-year-old female human cadaver', *Clinical Anatomy*, Vol. 21, No. 3, 2008, 259–60, 266–67; J.M. Taveras and M.D. Wood. *Diagnostic Neuroradiology*. 2nd edn. Vol. Section 1, Golden's Diagnostic Radiology. Baltimore: The Williams & Wilkins Company, 1976, 175.

143 G.J. Armelagos and O.D. Chrisman, 'Hyperostosis frontalis interna: A Nubian case', *American Journal of Physical Anthropology*, Vol. 76, 1988, 27; Moore, 1955, op. cit.; Salmi *et al.*, 1962, op. cit., 1039; Talarico Jr *et al.*, 2008, op. cit., 266; Taveras and Wood, 1976, op. cit., 175–78.

144 Henschen, 1949, op. cit., 85; Hershkovitz *et al.*, 1999, op. cit., 318; D.M. Mulhern *et al.*, 'Brief communication: Unusual finding at Pueblo Bonito: Multiple cases of hyperostosis frontalis interna', *American Journal of Physical Anthropology*, Vol. 130, No. 4, 2006, 480, 483; Ortner and Putschar, 1981, op. cit., 294; Salmi *et al.*, 1962, op. cit., 1032. Compare with A. Hrycek *et al.*, 'Morgagni–Stewart–Morel Syndrome in a young man', *Wiadomosci Lekarskie*, Vol. 42, Nos 19–21, 1989, 1060–63.

145 Ortner and Putschar, 1981, op. cit., 294.

146 T. Anderson, 'An Anglo-Saxon case of hyperostosis frontalis interna', *Archaeologia Cantiana*, Vol. 112 1993, 256; J. Gershon-Cohen *et al.*, 'Hyperostosis frontalis interna among the aged', *American Journal of Roentgenology, Radium Therapy & Nuclear Medicine*, Vol. 73 1955, 396–97; Henschen, 1949, op. cit.; Hershkovitz *et al.*, 1999, op. cit., 303, 318–19; H.L. Jaffe, *Metabolic, Degenerative and Inflammatory Diseases of Bones and Joints*. Philadelphia: Lea & Febiger, 1972, 272; Moore, 1955, op. cit., 180–81; Mulhern *et al.*, 2006, op. cit., 480; Ortner, 2003, op. cit., 416; Salmi, *et al.*, 1962, op. cit., 1033; Talarico Jr *et al.*, 2008, op. cit., 266; M. Verdy *et al.*, 'Prevalence of hyperostosis frontalis interna in relation to body weight', *American Journal of Clinical Nutrition*, Vol. 31, No. 11, 1978, 2002–4.

147 Rosatti 1972 in Armelagos and Chrisman, 1988, op. cit., 27; H. Glab *et al.*, 'Hyperostosis frontalis interna, a genetic disease?: Two medieval cases from Southern Poland', *Homo: Journal of Comparative Human Biology*, Vol. 57, No. 1, 2006, 19–27; M.F. Koller, A. Papassotiropoulos, K. Henke, B. Behrends, S. Noda, A. Kratzer, C. Hock and M. Hofmann, 'Evidence of a genetic basis of Morgagni–Stewart–Morel Syndrome: A case

report of identical twins', *Neurodegenerative Diseases*, Vol. 2, No. 2, 2005, 56–60; Mulhern *et al.*, 2006, op. cit., 483; A. Sperduti and G. Manzi, 'Hyperostosis frontalis interna in a cranial sample from the Roman population of Portus (Isola Sacra necropolis 1–111 Century AD)', *Rivista di Antropologia*, Vol. 68, 1990, 279.

148 35 or 83.3 per cent.

149 Lazer, 1995, op. cit., 251–54.

150 Henschen, 1949, op. cit., 3; Jaffe, 1972, op. cit., 272.

151 95.3 per cent.

152 Lazer, 1995, op. cit., 254.

153 Ortner, 2003, op. cit., 416.

154 Anderson, 1993, op. cit., 254–55; Armelagos and Chrisman, 1988, op. cit., 27; Henschen, 1949, op. cit., 62–64; Hershkovitz *et al.*, 1999, op. cit., 314; Manchester, 1983, op. cit., 71–75; Mulhern *et al.*, 2006, op. cit., 482; Ortner and Putschar, 1981, op. cit., 294–95, 298–300, 309, 315–17, 365–98; Ortner, 2003, op. cit., 415–16; Talarico Jr, *et al.*, 2008, op. cit., 263–65.

155 M.Y. El-Najjar and K.R. McWilliams, *Forensic Anthropology: The Structure, Morphology and Variation of Human Bone and Dentition*. Springfield, Illinois: Charles C. Thomas, 1978, 70.

156 Manchester, 1983, op. cit., 72; Ortner, 2003, op. cit., 506.

157 Brothwell, 1981, op. cit., 121; Lisowski, 1967, op. cit., 657; Ortner, 2003, op. cit., 171; White and Folkens, 2005, op. cit, 315.

158 This image was discovered on 22 August 1836 in *oecus* 11 (H. 1369). G.P. Carattelli (ed.), *Pompei: Pitture e Mosaici* (Rome: Istituto della Enciclopedia Italiana, 1993, 414, 417, Vol IV: VI7, 18). Colour picture published in reverse of the painting in *oecus* 11. This is an aquarelle by A. Abbate (ADS 202 Fot. Pedicini), 416 drawing of the painting ADS 203, B/W photo of the image is on page 417 (50 AFS A947(già A8096)); 286: tempera and ink colour image of the wall with the panel included (reproduced the right way round) *Soprintendenza Archeologica di Napoli* ADS 202 image by Abbate p. 290: full page image of squared drawing just of the toilet of Hermaphrodite, also by Abbate, pencil drawing is described on p. 291: *Soprintendenza Archeologica di Napoli* ADS 204 – this is probably the study for the painted image described above (painting h, 1369); P 833: drawing by Mastracchio, s. *Soprintendenza Archeologica di Napoli* ADS 20; M. Raoul-Rochette and M. Roux, *Choix de Peintures de Pompéi: Lithographiées en Couleur par M. Roux et Publiées avec l'Explication Archéologique de Chaque Peinture*. Paris: Adolphe Labitte, 1867, 136–37, Plate 10.

159 Raoul-Rochette, 1867, op. cit., 136–37, Plate 10.

160 H.J. Rose, *A Handbook of Greek Mythology*. New York: Dutton, 1959/1928, 148. Over one hundred years later, a completely different interpretation was offered for this figure when it was described as an example of incomplete testicular feminization. J. Kunze and I. Nippert, *Genetics and Malformations in Art*. Berlin: Grosse, 1986, 53, Fig. 61.

161 Examples of hermaphrodites in Pompeian wall paintings include Pan and Hermaphroditus from the atrium of the House of the Dioscuri (ref. no.), RP. Inv. No. 27700 Hermaphroditus struggling with a faun from Pompeii, RP. Inv. No. 110878, Faun and Hermaphroditus from Herculaneum, RP. Inv. No. 27701, illustrated in M. Grant, and A. Mulas. *Eros in Pompeii: The Erotic Art Collections of the Museum of Naples*. New edn. New York: Stewart, Tabori Chang, 1997, 147, 159 and 163 respectively.

162 As can be seen, for example, in the mosaic in *oecus* 11 in the *Casa del Menandro* (house reference), illustrated in Ling 2003: 28 and the paintings in the bath in the frigidarium in the *Terme del Sarno* (VII, ii, 17).

163 W.W. Eldridge and G. Holm, 'Incidence of hyperostosis frontalis interna in female patients admitted to a mental hospital', *American Journal of Roentgenology, Radium Therapy & Nuclear Medicine*, Vol. 43 1940, 356; Stewart, 1928, op. cit. 321–31; Salmi, *et al.*, 1962, op. cit., 1032; Talarico Jr, *et al.*, 2008, op. cit., 267.

164 Epistles 4.16 and 20.

165 16.19.

166 20.12.

167 Lazer, 1995, op. cit., 264–65.

168 Anderson, 1993, op. cit., 253–59; Armelagos and Chrisman, 1988, op. cit., 25–28; A.T. Chamberlain, *Demography in Archaeology*, Cambridge Manuals in Archaeology. Cambridge: Cambridge University Press, 2006, 55. J. Gladykowska-Rzecyscka, 'Is this a case of the Morgagni syndrome?', *Journal of Palaeopathology*, Vol. 1, 1988, 109–12.

169 For a summary of the cases that have been reported in the literature to date, see S.C. Antón, 'Endocranial Hyperostosis in Sangiran 2, Gibraltar 1, and Shanidar 5', *American Journal of Physical Anthropology*, Vol. 102, No. 1, 1997, 115; Hershkovitz *et al.*, 1999, op. cit., 321; Mulhern *et al.*, 2006, op. cit., 483; Talarico Jr, *et al.*, 2008, op. cit., 266. Also, see W. Devriendt *et al.*, 'Two Neolithic cases of hyperostosis frontalis interna', *International Journal of Osteoarchaeology*, Vol. 14, 2004: 414–18; Glab *et al.*, 2006, op. cit., 19–27.

170 Hershkovitz *et al.*, 1999, op. cit., 321.

171 Mulhern *et al.*, 2006, op. cit., 483.

172 F.J. Rühli *et al.*, 'Hyperostosis frontalis interna: Archaeological evidence of possible microevolution of human sex steroids?', *Homo: Journal of Comparative Human Biology*, Vol. 55, Nos 1–2, 2004, 91–99.

173 Belcastro *et al.*, 'Hyperostosis Frontalis Interna and Sex Identification of Two Skeletons', *International Journal of Osteoarchaeology*, Vol. 16, No. 6, 2006, 506–16; Sperduti and Manzi, 1990, op. cit., 279–86.

174 Capasso, 2001, op. cit., 170, 685.

175 Hershkovitz *et al.*, 1999, op. cit., 320–21.

176 Bisel 1988a, op. cit., 62, 65; Bisel 1988b, op. cit., 213–15; Bisel, 1991, op. cit., 11; Bisel and Bisel, 2002, op. cit., 457–58; Capasso, 2001, op. cit., 1065–67; M. Torino and G. Fornaciari, 'Paleopatologia degli individui nella Casa di Giulio Polibio', in *La Casa di Giulio Polibio: Studi Interdisciplinari*, ed. A. Ciarallo and E. De Carolas. Pompei: Centro Studi arti Figurative, Università di Tokio, 2001, 95–98; Petrone *et al.*, 2002b, op. cit., 78–80.

177 L.Z. Gannes *et al.*, 'Stable isotopes in animal ecology: Assumptions, caveats, and a call for more laboratory experiments', *Ecology*, Vol. 78, No. 4, 1997, 1271–76; P. Garnsey (Emeritus Professor of the History of Classical Antiquity, Faculty of Classics, Cambridge University) to E. Lazer, 2008, personal communication; F.M. Guarino *et al.*, 'Bone preservation in human remains from the Terme del Sarno at Pompeii using light microscopy and scanning electron microscopy', *Journal of Archaeological Science*, Vol. 33, 2006, 513–20; T.L. Prowse *et al.*, 'Isotopic paleodiet studies of skeletons from the Imperial Roman-age cemetery of Isola Sacra, Rome, Italy', *Journal of Archaeological Science*, Vol. 31, No. 3, 2004: 259–72; T.L. Prowse *et al.*, 'Isotopic evidence for age-related variation in diet from Isola Sacra, Italy', *American Journal of Physical Anthropology*, Vol. 128, 2005, 2–13; I. Reiche *et al.*, 'Trace element composition of archaeological bones and post–mortem alteration in the burial environment', *Nuclear Instruments and Methods in Physics Research B*, Vol. 150, 1999, 656–62; M.P. Richards *et al.*, 'Stable isotope analysis reveals variations in human diet at the Poundbury Camp Cemetery Site', *Journal of Archaeological Science*, Vol. 25, No. 12, 1998: 1247–52; H.P. Schwarcz and M.J. Schoeninger, 'Stable isotope analyses in human nutritional ecology', *Yearbook of Physical Anthropology*, Vol. 34, No. S13, 1991, 283–321; A. Sillen *et al.*, 'Chemistry and paleo-dietary research: No more easy answers', *American Antiquity*, Vol. 54, No. 3, 1989, 504–12.

178 See, for example, Robinson 2005, pp, 109–19.

179 For example, S.C. Gilfillan, 'Lead poisoning and the fall of Rome', *Journal of Occupational Medicine*, Vol. 7, 1965, 53–60.

180 For example, Bisel, 1983, op. cit., 7; Bisel and Bisel, 2002, op. cit., 459–60.

181 A.C. Aufderheide, 'Chemical analysis of skeletal remains', in *Reconstruction of Life from the Skeleton*, ed. M.Y. Iscan and K.A.R. Kennedy. New York: Alan R. Liss, 1989, 248, 251; Aufderheide and Rodríguez-Martin, 1998, op. cit., 318; Bisel and Bisel, 2002, op. cit.,

459; Gilfillan, 1965, op. cit., 53–54; T.H.G. Oettlé (former Director of the New South Wales Forensic Institute, Sydney) to E. Lazer, 1983, personal communication.

182 Gilfillan, 1965, op. cit., 53–54.

183 Aufderheide, 1989, op. cit., 251–52.

184 The Herculanean mean lead level for males (93.8 ppm; S.D. = 52.2; n = 49) was higher than that obtained for females (70.1 ppm; S.D. = 55.8; n = 43); Bisel, 1987, op. cit., 126; Bisel, 1988b, op. cit., 215; Bisel, 1991, op. cit., 12; Bisel and Bisel, 2002, op. cit., 459–60.

185 Bisel, 1991, op. cit., 13; Bisel and Bisel, 2002, op. cit., 460.

186 Bisel, 1991, op. cit., 13; Bisel and Bisel, 2002, op. cit., 460; Deiss, 1985, op. cit., 191; Vitruvius, 'De Architectura', in *Loeb Classical Library*. Cambridge, Massachusetts: Harvard University Press, 1934', VIII; CVI: 10.

187 For example, see Angel, 1969a, op. cit., 432; J.L. Angel, 'Palaeodemography and evolution', *American Journal of Physical Anthropology*, Vol. 31 1969b, 344; J.L. Angel, 'Ecology and population in the Eastern Mediterranean', *World Archaeology*, Vol. 4, 1972, 88–105; Bisel, 1991, op. cit., 2; Bisel and Bisel, 2002, op. cit., 453; Cook and Powell, 2006, op. cit., 300. Also, see Chapters 1 and 6.

188 Bisel and Bisel, 2002, op. cit., 453–54.

189 Capasso, 2001, op. cit., 973–78.

190 M. Henneberg *et al.*, 'Skeletal material from the house of C. Iulius Polybius in Pompeii, 79 AD', *Human Evolution*, Vol. 11, No. 3, 1996, 255; Henneberg and Henneberg, 2002, op. cit., 174.

191 For further consideration on the difficulties associated with studies to determine lifestyle and status, see T. Waldron, *Counting the Dead: The Epidemiology of Skeletal Populations*. Chichester: John Wiley & Sons, 1994, 98; and White and Folkens, 2005, op. cit, 331–32.

192 Bisel and Bisel, 2002, op. cit., 460–73; Capasso 2001 reconstructions of occupation and lifestyle indicators are in section that deals with individual skeletons, which occupies the major part of the book. Capasso, 2001, op. cit.

193 Erc 13 and Erc 98. Bisel and Bisel, 2002, op. cit., 466–67.

194 Erc 28 Bisel and Bisel, 2002, op. cit., 467.

195 Capasso, 2001, op. cit., 1042.

196 See, for example, Capasso *et al.*, 1999, op. cit., 132–42.

197 Capasso, 2001, op. cit., 172–83; Ercolano 14.

198 Capasso, 2001, op. cit., 181, Figs. 237 and 238.

9 The population

1 Strabo, *The Geography*. Translated by H.R. Jones. *Loeb Classical Library*. Cambridge, Massachusetts: Harvard University Press, 1988, V, IV, 8; Pliny the Elder, 'Natural Histories', in Loeb Classical Library. Cambridge, Massachusetts: Harvard University Press, 1938/1962, 3.60–62.

2 A.E. Cooley and M.G.L. Cooley, *Pompeii: A Sourcebook*. London: Routledge, 2004, 17.

3 M. Cipollaro *et al.*, 'Ancient DNA in human bone remains from Pompeii archaeological site', *Biochemical and Biophysical Research Communications*, Vol. 247, No. 3, 1998, 901–4; M. Cipollaro *et al.*, 'Histological analysis and ancient DNA amplification of human bone remains found in Caius Iulius Polybius House in Pompeii', *Croatian Medical Journal*, Vol. 40, No. 3, 1999, 392–97; R.M. Costantini and L. Capasso, 'Sulla Presenza di DNA endogeno nei resti scheletri dei fuggiaschi di Ercolano', in *I Fuggiaschi di Ercolano: Paleobiologia delle Vittime dell'Eruzione Vesuviana del 79 d.C., Appendix 3*, ed. L. Capasso. Rome: 'L'Erma' di Bretschneider, 2001, 1069–74; G. Geraci *et al.*, 'Le analisi paleogenetiche', in *Vesuvio 79 AD: Vita e Morte ad Ercolano*, eds P.P. Petrone and F. Fedele. Naples: Fredericiana Editrice Universitaria, 2002, 85–88; G. Di Bernardo *et al.*, 'Analisi dei reperti ossei della casa grado di conservazione ed amplificazione del DNA antico', in *La Casa di Giulio Polibio: Studi Interdisciplinari*, ed. A. Ciarallo and E. De Carolis. Pompei: Centro Studi arti

Figurative, Università di Tokio, 2001, 111–18. Note that there has been some success with DNA analysis of other mammalian species at Pompeii; see, for example, J.F. Bailey *et al.*, 'Monkey business in Pompeii: Unique find of a juvenile Barbary Macaque skeleton in Pompeii identified using osteology and ancient DNA techniques', *Molecular Biology and Evolution*, Vol. 16 1999, 1410–14; M. Sica *et al.*, 'Analysis of five ancient equine skeletons by mitochondrial DNA sequencing', *Ancient Biomolecules*, Vol. 4, No. 4, 2002, 179–84.

4 S.C. Bisel and J.F. Bisel, 'Health and nutrition at Herculaneum: An examination of human skeletal remains', in *The Natural History of Pompeii*, ed. W.F. Jashemski and F.G. Meyer. Cambridge: Cambridge University Press, 2002, 451–75; L. Capasso, *I Fuggiaschi di Ercolano: Paleobiologia delle Vittime dell'Eruzione Vesuviana del 79 d.C.* Roma: 'L'Erma' di Bretschneider, 2001, 927–33; C. D'Amore, 'Primi risultati degli studi sull'antropologia Pompeiana del 79 d.C.', in *La Regione Sotterrata dal Vesuvio: Studi e Prospettive, Atti del Convegno Internazionale 11–15 Novembre 1979*. Napoli: Università degli Studi, 1982, 927–43; G. Nicolucci, 'Crania Pompeiana: Descrizione de' crani umani rinvenuti fra le ruine dell' antica Pompei', *Atti della R. Accademia delle Scienze Fisiche e Matematiche,* Vol. 9, No. 10, 1882, 1–26.

5 See Chapter 3 for a discussion of why female skulls were traditionally excluded from population studies based on cranial measurements.

6 S.C. Bisel, 'The human skeletons of Herculaneum', *International Journal of Anthropology*, Vol. 6, No. 1, 1991, 4; Bisel and Bisel, 2002, op. cit., 454 –55; W.W. Howells, 'The early Christian Irish: The skeletons at Gallen Priory', *Proceedings of the Royal Irish Academy*, Vol. 46 (Section C) 1941, 103–219; W.W. Howells, *Skull Shapes and the Map: Craniometric Analyses in the Dispersion of Modern Homo*. Vol. 79, Papers of the Peabody Museum of Archaeology and Ethnology. Cambridge, Massachusetts: Harvard University, 1989, 91.

7 Bisel, 1991, op. cit., 1–20; W.W. Howells, 'Cranial Variation in Man: A Study by Multivariate Analysis of Patterns of Difference among Recent Populations'. Vol. 67, Papers of the Peabody Museum of Archaeology and Ethnology. Cambridge, Massachusetts: Harvard University, 1973; Bisel and Bisel, 2002, op. cit., 454 –55; Howells, 1989, op. cit.; E. Lazer, 'Human Skeletal Remains in Pompeii: Vols. I and II.' Unpublished PhD thesis, Department of Anatomy and Histology. Sydney: University of Sydney, 1995, 269–77; Nicolucci, 1882, op. cit. Note that because the Pompeian data set was not complete and the data sets of Nicolucci and Bisel did not contain all the measurements used by Howells, 1973, op. cit., Howells, 1989, op. cit., it was decided that the use of unpaired t–tests of the means for comparable measurements would be more appropriate than principal components analysis.

8 A.C. Berry and R.J. Berry, 'Epigenetic variation in the human cranium', *Journal of Anatomy*, Vol. 101 1967, 362–63; D.R. Brothwell (Institute of Archaeology, University College, London) to E. Lazer 1988, personal communication; T. Hanihara *et al.*, 'Characterization of biological diversity through analysis of discrete cranial traits', *American Journal of Physical Anthropology*, Vol. 121, No. 3, 2003, 247, 249; N.S. Ossenberg, 'The influence of artificial cranial deformation on discontinuous morphological traits', *American Journal of Physical Anthropology*, Vol. 33, 1970, 357; C. Pardoe, 'Prehistoric Human Morphological Variation in Australia', unpublished PhD thesis. Canberra: Australian National University, 1984, 14–20; S.R. Saunders, 'Nonmetric skeletal variation', in *Reconstruction of Life from the Skeleton*, eds. M.Y. Iscan and K.A.R. Kennedy. New York: Alan R. Liss, 1989, 103–6.

9 These included metopic suture, metopic fissure, supranasal suture, frontal grooves, trochlear spine, infraorbital suture, condylar facet, coronal ossicle, ossicle at bregma, sagittal ossicle, ossicle at lambda, lambdoid ossicles, ossicle at asterion, occipito-mastoid ossicles, inca bone, sutura mendosam pars incoidea, anterior ethmoid foramen, posterior ethmoid foramen, parietal foramina, occipital foramen, condylar canal, hypoglossal canal, infraorbital foramen, highest nuchal line, precondylar tubercle, palatine torus and auditory torus Lazer, 1995, op. cit., 227–313.

10 G. Hauser and G.F. de Stefano, *Epigenetic Variants of the Human Skull*. Stuttgart: Schweizerbart, 1989.

11 G.F. De Stefano *et al.*, 'Reflections on interobserver differences in scoring non–metric cranial traits (with practical examples)', *Journal of Human Evolution*, Vol. 13, 1984, 349–55; E. Gualdi-Russo *et al.*, 'Scoring of nonmetric cranial traits: A methodological approach', *Journal of Anatomy*, Vol. 195, No. 4, 1999, 543–50; F.W. Rösing, 'Discreta of the human skeleton: A critical review', *Journal of Human Evolution*, Vol. 13, 1984, 319–23; Saunders, 1989, op. cit., 102.

12 Capasso, 2001, op. cit., 981–97; Nicolucci, 1882, op. cit., 10.

13 See for example, Capasso, 2001, op. cit., 983–84.

14 Capasso, 2001, op. cit., 76, 981; Hauser and De Stefano, 1989, op. cit.

15 V. Higgins, 'A model for assessing health patterns from skeletal remains', in *Burial Archaeology: Current Research, Methods and Developments*, ed. C.A. Roberts, F. Lee and J. Bintliff, 211. Oxford: BAR, 1989, 175–76; V. Higgins, 'Rural Agricultural Communities of the Late Roman and Early Medieval Periods Including a Study of Two Skeletal Groups from San Vincenzo al Volturno', unpublished PhD thesis (Sheffield: University of Sheffield 1990); Higgins, 1989–90, op. cit.

16 M. Rubini *et al.*, 'Original research article biological divergence and equality during the first millennium BC in human populations of Central Italy', *American Journal of Human Biology*, Vol. 19, No. 1, 2007, 120.

17 L. Bondioli *et al.*, 'Familial segregation in the Iron-Age community of Alfedena, Abruzzo, Italy, based on osteo-dental trait analysis', *American Journal of Physical Anthropology*, Vol. 71, No. 4, 1986, 393–400; E. Bruner *et al.*, 'Endocranial traits. Prevalence and distribution in a recent human population', *European Journal of Anatomy*, Vol. 7, No. 1, 2003, 23–33; A. Coppa *et al.*, 'Dental anthropology of Central-Southern, Iron Age Italy: The evidence of metric versus nonmetric traits', *American Journal of Physical Anthropology*, Vol. 107, No. 4, 1998, 371–86; Gualdi-Russo *et al.*, 1999, op. cit., M. Rubini, 'Biological homogeneity and familial segregation in the Iron Age population of Alfedena (Abruzzo, Italy), based on cranial discrete traits analysis', *International Journal of Osteoarchaeology*, Vol. 6, No. 5, 1996: 454–62; M. Rubini *et al.*, 'Etruscan Biology: The Tarquinian population seventh to second century BC (Southern Etruria, Italy)', *International Journal of Osteoarchaeology*, Vol. 7, No. 3, 1997, 202–11; M. Rubini *et al.*, 'The population of East Sicily during the second and first millennium BC: The problem of the Greek colonies', *International Journal of Osteoarchaeology*, Vol. 9, No. 1, 1999, 8–17.

18 Brothwell, 1981, op. cit., 92; S. Eggen *et al.*, 'Variation in torus palatinus prevalence in Norway', *European Journal of Oral Sciences*, Vol. 102, No. 1, 1994, 54–59; Hauser and De Stefano, 1989, op. cit.; C.M. Halffman *et al.*, 'Palatine torus in the Greenlandic Norse', *American Journal of Physical Anthropology*, Vol. 88, No. 2, 1992, 145–61; C.M. Halffman and J.D. Irish. 'Palatine torus in the pre-conquest inhabitants of the Canary Islands', *Homo: Journal of Comparative Human Biology*, Vol. 55, No. 1–2, 2004, 101–11; T. Hanihara and H. Ishida. 'Os incae: Variation in frequency in major human population groups', *Journal of Anatomy*, Vol. 198, No. 2, 2001a, 137–52; T. Hanihara and H. Ishida. 'Frequency variations of discrete cranial traits in major human populations. I. Supernumerary ossicle variations', *Journal of Anatomy*, Vol. 198, No. 6, 2001b, 689–706; Hanihara *et al.*, 2003, op. cit., 241–51; J. Skrzat *et al.*, 'The morphological appearance of the palatine torus in the Cracovian skulls (XV–XVIII century)', *Folia Morphol*, Vol. 62, No. 3, 2003, 183–86.

19 Hauser and De Stefano, 1989, op. cit., 17.

20 Parametric tests, which assume normally distributed samples, were not used because these non-metric data do not tend to follow such distributions. Instead, non-parametric tests were applied. Spearman's rank correlation coefficients were calculated to identify side or intertrait association. The Mann–Whitney U test was used to discern relationships

between sex and specific traits. Spearman's rank correlation is based on ranks rather than raw scores and can be used to detect non-linear correlations, Stevens 1987: p. 100. The Mann–Whitney U test was designed to test for difference between the means of two independent samples. This test can be used to compare samples of unequal sizes (G. Stevens, *Statistics Course Notes*. Australia: Faculty of Architecture, University of Sydney, 1987, 127). As discussed in Chapter 6, sex determination was based on the sex index generated from the observations of features considered diagnostic on the skull.

21 Ossenberg, 1970, op. cit., 362–63.
22 Brothwell, 1981, op. cit., 95; L. Capasso *et al.*, *Atlas of Occupational Markers on Human Remains*, Journal of Paleontology: Monographic Publication 3. Teramo: Journal of Paleontology & Edigrafital, 1999, 16; Capasso *et al.*, 1999, 16; M.Y. El-Najjar and K.R. McWilliams. *Forensic Anthropology: The Structure, Morphology and Variation of Human Bone and Dentition*. Springfield, Illinois: Charles C. Thomas, 1978, 143–44; Hauser and De Stefano, 1989, op. cit., 17, 176–77; Halffman *et al.*, 1992, op. cit., 145–61; C.M. Halffman and J.D. Irish, 'Palatine torus in the pre-conquest inhabitants of the Canary Islands', *Homo: Journal of Comparative Human Biology*, Vol. 55, No. 1–2, 2004, 101–11; D. Kerdpon and S. Sirirungrojying. 'A clinical study of oral tori in southern Thailand, prevalence and the relation to parafunctional activity', *European Journal of Oral Sciences*, Vol. 107, No. 1, 1999, 9, 12–13.
23 Hauser and De Stefano, 1989, op. cit., 174, 176; Eggen *et al.*, 1994, op. cit.; 54; El-Najjar and McWilliams, 1978, op. cit., 143–44; Halffman *et al.*, 1992, op. cit., 154; Kerdpon and Sirirungrojying, 1999, op. cit., 9, 12. There are various views on the relationship between age and the expression of palatine torus but most scholars report a higher incidence in females than males, with the exception of J. Skrzat *et al.* who found equal incidence of this trait in males and females. J. Skrzat *et al.*, 'The morphological appearance of the palatine torus in the Cracovian skulls (XV–XVIII century)', *Folia Morphol*, Vol. 62, No. 3, 2003, 185.
24 Capasso, 2001, op. cit., 982.
25 Pardoe, 1984, op. cit., 115–17, Fig. 33.
26 Berry and Berry, 1967, op. cit., 376.
27 As in the case of Halffman and Irish, 2004, op. cit., 105.
28 J.B. Woelfel, *Dental Anatomy: Its Relevance to Dentistry*. 4th edn. Philadelphia: Lea & Febiger, 1990; 78.
29 C.G. Turner, II (Department of Anthropology, Arizona State University, USA) to E. Lazer, 1993, personal communication; G.R. Scott and C.G. Turner, *The Anthropology of Modern Human Teeth: Dental Morphology and Its Variation in Recent Human Populations*. Cambridge: Cambridge University Press, 1997, 322.
30 Berry and Berry, 1967, op. cit., 367; El-Najjar and McWilliams, 1978, op. cit., 122–23; Hauser and De Stefano, 1989, op. cit., 46–48; Ossenberg, 1970, op. cit., 361–62; Saunders, 1989, op. cit., 96.
31 Berry and Berry, 1967, op. cit., 367; Capasso, 2001, op. cit., 982, 984; Hauser and De Stefano, 1989, op. cit., 42–43; Nicolucci, 1882, op. cit., 10–11.
32 Hauser and De Stefano, 1989, op. cit., 99, 102; Hanihara and Ishida, 2001a, op. cit., 139–40. For scoring of inca bones in the Pompeian sample, see Lazer, 1995, op. cit., 460–62.
33 For a clear definition of how to distinguish inca bone variants from sutural bones, see Hanihara and Ishida, 2001a, op. cit., 140.
34 Nicolucci, 1882, op. cit., 11.
35 Hauser and De Stefano, 1989, op. cit., 103
36 Capasso, 2001, op. cit., 982; Rubini *et al.*, 1999, op. cit., 12; Rubini *et al.*, 2007, op. cit., 122–23.
37 Rubini *et al.*, 1999, op. cit., 12; Rubini *et al.*, 2007, op. cit., 122–23.
38 Berry and Berry, 1967, op. cit., 365; Hanihara and Ishida, 2001a, op. cit., 143–44; Hauser and De Stefano, 1989, op. cit., 102–3.

39 El-Najjar and McWilliams, 1978, op. cit., 123, 126, 129–30; Hanihara and Ishida, 2001b, op. cit., 690; Hauser and De Stefano, 1989, op. cit., 85–92; L.W. Konigsberg *et al.*, 'Cranial variation and nonmetric trait variation', *American Journal of Physical Anthropology*, Vol. 90, 1993, 35–48; Ossenberg, 1970, op. cit., 360; Pardoe, 1984, op. cit., 62.

40 M.Y. El-Najjar and G.L. Dawson, 'The effect of artificial cranial deformation on the incidence of wormian bones in the lambdoidal suture', *American Journal of Physical Anthropology*, Vol. 46, 1977, 155–60; El-Najjar and McWilliams, 1978, op. cit., 129–30; B. Cremin *et al.*, 'Wormian bones in osteogenesis imperfecta and other disorders', *Skeletal Radiology*, Vol. 8, 1982, 35–38; Konigsberg *et al.*, 1993, op. cit., 35–48.

41 Cremin *et al.*, 1982, op. cit., 35–48; El-Najjar and McWilliams, 1978, op. cit., 129–31; K. Kozlowski and P. Beighton, *Gamut Index of Skeletal Dysplasias: An Aid to Radiodiagnosis*. Berlin: Springer, 1984, 35–36; J. Musgrave (Department of Anatomy, University of Bristol) to E. Lazer, 1988/1989, personal communication.

42 Cremin et al., 1982, op. cit., 37–38; El-Najjar and McWilliams, 1978, op. cit., 130; Hanihara and Ishida, 2001n, op. cit., 690; Ossenberg, 1970, op. cit., 360; Pardoe, 1984, op. cit., 62.

43 Hauser and De Stefano, 1989, op. cit., 85.

44 Hauser and De Stefano, 1989, op. cit., 86; Ossenberg, 1970, op. cit., 361; Pardoe, 1984, op. cit., 63.

45 Berry and Berry, 1967, op. cit., 374; Hauser and De Stefano, 1989, op. cit., 93; W.L. Kellock and P.A. Parsons, 'Variation of minor non–metrical cranial variants in Australian Aborigines', *American Journal of Physical Anthropology*, Vol. 32, 1970, 409–21; Pardoe, 1984, op. cit., 70–72.

46 See Lazer, 1995, op. cit., 284–86, 448–59 for the scoring system that was employed.

47 Capasso, 2001, op. cit., 982–83.

48 The majority of cases for each side, namely, 28.6 per cent for the left and 35.7 per cent for the right, involved at least one medium-sized ossicle. One or more large ossicles were observed on 8 per cent of cases for the left and 12.5 per cent for the right side.

49 Capasso, 2001, op. cit., 982– 83; Nicolucci, 1882, op. cit., 11.

50 For example, Rubini *et al.*, 2007, op. cit., 122.

51 Capasso, 2001, op. cit., 982; Nicolucci, 1882, op. cit., 11.

52 Capasso, 2001, op. cit., 982; Nicolucci, 1882, op. cit., 11.

53 Capasso, 2001, op. cit., 982.

54 These were Allen's fossa, Poirier's facet, plaque, hypertrochanteric fossa, exostosis in the trochanteric fossa and third trochanter on the femur, medial and lateral squatting facets on the distal end of the tibia, and septal aperture and supracondyloid process in the humerus. Lazer, 1995, op. cit., 316–26.

55 Capasso, 2001, op. cit., 984–89.

56 Comparisons can also be made for some of the other non-metric traits. Septal aperture of the humerus was observed in the Pompeian sample with a frequency of 18.4 per cent in the left sample of 98 bones and 13.2 per cent of the right sample, which comprised 96 humeri. Capasso recorded 26 cases, 16 of which displayed bilateral expression in the sample of 160 individuals he examined for post-cranial non-metric traits. He calculated the frequency for this trait as 16 per cent. Two cases of supracondyloid process were observed in the Pompeian sample and one in that from Herculaneum. Six femoral non–metric traits were scored for 165 left femora from the Pompeian sample. Allen's fossa was observed with some degree of expression in 49.6 per cent of the Pompeian sample. There was an incidence of 12.8 per cent for Poirier's facet. Plaque was observed in 35.4 per cent of cases, hypertrochanteric fossa in 30.3 per cent, exostosis in trochanteric fossa in 64.19 per cent and third trochanter in 28.9 per cent of the Pompeian femoral sample. There were only three femoral traits in common for the Pompeian and Herculaneum studies. Capasso observed 15 cases of Poirier's facet in the Herculaneum left and right femora, which represented 16.per cent of the Herculaneum sample. Third trochanter was recorded

for three individuals or 1.9 per cent of the sample, and hypertrochanteric fossa was observed in five infants, which reflects a frequency of 3.1 per cent in the Herculaneum sample. While the humerus data is comparable for septal aperture, there seems to be a slightly higher incidence of supracondyloid process in the Pompeian sample. The observed frequency of Poirier's facet and third trochanter is considerably higher in the Pompeian sample, as is the incidence of hypertrochanteric fossa. Capasso, 2001, op. cit., 992–95; Lazer, 1995, op. cit., 316–26.

57 E.-L. Boulle, 'Evolution of two human skeletal markers of the squatting position: A diachronic study from antiquity to the modern age', *American Journal of Physical Anthropology*, Vol. 115, No. 1, 2001, 53–54; Capasso *et al.*, 1999, op. cit., 112; K.A.R. Kennedy, 'Skeletal markers of occupational stress', in *Reconstruction of Life from the Skeleton*, ed. M.Y. Iscan and K.A.R. Kennedy. New York: Alan R. Liss, 1989, 149–50.

58 Capasso, 2001, op. cit., 996; D. Donlon, 'The value of postcranial nonmetric variation in studies of global populations in modern homo sapiens', unpublished PhD thesis. Armidale: University of New England, 1990, 90.

10 The casts

1 The number of skeletons has been variously reported between eleven and twenty two – see, for example E.M. Moorman, 'Literary evocations of ancient Pompeii', in *Tales from an Eruption: Pompeii, Herculaneum, Oplontis: Guide to the Exhibition*, ed. P.G. Guzzo. Milan: Electa, 2003, 25, though the reported number is about 20 for the *cryptoporticus* corridor and two in the portico surrounding the garden. L. García y García, *Danni di Guerra a Pompei: Una Dolorosa Vicenda quasi Dimenticata*. Vol. 15, Studi della Soprintendenza Archeologica di Pompei. Roma: 'L'Erma' di Bretschneider, 2006, 188; T. Rocco, 'The Villa of Diomedes', in *Tales from an Eruption: Pompeii, Herculaneum, Oplontis: Guide to the Exhibition*, ed. P.G. Guzzo. Milan: Electa, 2003a, 92.

2 E.C.C. Corti, *The Destruction and Resurrection of Pompeii and Herculaneum*. Translated by K. Smith and R.G. Smith. London: Routledge & Kegan Paul, 1951, 191; W. Leppmann, *Pompeii in Fact and Fiction*. London: Elek, 1968, 169–70; H. Sigurdsson, S.N. Carey, W. Cornell and T. Pescatore, 'The eruption of Vesuvius in AD 79', *National Geographic Research*, Vol. 1, No. 3, 1985, 365–66.

3 E. De Carolis, G. Patricelli and A. Ciarallo, 'Rinvenimenti di corpi umani nell'area urbana di Pompei', *Rivista di Studi Pompeiani*, Vol. 9, 1998, 75; García y García, 2006, op. cit., 188; T. Rocco, 'La Villa di Diomede' in *Storie da un'Eruzione: Pompei, Ercolano, Oplontis: Guida alla Mostra*, ed. A. d'Ambrosio, P.G. Guzzo and M. Mastroroberto. Milano: Electa, 2003c, 229; T. Rocco, 2003a, op. cit., 92–93.

4 Rocco, 2003c, op. cit., 229.

5 García y García, 2006, op. cit., 182; M. Pagano, 'I calchi in archeologia: Ercolano e Pompei', in *Storie da un'Eruzione: Pompei, Ercolano, Oplontis: Guida alla Mostra*, ed. A. d'Ambrosio, P.G. Guzzo and M. Mastroroberto. Milano: Electa, 2003, 122.

6 De Carolis et al., 1998, op. cit., 75–77; E. De Carolis, and G. Patricelli. *Vesuvius, AD 79: The Destruction of Pompeii and Herculaneum*. Translated by The J. Paul Getty Trust. Rome: 'L'Erma' di Bretschneider, 2003b, 111–12.

7 Austen Henry Layard, *London Quarterly Review* (American Edition) 115, January–April 1864, 160–80, in E. Dwyer, *From fragments to icons: Stages in the making and exhibiting of the casts of Pompeian victims, 1863–1888* (2005); from *Interpreting Ceramics: Conference papers and presentations from the Fragmented Figure conference (Cardiff School of Art and Design on the 29th and 30th June 2005)*, 2005, http://www.uwic.ac.uk/ICRC/issue008/articles/06.htm (accessed 8 March 2007), endnote 2.

8 H. Sigurdsson and S.N. Carey, 'The eruption of Vesuvius in AD 79', in *The Natural History of Pompeii*, ed. W.F. Jashemski and F.G. Meyer. Cambridge: Cambridge University Press, 2002, 49, 57–58.

9 M. Monnier, *The Wonders of Pompeii by Marc Monnier* (Project Gutenberg, 2005/12/12 Release date), http://www.gutenberg.org/etext/17290 (accessed 4 July 2006), 240.

10 Anonymous, *Quarterly Review*, No. 230, p. 382 in T.H. Dyer, *Pompeii: Its History, Buildings and Antiquities*. 2nd edn. London: George Bell & Sons, 1883, 477.

11 De Carolis and Patricelli, 2003b, op. cit., 111.

12 M. Monnier, 'Tout du Monde', 1864, pp 415–16, in Adams, 1868, op. cit., 264–68; Monnier, 1871, op. cit., 239–43.

13 Anonymous, *Quarterly Review*, No. 230, p. 382 in Dyer, 1883, op. cit., 477–79.

14 P. Gusman, *Pompei: The City, its Life and Art*. Translated by F. Simmonds and M. Jourdain. London: Heinemann, 1900, 16–17.

15 Anonymous, *Quarterly Review*, No. 230, p. 382 in Dyer, 1883, op. cit., 477.

16 D.M. Brown (ed.), *Pompeii: The Vanished City*. Alexandria, Virginia: Time–Life Books, 1992, 40; A.T. Chamberlain and M.P. Pearson. *Earthly Remains: The History and Science of Preserved Bodies*. Oxford: Oxford University Press, 2001, 151; M. Grant, *Cities of Vesuvius: Pompeii and Herculaneum*. Middlesex: Penguin, 1976, 30.

17 For example, in S. Giuntoli, *Art and History of Pompeii*. Translated by E. Pauli, edited by M. Martinelli, Bonechi Art & History Collection. Florence: Casa Editrice Bonechi, 1995, 37; Grant, 1971, op. cit., 30.

18 For example, Brown, 1992, op. cit., 11; Moorman, 2003, op. cit., 15–16.

19 R. Etienne, *Pompeii: The Day a City Died*. Translated by C. Palmer. London: Thames & Hudson, 1992, 135.

20 A. Maiuri, *Pompeii: The New Excavations, the Villa dei Misteri, the Antiquarium*. Translated by V. Priestley, 7th edn. Roma: Istituto Poligrafico dello Stato, 1962, 69–70.

21 As can be seen in works like C. Amery and B. Curran. *The Lost World of Pompeii*. London: Frances Lincoln, 2002, 45; P. Wilkinson, *Pompeii: The Last Day*. London: BBC Books, 2003, 71.

22 Such as A.C. Aufderheide, *The Scientific Study of Mummies*. Cambridge: Cambridge University Press, 2003, 203; B. Brier, *The Encyclopedia of Mummies*. New York: Checkmark, 1998, 146–47; Chamberlain and Pearson, 2001, op. cit., 151–52.

23 B. Knight, *Forensic Pathology*. 2nd edn. London: Arnold, 1996, 309.

24 For example B. Conticello (Superintendent, Pompeii) to E. Lazer, 1994, personal communication; S. Pain, 'Pompeii's electronic guide', *New Scientist*, Vol. 1815, 1992, 22.

25 Conticello, 1994, op. cit.; Pain, 1992, op. cit., 22.

26 A. D'Ambrosio (Archaeological Superintendency of Pompeii) to E. Lazer, 2006, personal communication.

27 García y García, 2006, op. cit., 191.

28 Ibid., 192.

29 De Carolis *et al.*, 1998, op. cit., 100, 105.

30 García y García, 2006, op. cit., 191.

31 Ibid.

32 Gusman, 1900, op. cit., 17.

33 Dwyer, 2005, op. cit.

34 Ibid. and García y García, 2006, op. cit., 173.

35 For example Chamberlain and Pearson, 2001, op. cit., 151; De Carolis and Patricelli, 2003b, op. cit., 115; A. De Vos and M. De Vos. *Pompei, Ercolano, Stabia*. Rome: Laterza, 1982, 209; Giuntoli, 1995, op. cit., 37; Grant, 1976, op. cit., 37; A. King, 'Mammals: Evidence from wall paintings, sculpture, mosaics, faunal remains and ancient literary sources', in *The Natural History of Pompeii*, ed. W.F. Jashemski and F.G. Meyer. Cambridge: Cambridge University Press, 2002, 411; W.M.C. MacKenzie, *Pompeii: Painted by Alberto Pisa*. London: A. & C. Black, 1910, 172; Maiuri, 1962, op. cit., 103; J.B. Ward-Perkins and A. Claridge. *Pompeii AD 79: Treasures from the National Archaeological Museum, Naples and the Pompeii Antiquarium, Italy*. 2nd edn. Sydney: Australian Gallery Directors' Council, 1980, 95.

36 S. De Caro and A. Casale, *Boscoreale e le Sue Testimonianze Archeologiche: Villa Rustica in Località Villa Regina*. Napoli: Commune di Boscoreale, Assessorato ai Beni Culturali e Ambientali, 1988, 11; King, 2002, op. cit., 411, 444.

37 W.F. Jashemski, *The Gardens of Pompeii, Herculaneum and the Villas Destroyed by Vesuvius*. New York: Caratzas Brothers, 1979a, 23–24; W.F. Jashemski, 'The Vesuvian sites before AD 79: The archaeological, literary and epigraphical evidence', in *The Natural History of Pompeii*, ed. W.F. Jashemski and F.G. Meyer. Cambridge: Cambridge University Press, 2002, 16.

38 Monnier, 1864, pp 415–16 in Adams, 1868, op. cit., 264–66.

39 P.J. Baxter, 'Medical effects of volcanic eruptions', *Bulletin of Volcanology*, Vol. 52, 1990, 532–44.

40 For example, C. D'Amore *et al.*, 'Antropologia pompeiana del 79 d.C.: Sesso ed età di morte', *Archivio per l'Antropologia e la Etnologia*, Vol. 109, 1979, 300.

41 Brier, 1998, op. cit., 147; Chamberlain and Pearson, 2001, op. cit., 150; Grant, 1976, op. cit., 34.

42 Dr Mario Benanzio, orthopaedic surgeon, Dr Michael Houang, radiologist, Dr Chris Griffiths, of the then NSW Forensic Institute, Ian White, from the then NSW Forensic Institute, Dr Greg Doran, then from Anatomy and Histology, University of Sydney and a team of radiographers. E. Lazer, 'Human Skeletal Remains in Pompeii: Vols. I and II', unpublished PhD thesis, Department of Anatomy and Histology. Sydney: The University of Sydney, 1995, 376–79.

43 A. D'Ambrosio, 'The lady from Oplontis', in *Rediscovering Pompeii: IBM Gallery of Science and Art*, ed. B. Conticello. Rome: 'L'Erma' di Bretschneider, 1990, 133; De Carolis and Patricelli, 2003b, op. cit., 63, 91.

44 D'Ambrosio, 1990, op. cit., 133; A. Civale, 'Oplontis: The villa of Lucius Crassius Tertius', in *Tales from an Eruption: Pompeii, Herculaneum, Oplontis: Guide to the Exhibition*, ed. P. G. Guzzo. Milan: Electa, 2003b, 78.

45 B. Conticello (Superintendent, Pompeii) to E. Lazer, 1994, personal communication; C. Griffiths (New South Wales Institute of Forensic Science, Sydney) to E. Lazer, 1994, personal communication.

46 D'Ambrosio, 1990, op. cit., 133.

47 D.R. Brothwell, *Digging up Bones: The Excavation, Treatment and Study of Human Skeletal Remains*. 3rd edn. London: British Museum (Natural History) & Oxford University Press, 1981/1965, 155.

48 G. Doran (Department of Anatomy & Histology, The University of Sydney, Australia) to E. Lazer, 1994, personal communication; Griffiths, 1994, op. cit.

49 Caries cavities could be observed on the upper right second premolar, first and second molars and upper left first molar. Griffiths, 1994, op. cit.

50 Carious lesions that involved the entire crown were observed on the upper right second premolar and the upper left first molar. Griffiths, 1994, op. cit.

51 M. Houang (Radiologist, St Luke's Hospital, Sydney) to E. Lazer, 1994, personal communication; C. Roberts, 'Trauma and treatment in the British Isles in the historic period: A design for multidisciplinary research', in *Human Palaeopathology: Current Syntheses and Future Options*, ed. D.J. Ortner and A.C. Aufderheide. Washington, DC: Smithsonian Institution Press, 1991, 232.

52 These include the 17 humans that were cast from 1963, the nine individuals that were cast in the garden of the House of the Cryptoporticus in 1914, plus the 13 that were produced in the Garden of the Fugitives in 1961. A further 10 victims were cast between 1958 and the mid-1970s in the *Casa del Bracciale d'Oro, Casa di Ma. Castricius* and the Villa of M. Fabius Rufus. A number of casts were made of the 21 bodies that were found outside the Porta Nola between 1908 and 1911 and ten bodies were cast from the ten bodies found in August 1989 in Insula 22 of Region 1. De Carolis et al, 1998, op. cit., 77; García y García, 2006, op. cit., 188–95.

11 Making sense

1 Such as Public Law 101–601, the Native American Graves Protection and Repatriation Act, approved by President Bush in 1990. T.D. White and P.A. Folkens. *The Human Bone Manual*. Boston: Academic Press, 2005, 28.

2 See, for example, S. Colley, *Uncovering Australia: Archaeology, Indigenous People and the Public*. Sydney: Allen & Unwin, 2002, 56–58.

3 For example, A. Bickford *et al.*, 'Skeletal Remains: Guidelines for the Management of Human Skeletal Remains under the Heritage Act 1999'. Sydney: New South Wales Heritage Office, 1998; S. Mays, *The Archaeology of Human Bones*. London: Routledge, 1998.

4 J.B.d.C.M. Saunders and C.D. O'Malley, *The Anatomical Drawings of Andreas Vesalius*. New York: Bonanza Books, 1982; A.T. Chamberlain, and M.P. Pearson. *Earthly Remains: The History and Science of Preserved Bodies*. Oxford: Oxford University Press, 2001, 8, Fig. 1.

5 A.C. Aufderheide, *The Scientific Study of Mummies*. Cambridge: Cambridge University Press, 2003, 192–203.

6 R. Cordovani, *La Cripta dei Cappuccini. Chiesa dell'Immacolata Conzezione Via Vittorio Veneto-Roma*. Rome: Provincia Romana dei Frati Minori Cappuccini, 2005.

7 S. Court (Herculaneum Conservation Project Research and Outreach Coordinator) to E. Lazer, 2006, *personal communication*; J. Thompson (Project Manager Herculaneum Conservation Project) to E. Lazer, 15 October 2007, *personal communication*.

Glossary

1 W.M. Bass, *Human Osteology: A Laboratory and Field Manual of the Human Skeleton*, 2nd edn. Columbia: Missouri Archaeological Society, 1984, 291–93; J.G. Clement and D.L. Ranson (eds), *Craniofacial Identification in Forensic Medicine*. London: Arnold, 1998, 297–98; E. De Carolis and G. Patricelli, *Vesuvius, AD 79: The Destruction of Pompeii and Herculaneum*, translated by The J. Paul Getty Trust, Rome: 'L'Erma' di Bretschneider, 2003b, 127–28; Freeman, 'Glossary of Histological and Microanatomical Terms Including Historical Origins and Eponyms'. Sydney: School of Anatomy, University of New South Wales, 2000; S. Hilson, *Dental Anthropology*. Cambridge: Cambridge University Press, 1996; L. Scheuer, and S. Black, *The Juvenile Skeleton*. Amsterdam: Elsevier, 2004, 2–3; H. Sigurdsson, *Melting the Earth: The History of Ideas on Volcanic Eruptions*, Oxford: Oxford University Press, 1999: T.D. White, *Human Osteology*, 1st edn. San Diego, California: Academic Press, 2000.

2 A.C. Aufderheide and C. Rodriguez-Martin, *The Cambridge Encyclopaedia of Human Palaeopathology*, Cambridge: Cambridge University Press, 1998, 84.

3 A.T. Chamberlain, *Demography in Archaeology*, Cambridge Manuals in Archaeology. Cambridge: Cambridge University Press, 2006, 26–27.

4 Ibid.

Appendix 1

1 Based on J.W. Alexander, 'The impact of discoveries', in *The Buried Cities and the Eruption of Vesuvius: The 1900th Anniversary*, ed. H.W. Benario and G.W. Lawall. Amherst: NECN and University of Massachusetts, 1979, 23–29; C. Amery, and B. Curran, *The Lost World of Pompeii*. London: Frances Lincoln, 2002, 30–47, 148–67; M. Brion, *Pompeii and Herculaneum, The Glory and the Grief*. London: Cardinal, 1973/1960, 42–72; B. Conticello, 'Rediscovering Pompeii', in *Rediscovering Pompeii: IBM Gallery of Science and Art*, ed. B. Conticello. Rome: 'L'Erma' di Bretschneider, 1990, 2–25; A.E. Cooley, *Pompeii*. London: Duckworth, 2003, 65–125; E.C.C. Corti, *The Destruction and Resurrection of Pompeii and Herculaneum*. Translated by K. Smith and R.G. Smith. London: Routledge & Kegan Paul, 1951, 81–209; J.-P. Descœudres, 'Discovery and excavation', in *Pompeii Revisited: The Life*

and Death of a Roman Town, ed. D. Harrison. Sydney: Meditarch, 1994b, 41–53; R. Etienne, *Pompeii: The Day a City Died*. Translated by C. Palmer. London: Thames & Hudson, 1992, 16–41; W. Leppmann, *Pompeii in Fact and Fiction*. London: Elek, 1968, 48–154, R. Ling, *Pompeii: History, Life and Afterlife*. Stroud, Gloucestershire: Tempus, 2005, 157–70; R. Trevelyan, *The Shadow of Vesuvius: Pompeii AD 79*. London: Michael Joseph, 1976, 37–100; The British School at Rome, *Herculaneum: The Herculaneum Conservation Project* (2007), http://www.bsr.ac.uk/BSR/sub_arch/BSR_Arch_03Herc.htm (accessed 2 October 2008).

BIBLIOGRAPHY

Ancient sources

Anonymous, 'The Etna Poem', in *Minor Latin Poets in Two Volumes*, *Loeb Classical Library*. Cambridge, Massachusetts: Harvard University Press, 1982.

Augustus, 'Ius Trium Liberorum', in *The Oxford Classical Dictionary*, ed. Hammond, N.G.L. and H.H. Scullard. Oxford: Oxford University Press, 1970.

Celsus, 'De Medicina', in *Loeb Classical Library*. Cambridge, Massachusetts: Harvard University Press, 1938.

Dio Cassius, 'Dio's Roman history', in *Loeb Classical Library*. Cambridge, Massachusetts: Harvard University Press, 1914–27.

Diodorus Siculus, 'Diodorus Siculus', in *Loeb Classical Library*. Cambridge, Massachusetts: Harvard University Press, 1933–67.

Martial, 'Epigrammata: English and Latin Selections'. London: Hart-Davis, MacGibbon, 1973.

Ovid, 'The Art of Love', in *Loeb Classical Library*. Cambridge, Massachusetts: Harvard University Press, 1957.

Plautus, 'The Haunted House', in *Loeb Classical Library*. Cambridge, Massachusetts: Harvard University Press, 1957.

Pliny the Elder, 'Natural Histories', in *Loeb Classical Library*. Cambridge, Massachusetts: Harvard University Press, 1938/1962.

Pliny the Younger, 'Letters and Panegyrics', in *Loeb Classical Library*. Cambridge, Massachusetts: Harvard University Press, 1969.

Plutarch, *Makers of Rome: Nine Lives*. Translated by Scott-Kilvert, I. Harmondsworth, England: Penguin, 1965.

Seneca, 'Naturales Quaestiones', in *Loeb Classical Library*. Cambridge, Massachusetts: Harvard University Press, 1972.

Strabo, *The Geography*. Translated by Jones, H.R., *Loeb Classical Library*. Cambridge, Massachusetts: Harvard University Press, 1988.

Suetonius, 'The Twelve Caesars'. Middlesex: Penguin, 1957.

Tacitus, 'Annals of Imperial Rome'. Middlesex: Penguin, 1971.

Vitruvius, 'De Architectura', in *Loeb Classical Library*. Cambridge, Massachusetts: Harvard University Press, 1934.

References

Anonymous, *Documentazione nell'opera di disengnatori e pittori dei secoli XVII e XIX*, 1990.

Adam, J.–P., 'Observations techniques sur les suites du séisme de 62 à Pompéi', in *Tremblements de Terre, Éruptions Volcaniques et Vie des Hommes dans la Campanie Antique*, ed. Albore Livadie, C. Naples: Centre Jean Bâerard, 1986, 67–87.

Adams, W.H.D. *The Buried Cities of Campania, or, Pompeii and Herculaneum: Their History, Their Destruction, and Their Remains*. London: T. Nelson & Sons, Paternoster Row, 1868.

Ahlqvist, J. and D. Damsten, 'A modification of Kerley's method for the microscopic determination of age in human bone', *Journal of Forensic Sciences*, Vol. 14, 1969: 205–12.

Alexander, J.W., 'The impact of discoveries', in *The Buried Cities and the Eruption of Vesuvius: The 1900th Anniversary*, ed. Benario, H.W. and G.W. Lawall. Amherst: NECN & University of Massachusetts, 1979, 23–29.

Allison, P.M., 'Artefact assemblages: Not the "Pompeii Premise"', in *Papers of the Fourth Conference of Italian Archaeology, University of London, 1990*, ed. Herring, E., R. Whitehouse and J. Wilkins. London: Accordia Research Centre, 1992a, 49–56.

——'The Distribution of Pompeiian House Contents and Its Significance. Vols. I and II', unpublished PhD thesis, School of Archaeology, Classics and Ancient History. Sydney: The University of Sydney, 1992b.

——'On-going seismic activity and its effects on the living conditions in Pompeii in the last decades', in *La Regione Vesuviana dal 62 al 79 d.C.: Problemi Archeologici e Sismologici*, ed. Frölich, T. and L. Jacobelli. Munich: 1995, 162–69.

——'Placing individuals: Pompeian epigraphy in context', *Journal of Mediterranean Archaeology*, Vol. 14, No. 1, 2001: 53–74.

——'Recurring tremors: The continuing impact of the AD 79 eruption of Mt Vesuvius', in *Natural Disasters and Cultural Change*, ed. Torrence, R. and J. Gratton. London: Routledge, 2002, 107–25.

——*Pompeian Households: An Analysis of the Material Culture*, Monograph 42. Los Angeles: Cotsen Institute for Archaeology, University of California, 2004.

Amery, C. and B. Curran, *The Lost World of Pompeii*. London: Frances Lincoln, 2002.

Anderson, B.E., 'Ventral arc of the os pubis: Anatomical and developmental considerations', *American Journal of Physical Anthropology*, Vol. 83, 1990: 449–58.

Anderson, T., 'An Anglo-Saxon case of hyperostosis frontalis interna', *Archaeologia Cantiana*, Vol. 112, 1993: 253–59.

Andreau, J., 'Il terremoto del 62', in *Pompei 79: Raccolta di Studi per il Decimonono Centenario dell'Eruzione Vesuviana*, ed. Zevi, F. Naples: Gaetano Macchiaroli, 1979, 40–44.

Andrews, I., *Pompeii*, Cambridge Introduction to the History of Mankind. Cambridge: Cambridge University Press, 1978.

Angel, J.L., 'A racial analysis of the ancient Greeks: An essay on the use of morphological types', *American Journal of Physical Anthropology*, Vol. 2, 1944: 329–76.

——'Skeletal material from Attica', *Hesperia*, Vol. 14, 1945: 279–363.

——'Skeletal change in ancient Greece', *American Journal of Physical Anthropology*, Vol. 4 1946: 69–97.

——'Porotic hyperostosis, anemias, malarias and marshes in the prehistoric Eastern Mediterranean', *Science*, Vol. 153, 1966: 760–63.

——'Porotic hyperostosis or osteoporosis symmetrica', in *Diseases in Antiquity*, ed. Brothwell, D.R. and A.T. Sandison. Springfield, Illinois: Charles C. Thomas, 1967, 378–89.

——'The bases of palaeodemography', *American Journal of Physical Anthropology*, Vol. 30 1969a: 427–37.

——'Palaeodemography and evolution', *American Journal of Physical Anthropology*, Vol. 31 1969b: 343–53.

——'Ecology and population in the Eastern Mediterranean', *World Archaeology*, Vol. 4, 1972: 88–105.

Angel, J.L., J.O. Kelley, M. Parrington and S. Pinter, 'Life stresses of the free black community as represented by the First African Baptist Church, Philadelphia, 1823–41', *American Journal of Physical Anthropology*, Vol. 74, No. 2, 1987: 213–29.

Anton, S.C., 'Endocranial Hyperostosis in Sangiran 2, Gibraltar 1, and Shanidar 5', *American Journal of Physical Anthropology*, Vol. 102, No. 1, 1997: 111–22.

Ariëns Kappers, C.U. and L.W. Parr. *An Introduction to the Anthropology of the Near East in Ancient and Recent Times*. Amsterdam: Noord-Hollandsche, 1934.

Armelagos, G.J. and O.D. Chrisman. 'Hyperostosis frontalis interna: A Nubian case', *American Journal of Physical Anthropology*, Vol. 76, 1988: 25–28.

Arnold, M.A. and B. Freeman (additions), 'Glossary of anatomical terms', in *Unpublished Class Notes*. Sydney: The University of New South Wales, Faculty of Medicine, School of Medical Sciences, Department of Anatomy, 2002.

Arriaza, B.T., C.F. Merbs and B.M. Rothschild, 'Diffuse idiopathic skeletal hyperostosis in Meroitic Nubians from Semna South, Sudan', *American Journal of Physical Anthropology*, Vol. 92, 1993: 243–48.

Ascenzi, A., 'Physiological relationship and pathological interferences between bone tissue and marrow', in *The Biochemistry and Physiology of Bone*, ed. Bourne, G.H. New York: Academic Press, 1976, 403–45.

——'A problem in palaeopathology: The origin of thalassemia in Italy', *Virchows Archiv A: Pathological Anatomy and Histopathology*, Vol. 384, 1979: 121–30.

——'Microscopy and ultramicroscopy in palaeopathology', in *Innovative Trends in Prehistoric Anthropology: Contributions to an International Symposium from February 26th to March 1st 1986 in Berlin (West)*, ed. Hänsel, B. and B. Herrmann, *Mitteilungen der Berliner Gesellschaft für Anthropologie, Ethnologie und Urgeschichte*, Berlin: 1986, 149–56.

Ascenzi, A. and P. Balistreri. 'Aural exostoses in a Roman skull excavated at the "Baths of the Swimmer" in the ancient town of Ostia', *Journal of Human Evolution*, Vol. 4, 1975: 579–84.

Ascenzi, A., M. Brunori, G. Citro and R. Zito, 'Immunological detection of haemoglobin in bones of ancient Roman times and of Iron and Eneolithic Ages', *Proceedings of the National Academy of Science, USA*, Vol. 82, 1985: 7170–72.

Ascher, R., 'Analogy in archaeological interpretation', *Southwestern Journal of Anthropology*, Vol. 17, 1961: 317–25.

Ashley Montagu, M.F., *Man's Most Dangerous Myth: The Fallacy of Race*. 3rd edn. New York: Harper & Brothers, 1952.

——(ed.), *The Concept of Race*. New York: Free Press, 1964.

Aufderheide, A.C., 'Chemical analysis of skeletal remains', in *Reconstruction of Life from the Skeleton*, ed. Iscan, M.Y. and K.A.R. Kennedy. New York: Alan R. Liss, 1989, 237–60.

——*The Scientific Study of Mummies*. Cambridge: Cambridge University Press, 2003.

Aufderheide, A.C. and C. Rodriguez-Martin, *The Cambridge Encyclopaedia of Human Palaeopathology*. Cambridge: Cambridge University Press, 1998.

Bailey, J.F., M. Henneberg, I.B. Colson, A. Ciarollo, R.E.M. Hedges and B. Sykes, 'Monkey business in Pompeii: Unique find of a juvenile Barbary Macaque skeleton in Pompeii identified using osteology and ancient DNA techniques', *Molecular Biology and Evolution*, Vol. 16, 1999: 1410–14.

Barber, G., I. Watt, and J. Rogers, 'A comparison of radiological and palaeopathological diagnostic criteria for hyperostosis frontalis interna', *International Journal of Osteoarchaeology*, Vol. 7, 1998: 157–64.

Barker, B.C.W., 'Concerning the possibility of estimating the original dimensions of worn Aboriginal teeth', *Australian Dental Journal*, Vol. 17, 1972: 448–53.

Barnicot, N.A. and D.R. Brothwell, 'The evaluation of metrical data in the comparison of ancient and modern bones', in *CIBA Foundation Symposium on Medical Biology and Etruscan Origins*, ed. Wolstenholme, G.E.W. and C.M. O'Connor. London: J. & A. Churchill, 1959, 131–48.

Bass, W.M., *Human Osteology: A Laboratory and Field Manual of the Human Skeleton*. 2nd edn. Columbia: Missouri Archaeological Society, 1984.

Bastet, F.L. and M. De Vos. *Proposta per una Classificazione del Terzo Stile Pompeiano*. Translated by De Vos, A. Vol. 4, Archeologische Studien van het Nederlands Instituut te Rome. s-Gravenhage: Staatsuitgeverij, 1979.

Baxter, P.J. 'Medical effects of volcanic eruptions', *Bulletin of Volcanology*, Vol. 52, 1990: 532–44.

Baxter, P.J., R.S. Bernstein, H. Falk, J. French and R. Ing, 'Medical aspects of volcanic disasters: An outline of the hazards and emergency response measures', *Disasters*, Vol. 6, No. 4, 1982: 268–76.

Baxter, P.J., R. Boyle, P. Cole, A. Neri, R. Spence and G. Zuccaro, 'The impacts of pyroclastic surges on buildings at the eruption of the Soufrière Hills Volcano, Montserrat', *Bulletin of Volcanology*, Vol. 67, No. 4, 2005: 292–313.

Baxter, P.J., A. Neri and M. Todesco, 'Physical modelling and human survival in pyroclastic flows', *Natural Hazards*, Vol. 17, No. 2, 1998: 163–76.

Baxter, P.J., R.E. Stoiber and S.N. Williams, 'Volcanic gases and health: Masaya Volcano, Nicaragua', *The Lancet*, Vol. 320, No. 8290, 1982: 150–51.

Becker, M.J. 'Calculating stature from in situ measurements of skeletons and from long bone lengths: An historical perspective leading to a test of Formicola's hypothesis at 5th century BCE Satricum, Lazio, Italy', *Rivista di Antrolopologia*, Vol. 77, 1999: 225–47.

——'Review [untitled]', Rev. of I Fuggiaschi di Ercolano: Paleobiologia delle vittime dell'eruzione Vesuviana del 79 D.C. by Capasso, L. Rome: L'Erma di Bretschneider, 2001), *Journal of Roman Studies*, Vol. 93, 2003: 404–6.

Bedford, M.E., K.F. Russell, C.O. Lovejoy, R.S. Meindl, S.W. Simpson and P.L. Stuart-Macadam, 'Test of the multifactorial aging method using skeletons with known ages-at-death from the Grant Collection', *American Journal of Physical Anthropology*, Vol. 91, 1993: 287–97.

Belcastro, M.G., F. Facchini and E. Rastelli. '*Hyperostosis Frontalis Interna* and Sex Identification of Two Skeletons', *International Journal of Osteoarchaeology*, Vol. 16, No. 6, 2006: 506–16.

Beloch, J. *Campanien: Geschichte und Topographie des Antiken Neapel und Seiner Umgebung*. 2nd edn. Breslau: E. Morganstern, 1890.

Benario, H.W., 'The land, the cities, the event', in *The Buried Cities and the Eruption of Vesuvius: The 1900th Anniversary*, ed. Benario, H.W. and G.W. Lawall, *Lectures presented at Emory University on May 7, 1979 in a symposium sponsored by the Dept. of Modern Languages and Classics, Alpha Sigma chapter of Eta Sigma Phi, and the Atlanta Society of the Archaeological Institute of America*. Amherst: NECN & University of Massachusetts, 1979, 1–6.

Berry, A.C. and R.J. Berry, 'Epigenetic variation in the human cranium', *Journal of Anatomy*, Vol. 101, 1967: 361–79.

Bickford, A., D. Donlon and S. Lavelle, 'Skeletal Remains: Guidelines for the Management of Human Skeletal Remains under the Heritage Act 1999'. Sydney: New South Wales Heritage Office, 1998.

Biddle, M., 'The archaeology of Winchester', *Scientific American*, Vol. 230, No. 5, 1974: 32–43.

Binford, L.R., 'Behavioural archaeology and the "Pompeii Premise" in archaeology', *Journal of Anthropological Research*, Vol. 37, 1981: 195–208.

Bisel, S.C., 'The Herculaneum Project: Preliminary Report', *Palaeopathology Newsletter*, Vol. 41, 1983: 6–7.

——'The people of Herculaneum', *Helmartica*, Vol. 37, 1986: 11–23.

——'Human bones at Herculaneum', *Rivista di Studi Pompeiani*, Vol. 1, 1987: 123–31.

——'Nutrition in first century Herculaneum', *Anthropologie*, Vol. 26, 1988a: 61–66.

——'The skeletons of Herculaneum, Italy', in *Wet Site Archaeology: Proceedings of the International Conference on Wet Site Archaeology, Gainesville, Florida, December 12–14, 1986; sponsored by the National Endowment for the Humanities and University of Florida*, ed. Purdy, B.A. Caldwell, New Jersey: Telford Press, 1988b.

——'The human skeletons of Herculaneum', *International Journal of Anthropology*, Vol. 6, No. 1, 1991: 1–20.

Bisel, S.C. and J.F. Bisel, 'Health and nutrition at Herculaneum: An examination of human skeletal remains', in *The Natural History of Pompeii*, ed. Jashemski, W.F. and F.G. Meyer. Cambridge: Cambridge University Press, 2002, 451–75.

Bisel, S.C., J.F. Bisel and S. Tanaka, *The Secrets of Vesuvius*. Toronto: Madison Press, 1990.

Bleibtreu, H.K. (ed.), *Evolutionary Anthropology: A Reader in Human Biology* Boston: Allyn & Bacon, 1969.

Bliquez, L.J., *Roman Surgical Instruments and Other Minor Objects in the National Museum of Naples*. Mainz, Germany: Philipp von Zabern, 1994.

Blong, R.J., *Volcanic Hazards: A Sourcebook on the Effects of Eruptions*. Sydney: Academic Press, 1984.

Boas, F., 'Changes in bodily form of descendants of immigrants (reprint of 1912 article)', in *Frontiers of Anthropology*, ed. Ashley Montagu, M.F. New York: Capricorn Books, 1974, 321–32.

Bocquet-Appel, J.P. and C. Masset, 'Paleodemography: Resurrection or Ghost?', *Journal of Human Evolution*, Vol. 14, No. 2, 1985: 107–11.

——'Farewell to paleodemography', *Journal of Human Evolution*, Vol. 11, 1982: 321–33.

Boldsen, J.L., G.R. Milner, L.W. Konigsberg and J.W. Wood, 'Transition analysis: A new method for estimating age from skeletons', in *Paleodemography: Age Distributions from Skeletal Samples*, ed. Hoppa, R.D. and J.W. Vaupel, *Cambridge Studies in Biological and Evolutionary Anthropology*. Cambridge: Cambridge University Press, 2002, 73–106.

Bologna, F., 'The rediscovery of Herculaneum and Pompeii in the artistic culture of Europe in the eighteenth century', in *Rediscovering Pompeii: IBM Gallery of Science and Art,* ed. Conticello, B. Rome: 'L'Erma' di Bretschneider, 1990, 79–91.

Bondioli, L., R.S. Corruccini and R. Macchiarelli, 'Familial segregation in the Iron-Age community of Alfedena, Abruzzo, Italy, based on osteo-dental trait analysis', *American Journal of Physical Anthropology*, Vol. 71, No. 4, 1986: 393–400.

Bonfiglioli, B., P. Brasili and M.G. Belcastro, 'Dento-alveolar lesions and nutritional habits of a Roman Imperial age population (1st–4th c. AD): Quadrella (Molise, Italy)', *Homo: Journal of Comparative Human Biology*, Vol. 54, No. 1, 2003: 36–56.

Boulle, E.-L., 'Evolution of two human skeletal markers of the squatting position: A dia-chronic study from antiquity to the modern age', *American Journal of Physical Anthropology*, Vol. 115, No. 1, 2001: 50–56.

Bowden, K.M., *Forensic Medicine*. 2nd edn. Brisbane: Jacaranda, 1965.

Bowler, S., 'Earthquakes and volcanoes', *New Scientist*, Vol. 139, No. 1891: Inside Science Supplement 64, 1993: 1–4.

——'Earth's fireworks', Rev. of P. Francis, Volcanoes: A Planetary Perspective, Oxford University Press, 1993, *New Scientist*, Vol. 139, No. 1891, 1993: 40–41.

Boyd, W.C., *Genetics and the Races of Man*. Boston: Little, Brown & Co., 1950.

Breathnach, A.S. (ed.), *Frazer's Anatomy of the Human Skeleton*. London: J. & A. Churchill, 1965.

Brier, B., *The Encyclopedia of Mummies*. New York: Checkmark, 1998.

——*Egyptian Mummies: Unravelling the Secrets of an Ancient Art*. London: Brockhampton Press, 1999/1994.

Briggs, C.A., 'Anthropological assessment', in *Craniofacial Identification in Forensic Medicine*, ed. Clement, J.G. and D.L. Ranson. London: Arnold, 1998, 49–61.

Brion, M., *Pompeii and Herculaneum: The Glory and the Grief*. London: Cardinal, 1973/1960.

Brooks, S. and J.M. Suchey. 'Skeletal age determination based on the *os pubis*: A comparison of the Acsádi–Nemeskéri and Suchey–Brooks methods', *Human Evolution*, Vol. 5, No. 3, 1990: 227–38.

Brothwell, D.R., *Digging up Bones: The Excavation, Treatment and Study of Human Skeletal Remains*. 3rd edn. London: British Museum (Natural History) & Oxford University Press, 1981.

——*The Bog Man and the Archaeology of People*. London: British Museum Publications, 1986.

Brothwell, D.R., E. Higgs and G. Clark (eds), *Science in Archaeology: A Comprehensive Survey of Progress and Research*. New York: Basic Books, 1963.

Brothwell, D.R. and A.T. Sandison. *Diseases in Antiquity*. Springfield, Illinois: Basic Books, 1967.

Brown, D.M. (ed.), *Pompeii: The Vanished City*. Alexandria, Virginia: Time–Life Books, 1992.

Brown, J.M., 'Eyewitness memory for arousing events: putting things into context', *Applied Cognitive Psychology*, Vol. 17, No. 1, 2003: 93–106.

Brues, A.M., *People and Races*. New York: Macmillan, 1977.

Bruner, E., M. Averini, and G. Manzi, 'Endocranial traits. Prevalence and distribution in a recent human population', *European Journal of Anatomy*, Vol. 7, No. 1, 2003: 23–33.

Buikstra, J.E., 'Repatriation and bioarchaeology: Challenges and opportunities', in *Bioarchaeology: The Contextual Analysis of Human Remains*, ed. Buikstra, J.E. and L.A. Beck. Amsterdam: Academic Press, 2006), 389–415.

Buikstra, J.E. and D.H. Ubelaker (eds), *Standards for Data Collection from Human Skeletal Remains: Proceedings of a Seminar at the Field Museum of Natural History Organized by Jonathon Haas*. Fayetteville, Arkansas, 1994.

Bullard, F.M., 'Volcanoes and their activity', in *Volcanic Activity and Human Ecology*, ed. Sheets, P.D. and D.K. Grayson. New York: Academic Press, 1979, 9–48.

——*Volcanoes of the Earth*. Austin: University of Texas Press, 1984.

Bulwer-Lytton, E. *Paul Clifford*. London: Routledge, 1875.

——*The Last Days of Pompeii*. New York: Putnam, 1897.

—— C. Frères (illustrations) and H. Rouillard (adapted by). *Les Derniers Jours de Pompéi*, Bibliothèque Juventa. Paris: Librairie Delagrave, 1936.

Busignani, A., *Botticelli: The Life and Work of the Artist*. London: Thames & Hudson, 1968.

353

Butterworth, A. and R. Laurence, *Pompeii: The Living City*. London: Weidenfeld & Nicolson, 2005.

Buzarbaruah, P.M., 'Changes in anthropometric measurements due to migration and environment: A preliminary observation', *Anthropologie*, Vol. 30, No. 2, 1992: 189–95.

Cabell, C.H., E. Abrutyn, and A.W. Karchmer, 'Bacterial endocarditis: The disease, treatment, and prevention', in *Circulation*, Vol. 107, American Heart Association, 2003; e185–e7.

Calcagno, J.M., 'On the applicability of sexing human skeletal material by discriminant function analysis', *Journal of Human Evolution*, Vol. 10, 1981: 189–98.

Cammisa, M., A. De Serio and G. Guglielmi. 'Diffuse idiopathic skeletal hyperostosis', *European Journal of Radiology*, Vol. 27, No. Supplement 1, 1998: 7–11.

Campbell, J.L., *Edward Bulwer-Lytton*. Boston: Twayne, 1986.

Capasso, L., 'Brucellosis at Herculaneum (79 AD)', *International Journal of Osteoarchaeology*, Vol. 9, 1999: 277–88.

——'Herculaneum victims of the volcanic eruptions of Vesuvius in 79 AD', *The Lancet*, Vol. 356, No. 9238, 2000a: 1344–46.

——'Indoor pollution and respiratory diseases in ancient Rome', *The Lancet*, Vol. 356, No. 9243, 2000b: 1774.

——*I Fuggiaschi di Ercolano: Paleobiologia delle Vittime dell'Eruzione Vesuviana del 79 d.C.* Roma: 'L'Erma' di Bretschneider, 2001.

——'Bacteria in two-millennia-old cheese, and related epizoonoses in Roman populations', *Journal of Infection*, Vol. 45, No. 2, 2002: 122–27.

——'Infectious diseases and eating habits at Herculaneum (1st century AD, Southern Italy)', *International Journal of Osteoarchaeology*, Vol. 17, No. 4, 2007: 350–57.

Capasso, L. and L. Capasso, 'Mortality in Herculaneum before volcanic eruption in 79 AD', *The Lancet*, Vol. 354, No. 9192, 1999: 1826.

Capasso, L. and L. Di Domenicantonio, 'Work-related syndesmoses on the bones of children who died at Herculaneum', *The Lancet*, Vol. 352, No. 9140, 1998: 1634.

Capasso, L. and G. Di Tota, 'Lice buried under the ashes of Herculaneum', *The Lancet*, Vol. 351, No. 9107, 1998: 992.

——'Tuberculosis in Herculaneum (79 AD)', in *Tuberculosis Past and Present*, ed. Pálfi, G., O. Dutour, J. Deák and I. Hutás. Budapest: Golden Books & Tuberculosis Foundation, 1999, 463–67.

Capasso, L., K.A.R. Kennedy and C.A. Wilczak, *Atlas of Occupational Markers on Human Remains*, *Journal of Paleopathology*: Monographic Publication 3. Teramo: Journal of Paleopathology & Edigrafital, 1999.

Carafa, P., 'Recent work on early Pompeii', in *The World of Pompeii*, ed. Dobbins, J.J. and P. W. Foss (London: Routledge, 2007), 63–72.

Carattelli, G.P. (ed.), *Pompei: Pitture e Mosaici*. (Rome: Istituto della Enciclopedia Italiana, 1993.

Carey, S. and H. Sigurdsson. 'Temporal variations in column height and magma discharge rate during the AD 79 eruption of Vesuvius', *Geological Society of America Bulletin*, Vol. 99, 1987: 303–14.

Carrington, R.C., *Pompeii*. Oxford: Clarendon Press, 1936.

Cartmill, M. and K. Brown, 'Surveying the race concept: A reply to Lieberman, Kirk, and Littlefield', *American Anthropologist*, Vol. 105, No. 1, 2003: 114–15.

Caspari, R., 'From types to populations: A century of race, physical anthropology, and the American Anthropological Association', *American Anthropologist*, Vol. 105, No. 1, 2003: 65–76.

Cassanelli, R., 'Images of Pompeii: From engraving to photography', in *Houses and Monuments of Pompeii: The Works of Fausto and Felice Niccolini*, ed. Cassanelli, R., P.L. Ciapparelli, E. Colle and M. David. Los Angeles: The J. Paul Getty Museum, 2002, 48–51.

Cassanelli, R., P.L. Ciapparelli, E. Colle and M. David, *Houses and Monuments of Pompeii: The Works of Fausto and Felice Niccolini*. Translated by T.M. Hartmann. Los Angeles: The J. Paul Getty Museum, 2002.

Caton, R. 'Notes on a group of medical and surgical instruments found near Kolophon', *Journal of Hellenic Studies*, Vol. 34, 1914: 114–18.

Cerulli Irelli, M.G., 'Intorno al problema della rinascita di Pompei', in *Neue Forschungen in Pompeji*, ed. Andreae, B. and H. Kyrieleis. Recklinghausen: Aurel Bongers, 1975, 291–98.

——'Der letzten Pompejanische stil', in *Pompejianische Wandmalerei*, ed. Cerulli Irelli, G., M. Aoyagi and D. Stefano. Zürich: Belser, 1990, 233–38.

Chamberlain, A.T., *Demography in Archaeology*, Cambridge Manuals in Archaeology. Cambridge: Cambridge University Press, 2006.

Chamberlain, A.T. and M.P. Pearson, *Earthly Remains: The History and Science of Preserved Bodies*. Oxford: Oxford University Press, 2001.

Ciarello, A.M. and E. De Carolis, 'La data dell' eruzione', *Rivista di Studi Pompeiani*, Vol. 9, 1998: 63–73.

Cipollaro, M., G. Di Bernardo, A. Forte, G. Galano, L. De Masi, U. Galderisi, F.M. Guarino, F. Angelini and A. Cascino, 'Histological analysis and ancient DNA amplification of human bone remains found in Caius Iulius Polybius House in Pompeii', *Croatian Medical Journal*, Vol. 40, No. 3, 1999: 392–97.

Cipollaro, M., G. Di Bernardo, G. Galano, U. Galderisi, F.M. Guarino, F. Angelini and A. Cascino, 'Ancient DNA in human bone remains from Pompeii archaeological site', *Biochemical and Biophysical Research Communications*, Vol. 247, No. 3, 1998: 901–4.

Ciprotti, P., *Pompei*, Universale Studium: 86. Rome: Studium, 1962.

——'Der letzte tag von Pompeji', *Altertum*, Vol. 10, 1964: 40–54.

Civale, A., 'Oplontis: Introduction', in *Tales from an Eruption: Pompeii, Herculaneum, Oplontis: Guide to the Exhibition*, ed. Guzzo, P.G. Milan: Electa, 2003a, 72–73.

——'Oplontis: The villa of Lucius Crassius Tertius', in *Tales from an Eruption: Pompeii, Herculaneum, Oplontis: Guide to the Exhibition*, ed. Guzzo, P.G. Milan: Electa, 2003b, 74–79.

——'Pompeii: Caupona (V, 1, 13)', in *Tales from an Eruption: Pompeii, Herculaneum, Oplontis: Guide to the Exhibition*, ed. Guzzo, P.G. Milan: Electa, 2003c, 106–7.

——'Pompeii: The harbour gate', in *Tales from an Eruption: Pompeii, Herculaneum, Oplontis: Guide to the Exhibition*, ed. Guzzo, P.G. Milan: Electa, 2003d, 151–52.

——'Pompeii: The house of Julius Polybius (IX, 13, 1–3)', in *Tales from an Eruption: Pompeii, Herculaneum, Oplontis: Guide to the Exhibition*, ed. Guzzo, P.G. Milan: Electa, 2003e, 163–65.

——'Pompeii: The house of Oppius Gratus (IX, 6, 5)', in *Tales from an Eruption: Pompeii, Herculaneum, Oplontis: Guide to the Exhibition*, ed. Guzzo, P.G. Milan: Electa, 2003f, 113–15.

——'Pompeii: The house of the centenary (IX, 8, 3–5)', in *Tales from an Eruption: Pompeii, Herculaneum, Oplontis: Guide to the Exhibition*, ed. Guzzo, P.G. Milan: Electa, 2003g, 116–19.

——'Pompeii: The House of the Craftsman (I, 10, 7)', in *Tales from an Eruption: Pompeii, Herculaneum, Oplontis: Guide to the Exhibition*, ed. Guzzo, P.G. Milan: Electa, 2003h, 140–42.

——'Pompeii: The house of the Menander (I, 10, 4)', in *Tales from an Eruption: Pompeii, Herculaneum, Oplontis: Guide to the Exhibition*, ed. Guzzo, P.G. Milan: Electa, 2003i, 137–39.

——'Pompeii: The Nolan Gate', in *Tales from an Eruption: Pompeii, Herculaneum, Oplontis: Guide to the Exhibition*, ed. Guzzo, P.G. Milan: Electa, 2003j, 120–23.

——'Pompeii: The Vesuvius Gate', in *Tales from an Eruption: Pompeii, Herculaneum, Oplontis: Guide to the Exhibition*, ed. Guzzo, P.G. Milan: Electa, 2003k, 124–25.

——'Pompeii: The villa of the mysteries', in *Tales from an Eruption: Pompeii, Herculaneum, Oplontis: Guide to the Exhibition*, ed. Guzzo, P.G. Milan: Electa, 2003l, 134–36.

——'Pompeii: Via Dell'Abbondanza', in *Tales from an Eruption: Pompeii, Herculaneum, Oplontis: Guide to the Exhibition*, ed. Guzzo, P.G. Milan: Electa, 2003m, 130–31.

——'Pompeii: Vicolo di Tesmus', in *Tales from an Eruption: Pompeii, Herculaneum, Oplontis: Guide to the Exhibition*, ed. Guzzo, P.G. Milan: Electa, 2003n, 110–12.

——'Pompeii: Introduction', in *Tales from an Eruption: Pompeii, Herculaneum, Oplontis: Guide to the Exhibition*, ed. Guzzo, P.G. Milan: Electa, 2003o, 90–91.

——'Pompeii: The Temple of Isis', in *Tales from an Eruption: Pompeii, Herculaneum, Oplontis: Guide to the Exhibition*, ed. Guzzo, P.G. Milan: Electa, 2003p, 95–97.

——'Pompeii: Vicolo degli Scheletri (VII, 13, 19)', in *Tales from an Eruption: Pompeii, Herculaneum, Oplontis: Guide to the Exhibition*, ed. Guzzo, P.G. Milan: Electa, 2003q, 103–5.

——'Terzigno: Introduction', in *Tales from an Eruption: Pompeii, Herculaneum, Oplontis: Guide to the Exhibition*, ed. Guzzo, P.G. Milan: Electa, 2003r, 80–85.

——'Terzigno: Villa 6', in *Tales from an Eruption: Pompeii, Herculaneum, Oplontis: Guide to the Exhibition*, ed. Guzzo, P.G. Milan: Electa, 2003s, 86–89.

Clarke, N.G., S.E. Carey, W. Srikandi, R.S. Hirsch, and P.I. Leppard. 'Periodontal disease in ancient populations', *American Journal of Physical Anthropology*, Vol. 71, 1986: 173–83.

Clay, E. and M. Fredericksen (eds), 'Sir William Gell in Italy: Letters to the Society of Dilettanti, 1831–35'. London: Hamilton, 1976.

Clement, J.G., 'Dental identification', in *Craniofacial Identification in Forensic Medicine*, ed. Clement, J.G. and D.L. Ranson. London: Arnold, 1998, 63–81.

Cocheton, J.J., L. Fineltain, and J. Poulet, 'Le syndrome de Morgagni-Stewart-Morel: Mythe ou réalité?', *Semaine des Hôpitaux*, Vol. 50, 1974: 2945–50.

Cockburn, A., E. Cockburn, and T.A. Reyman (eds), *Mummies, Disease and Ancient Cultures*. Cambridge: Cambridge University Press, 1998.

Cohen, I.B., *The Triumph of Numbers: How Counting Shaped Modern Life*. New York: WW Norton & Company, 2005.

Colley, S. *Uncovering Australia: Archaeology, Indigenous People and the Public*. Sydney: Allen & Unwin, 2002.

Collins, D.H., *Pathology of Bone*. London: Butterworths, 1966.

Colliton, J., 'Back pain and pregnancy: Active management strategies', in *The Physician and Sportsmedicine* (1996 July).

Comas, J., *Manual of Physical Anthropology*. Springfield, Illinois: Charles C. Thomas, 1960.

Conticello, B. *Villa dei Misteri*. Milan: FMR/Museum, 1987.

——'Rediscovering Pompeii', in *Rediscovering Pompeii: IBM Gallery of Science and Art* ed. Conticello, B. (Rome: 'L'Erma' di Bretschneider, 1990), 2–25.

Cook, D.C., 'The old physical anthropology and the New World: A look at the accomplishments of an antiquated paradigm', in *Bioarchaeology: The Contextual Analysis of Human Remains*, ed. Buikstra, J.E. and L.A. Beck. Amsterdam: Academic Press, 2006, 27–72.

Cook, D.C. and M.L. Powell, 'The evolution of American paleopathology', in *Bioarchaeology: The Contextual Analysis of Human Remains*, ed. Buikstra, J.E. and L.A. Beck. Amsterdam: Academic Press, 2006, 281–322.

Cooley, A.E., *Pompeii*. London: Duckworth, 2003.

Cooley, A.E. and M.G.L. Cooley, *Pompeii: A Sourcebook*. London: Routledge, 2004.

Coon, C.S., *The Races of Europe*. New York: Macmillan, 1939.

——*The Origin of Races*. London: Jonathan Cape, 1963.

Coon, C.S. and E.E. Hunt (eds), *The Living Races of Man*. London: Jonathan Cape, 1965.

Coppa, A., A. Cucina, D. Mancinelli, R. Vargiu, and J.M. Calcagno, 'Dental anthropology of Central-Southern, Iron Age Italy: The evidence of metric versus nonmetric traits', *American Journal of Physical Anthropology*, Vol. 107, No. 4, 1998: 371–86.

Cordovani, R., *La Cripta dei Cappuccini. Chiesa dell'Immacolata Concezione Via Vittorio Veneto-Roma*. Rome: Provincia Romana dei Frati Minori Cappuccini, 2005.

Corruccini, R.S., 'An examination of the meaning of cranial discrete traits for human skeletal biological studies', *American Journal of Physical Anthropology*, Vol. 40, 1974: 425–45.

Corti, E.C.C., *The Destruction and Resurrection of Pompeii and Herculaneum*. Translated by Smith, K. and R.G. Smith. London: Routledge & Kegan Paul, 1951.

Costantini, R.M. and L. Capasso, 'Sulla Presenza di DNA endogeno nei resti scheletri dei fuggiaschi di Ercolano', in *I Fuggiaschi di Ercolano: Paleobiologia delle Vittime dell'Eruzione Vesuviana del 79 d.C., Appendix 3*, ed. Capasso, L. Rome: 'L'Erma' di Bretschneider, 2001, 1069–74.

Council for British Archaeology, *Handbook of Scientific Aids and Evidence for Archaeologists*. London: Council for British Archaeology, 1970.

Court, S., 'Teaching archaeology of human remains to students: The perspective of the Nicholson Museum Education Program', *Teaching History (History Teachers' Association of NSW)*, Vol. 40, No. 1, 2006: 34–35.

Cox, M. and A. Scott, 'Evaluation of the obstetric significance of some pelvic characters in an 18th century British sample of known parity status', *American Journal of Physical Anthropology*, Vol. 89, 1992: 431–40.

Cremin, B., H. Goodman, J. Spranger and P. Beighton, 'Wormian bones in osteogenesis imperfecta and other disorders', *Skeletal Radiology*, Vol. 8, 1982: 35–38.

Cucina, A., R. Vargiu, D. Mancinelli, R. Ricci, E. Santandrea, P. Catalano, and A. Coppa, 'The Necropolis of Vallerano (Rome, 2nd–3rd Century AD): An anthropological perspective on the Ancient Romans in the Suburbium', *International Journal of Osteoarchaeology*, Vol. 16, No. 2, 2006: 104–16.

Cutler, B.L., S.D. Penrod and T.K. Martens, 'The reliability of eyewitness identification', *Law and Human Behavior*, Vol. 11, No. 3, 1987: 233–58.

Daintith, J. and J.O.E. Clark, *The Facts on File Dictionary of Mathematics*. 3rd edn. New York: Checkmark, 1999.

Damasio, A.R. and H. Damasio. 'Brain and language', *Scientific American*, Vol. 267, No. 3, 1992: 62–71.

D'Ambrosio, A., 'The lady from Oplontis', in *Rediscovering Pompeii: IBM Gallery of Science and Art* ed. Conticello, B. (Rome: 'L'Erma' di Bretschneider, 1990), 133.

D'Amore, C., M. Carfagna and G. Matarese, 'Definizione antropologica della popolazione adulta di un commune della provincia di Napoli', in *Rendiconto dell'Accademia delle Scienze, Fisiche e Matematiche della Società Nazionale di Scienze, Lettere ed Arti in Napoli, Serie IV, XXXI* Naples: 1964.

D'Amore, C. and T. De Leo. 'Antropologia Pompeiana del 79 d.C., Paleodietica. Nota I: generalità', *Archivio per l'Antropologia e la Etnologia*, Vol. 116, 1986: 81–106.

D'Amore, C., F. Mallegni and M. Schiano di Zenise, 'Antropologia pompeiana del 79 d.C.: Sesso ed età di morte', *Archivio per l'Antropologia e la Etnologia*, Vol. 109, 1979: 297–308.

357

——'Primi risultati degli studi sull'antropologia Pompeiana del 79 d.C.', in *La Regione Sotterrata dal Vesuvio: Studi e Prospettive, Atti del Convegno Internazionale 11–15 Novembre 1979*. Napoli: Università degli Studi, 1982, 927–43.

Daniel, G.E., *The Origins and Growth of Archaeology*. Middlesex: Penguin, 1967.

——*A Hundred and Fifty Years of Archaeology*. 2nd edn. London: Duckworth, 1975.

——*A Short History of Archaeology*. London: Thames & Hudson, 1981.

D'Arms, J.H., *Romans on the Bay of Naples: A Social and Cultural Study of the Villas and their Owners from 150 BC to AD 400*. Cambridge Massachusetts: Harvard University Press, 1970.

David, A.R. and R. Archbold, *Conversations with Mummies: New Light on the Lives of the Ancient Egyptians*. Sydney: Allen & Unwin, 2000.

David, M., 'Fiorelli and documentation methods in archaeology, photography', in *Houses and Monuments of Pompeii: The Works of Fausto and Felice Niccolini*, ed. Cassanelli, R., P.L. Ciapparelli, E. Colle and M. David. Los Angeles: The J. Paul Getty Museum, 2002, 52–57.

De Caro, S. and A. Casale, *Boscoreale e le Sue Testimonianze Archeologiche: Villa Rustica in Località Villa Regina*. Naples: Commune di Boscoreale, Assessorato ai Beni Culturali e Ambientali, 1988.

De Carolis, E. and G. Patricelli, 'Le vittime dell'eruzione', in *Storie da un'Eruzione: Pompei, Ercolano, Oplontis: Guida alla Mostra*, ed. d'Ambrosio, A., P.G. Guzzo and M. Mastroroberto. Milan: Electa, 2003a, 56–72.

——*Vesuvius, AD 79: The Destruction of Pompeii and Herculaneum*. Translated by The J. Paul Getty Trust. Rome: 'L'Erma' di Bretschneider, 2003b.

De Carolis, E., G. Patricelli and A. Ciarallo, 'Rinvenimenti di corpi umani nell'area urbana di Pompei', *Rivista di Studi Pompeiani*, Vol. 9, 1998: 75–123.

De Franciscis, A., *The Pompeian Wall Paintings in the Roman Villa of Oplontis*. Recklinghausen, Germany: Aurel Bongers, 1975.

De Kind, R.E.L.B., 'Two Tondo heads in the Casa dell'Atrio a Mosaico (IV,1–2) at Herculaneum: Some remarks on portraits in Campanian wall paintings', *Kölner Jahrbuch für Vor–und Frühgeschichte*, Vol. 24, 1991: 165–69.

De Simone, A., 'Archaeology and science', in *Rediscovering Pompeii: IBM Gallery of Science and Art*, ed. Conticello, B. Rome: 'L'Erma' di Bretschneider, 1990, 62–77.

——'I siti archeologici Vesuviani sepolti dalla eruzione del Somma–Vesuvio', in *Vesuvio 79 AD: Vita e Morte ad Ercolano: Mostra Fotografica e di Reperti Archeologici*, ed. Petrone, P.P. and F. Fedele. Naples: Fredericiana Editrice Universitaria, 2002, 93–104.

De Stefano, G.F., G. Hauser, A. Guidotti, E. Gualdo Russo and P. Brasili Gualandi, 'Reflections on interobserver differences in scoring non-metric cranial traits (with practical examples)', *Journal of Human Evolution*, Vol. 13, 1984: 349–55.

De Vos, A., 'Casa dei quadretti teatrali', in *Pompei: Pitture e Mosaici*. Rome: Istituto dell'Enciclopedia, 1990, 361–96.

De Vos, A. and M. De Vos, *Pompei, Ercolano, Stabia*. Rome: Laterza, 1982.

De Waele, J.A.K., 'The "doric" temple in the Forum Triangulare', in *Pompeii, Opuscula Pompeiana*, *III* (1993), 105–18.

Deevey, E.S., 'The human population', *Scientific American*, Vol. 203, 1960: 194–204.

Deiss, J.J., *Herculaneum: Italy's Buried Treasure*. 2nd edn. New York: Harper & Row, 1985.

Della Corte, M., *Casa ed Abitanti di Pompei*. 3rd edn. Naples: Fausto Fiorentino, 1965.

Delle Chiaie, S., 'Cenno notomico-patologico sulle ossa umane scavate in Pompei: Letto dal Socio ordinario Stefano Delle Chiaie nella tornata de' 15 settembre 1853', *Filiatre-Sebezio*, Vol. 48, 1854: 3–30.

Descœudres, J.-P., 'A Pompeian house revisited', *Australian Natural History*, Vol. 20, No. 4, 1980: 117–22.

——'Rome and Roman art', in *The Enduring Past: Archaeology of the Ancient World for Australians*, ed. Cremin, A. Sydney: NSW University Press, 1987, 164–209.

——'Did some Pompeians return to their city after the eruption of Mt. Vesuvius in AD 79? Observations in the house of the coloured capitals', in *Ercolano 1738–1988: 250 Anni di Ricerca Archeologica*, ed. Dell'Orto, L.F. Rome: "L'Erma" di Bretschneider, 1993, 165–78.

——'A brief history of Pompeii', in *Pompeii Revisited: The Life and Death of a Roman Town*, ed. Harrison, D. Sydney: Meditarch, 1994a, 1–39.

——'Discovery and excavation', in *Pompeii Revisited: The Life and Death of a Roman Town*, ed. Harrison, D. Sydney: Meditarch, 1994b, 41–53.

——*Pompeii Revisited: The Life and Death of a Roman Town*. Sydney: Meditarch, 1994c.

Devriendt, W., M.D. Piercecchi-Marti, P. Adalian, A. Sanvoisin, O. Dutour and G. Leonetti. 'Hyperostosis frontalis interna: Forensic issues', *Journal of Forensic Science*, Vol. 50, No. 1, 2005: 143–46.

Devriendt, W., M.D. Piercecchi-Marti, Y. Ardagna, E. Mahieu, I. Hershkovitz, M. Signoli and O. Dutour, 'Two Neolithic cases of hyperostosis frontalis interna', *International Journal of Osteoarchaeology*, Vol. 14, 2004: 414–18.

Di Bernardo, G., S. Del Gaudio, M. Cammarota, U. Galderisi, A. Cascino and M. Cipollaro, 'Enzymatic repair of selected cross-linked homoduplex molecules enhances nuclear gene rescue from Pompeii and Herculaneum remains', in *Nucleic Acids Research*, Vol. 30(4), 2002: e16.

Di Bernardo, G., G. Galano, U. Galderisi, A. Cascino, F.M. Guarino, F. Angelini and M. Cipollaro, 'Analisi dei reperti ossei della casa grado di conservazione ed amplificazione del DNA antico', in *La Casa di Giulio Polibio: Studi Interdisciplinari*, ed. Ciarallo, A. and E. De Carolis. Pompei: Centro Studi arti Figurative, Università di Tokio, 2001, 111–18.

Diamond, J., 'Race without colour', *Discover*, Vol. 15, No. 11, 1994: 82–89.

Dilke, O.A.W. and M.S. Dilke, 'Vesuvius, August 79: First recorded eruption', *Geographical Magazine*, Vol. 51, No. 51, 1979: 743–49.

Dittirick, J. and J.M. Suchey, 'Sex determination of prehistoric central California skeletal remains using discriminant analysis of the femur and humerus', *American Journal of Physical Anthropology*, Vol. 70, 1986: 3–9.

Dobbins, J.J., 'Problems of chronology, decoration and urban design in the forum at Pompeii', *American Journal of Archaeology*, Vol. 98, 1994: 629–94.

——'The Pompeii Forum Project 1994–95', in *Sequence and Space in Pompeii*, ed. Bon, S.E. and R. Jones. Oxford: Oxbow Monograph 77, 1997, 73–87.

——'The forum and its dependencies', in *The World of Pompeii*, ed. Dobbins, J.J. and P.W. Foss. London: Routledge, 2007, 150–83.

Dobzhansky, T., 'On species and races of living and fossil man', *American Journal of Physical Anthropology*, Vol. 2, 1944: 251–65.

Donlon, D., 'The Value of Postcranial Nonmetric Variation in Studies of Global Populations in Modern Homo Sapiens', unpublished PhD thesis. Armidale: University of New England, 1990.

D'Orta, P. and E. D'Orta., *Come Visitare Pompei*. Pompeii: Falanga, 1982.

Dow, S., 'A century of humane archaeology', *Archaeology*, Vol. 33, 1980: 42–51.

Drackett, P., *The Book of Great Disasters*. Berkshire: Purnell, 1977.

Dunnell, R.C., 'Americanist archaeology: The 1979 contribution', *American Journal of Archaeology*, Vol. 84, 1980: 463–78.

Dwyer, E., 'From fragments to icons: Stages in the making and exhibiting of the casts of Pompeian victims, 1863–88', in *Interpreting Ceramics: Conference papers and presentations from the Fragmented Figure conference (Cardiff School of Art and Design on the 29th and 30th June 2005)* (2005).

Dyer, T.H., *Pompeii: Its History, Buildings and Antiquities*. 2nd edn. London: George Bell & Sons, 1883.

Dyson, S.L., *Community and Society in Roman Italy*. Baltimore: Johns Hopkins University Press, 1992.

Eco, U., 'A portrait of the Elder as a Young Pliny: How to build fame', in *On Signs*, ed. Blonsky, M. (Oxford: Blackwell, 1985), 289–302.

Edwards, C., 'The roads to Rome', in *Imagining Rome: British Artists and Rome in the Nineteenth Century*, ed. Liversidge, M.J.H. and C. Edwards. London: Merrell Holberton, 1996, 8–19.

Eggen, S., B. Natvig and J. Gasemyr, 'Variation in torus palatinus prevalence in Norway', *European Journal of Oral Sciences*, Vol. 102, No. 1, 1994: 54–59.

Ehrhardt, W., *Stilgeschichte Untersuchungen an Römischen Wandmalereien von der Späten Republik bis zur zeit Neros*. Mainz am Rhein: Philip von Zabern, 1987.

Eisele, J.W., R.L. O'Halloran, D.T. Reay, G.R. Lindholm, L.V. Lewman and W.J. Brady, 'Deaths during the May 18, 1980, eruption of Mt St Helens', *The New England Journal of Medicine*, Vol. 305, No. 16, 1981: 931–36.

Eldridge, W.W. and G. Holm, 'Incidence of hyperostosis frontalis interna in female patients admitted to a mental hospital', *American Journal of Roentgenology, Radium Therapy & Nuclear Medicine*, Vol. 43, 1940: 356–59.

El-Najjar, M.Y. and G.L. Dawson, 'The effect of artificial cranial deformation on the incidence of wormian bones in the lambdoidal suture', *American Journal of Physical Anthropology*, Vol. 46, 1977: 155–60.

El-Najjar, M.Y. and K.R. McWilliams, *Forensic Anthropology: The Structure, Morphology and Variation of Human Bone and Dentition*. Springfield, Illinois: Charles C. Thomas, 1978.

Engelmann, W. *New Guide to Pompeii*. Leipzig: Wilhelm Engelmann, 1925.

Eschebach, H., L. Eschebach, and J. Adamiak, *Pompeji: Erlebte Antike Welt*. Leipzig: Seeman, VEB, 1978.

Etani, H., S.S. Yuichi, Y. Shigematsu and V. Iorio, 'La campagna di scavo del Japan Institute of Palaeological Studies di Kyoto del 2002', *Opuscula Pompeiana*, Vol. 12, 2004: 125–37.

Etienne, R., 'L'Eruzione del 79', in *Pompei 79: Raccolta di Studi per il Decimonono Centenario dell'Eruzione Vesuviana*, ed. Zevi, F. Naples: Gaetano Macchiarolo Editore, 1979, 289–92.

——*Pompeii: The Day a City Died*. Translated by Palmer, C. London: Thames & Hudson, 1992.

Feder, T. *Great Treasures of Pompeii and Herculaneum*. New York: Abbeville Press, 1978.

Feinberg, A. *Human Anatomy 1: Muscular and Skeletal System*. New York: Data Guide, 1958.

Ferembach, D., I. Schwidetzky and M. Stloukal. 'Recommendations for age and sex diagnoses of skeletons (Workshop of European Anthropologists)', *Journal of Human Evolution*, Vol. 9, No. 7, 1980: 517–49.

Fergola, L., 'Oplontis', in *Storie da un'Eruzione: Pompei, Ercolano, Oplontis*, ed. d'Ambrosio, A., P.G. Guzzo and M. Mastroroberto. Milan: Electa, 2003, 152–64.

Ferguson, J., 'The laboratory of racism', *New Scientist*, Vol. 103 1984: 18–20.

Fernandez-Nogueras, F.J. and V.J. Fernandez-Nogueras, 'The Stewart–Morel Syndrome in the differential diagnosis of patients with frontal headache', *Anales Ortorrinolaringologicos Ibero-Americanos*, Vol. 20, No. 4, 1993: 383–91.

Fforde, C., *Collecting the Dead: Archaeology and the Reburial Issue*. London: Duckworth, 2004.

Filer, J., *Disease*, Egyptian Bookshelf. London: British Museum, 1995.

Finnegan, M., 'Non-metric variation of the infracranial skeleton', *Journal of Anatomy*, Vol. 125, 1978: 23–37.

Finnegan, M. and K. Cooprider, 'Empirical comparison of distance equations using discrete traits', *American Journal of Physical Anthropology*, Vol. 49, 1978: 39–46.

Fiorelli, G., *Gli Scavi di Pompei dal 1861 al 1872*. Naples: Tipografica nel Liceo V. Emmanuele, 1873.

FitzGerald, C., S.R. Saunders, L. Bondioli, and R. Macchiarelli, 'Health of infants in an Imperial Roman skeletal sample: Perspective from dental microstructure', *American Journal of Physical Anthropology*, Vol. 130, 2006: 179–89.

Flury, B. and H. Riedwyl, *Multivariate Statistics: A Practical Approach*. London: Chapman & Hall, 1988.

Formicola, V., 'Stature reconstruction from long bones in ancient population samples: An approach to the problem of its reliability', *American Journal of Physical Anthropology*, Vol. 90, No. 3, 1993: 351–58.

Fornaciari, G. and F. Mellegni, 'Palaeonutritional studies on skeletal remains of ancient populations from the Mediterranean area: An attempt to [sic] interpretation', *Anthropologischer Anzeiger*, Vol. 45, No. 4, 1987: 361–70.

France, D.L., 'Osteometry at muscle origin and insertion in sex determination', *American Journal of Physical Anthropology*, Vol. 76, 1988: 515–26.

Francis, K.J., 'The Pompeian Bust Medallion', unpublished MA thesis, Department of Archaeology. Sydney: University of Sydney, 1983.

Francis, P., 'Vesuvius inquest: August 1979', *Geographical Magazine*, Vol. 51, 1979: 750–55.

——*Volcanoes: A Planetary Perspective*. Oxford: Clarendon Press, 1993.

Frederikson, M. and N. Purcell, *Campania*. Rome: The British School at Rome, 1984.

Freeman, B., 'Glossary of Histological and Microanatomical Terms Including Historical Origins and Eponyms'. Sydney: School of Anatomy, University of New South Wales, 2000.

Fürst, C.M., 'Zur anthropologie der prähistorischen Griechen in Argolis', *Lunds Arsskrift*, Vol. 26, No. 8, 1930: 130.

——'Zur Kenntniss der anthropologie prähistorischen bevölkerung der Insel Cypern', *Lunds Arsskrift*, Vol. 29, No. 6, 1933: 1–106.

Gannes, L.Z., D.M. O'Brien and C. Martinez del Rio, 'Stable isotopes in animal ecology: Assumptions, caveats, and a call for more laboratory experiments', *Ecology*, Vol. 78, No. 4, 1997: 1271–76.

García y García, L., *Danni di Guerra a Pompei: Una Dolorosa Vicenda quasi Dimenticata*. Vol. 15, Studi della Soprintendenza Archeologica di Pompei. Rome: 'L'Erma' di Bretschneider, 2006.

Garn, S.M. (ed.), *Readings on Race*. Springfield, Illinois: Charles C. Thomas, 1960.

——*Human Races*. 3rd edn. Springfield, Illinois: Charles C. Thomas, 1971.

Gautier, T., *The Mummy's Foot*. Translated by De Sumichrast, F.C. 1901 edn. New York: C.T. Brainard.

——*Romance of a Mummy*. New York: C.T. Brainard, 1898.

——*Arria Marcella: A Souvenir of Pompeii*. Translated by De Sumichrast, F.C. New York: C.T. Brainard, 1901.

Gell, W., *Pompeiana: The Topography, Edifices and Ornaments of Pompeii: The Results of Excavations since 1819*. London: Jennings & Chaplin, 1832.

Gell, W. and J.P. Gandy, *Pompeiana: The Topography, Edifices and Ornaments of Pompeii*. 2nd edn. London: Rodwell & Martin, 1821.

Gendron, R., D. Grenier and L.F. Maheu-Robert, 'The oral cavity as a reservoir of bacterial pathogens for focal infections', *Microbes and Infection*, Vol. 2, No. 8, 2000: 897–906.

Genovés, S., 'Sex determination in earlier man', in *Science in Archaeology: A Survey of Progress and Research*, ed. Brothwell, D. and E. Higgs. London: Thames & Hudson, 1969a, 429–39.

——'Estimation of age and mortality', in *Science in Archaeology: A Survey of Progress and Research*, ed. Brothwell, D. and E. Higgs. London: Thames & Hudson, 1969b, 440–52.

Geraci, G., R. del Gaudio and R. di Giaimo, 'Le analisi paleogenetiche', in *Vesuvio 79 AD: Vita e Morte ad Ercolano*, ed. Petrone, P.P. and F. Fedele. Naples: Fredericiana Editrice Universitaria, 2002), 85–88.

Gershon-Cohen, J., H. Schraer and N. Blumberg. 'Hyperostosis frontalis interna among the aged', *American Journal of Roentgenology, Radium Therapy & Nuclear Medicine*, Vol. 73 1955: 396–97.

Giacomelli, L., A. Perrotta, R. Scandone and C. Scarpati, 'The eruption of Vesuvius of AD 79 and its impact on human environment in Pompeii', *Episodes*, Vol. 26, No. 3, 2003: 234–38.

Giannecchini, M. and J. Moggi-Cecchi. 'Stature in archeological samples from Central Italy: Methodological issues and diachronic changes', *American Journal of Physical Anthropology*, Vol. 135, No. 3, 2008: 284–92.

Giannelli, G. (ed.), *The World of Ancient Rome*. London: Macdonald, 1963.

Gilbert, B.M. and T.W. McKern, 'A method for aging the female *os pubis*', *American Journal of Physical Anthropology*, Vol. 38, 1973: 31–38.

Gilfillan, S.C., 'Lead poisoning and the fall of Rome', *Journal of Occupational Medicine*, Vol. 7, 1965: 53–60.

Ginge, B., M.J. Becker and P. Guldager, 'Of Roman extraction', *Archaeology*, Vol. 42, No. 4, 1989: 34–37.

Giordano, C. and I. Kahn, *The Jews in Pompeii, Herculaneum, Stabiae and in the Cities of Campania Felix*. Napoli: Procaccini, 1979.

Giuntoli, S., *Art and History of Pompeii*. Translated by Pauli, E. Edited by Martinelli, M., Bonechi Art & History Collection. Florence: Casa Editrice Bonechi, 1995.

Glab, H., K. Szostek and K. Kaczanowski, 'Hyperostosis frontalis interna, a genetic disease?: Two medieval cases from Southern Poland', *Homo: Journal of Comparative Human Biology*, Vol. 57, No. 1, 2006: 19–27.

Gladykowska-Rzecyscka, J., 'Is this a case of the Morgagni syndrome?', *Journal of Palaeopathology*, Vol. 1, 1988: 109–12.

Goethe, J.W., *Italian Journey (1786–1788)*. Translated by Auden, W.H. and E. Mayer. Middlesex: Penguin, 1970.

Goldstein, M.S., 'The palaeopathology of human skeletal remains', in *Science in Archaeology: A Survey of Progress and Research*, eds. Brothwell, D. and E. Higgs. London: Thames & Hudson, 1969, 480–89.

Goodman, A.H. and G.J. Armelagos, 'Factors affecting the distribution of enamel hypoplasias within the human permanent dentition', *American Journal of Physical Anthropology*, Vol. 68, 1985: 479–93.

Gore, R., 'After 2000 years of silence: The dead do tell tales at Vesuvius', *National Geographic*, Vol. 165, No. 5, 1984: 556–613.

Gould, S.J., 'Morton's ranking of races by cranial capacity: Unconscious manipulation of data may be a scientific norm', *Science*, Vol. 200, No. 4341, 1978: 503–9.

——*The Mismeasure of Man*. Middlesex: Pelican, 1984.

——'The geometer of race', *Discover*, Vol. 15, No. 11, 1994: 65–69.

Grant, M., *Cities of Vesuvius: Pompeii and Herculaneum*. Middlesex: Penguin, 1976.

——*Anatomy, Descriptive and Surgical*. 15th edn. New York: Bounty Books, 1977.

Grant, M. and A. Mulas, *Eros in Pompeii: The Erotic Art Collections of the Museum of Naples*. New edn. New York: Stewart, Tabori & Chang, 1997.

Gravlee, C.C., H.R. Bernard and W.R. Leonard, 'Boas's changes in bodily form: The immigrant study, cranial plasticity, and Boas's physical anthropology', *American Anthropologist*, Vol. 105, No. 2, 2003: 326–32.

Gray, H., *Anatomy, Descriptive and Surgical*. Revised American from the 15th English edn. New York: Bounty Books, 1977.

Grayson, D.K. and P.D. Sheets, 'Volcanic disasters and the archaeological record', in *Volcanic Activity and Human Ecology*, ed. Sheets, P.D. and D.K. Grayson. New York: Academic Press, 1979, 623–32.

Greenberg, M.S., D.R. Westcott and S.E. Bailey, 'When believing is seeing: The effect of scripts on eyewitness memory', *Law and Human Behavior*, Vol. 22, No. 6, 1998: 685–94.

Grmek, M.D., *Diseases in the Ancient Greek World*. Translated by Muellner, M. and L. Muellner. Baltimore: Johns Hopkins University Press, 1989.

Gros, C., J.P. Walter, J. Girardie and A. Schmeltzer, 'Écoulements mamelonnaires lactoides et endostose cranienne', *Journal de Radiologie, d'Électrologie, et de Médecine Nucléaire*, Vol. 46, No. 12, 1965: 827–34.

Grosskopf, B., 'Individualaltersbestimmung mit hilfe von zuwachsringen im zement bodengelagerter menschlicher zähne', *Zeitschrift für Rechtsmedizin*, Vol. 103, No. 5, 1990: 351–59.

Grosvenor, G.M., 'An exciting year of discovery', *National Geographic*, Vol. 162, No. 6, 1982: 820–21.

Grupe, G., 'Impact of the choice of bone samples on trace element data in excavated human skeletons', *Journal of Archaeological Science*, Vol. 15, 1988: 123–29.

Gualdi-Russo, E., M.A. Tasca, and P. Brasili, 'Scoring of nonmetric cranial traits: A methodological approach', *Journal of Anatomy*, Vol. 195, No. 4, 1999: 543–50.

Guarino, F.M., F. Angelini, C. Vollono and C. Orefice, 'Bone preservation in human remains from the Terme del Sarno at Pompeii using light microscopy and scanning electron microscopy', *Journal of Archaeological Science*, Vol. 33, 2006: 513–20.

Gurioli, L., M.T. Pareschi, E. Zanella, R. Lanza, E. Deluca and M. Bisso, 'Interaction of pyroclastic density currents with human settlements: Evidence from ancient Pompeii', *Geology*, Vol. 33, No. 6, 2005: 441–44.

Gusman, P., *Pompei: The City, its Life and Art*. Translated by Simmonds, F. and M. Jourdain. London: Heinemann, 1900.

Gustafson, G., *Forensic Odontology*. London: Staples Press, 1966.

Guzzo, P.G., A. D'Ambrosio and M. Mastroroberto (eds), *Storie da un'Eruzione: Pompei, Ercolano, Oplontis: Guida alla Mostra*. Milan: Electa, 2003.

Haddon, A.C., *The Races of Man and Their Distribution*. Halifax, Nova Scotia: Milner, 1912.

Haglund, W., 'Forensic "art" in human identification', in *Craniofacial Identification in Forensic Medicine*, ed. Clement, J.G. and D.L. Ranson. London: Arnold, 1998, 235–43.

Halffman, C.M. and J.D. Irish, 'Palatine torus in the pre-conquest inhabitants of the Canary Islands', *Homo: Journal of Comparative Human Biology*, Vol. 55, No. 1–2, 2004: 101–11.

Halffman, C.M., G.R. Scott and P.O. Pedersen, 'Palatine torus in the Greenlandic Norse', *American Journal of Physical Anthropology*, Vol. 88, No. 2, 1992: 145–61.

Hamilton, W., *Observations on Mt Vesuvius, Mt Etna and Other Volcanoes in a Series of Letters Addressed To the Royal Society ... To Which Are Added Notes by the Author, Hitherto Unpublished*. London: Royal Society, 1774.

Hammond, N., 'Ancient cities', *Scientific American*, Vol. 5, No. 1: Special Issue, 1994: 4–9.

Hanihara, T. and H. Ishida, 'Os incae: Variation in frequency in major human population groups', *Journal of Anatomy*, Vol. 198, No. 2, 2001a: 137–52.

——'Frequency variations of discrete cranial traits in major human populations. I. Supernumerary ossicle variations', *Journal of Anatomy*, Vol. 198, No. 6, 2001b: 689–706.

Hanihara, T., H. Ishida and Y. Dodo, 'Characterization of biological diversity through analysis of discrete cranial traits', *American Journal of Physical Anthropology*, Vol. 121, No. 3, 2003: 241–51.

Hansell, A. and C. Oppenheimer, 'Health hazards from volcanic gases: A systematic literature review', *Archives of Environmental Health*, Vol. 59, No. 12, 2004: 628–39.

Hansell, A.L., C.J. Horwell and C. Oppenheimer, 'The health hazards of volcanoes and geothermal areas', *Occupational & Environmental Medicine*, Vol. 63, No. 2, 2006: 149–56.

Harman, M., T.I. Molleson and J.L. Price, 'Burials, bodies and beheadings in Romano-British and Anglo-Saxon cemeteries', *Bulletin of the British Museum of Natural History (Geology)*, Vol. 35, No. 3, 1981: 145–88.

Harrison, G.A., J.S. Weiner, J.M. Tanner and N.A. Barnicot, *Human Biology: An Introduction to Human Evolution and Growth*. Oxford: Clarendon Press, 1964.

Hauser, G. and G.F. de Stefano, *Epigenetic Variants of the Human Skull*. Stuttgart: Schweizerbart, 1989.

Hauser, G., A. Vienna and G.F. de Stefano, 'Epigenetic cranial traits in Etruscan skulls', *Anthropologie*, Vol. 30, No. 1, 1992: 75–80.

Hay, J. *Ancient China*. London: Bodley Head, 1973.

Henneberg, M. and R. Henneberg, 'Skeletal material from the house of C. Iulius Polybius in Pompei, 79 AD', in *La Casa di Giulio Polibio: Studi Interdisciplinari*, ed. Ciarallo, A. and E. De Carolis. Pompei: Centro Studi arti Figurative, Università di Tokio, 2001, 79–92.

Henneberg, M. and R.J. Henneberg, 'Reconstructing medical knowledge in ancient Pompeii from the hard evidence of bones and teeth (Presented at a conference at Deutsches Museum, Munich 21–22 March 2000)', in *Homo Faber: Studies in Nature, Technology and Science at the Time of Pompeii*, ed. Renn, J. and G. Castagnetti. Rome: L'Erma di Bretschneider, 2002, 169–87.

Henneberg, M., R.J. Henneberg and A. Ciarallo, 'Skeletal material from the house of C. Iulius Polybius in Pompeii, 79 AD', *Human Evolution*, Vol. 11, No. 3, 1996: 249–59.

Henschen, F., *Morgagni's Syndrome: Hyperostosis Frontalis Interna, Virilismus, Obesitas*. Edinburgh: Oliver & Boyd, 1949.

Herbet, D. and F. Bardossi, *Kilauea: Case History of a Volcano*. New York: Harper & Row, 1968.

Herrmann, N.P. and L.W. Konigsberg, 'A re-examination of the age-at-death distribution of Indian Knoll', in *Paleodemography: Age Distributions from Skeletal Samples*, ed. Hoppa, R.D. and J.W. Vaupel, *Cambridge Studies in Biological and Evolutionary Anthropology*. Cambridge: Cambridge University Press, 2002, 243–57.

Hershkovitz, I., C. Greenwald, B.M. Rothschild, B. Latimer, O. Dutour, L.M. Jellema and S. Wish-Baratz, 'Hyperostosis frontalis interna: An anthropological perspective', *American Journal of Physical Anthropology*, Vol. 109, 1999: 303–25.

Hicks, M., 'Exhibiting human remains: A provocative seminar', in *Collected Papers from Exhibiting Human Remains, a Seminar on 12 May 2000*. The Powerhouse Museum, Sydney: Health & Medicine Museums, 2001.

——'Displaying the dead', *History Teachers' Association of New South Wales*, Vol. 40, No. 1, 2006: 30–32.

Higgins, V., 'A preliminary analysis of some of the early medieval human skeletons from San Vincenzo al Volturno', in *San Vincenzo al Volturno: The Archaeology, Art and Territory of an Early Medieval Monastery*, ed. Hodges, R. and J. Mitchell, *B.A.R. International Series 252*. Oxford: British School at Rome (BAR), 1985, 111–22.

——'A model for assessing health patterns from skeletal remains', in *Burial Archaeology: Current Research, Methods and Developments*, ed. Roberts, C.A., F. Lee and J. Bintliff, *211* Oxford: BAR, 1989, 175–204.

—— 'Rural agricultural communities of the late Roman and early Medieval periods including a study of two skeletal groups from San Vincenzo al Volturno', unpublished PhD thesis Sheffield: University of Sheffield, 1990.

Hillson, S., *Teeth*, Cambridge Manuals in Archaeology. Cambridge: Cambridge University Press, 1986.

——*Dental Anthropology*. Cambridge: Cambridge University Press, 1996.

Hoffman, A., *A History of Dentistry*. Translated by Koehler, H.M. Chicago, Illinois: Quintessence Publishing Co, 1981.

Holcomb, S.M.C. and L.W. Konigsberg. 'Statistical study of sexual dimorphism in the human foetal sciatic notch', *American Journal of Physical Anthropology*, Vol. 97, 1995: 113–25.

Holman, D.J., J.W. Wood and K.A. O'Connor, 'Estimating age-at-death distributions from skeletal samples: Multivariate latent-trait approach', in *Paleodemography: Age Distributions from Skeletal Samples*, ed. Hoppa, R.D. and J.W. Vaupel, *Cambridge Studies in Biological and Evolutionary Anthropology*. Cambridge: Cambridge University Press, 2002, 193–221.

Holt, C.A., 'A re-examination of parturition scars on the human female pelvis', *American Journal of Physical Anthropology*, Vol. 49, 1978: 91–94.

Hoppa, R.D., 'Paleodemography: Looking back and thinking ahead', in *Paleodemography: Age Distributions from Skeletal Samples*, ed. Hoppa, R.D. and J.W. Vaupel, *Cambridge Studies in Biological and Evolutionary Anthropology*. Cambridge: Cambridge University Press, 2002, 9–28.

Hoppa, R.D. and J.W. Vaupel (eds), *Paleodemography: Age Distributions from Skeletal Samples* Cambridge: Cambridge University Press, 2002.

——'The Rostock Manifesto for paleodemography: The way from stage to age', in *Paleodemography: Age Distributions from Skeletal Samples*, ed. Hoppa, R.D. and J.W. Vaupel, *Cambridge Studies in Biological and Evolutionary Anthropology*. Cambridge: Cambridge University Press, 2002, 1–8.

Houghton, P., 'The relationship of the pre-auricular groove of the ilium to pregnancy', *American Journal of Physical Anthropology*, Vol. 41, 1974: 381–89.

Howells, W.W., 'The early Christian Irish: The skeletons at Gallen Priory', *Proceedings of the Royal Irish Academy*, Vol. 46 (Section C), 1941: 103–219.

——'Criteria for selection of osteometric dimensions', *American Journal of Physical Anthropology*, Vol. 30, 1969: 451–57.

——'The use of multivariate techniques in the study of skeletal populations', *American Journal of Physical Anthropology*, Vol. 31, 1969: 311–14.

——*Cranial Variation in Man: A Study by Multivariate Analysis of Patterns of Difference among Recent Populations*. Vol. 67, Papers of the Peabody Museum of Archaeology and Ethnology. Cambridge, Massachusetts: Harvard University, 1973.

——*Skull Shapes and the Map: Craniometric Analyses in the Dispersion of Modern Homo*. Vol. 79, Papers of the Peabody Museum of Archaeology and Ethnology. Cambridge, Massachusetts: Harvard University, 1989.

Hrycek, A., B. Bloch and I. Szoltysik, 'Morgagni–Stewart–Morel Syndrome in a young man', *Wiadomosci Lekarskie*, Vol. 42, No. 19–21, 1989: 1060–63.

Huybers, J.A., 'Within the enclosure at Pompeii: Some recent excavations', *The Nation*, Vol. 101, No. 2635, 1915: 788.

Ikram, S. and A. Dodson, *The Mummy in Ancient Egypt: Equipping the Dead for Eternity*. London: Thames & Hudson, 1998.

Iscan, M.Y. and S.R. Loth, 'Osteological manifestations of age in the adult', in *Reconstruction of Life from the Skeleton*, ed. Iscan, M.Y. and K.A.R. Kennedy. New York: Alan R. Liss, 1989, 23–40.

Jackes, M.K., 'Paleodemography: Problems and techniques', in *Skeletal Biology of Past Peoples: Research Methods*, ed. Saunders, S.R. and M.A. Katzenberg. New York: Wiley-Liss, 1992, 189–224.

Jackson, R., 'Roman doctors and their instruments: Recent research into ancient practice', *Journal of Roman Archaeology*, Vol. 3, 1990: 5–27.

Jackson, R. and S. La Niece, 'A set of Roman medical instruments from Italy', *Britannia*, Vol. 17, 1986: 119–67.

Jacobssen, H. and M. Haverling, 'Hyperostosis cranii: Radiography and scintigraphy compared', *Acta Radiologica*, Vol. 29, 1998: 223–26.

Jaffe, H.L. *Metabolic, Degenerative and Inflammatory Diseases of Bones and Joints*. Philadelphia: Lea & Febiger, 1972.

Janssens, P.A., *Palaeopathology: Diseases and Injuries of Prehistoric Man*. London: Baker, 1970.

Jashemski, W.F., *The Gardens of Pompeii, Herculaneum and the Villas Destroyed by Vesuvius*. New York: Caratzas Brothers, 1979a.

——'Pompeii and Mt Vesuvius AD 79', in *Volcanic Activity and Human Ecology*, ed. Sheets, P. D. and D.K. Grayson. New York: Academic Press, 1979b, 587–622.

——'The Vesuvian sites before AD 79: The archaeological, literary and epigraphical evidence', in *The Natural History of Pompeii*, ed. Jashemski, W.F. and F.G. Meyer. Cambridge: Cambridge University Press, 2002, 6–28.

Jongman, W., 'Gibbon was right: The decline and fall of the Roman economy', in *Crises and the Roman Empire. Proceedings of the Seventh Workshop of the International Network Impact of Empire (Nijmegen, June 20–24, 2006)*, ed. Hekster, O., G. de Kleijn and D. Slootjes. Leiden: Brill, 2007.

Jongman, W., P.W. De Neeve and H.W. Pleket (eds), *The Economy and Society of Pompeii*. Vol. 4, Dutch Monographs on Ancient History and Archaeology. Amsterdam: J.C. Gieber, 1988.

Judge, J., 'On the slope of Vesuvius a buried town gives up its dead', *National Geographic*, Vol. 162, No. 6, 1982: 686–93.

Junqueira, L.C.U., J. Carneiro and A.N. Contopoulos. *Basic Histology*. California: Lange Medical, 1975.

Kamminga, J. and R.V.S. Wright. 'The upper cave at Zhoukoudian and the origins of the Mongoloids', *Journal of Human Evolution*, Vol. 17, 1988: 739–67.

Kappers, C.U.A. and L.W. Parr, *An Introduction to the Anthropology of the Near East in Ancient and Recent Times*. Amsterdam: Noord-hollandsche uitgeversmaatschappij, 1934.

Kaszycka, K.A. and J. Strziko. '"Race" – Still an issue for physical anthropology? Results of Polish studies seen in the light of the US findings', *American Anthropologist*, Vol. 105, No. 1, 2003: 116–24.

Katz, D. and J.M. Suchey, 'Age determination of the male os pubis', *American Journal of Physical Anthropology*, Vol. 69, 1986: 427–35.

Katzenberg, M.A. and R. White, 'A paleodemographic analysis of *os coxae* from Ossossane Ossuary', *Canadian Review of Physical Anthropology*, Vol. 1, 1979: 10–28.

Kayshap, V.K. and N.R. Koteswara Rao, 'A modified Gustafson method of age estimation from teeth', *Forensic Science International*, Vol. 47, No. 3, 1990: 237–47.

Kelley, M.A., 'Phenice's visual sexing technique for the os pubis: A critique', *American Journal of Physical Anthropology*, Vol. 48, 1978: 121–22.

——'Parturition and pelvic changes', *American Journal of Physical Anthropology*, Vol. 51, 1979: 541–46.

Kellock, W.L. and P.A. Parsons, 'Variation of minor non-metrical cranial variants in Australian Aborigines', *American Journal of Physical Anthropology*, Vol. 32, 1970: 409–21.

Kemkes-Grottenthaler, A., 'Aging through the ages: Historical perspectives on age indicator methods', in *Paleodemography: Age Distributions from Skeletal Samples*, ed. Hoppa, R.D. and J. W. Vaupel, *Cambridge Studies in Biological and Evolutionary Anthropology*. Cambridge: Cambridge University Press, 2002, 48–72.

Kendall, M.G., *A Course in Multivariate Analysis*. London: Griffin, 1972.

Kennedy, G.E., 'The relationship between auditory exostoses and cold water: A latitudinal analysis', *American Journal of Physical Anthropology*, Vol. 71, 1986: 401–15.

Kennedy, K.A.R., 'Skeletal markers of occupational stress', in *Reconstruction of Life from the Skeleton*, ed. Iscan, M.Y. and K.A.R. Kennedy. New York: Alan R. Liss, 1989, 129–60.

Kerdpon, D. and S. Sirirungrojying, 'A clinical study of oral tori in southern Thailand, prevalence and the relation to parafunctional activity', *European Journal of Oral Sciences*, Vol. 107, No. 1, 1999: 9–13.

Kerley, E.R., 'The microscopic determination of age in human bone', *American Journal of Physical Anthropology*, Vol. 23, 1965: 149–64.

Kimball, J.W., *Kimball's Biology Pages: Hormones of the Reproductive System: Females* (2008 July 29: latest update), http://users.rcn.com/jkimball.ma.ultranet/BiologyPages/S/SexHormones. html (accessed 30 July 2008).

King, A., 'Mammals: Evidence from wall paintings, sculpture, mosaics, faunal remains and ancient literary sources', in *The Natural History of Pompeii*, ed. Jashemski, W.F. and F.G. Meyer. Cambridge: Cambridge University Press, 2002, 401–50.

Kirkup, J. *The Evolution of Surgical Instruments: An Illustrated History from Ancient Times to the Twentieth Century*. Novato, California: Norman Publishing, 2006.

Kiss, C., T.W. O'Neill, M. Mituszova, M. Szilágyi, and G. Poór, 'The prevalence of diffuse idiopathic skeletal hyperostosis in a population-based study in Hungary', *Scandinavian Journal of Rheumatology*, Vol. 31, No. 4, 2002: 226–29.

Kiss, C., M. Szilágyi, A. Paksy, and G. Poór, 'Risk factors for diffuse idiopathic skeletal hyperostosis: A case-control study', *Rheumatology*, Vol. 41, No. 1, 2002: 27–30.

Knight, B., *Forensic Pathology*. 2nd edn. London: Arnold, 1996.

Koller, M.F., A. Papassotiropoulos, K. Henke, B. Behrends, S. Noda, A. Kratzer, C. Hock and M. Hofmann, 'Evidence of a genetic basis of Morgagni–Stewart–Morel Syndrome: A case report of identical twins', *Neurodegenerative Diseases*, Vol. 2, No. 2, 2005: 56–60.

Kollin, E. and T. Fehér, 'Androgens, bone mineral content and hyperostosis frontalis interna in pre-menopausal women', *Experimental Clinical Endocrinology*, Vol. 87, 1986: 211–14.

Konigsberg, L.W. and N.P. Herrmann, 'Markov Chain Monte Carlo estimation of hazard model parameters in paleodemography', in *Paleodemography: Age Distributions from Skeletal Samples*, ed. Hoppa, R.D. and J.W. Vaupel, *Cambridge Studies in Biological and Evolutionary Anthropology*. Cambridge: Cambridge University Press, 2002, 222–42.

Konigsberg, L.W., L.A.P. Kohn and J.M. Chevrud, 'Cranial variation and nonmetric trait variation', *American Journal of Physical Anthropology*, Vol. 90, 1993: 35–48.

Kosloski-Ostrow, A., *The Sarno Bath Complex: Architecture in Pompeii's Last Years*. Monographie 4, Ministero per i Beni Culturali ed Ambientali, Soprintendenza Archeologia di Pompei. Rome: 'L'Erma' di Bretschneider, 1990.

Kowalski, C.J., 'A commentary on the use of multivariate statistical methods in anthropometric research', *American Journal of Physical Anthropology*, Vol. 36, 1972: 119–31.

Kozlowski, K. and P. Beighton, *Gamut Index of Skeletal Dysplasias: An Aid to Radiodiagnosis*. Berlin: Springer, 1984.

Krafft, M., *Volcanoes: Fire from the Earth*. Translated by Bahn, P.G. London: Thames & Hudson, 1993.

Kroeber, A.L., *Anthropology: Race, Language, Culture, Psychology, Prehistory*. 2nd edn. New York: Harcourt Brace, 1948.

Krogman, W.M., 'The concept of race', in *The Science of Man in the World Crisis*, ed. Linton, R. New York: Columbia University Press, 1945, 38–62.

——*The Human Skeleton in Forensic Medicine*. Springfield, Illinois: Charles C. Thomas, 1962.

Krogman, W.M. and M.Y. Iscan, *The Human Skeleton in Forensic Medicine*. 2nd edn. Springfield, Illinois: Charles, C. Thomas, 1986.

Kunze, J. and I. Nippert, *Genetics and Malformations in Art*. Berlin: Grosse, 1986.

Kunze, M., 'Zu Winckelmann's Schriften über Herkulaneum und Pompeji', in *Pompeji: 79– 1979: Beiträge Zum Vesuvausbruch und seiner Nachwirkung*, ed. Kunze, M. Stendal: Beiträge der Winckelmann Gesellschaft, 1982, 25–39.

La Rocca, E., M. De Vos, and A. De Vos, *Guida Archeologica di Pompei*. 1st edn. Verona, Italy: Arnoldo Mondadori, 1976.

Langsjoen, O., 'Diseases of the dentition', in *The Cambridge Encyclopedia of Human Paleopathology*, ed. Aufderheide, A.C. and C. Rodriguez-Martin. Cambridge: Cambridge University Press, 1998, 393–412.

Lasker, G.W., *Physical Anthropology*. 2nd edn. New York: Holt, Rinehart & Winston, 1976.

Laurence, R., *Roman Pompeii: Space and Society*. London: Routledge, 1994.

Lazer, E., 'The people of Pompeii', in *Pompeii Revisited: The Life and Death of a Roman Town*, ed. Harrison, D. Sydney: Meditarch, 1994, 144–49.

——'Human Skeletal Remains in Pompeii: Vols. I and II.' unpublished PhD thesis, Department of Anatomy and Histology. Sydney: University of Sydney, 1995.

——'Revealing secrets of a lost city', *The Medical Journal of Australia*, Vol. 165, No. 11/12, 1996: 620–23.

——'Pompeii AD 79: A population in flux?', in *Sequence and Space in Pompeii*, ed. Bon, S.E. and R. Jones. Oxford: Oxbow Monograph 77, 1997a, 102–20.

——'Human skeletal remains in the Casa del Menandro: Appendix F', in *The Insula of the Menander at Pompeii*, ed. Ling, R. Oxford: Clarendon Press, 1997b, 342–43.

——'"Human skeletal remains in Pompeii: A physical anthropological study of the victims of the AD 79 eruption of Mt Vesuvius" in Abstracts from XV Congress of the International Federation of Associations of Anatomists and the 4th International Malpighi Symposium', *Italian Journal of Anatomy and Embryology*, Vol. 104 (Supplement No.1) 1999: 388.

——*Report on the Excavation of the Cadia Cemetery, Cadia Road, Cadia, NSW, 1997–98*. Vol. 4: Skeletal Report: Unpublished report for Cadia Holdings. Orange, NSW: Edward Higginbotham & Associates, 2001.

——'Resti umani scheletrici nella Casa del Menandro', in *Menander: La Casa del Menandro di Pompei*, ed. Stefani, G. Milan: Electa, 2003, 64–69.

——'Victims of the cataclysm', in *The World of Pompeii*, ed. Foss, P.W. and J.J. Dobbins. London: Routledge, 2007.

Leppmann, W., *Pompeii in Fact and Fiction*. London: Elek, 1968.

Lichtenstein, L., *Diseases of Bone and Joints*. Saint Louis, Missouri: Mosby, 1970.

Lieberman, L., R.C. Kirk and A. Littlefield, 'Exchange across difference: The status of the race concept – Perishing paradigm: Race – 1931–99', *American Anthropologist*, Vol. 105, No. 1, 2003: 110–13.

Limeback, H., 'The relationship between oral health and systemic infections among elderly residents of chronic care facilities: A review 1', *Gerodontology*, Vol. 7, No. 3–4, 1988: 131–37.

Ling, R., 'The Insula of the Menander at Pompeii: Interim report', *Antiquity Journal*, Vol. 63, 1983: 34–57.

——'La Casa del Menandro', in *Menander: La Casa del Menandro di Pompei*, ed. Stefani, G. Milan: Electa, 2003, 10–45.

——*Pompeii: History, Life and Afterlife*. Stroud, Gloucestershire: Tempus, 2005.

Lirer, L., T. Pescatore, B. Booth, and G.L. Walker, 'Two Plinian pumice-fall deposits from Somma-Vesuvius, Italy', *Geological Society of America Bulletin*, Vol. 84, 1973: 759–72.

Lisowski, F.P., 'Prehistoric and early trepanation', in *Diseases in Antiquity: A Survey of the Diseases, Injuries and Surgery of Early Populations*, ed. Brothwell, D.R. and A.T. Sandison. Springfield, Illinois: Charles C. Thomas, 1967, 651–72.

Liversidge, H.M., 'Accuracy of age estimation from developing teeth of a population of known age (0–5.4 years)', *International Journal of Osteoarchaeology*, Vol. 4, 1994: 37–45.

Liversidge, M.J.H., 'Representing Rome: Catalogue I', in *Imagining Rome: British Artists and Rome in the Nineteenth Century*, ed. Liversidge, M.J.H. and C. Edwards. London: Merrell Holberton, 1996, 70–134.

Lorentsen, M. and T. Solheim, 'Age assessment based on translucent dentine', *Journal of Forensic Odontostomatology*, Vol. 7, No. 2, 1989: 3–9.

Love, B. and H.G. Müller, 'A solution to the problem of obtaining a mortality schedule for paleodemographic data', in *Paleodemography: Age Distributions from Skeletal Samples*, ed. Hoppa, R.D. and J.W. Vaupel, *Cambridge Studies in Biological and Evolutionary Anthropology* Cambridge: Cambridge University Press, 2002, 181–92.

Lovejoy, C.O., 'Dental wear in the Libben population: Its functional pattern and role in the determination of adult skeletal age at death', *American Journal of Physical Anthropology*, Vol. 68, 1985: 47–56.

Lovejoy, C.O., R.S. Meindl, R.P. Mensworth and T.J. Barton, 'Multifactorial determination of skeletal age at death: A method and blind tests of its accuracy', *American Journal of Physical Anthropology*, Vol. 68, 1985a: 1–14.

Lovejoy, C.O., R.S. Meindl, T.R. Pryzbeck and R.P. Mensworth, 'Chronological metamorphosis of the auricular surface of the ilium: A new method for the determination of adult skeletal age at death', *American Journal of Physical Anthropology*, Vol. 68, 1985b: 15–28.

Lullies, R. and W. Schiering, *Archäologenbildnisse: Porträts und Kurzbiograhien von Klassischen Archäologen Deutscher Sprache*. Zabern: Verlag, 1988.

Luongo, G., A. Perrotta and C. Scarpati, 'Impact of the AD 79 explosive eruption on Pompeii, I: Relations amongst the depositional mechanisms of the pyroclastic products, the framework of the buildings and the associated destructive events', *Journal of Volcanology and Geothermal Research*, Vol. 126, No. 3–4, 2003a: 201–23.

Luongo, G., A. Perrotta, C. Scarpati, E. De Carolis, G. Patricelli and A. Ciarallo, 'Impact of the AD 79 explosive eruption on Pompeii, II: Causes of death of the inhabitants inferred by stratigraphic analysis and areal distribution of the human casualties', *Journal of Volcanology and Geothermal Research*, Vol. 126, No. 3–4, 2003b: 169–200.

MacKenzie, W.M.C., *Pompeii: Painted by Alberto Pisa*. London: A. & C. Black, 1910.

MacLaughlin, S.M. and M.F. Bruce, 'A simple univariate technique for determining sex from fragmentary femora: Its application to a Scottish short cist population', *American Journal of Physical Anthropology*, Vol. 67, 1985: 413–17.

Maiuri, A., *La Casa del Menandro e il Suo Tesoro di Argenteria*. Rome: La Libreria dello Stato, 1933.

——*Pompei*. 2nd edn. Novara, Italy: Istituto Geografico de Agostini, 1943.

——'Last moments of the Pompeians', *National Geographic*, Vol. 120, 1961: 651–69.

——*Pompeii: The New Excavations, the Villa dei Misteri, the Antiquarium*. Translated by Priestley, V. 7th edn. Rome: Istituto Poligrafico dello Stato, 1962.

——'Pompeii (Reprinted from 1958 issue)', *Scientific American*, Vol. Special Issue 1994: 78–85.

Majno, G., *The Healing Hand: Man and Wound in the Ancient World*. 1991 edn. Cambridge, Massachusetts: Harvard University Press, 1975.

Manchester, K., *The Archaeology of Disease*. Bradford: University of Bradford, 1983.

Manly, B.F.J., *Multivariate Statistical Methods: A Primer*. London: Chapman & Hall, 1986.

Margetts, E.L., 'Trepanation of the skull by the medicine men of primitive cultures, with particular reference to present-day native East African practice', in *Diseases in Antiquity: A Survey of the Diseases, Injuries and Surgery of Early Populations*, ed. Brothwell, D.R. and A.T. Sandison. Springfield, Illinois: Charles C. Thomas, 1967, 673–701.

Martin, L.D., A.H. Goodman, G.J. Armelagos and A.L. Magennis, *Black Mesa Anasazi Health: Reconstructing Life from Patterns of Death and Disease*. Vol. 14, Occasional Paper Carbonale, Illinois: Center for Archaeological Investigations: Southern Illinois University at Carbondale, 1991.

Martin, R. and K. Saller, *Lehrbuch der Anthropologie in Systematischer Darstellung mit Besonderer Berucksichtigung der Anthropologischen Methoden*. Vol. 2. Stuttgart: Fisher, 1959.

Massa, A., *The World of Pompeii*. London: Routledge, 1972.

Mastrolorenzo, G. and P.P. Petrone, 'Nuove evidenze sugli effetti dell'eruzione del 79d.C. ad Ercolano da ricerche biogeoarcheologiche', *Forma Urbis*, Vol. 10, No. 3: Edizione speciale: La rinascita di Ercolano, 2005: 31–34.

Mastrolorenzo, G., P.P. Petrone, M. Pagano, A. Icoronato, P.J. Baxter, A. Canzanella and L. Fattore, 'Archaeology: Herculaneum victims of Vesuvius in AD 79', *Nature*, Vol. 410, No. 6830, 2001: 769–70.

Mau, A., *Pompeii: Its Life and Art*. Translated by Kelsey, F.W. 1907 edn. London: Macmillan, 1907.

Maulucci, F.P., *Pompeii*. Naples: Carcavallo, 1987.

Mays, S., *The Archaeology of Human Bones*. London: Routledge, 1998.

McGeorge, P.J.P., 'The interpretation of social structure through the analysis of non-metrical skeletal variation in the LM III population at Armenoi Rethymnon, Abstract', in *Future Directions in Greek Archaeology Conference, 28th–30th August*, ed. Renfrew, A.C. and A.M. Snodgrass. Cambridge: Cambridge University Press, 1986.

McKern, S.S. and T.W. McKern, *Living Prehistory: An Introduction to Physical Anthropology and Archaeology*. California: Cummings, 1974.

McKern, T.W. and T.D. Stewart, 'Skeletal Age Changes in Young American Males Analysed from the Standpoint of Age Identification: Technical Report EP-45', Natick, Massachusetts: Headquarter Quarter Master Research and Development Command, 1957.

MedicineNet, *Definition of Relaxin* (2000 8 June: latest update); from *MedicineNet.com: Online Medical Dictionary and Glossary*, http://www.medterms.com/script/main/art.asp?articlekey=1 3411 (accessed 30 July 2008).

Meindl, R.S. and C.O. Lovejoy, 'Ectocranial suture closure: A revised method for the determination of skeletal age at death based on the lateral-anterior sutures', *American Journal of Physical Anthropology*, Vol. 68, 1985: 57–66.

Meindl, R.S., C.O. Lovejoy, R.P. Mensforth and R.A. Walker, 'A revised method of age determination using the os pubis, with a review and tests of accuracy of other current methods of pubic symphyseal aging', *American Journal of Physical Anthropology*, Vol. 68, No. 1, 1985: 29–45.

Merbs, C.F., 'Trauma', in *Reconstruction of Life from the Skeleton*, ed. Iscan, M.Y. and K.A.R. Kennedy. New York: Alan R. Liss, 1989, 161–89.

Meyer, D.H. and P.M. Fives-Taylor, 'Oral pathogens: from dental plaque to cardiac disease', *Current Opinion in Microbiology*, Vol. 1, No. 1, 1998: 88–95.

Miles, A.E.W., 'Assessment of the ages of a population of Anglo-Saxons from their dentitions', *Proceedings of the Royal Society of Medicine*, Vol. 55, 1962: 881–86.

——'Teeth as an indicator of age in man', in *Development, Function and Evolution of Teeth*, ed. Butler, P.M. and K.A. Joysey. New York: Academic Press, 1978, 455–64.

Mittler, D.M. and D.P. van Gerven, 'Developmental, diachronic, and demographic analysis of cribra orbitalia in the medieval Christian populations of Kulubnarti', *American Journal of Physical Anthropology*, Vol. 93, 1994: 287–97.

Molleson, T., M. Cox, A.H. Waldron and D.K. Whittaker, *The Spitalfields Project*. Vol. 2: The Anthropology: The Middling Sort, Council for British Archaeology Research Report 86. York, UK: Council for British Archaeology, 1993.

Molleson, T.I., 'The archaeology and anthropology of death: What the bones tell us', in *Mortality and Immortality: The Anthropology and Archaeology of Death*, ed. Humphreys, S.C. and H. King. London: Academic Press, 1981, 15–32.

——'Urban bones: The skeletal evidence for environmental change', in *Actes des Troisièmes Journées Anthropologiques de Valbonne, Notes et Monographies Techniques*. Paris: Editions du CNRS, 1987, 143–58.

——, 'Social implications of mortality patterns of juveniles from Poundbury Camp, Romano–British Cemetery', *Anthropologischer Anzeiger*, Vol. 47, 1989: 27–38.

Molloy, J., L.F. Wolff, A. Lopez-Guzman, and J.S. Hodges, 'The association of periodontal disease parameters with systemic medical conditions and tobacco use', *Journal Of Clinical Periodontology*, Vol. 31, No. 8, 2004: 625–32.

Molnar, S., *Races, Types and Ethnic Groups: The Problems of Human Variation*. New Jersey: Prentice-Hall, 1975.

Monnier, M., *The Wonders of Pompeii by Marc Monnier* (Project Gutenberg, 2005/12/12 Release date), http://www.gutenberg.org/etext/17290 (accessed 4 July 2006).

Moore, S., *Hyperostosis Cranii (Stewart–Morel Syndrome, Metabolic Craniopathy, Morgagni's Syndrome, Stewart–Morel–Moore Syndrome (Ritvo), le Syndrome de Morgagni–Morel)*. Springfield, Illinois: Charles C. Thomas, 1955.

Moorman, E.M., 'Literary evocations of ancient Pompeii', in *Tales from an Eruption: Pompeii, Herculaneum, Oplontis: Guide to the Exhibition*, ed. Guzzo, P.G. Milan: Electa, 2003, 14–33.

Morant, G.M., *The Races of Europe*. London: Allen & Unwin, 1939.

Moroney, M.J., *Facts from Figures*. 1st edn. Middlesex: Penguin, 1955.

Morton, S.G., *Crania Americana or, a Comparative View of the Skulls of Various Aboriginal Nations of North and South America*. Philadelphia: John Pennington, 1839.

—— *Crania Aegyptiaca; or Observations on Egyptian Ethnography Derived from Anatomy, History and the Monuments*. Philadelphia: John Pennington, 1844.

Moscati, S., 'Pompeii: The resurrection of a city', in *Vanished Civilizations*, ed. Readers' Digest Association. Sydney: Readers' Digest, 1983.

Moss, M.L. 'The pathogenesis of artificial cranial deformation', *American Journal of Physical Anthropology*, Vol. 16, 1958: 269–86.

371

Mulhern, D.M., C.A. Wilczak and J.C. Dudar, 'Brief communication: Unusual finding at Pueblo Bonito: Multiple cases of hyperostosis frontalis interna', *American Journal of Physical Anthropology*, Vol. 130, No. 4, 2006: 480–84.

Nappo, S.C., 'Il rinvenimento delle vittime dell'eruzione del 79 d.C. nella Regio 1 insula 22', *Hydria*, Vol. 63, No. 19, 1992: 16–18.

Neidburger, E.J. 'Enamel hypoplasias: Poor indicators of dietary stress', *American Journal of Physical Anthropology*, Vol. 82, 1990: 231–32.

Néret, G. (ed.), *Napoleon and the Pharaohs: Description of Egypt*. Cologne: Taschen, 2001.

Neumann, K., *Rabaul: Yu Swit Moa Yet: Surviving the 1994 Volcanic Eruption*. Oxford: Oxford University Press, 1996.

Nicolucci, G., 'Crania Pompeiana: Descrizione de' crani umani rinvenuti fra le ruine dell' antica Pompei', *Atti della R. Accademia delle Scienze Fisiche e Matematiche*, Vol. 9, No. 10, 1882: 1–26.

Nolan, M.L., 'Impact of paricutin on five communities', in *Volcanic Activity and Human Ecology*, ed. Sheets, P.D. and D.K. Grayson. New York: Academic Press, 1979, 293–338.

Oliver, G., *Practical Anthropology*. Springfield, Illinois: Charles C. Thomas, 1969.

O'Reilly, P.G. and N.M. Claffey, 'A history of oral sepsis as a cause of disease', *Periodontology 2000*, Vol. 23, No. 1, 2000: 13–18.

Oriente, P., A. Del Puente, A. Lorizio and A. Brunetti, 'Studio della densità minerale ossea negli scheletri di età Romana rinvenuti in Pompei nella Casa di Polibio', in *La Casa di Giulio Polibio: Studi Interdisciplinari*, ed. Ciarallo, A. and E. De Carolis. Pompei: Centro Studi arti Figurative, Università di Tokio, 2001, 107–10.

Ortner, D.J., *Identification of Pathological Conditions in Human Skeletal Remains*. 2nd edn. San Diego: Academic Press, 2003.

Ortner, D.J. and W.G.J. Putschar, *Identification of Pathological Conditions in Human Skeletal Remains*. Vol. 28, Smithsonian Contributions to Anthropology. Washington: Smithsonian Institution Press, 1981.

Osborne, D., 'The archaeological determination of diet and natural resources and the case for cooperation', *American Journal of Physical Anthropology*, Vol. 30, 1969: 439–42.

Ossenberg, N.S., 'The influence of artificial cranial deformation on discontinuous morphological traits', *American Journal of Physical Anthropology*, Vol. 33, 1970: 357–71.

Owings Webb, P.A. and J.M. Suchry, 'Epiphyseal union of the anterior iliac crest and the medial clavicle in a modern multiracial sample of American males and females', *American Journal of Physical Anthropology*, Vol. 68, 1985: 457–66.

Pagano, M., 'L'antica Ercolano', in *Vesuvio 79 AD: Vita e Morte ad Ercolano*, ed. Petrone, P.P. and F. Fedele. Naples: Fredericiana Editrice Universitaria, 2002, 55–66.

——'I calchi in archeologia: Ercolano e Pompei', in *Storie da un'Eruzione: Pompei, Ercolano, Oplontis: Guida alla Mostra*, ed. d'Ambrosio, A., P.G. Guzzo and M. Mastroroberto. Milan: Electa, 2003, 122–23.

Pain, S., 'Pompeii's electronic guide', *New Scientist*, Vol. 1815, 1992: 22–23.

Paine, R.R. and J.L. Boldsen, 'Linking age-at-death distributions and ancient population dynamics', in *Paleodemography: Age Distributions from Skeletal Samples*, ed. Hoppa, R.D. and J.W. Vaupel. Cambridge: Cambridge University Press, 2002, 169–80.

Pal, G.P., B.P. Tamankar, R.V. Routal and S.S. Bhagwat, 'The ossification of the membranous part of the squamous occipital bone in man', *Journal of Anatomy*, Vol. 138, 1984: 259–66.

Pappalardo, U., 'L'eruzione pliniana del Vesuvio nel 79 d.C.: Ercolano', in *Volcanology and Archaeology*, ed. Albore Livadie, C. and F. Widerman. Strasburg: Council of Europe, 1900, 197–215.

Pardoe, C., 'Prehistoric Human Morphological Variation in Australia', unpublished PhD thesis. Canberra: Australian National University, 1984.

Parkin, T.G., *Demography and Roman Society*. Baltimore: Johns Hopkins University Press, 1992.

——*Old Age in the Roman World: A Cultural and Social History*. Baltimore: Johns Hopkins University Press, 2003.

Parslow, C.C., *Rediscovering Antiquity: Karl Weber and the Excavation of Herculaneum, Pompeii and Stabiae*. Cambridge: Cambridge University Press, 1995.

Patrik, L.E., 'Is there an archaeological record?', in *Advances in Archaeological Method and Theory*, ed. Schiffer, M.B. Orlando, Florida: Academic Press, 1985), 27–62.

Pawlikowski, M. and J. Komorowski, 'Hyperostosis frontalis interna and the Morgagni–Stewart–Morel Syndrome', *Lancet*, Vol. 1, No. 8322, 1983: 474.

Pellegrino, C., *Ghosts of Vesuvius: A New Look at the Last Days of Pompeii, How Towers Fall, and Other Strange Connections*. New York: William Morrow, 2004.

Pereira, A., *Naples, Pompeii and Southern Italy*. London: Batsford, 1977.

Perl, G., 'Pompeji-geschichte und untergang', in *Pompeji: 79–1979: Beiträge Zum Vesuvausbruch und seiner Nachwirkung*, ed. Kunze, M. Stendal: Beiträge der Winckelmann Gesellschaft, 1982, 9–24.

Pesando, F., 'Shadows of light: Cinema, peplum and Pompeii', in *Tales from an Eruption: Pompeii, Herculaneum, Oplontis: Guide to the Exhibition*, ed. Guzzo, P.G. Milan: Electa, 2003, 34–45.

Petrone, P.P., 'Le Vittime dell'Eruzione del 79 AD', in *Storie da un'Eruzione: Pompei, Ercolano, Oplontis: Guida alla Mostra*, ed. d'Ambrosio, A., P.G. Guzzo and M. Mastroroberto. Milan: Electa, 2003, 31–44.

——'Le vittime dell'eruzione del 79 AD', in *Storie da un'Eruzione: Pompei, Ercolano, Oplontis: Guida alla Mostra, Atti della Tavola Rotonda, Napoli, 2003, Associazione Internazionale Amici di Pompei, Dipartimento di Discipline Storiche, Università degli Studi di Napoli Federico II*, ed. Guzzo, P.G. Pompei: Litografia Sicignano, 2005, 31–44.

Petrone, P.P., A. Coppa and L. Fattore, 'La popolazione di Ercolano', in *Vesuvio 79 AD: Vita e Morte ad Ercolano*, ed. Petrone, P.P. and F. Fedele. Naples: Fredericiana Editrice Universitaria, 2002a, 67–73.

Petrone, P.P., L. Fattore and V. Monetti, 'Alimentazione e malattie ad Ercolano', in *Vesuvio79 AD: Vita e Morte ad Ercolano*, ed. Petrone, P.P. and F. Fedele. Naples: Fredericiana Editrice Universitaria, 2002b, 75–83.

Pfeiffer, S., 'Assignment of sex to adult femora from an ossuary population', *Canadian Review of Physical Anthropology*, Vol. 1, 1979: 55–62.

——'Comparison of adult age estimation techniques using an ossuary sample', *Canadian Review of Physical Anthropology*, Vol. 4, No. 1, 1985: 21–25.

——'Morbidity and mortality in the Uxbridge Ossuary', *Canadian Review of Physical Anthropology*, Vol. 5, 1986: 23–31.

Pheasant, S., *Bodyspace: Anthropology, Ergonomics and Design*. London: Taylor & Francis, 1986.

——*Ergonomic Standards and Guidelines for Design*. Milton Keynes: British Standards Institution, 1987.

Phenice, T.W., 'A newly developed visual method of sexing the os pubis', *American Journal of Physical Anthropology*, Vol. 30, 1967: 297–301.

Plueckhahn, V.D., *Ethics, Legal Medicine and Forensic Pathology*. Carlton, Victoria: Melbourne University Press, 1983.

Pollard, A.H., *Introductory Statistics: A Service Course*. 2nd edn. Rushcutters Bay, NSW: Pergamon (Australia), 1972.

Prettejohn, E., 'Recreating Rome in Victorian painting: From history to genre', in *Imagining Rome: British Artists and Rome in the Nineteenth Century*, ed. Liversidge, M.J.H. and C. Edwards. London: Merrell Holberton, 1996a, 54–69.

——'Recreating Rome: Catalogue II', in *Imagining Rome: British Artists and Rome in the Nineteenth Century*, ed. Liversidge, M.J.H. and C. Edwards. London: Merrell Holberton, 1996b, 125–70.

Pringle, H. *The Mummy Congress: Science, Obsession, and the Everlasting Dead*. London: Fourth Estate, 2001.

Prowse, T.L., H.P. Schwarcz, S. Saunders, R. Macchiarelli and L. Bondioli, 'Isotopic paleodiet studies of skeletons from the Imperial Roman-age cemetery of Isola Sacra, Rome, Italy', *Journal of Archaeological Science*, Vol. 31, No. 3, 2004: 259–72.

Prowse, T.L., H.P. Schwarcz, S.R. Saunders, R. Macchiarelli, and L. Bondioli. 'Isotopic evidence for age-related variation in diet from Isola Sacra, Italy', *American Journal of Physical Anthropology*, Vol. 128, 2005: 2–13.

Puech-Rochette, M., C. Serratrice and F.F. Leek, 'Tooth wear as observed on ancient Egyptian skulls', *Journal of Human Evolution*, Vol. 12, 1983: 617–29.

Punongbayan, R.S. and R.I. Tilling, 'Some recent case histories', in *Volcanic Hazards*, ed. Tilling, R.I., *Short Course in Geology*. Washington DC American Geophysical Union, 1989, 81–101.

Raoul-Rochette, M. and M. Roux, *Choix de Peintures de Pompéi: Lithographiées en Couleur par M. Roux et Publiées avec l'Explication Archéologique de Chaque Peinture*. Paris: Adolphe Labitte, 1867.

Reiche, I., L. Favre-Quattropani, T. Calligaro, J. Salomon, H. Bocherens, L. Charlet and M. Menu, 'Trace element composition of archaeological bones and post-mortem alteration in the burial environment', *Nuclear Instruments and Methods in Physics Research B*, Vol. 150, 1999: 656–62.

Renfrew, C. and P. Bahn, *Archaeology: Theory, Methods and Practice*. London: Thames & Hudson, 1991.

Richards, M.P., R.E.M. Hedges, T.I. Molleson and J.C. Vogel, 'Stable isotope analysis reveals variations in human diet at the Poundbury Camp Cemetery Site', *Journal of Archaeological Science*, Vol. 25, No. 12, 1998: 1247–52.

Richardson, L., 'Life as it appeared when Vesuvius engulfed Pompeii', *Smithsonian*, Vol. 9, No. 1, 1978: 84–93.

——*Pompeii: An Architectural History*. Baltimore: Johns Hopkins University Press, 1988.

Ripley, W.Z., *The Races of Europe: A Sociological Study*. London: Kegan Paul, 1899.

Roberts, C., 'Trauma and treatment in the British Isles in the historic period: A design for multidisciplinary research', in *Human Palaeopathology: Current Syntheses and Future Options*, ed. Ortner, D.J. and A.C. Aufderheide. Washington, DC: Smithsonian Institution Press, 1991, 225–40.

Roberts, C. and K. Manchester, *The Archaeology of Disease*. 2nd edn. Ithaca, New York: Cornell University Press, 1995.

Roberts, C.A., 'A view from afar: Bioarchaeology in Britain', in *Bioarchaeology: The Contextual Analysis of Human Remains*, ed. Buikstra, J.E. and L.A. Beck. Amsterdam: Academic Press, 2006, 417–39.

Robinson, M.A., 'Fosse, piccole fosse e peristili a Pompei', in *Nuove ricerche archeologiche a Pompei ed Ercolano*, ed. Guzzo, P.G. and M.P. Guidobaldi. Naples: Electa, 2005, 109–19.

Rocco, T., 'The Villa of Diomedes', in *Tales from an Eruption: Pompeii, Herculaneum, Oplontis: Guide to the Exhibition*, ed. Guzzo, P.G. Milan: Electa, 2003a, 92–94.

——'The Quadriporticus of the theatres (VIII, 7, 16–17)', in *Tales from an Eruption: Pompeii, Herculaneum, Oplontis: Guide to the Exhibition*, ed. Guzzo, P.G. Milan: Electa, 2003b, 99–102.

Rogers, J. and T. Waldron, 'DISH and the monastic way of life', *International Journal of Osteoarchaeology*, Vol. 11, 2001.

Rogers, J., T. Waldron, P. Dieppe and I. Watt, 'Arthropathies in palaeopathology: The basis of classification according to most probable cause', *Journal of Archaeological Science*, Vol. 14, 1987: 179–93.

Rosci, M., *Leonardo*. New York: Mayflower Books, 1981.

Rose, H.J., *A Handbook of Greek Mythology*. New York: Dutton, 1959/1928.

Rosi, M. and R. Santacroce, 'L'eruzione di Pompei del 79 d.C.', in *Tremblements de Terre, Éruptions Volcaniques et Vie des Hommes dans la Campanie Antique*, ed. Albore Livadie, C. Naples: Publications du Centre Jean Berard, 1986, 24–26.

Rösing, F.W., 'Sexing immature human skeletons', *Journal of Human Evolution*, Vol. 12, 1983: 149–55.

——'Discreta of the human skeleton: A critical review', *Journal of Human Evolution*, Vol. 13, 1984: 319–23.

Rothschild, B., 'Porotic hyperostosis as a marker of health and nutritional conditions', *American Journal of Human Biology*, Vol. 14, No. 4, 2002: 417–18.

Rothschild, B.M., F.J. Rühli, J. Sebes, V. Naples and M. Billard, *Relationship between porotic hyperostosis and cribra orbitalia?* (2004); from *PaleoBios*, http://anthropologie-et-paleopatholo gie.univ-lyon1.fr/ (accessed 4 April 2005).

Rubin, P., *Dynamic Classification of Bone Dysplasias*. Chicago: Year Book Medical Publishers, 1972/1964.

Rubini, M., 'Biological homogeneity and familial segregation in the Iron Age population of Alfedena (Abruzzo, Italy), based on cranial discrete traits analysis', *International Journal of Osteoarchaeology*, Vol. 6, No. 5, 1996: 454–62.

Rubini, M., E. Bonafede and S. Mogliazza, 'The population of East Sicily during the second and first millennium BC: The problem of the Greek colonies', *International Journal of Osteoarchaeology*, Vol. 9, No. 1, 1999: 8–17.

Rubini, M., E. Bonafede, S. Mogliazza and L. Moreschini, 'Etruscan Biology: The Tarquinian population seventh to second century BC (Southern Etruria, Italy)', *International Journal of Osteoarchaeology*, Vol. 7, No. 3, 1997: 202–11.

Rubini, M., S. Mogliazza and R.S.T. Corruccini, 'Biological divergence and equality during the first millennium BC in human populations of Central Italy', *American Journal of Human Biology*, Vol. 19, No. 1, 2007: 119–31.

Rühli, F.J., T. Böni and M. Henneberg, 'Hyperostosis frontalis interna: Archaeological evidence of possible microevolution of human sex steroids?', *Homo: Journal of Comparative Human Biology*, Vol. 55, No. 1–2, 2004: 91–99.

Rühli, F.J. and M. Henneberg, 'Are hyperostosis frontalis interna and leptin linked? A hypothetical approach about hormonal influence on human microevolution', *Medical Hypotheses*, Vol. 58, No. 5, 2002: 378–81.

Russell, J.C., *The Control of Late Ancient and Medieval Population*. Philadelphia: The American Philosophical Society, 1985.

Sadler, T.W., *Langman's Medical Embryology*. 10th edn. Philadelphia: Lippincott Williams & Wilkins, 2006.

Salmi, A., A. Voutilainen, L.R. Holsti and C.-E. Unnerus, 'Hyperostosis cranii in a normal population', *American Journal of Roentgenology, Radium Therapy & Nuclear Medicine*, Vol. 87, 1962: 1032–40.

Saunders, J.B.d.C.M. and C.D. O'Malley, *The Anatomical Drawings of Andreas Vesalius*. New York: Bonanza Books, 1982.

Saunders, S.R., 'Nonmetric skeletal variation', in *Reconstruction of Life from the Skeleton*, ed. Iscan, M.Y. and K.A.R. Kennedy. New York: Alan R. Liss, 1989, 95–108.

Schefold, K., *Die Wände Pompejis*. Berlin: Topographisches Verzeichnis der Bildemotive, 1957.

——'Die bedeutung der malerei Pompejis', in *Pompejanische Wandmalerei*, ed. Cerulli Irelli, G., M. Aoyagi and D. Stefano. Zurich: Belser, 1990, 107–14

Scheuer, L. and S. Black, *The Juvenile Skeleton*. Amsterdam: Elsevier, 2004.

Schiering, W., 'Johann Joachim Winckelmann', in *Archäologenbildnisse: Porträts und Kurzbiographien von Klassischen Archäologen Deutscher Sprache mit Beiträgen Zahlreichen Fachgenossen Herausgegeben*, ed. Lullies, R. and W. Schiering. Mainz: Philipp von Zabern, 1988, 5–7.

Schiffer, M.B., 'Is there a "Pompeii Premise" in archaeology?', *Journal of Anthropological Research*, Vol. 41, 1985: 18–41.

——*Formation Processes of the Archaeological Record*. Albuquerque, New Mexico: University of New Mexico, 1987.

Schutkowski, H., 'Sex determination of infant and juvenile skeletons: 1. Morphognostic features', *American Journal of Physical Anthropology*, Vol. 90, 1993: 199–205.

Schwarcz, H.P. and M.J. Schoeninger, 'Stable isotope analyses in human nutritional ecology', *Yearbook of Physical Anthropology*, Vol. 34, No. S13, 1991: 283–321.

Scobie, A., 'Slums, sanitation, and mortality in the Roman world', *Klio*, Vol. 68, No. 2, 1986: 399–433.

Scott, G.R. and C.G. Turner, *The Anthropology of Modern Human Teeth: Dental Morphology and Its Variation in Recent Human Populations*. Cambridge: Cambridge University Press, 1997.

Scott, J.H. and N.B.B. Symons, *Introduction to Dental Anatomy*. 7th edn. Edinburgh: Churchill Livingstone, 1974.

Scott, W.E., 'Volcanic and related hazards', in *Volcanic Hazards*, ed. Tilling, R.I., *Short Course in Geology*, Washington DC: American Geophysical Union, 1989, 9–23.

Sekla, B. and F. Soukup, 'Inheritance of the cephalic index', *American Journal of Physical Anthropology*, Vol. 30, 1969: 137–40.

Sheets, P.D., 'Environmental and cultural effects of the Ilopango eruption in Central America', in *Volcanic Activity and Human Ecology*, ed. Sheets, P.D. and D.K. Grayson (New York: Academic Press, 1979), 525–64.

Sheridan, M.F. and F. Barberi (eds), *Explosive Volcanism*, Amsterdam: Elsevier, 1983.

Shipman, P., *The Evolution of Racism: Human Differences and the Use and Abuse of Science*. New York: Simon & Schuster, 1994.

Shipman, P., A. Walker and D. Bichell, *The Human Skeleton*. Cambridge, Massachusetts: Harvard University Press, 1985.

Sica, M., S. Aceto, A. Genovese and L. Gaudio, 'Analysis of five ancient equine skeletons by mitochondrial DNA sequencing', *Ancient Biomolecules*, Vol. 4, No. 4, 2002: 179–84.

Sigurdsson, H., *Melting the Earth: The History of Ideas on Volcanic Eruptions*. Oxford: Oxford University Press, 1999.

——'Mount Vesuvius before the disaster', in *The Natural History of Pompeii*, ed. Jashemski, W. F. and F.G. Meyer. Cambridge: Cambridge University Press, 2002, 29–36.

——'The environmental and geomorphological context of the volcano', in *The World of Pompeii*, ed. Foss, P.W. and J.J. Dobbins. London: Routledge, 2007, 43–62.

Sigurdsson, H. and S.N. Carey, 'The eruption of Vesuvius in AD 79', in *The Natural History of Pompeii*, ed. Jashemski, W.F. and F.G. Meyer. Cambridge: Cambridge University Press, 2002, 37–64.

Sigurdsson, H., S.N. Carey, W. Cornell and T. Pescatore, 'The Eruption of Vesuvius in AD 79', *National Geographic Research* Vol. 1, No. 3, 1985: 332–87.

Sigurdsson, H., S. Cashdollar, and S.R.J. Sparks, 'The eruption of Vesuvius in AD 79: Reconstruction from historical and volcanological evidence', *American Journal of Archaeology*, Vol. 86, 1982: 39–51.

Sillen, A., J.C. Sealy, and N.J. van der Merwe, 'Chemistry and paleodietary research: No more easy answers', *American Antiquity*, Vol. 54, No. 3, 1989: 504–12.

Skrzat, J., D. Holiat, and J. Walocha, 'The morphological appearance of the palatine torus in the Cracovian skulls (XV–XVIII century)', *Folia Morphol*, Vol. 62, No. 3, 2003: 183–86.

Smith, G.E., *The Royal Mummies: Catalogue Général des Antiquités Égyptiennes du Musée du Caire, Nos 61051–61100*. 2000 edn. London: Duckworth, 1912.

Smith, G.E. and W.R. Dawson, *Egyptian Mummies*. London: George Allen & Unwin, 1924.

Sogliano, A., *Guida di Pompei*. 3rd edn. Milan: Antonio Vallardi, 1922.

Sperduti, A. and G. Manzi, 'Hyperostosis frontalis interna in a cranial sample from the Roman population of Portus (Isola Sacra necropolis 1–111 Century AD)', *Rivista di Antropologia*, Vol. 68 1990: 279–86.

Srb, A.M., R.D. Owen and R.S. Edgar, *General Genetics*. 2nd edn. San Francisco: Freeman, 1965.

St Hoyme, L.E. and M.Y. Iscan, 'Determination of sex and race: Accuracy and assumptions', in *Reconstruction of Life from the Skeleton*, ed. Iscan, M.Y. and K.A.R. Kennedy. New York: Alan R. Liss, 1989, 53–93.

Steele, D.G. and C.A. Bramblett, *The Anatomy and Biology of the Human Skeleton*. College Station: Texas A & M University Press, 1988.

Stefani, G., 'La vera data dell'eruzione', *Archeo*, Vol. 260, No. 10, 2006: 10–13.

Steinbock, R.T., *Paleopathological Diagnosis and Interpretation: Bone Diseases in Ancient Human Populations*. Springfield, Illinois: Charles C. Thomas, 1976.

Stevens, G., *Statistics Course Notes*. Sydney: Faculty of Architecture, University of Sydney, 1987.

Stewart, R.M., 'Localised cranial hyperostosis in the insane', *The Journal of Neurology and Psychopathology*, Vol. 8, 1928: 321–31.

Stewart, T.D., 'Distortion of the pubic symphyseal surface in females and its effect on age determination', *American Journal of Physical Anthropology*, Vol. 15, 1957: 9–18.

——'The effects of pathology on skeletal populations', *American Journal Physical Anthropology*, Vol. 30, 1969: 443–50.

Stone, A.C., G.R. Milner, S. Pääbo, and M. Stoneking, 'Sex determination of ancient human skeletons using DNA', *American Journal of Physical Anthropology*, Vol. 99, 1996: 231–38.

Stuart-Macadam, P., 'Porotic hyperostosis: Representative of a childhood condition', *American Journal of Physical Anthropology*, Vol. 66, 1985: 391–98.

——'Porotic hyperostosis: Changing interpretations', in *Human Palaeopathology: Current Syntheses and Future Options*, ed. Ortner, D.J. and A.C. Aufderheide. Washington: Smithsonian Institution Press, 1991, 36–39.

Suchey, J.M. 'Problems in the aging of females using the os pubis', *American Journal of Physical Anthropology*, Vol. 51, 1979: 467–70.

Suchey, J.M. and D. Katz, 'Skeletal age standards derived from an extensive multiracial sample of modern Americans (unpublished paper)', in *The Fifty-Fifth Annual Meeting of the American Association of Physical Anthropologists*. Albuquerque, New Mexico: 1986.

Suchey, J.M., S.T. Brooks and D. Katz, *Instructions for the Use of the Suchey–Brooks System for Age Determination of the Female Os Pubis*, instructional materials accompanying female pubic symphyseal models of the Suchey–Brooks System, 1988.

Suchey, J.M., D.V. Wiseley, R.F. Green and T.T. Noguchi, 'Analysis of dorsal pitting in the os pubis in an extensive sample of modern American females', *American Journal of Physical Anthropology*, Vol. 51, 1979: 517–39.

Suchey, J.M., D.V. Wiseley and D. Katz, 'Evaluation of the Todd and McKern–Stewart methods for aging the male os pubis', in *Forensic Osteology: Advances in the Identification of Human Remains*, ed. Reichs, K.J. Springfield, Illinois: Charles C. Thomas, 1986, 33–67.

Sunderland, E., 'Biological components of the races of man', in *Racial Variation in Man: Proceedings of a Symposium held at the Royal Geographical Society, London 19–20 September, 1974*, ed. Ebling, F.J. London: The Institute of Biology, 1975, 9–25.

Sutherland, F.L., 'The volcanic fall of Pompeii', in *Pompeii Revisited: The Life and Death of a Roman Town*, ed. Harrison, D. Sydney: Meditarch, 1994, 72–75.

Tague, R.G., 'Bone resorption of the pubis and preauricular area in humans and nonhuman mammals', *American Journal of Physical Anthropology*, Vol. 76, 1988: 251–67.

Talarico Jr, E.F., A.D. Prather and K.D. Hardt, 'A case of extensive hyperostosis frontalis interna in an 87-year-old female human cadaver', *Clinical Anatomy*, Vol. 21, No. 3, 2008: 259–68.

Tanguy, J.-C., C. Ribière, A. Scarth and W.S. Tjetjep, 'Victims from volcanic eruptions: A revised database', *Bulletin of Volcanology*, Vol. 60, No. 2, 1998: 137–44.

Taveras, J.M. and M.D. Wood, *Diagnostic Neuroradiology*. 2nd edn. Section 1, Golden's Diagnostic Radiology. Baltimore: The Williams & Wilkins Company, 1976.

Taylor, K.T., *Forensic Art and Illustration*. Boca Raton, Florida: CRC Press, 2001.

Taylor, R.M.S., 'Assault or accident', *British Dental Journal*, Vol. 131, 1971: 419–20.

The British School at Rome, *Herculaneum: The Herculaneum Conservation Project* (2007), http://www.bsr.ac.uk/BSR/sub_arch/BSR_Arch_03Herc.htm (accessed 2 October 2008).

Thomas, D.L., 'Portraiture at Pompeii', in *Pompeii and the Vesuvian Landscape*, ed. AIA Washington, DC: The Archaeological Institute of America & The Smithsonian, 1979.

Torino, M. and G. Fornaciari, 'Gli Scheletri di Ercolani: Richerche paleopatologiche', in *Gli Antichi Ercolanesi: Antropologia, Società, Economia*, ed. Pagano, M. Naples: Electa, 2000, 60–63.

——'Paleopatologia degli individui nella Casa di Giulio Polibio', in *La Casa di Giulio Polibio: Studi Interdisciplinari*, ed. Ciarallo, A. and E. De Carolis. Pompei: Centro Studi arti Figurative, Università di Tokio, 2001, 93–106.

Tran Tam Tinh, V., *Essai sur le Culte d'Isis à Pompei*. Paris: de Boccard, 1964.

Trevelyan, R., *The Shadow of Vesuvius: Pompeii AD 79*. London: Michael Joseph, 1976.

Trotter, M., 'Estimation of stature from intact long bones', in *Personal Identification in Mass Disasters*, ed. Stewart, T.D. Washington, DC: Smithsonian Institution Press, 1970, 71–83.

Trotter, M. and G.C. Gleser, 'Estimation of stature from long bones of American Whites and Negroes', *American Journal of Physical Anthropology*, Vol. 10, 1952: 463–514.

——'A re-evaluation of estimation of stature based on measurements of stature taken during life and of long bones after death', *American Journal of Physical Anthropology*, Vol. 16, 1958: 79–123.

——'Corrigenda to "estimation of stature from long limb bones of American Whites and Negroes", *American Journal Physical Anthropology* (1952)', *American Journal Physical Anthropology*, Vol. 47, No. 2, 1977: 355–56.

Turner, C.G., II, C.R. Nichol and G.R. Scott, 'Scoring procedures for key morphological traits of the permanent dentition: The Arizona State University Dental System', in *Advances in Dental Anthropology*, ed. Kelley, M.A. and C.S. Larsen. New York: Wiley–Liss, 1991, 13–32.

Tutt, P. and D. Adler (eds), *New Metric Handbook*. London: Architectural Press, 1979.

Twain, M., *The Innocents Abroad*. New York: Harper & Brothers, 1903.

Tyldesley, J. *The Mummy: Unwrap the Ancient Secrets of the Mummies' Tombs*. London: Carlton, 1999.

Tyson, R.A. and E.S.D. Alcauskas (eds), *Catalogue of the Hrdlicka Paleopathology Collection*. San Diego, California: San Diego Museum of Man, 1980.

Ubelaker, D.H., *Human Skeletal Remains: Excavation, Analysis, Interpretation*. 2nd edn. Vol. 2, Manuals on Archaeology. Washington: Taraxacum, 1989.

Usher, B.M., 'Reference samples: The first step in linking biology and age in the human skeleton', in *Paleodemography: Age Distributions from Skeletal Samples*, ed. Hoppa, R.D. and J. W. Vaupel. Cambridge: Cambridge University Press, 2002, 29–47.

Vallois, H.V., 'Vital statistics in prehistoric population as determined from archaeological data', in *The Application of Quantitative Methods in Archaeology*, ed. Heizer, R.F. and S.F. Cook. Chicago: Quadrangle, 1960, 186–222.

——'Race', in *Anthropology Today: Selections*, ed. Tax, S. Chicago: University of Chicago Press, 1962, 46–64.

van Gerven, D.P., 'The contribution of size and shape variation to patterns of sexual dimorphism of the human femur', *American Journal of Physical Anthropology*, Vol. 37, 1972: 49–60.

van Gerven, D.P. and G.J. Armelagos, '"Farewell to paleodemography?" Rumours of its death have been greatly exaggerated', *Journal of Human Evolution*, Vol. 12, 1983: 353–60.

Verdy, M., J. Guimond, P. Fauteux and M. Aube. 'Prevalence of hyperostosis frontalis interna in relation to body weight', *American Journal of Clinical Nutrition*, Vol. 31, No. 11, 1978: 2002–4.

Wakely, J. and C. Duhig, 'A comparative microscopical study of three European trephined skulls', *International Journal of Osteoarchaeology*, Vol. 2, 2005: 337–40.

Waldron, T., *Counting the Dead: The Epidemiology of Skeletal Populations*. Chichester: John Wiley & Sons, 1994.

Waldstein, C. and L. Shoobridge, *Herculaneum: Past, Present and Future*. London: Macmillan, 1908.

Wallace, B., *Genetics, Evolution, Race, Radiation Biology*. Vol. 2, Essays in Social Biology. New Jersey: Prentice–Hall, 1972.

Wallace-Hadrill, A., 'Houses and households: Sampling Pompeii and Herculaneum', in *Marriage, Divorce and Children in Ancient Rome*, ed. Rawson, B. Oxford: Oxford University Press, 1991, 191–227.

——*Houses and Society in Pompeii and Herculaneum*. Princeton, New Jersey: Princeton University Press, 1994.

Wapler, U., E. Crubézy, and M. Schultz, 'Is cribra orbitalia synonymous with anemia? Analysis and interpretation of cranial pathology in Sudan', *American Journal of Physical Anthropology*, Vol. 123, No. 4, 2004: 333–39.

Ward-Perkins, J.B. and A. Claridge. *Pompeii AD 79: Treasures from the National Archaeological Museum, Naples and the Pompeii Antiquarium, Italy*. 2nd edn. Sydney: Australian Gallery Directors' Council, 1980.

Weinberger, B.W., *An introduction to the history of dentistry*, St Louis, Missouri: Mosby, 1948: 99–365.

Weinfeld, R.M., P.N. Olson, D.D. Mak, and H.J. Griffiths, 'The prevalence of diffuse idiopathic skeletal hyperostosis (DISH) in two large American Midwest metropolitan hospital populations', *Skeletal Radiology*, Vol. 26, No. 4, 1997: 222–25.

Weiss, K.M., 'On the systematic bias in skeletal sexing', *American Journal of Physical Anthropology*, Vol. 37, 1972: 239–49.

Wells, C.H., *Bones, Bodies and Disease: Evidence of Disease and Abnormality in Early Man*. London: Thames & Hudson, 1964.

Wells, L.H., 'Stature in earlier races of mankind', in *Science in Archaeology: A Survey of Progress and Research*, ed. Brothwell, D. and E. Higgs. London: Thames & Hudson, 1969, 453–67.

White, T.D., *Human Osteology*. 1st edn. San Diego, California: Academic Press, 1991.

——*Human Osteology*. 2nd edn. San Diego, California: Academic Press, 2000.

White, T.D. and P.A. Folkens, *The Human Bone Manual*. Boston: Academic Press, 2005.

Widemann, F., 'Les effets économiques de l'éruption de 79: Nouvelles données et nouvelles approches', in *Tremblements de Terre, Éruptions Volcaniques et Vie des Hommes dans la Campanie Antique*, ed. Albore Livadie, C. Naples: Publications du Centre Jean Berard, 1986, 107–12.

Wilkinson, P., *Pompeii: The Last Day*. London: BBC Books, 2003.

Williams, D.R. and C.M. Woodhead, 'Attrition: A contemporary dental viewpoint', in *Teeth and Anthropology*, ed. Cruwys, E. and R.A. Foley, 291. Oxford: British Anthropological Reports International, 1986, 109–21.

Witt, R.E., *Isis in the Graeco-Roman World*. London: Thames & Hudson, 1971.

Wittwer-Backofen, U. and H. Buba, 'Age estimation by tooth cementum annulation: Perspectives of a new validation study', in *Paleodemography: Age Distributions from Skeletal Samples*, ed. Hoppa, R.D. and J.W. Vaupel. Cambridge: Cambridge University Press, 2002, 107–28.

Woelfel, J.B., *Dental Anatomy: Its Relevance to Dentistry*. 4th edn. Philadelphia: Lea & Febiger, 1990.

Wood, J.W., D.J. Holman, K.A. O'Connor and R.J. Ferrell, 'Mortality models for paleodemography', in *Paleodemography: Age Distributions from Skeletal Samples*, ed. Hoppa, R.D. and J.W. Vaupel, *Cambridge Studies in Biological and Evolutionary Anthropology*. Cambridge: Cambridge University Press, 2002, 129–68.

Wood-Jones, F., 'The non-metrical morphological characters of the skull as criteria for racial diagnosis', *Journal of Anatomy*, Vol. 65, 1931: 179–95.

Wyke, M., *Projecting the Past: Ancient Rome, Cinema, and History*. London: Routledge, 1997.

Zihlman, A.L., *The Human Evolution Colouring Book*. New York: Barnes & Noble, 1982.

INDEX

abandonment of Pompeii, 70–73, 315 (n.166)

Academy of Herculaneum, 7

achondroplastic dwarves, *see* pygmies

agriculture in Pompeii, 75

Alcubierre R.J., 6, 284–85

Allison, P.M., 68–69

Alma Tadema, Lawrence, 19

African populations, 121, 126, 154, 181, 223, 226–27, 232, 235, 237–39, 241–43

'African' skull, 48, 54–55, 134–35

American populations, Black, 179–81; Native, 142–43, 169, 171, 173–74, 195, 212, 236; White, 57, 142–43, 179–81, 244

amphitheatre, 22, 27, 73–74

anaemia, 197–99, 214

ancient populations, 160, 179, 195, 212, 226; in Egypt, 195, 226; in Greece, 49, 63, 195; in Italy, 50, 58–61, 161, 170–71, 212, 226, 232

androgyny, 123, 137

Angel, J. Lawrence, 49, 63, 199

Antiquarium, Pompeii, 258

Asian populations, 30, 119, 179, 232

asphyxiation, 84–85, 87, 91

Augustus, Emperor, 31, 79, 155, 215

Australian Aboriginal populations, 119, 228, 237

Barnicot, N.A. and Brothwell, D.R., 58–59

Baths, *see* Central, Forum, Sarno

Baxter, P.J., 87–88, 260

Becker, M.J, 203

Beloch (1898), 74

Belzoni, G.B, 38–40

Berry, A.C. and Berry, R.J., 228, 233, 235

birth rate, 215

Bisel, Sara, popular works, 28–30; scientific work, 62–63, 123, 130, 136, 157–58, 162–65, 170–76, 183, 184, 194, 199–200, 202–3, 213–14, 216–20, 223

Blong, R.J., 77

Blumenbach, J.F., 38, 57

bone hinges, 104–*105*, 127, 195

Bonucci, Antonio, 26, 76, 285

Bourbon kings, 7, 8, 15, 47, 285

Bourbon Museum, 47

Boscoreale, *53*, 258

British Museum, 7, 37, 40

Broca, Paul, 57

Broca's area, 91

Brothwell scheme, 151–52

brucellosis, 197, 219

Bullard, F.M., 81

Bulwer-Lytton, Edward, 14, 19, 26–28, 30, 64, 76, 101, 104, 249–51, 265, 286, 299 (n. 57), 300 (n.80)

burns, 85, 89

Butterworth, A. and Laurence, R., 33–35

cadaveric spasm, 88

Caffey's disease, 208

Capasso, Luigi *et al.*, 63–64, 90–91, 136, 157, 163–65, 170–72, 174–76, 183, 184, 195, 196–97, 199–200, 203, 217–20, 222, 225–27, 233, 234, 237–44